# A DATA-BASED ASSESSMENT OF RESEARCH-DOCTORATE PROGRAMS IN THE UNITED STATES

Committee on an Assessment of Research Doctorate Programs

Jeremiah P. Ostriker, Charlotte V. Kuh, and James A. Voytuk, *Editors*

Board on Higher Education and Workforce
Policy and Global Affairs

NATIONAL RESEARCH COUNCIL
*OF THE NATIONAL ACADEMIES*

THE NATIONAL ACADEMIES PRESS
Washington, D.C.
*www.nap.edu*

THE NATIONAL ACADEMIES PRESS    500 Fifth Street, N.W.    Washington, DC 20001

NOTICE: The project that is the subject of this report was approved by the Governing Board of the NRC, whose members are drawn from the councils of the National Academy of Sciences, the National Academy of Engineering, and the Institute of Medicine. The members of the committee responsible for the report were chosen for their special competences and with regard for appropriate balance.

This project was supported by the Andrew W. Mellon Foundation, the Alfred P. Sloan Foundation, the U.S. Department of Energy (Grant DE-FG02-07ER35880), the National Institutes of Health (Grant N01-OD-4-2139, TO#170), the National Science Foundation (Grant OIA-0540823), the National Research Council, and contributions from 212 U.S. universities. Any opinions, findings, conclusions, or recommendations expressed in this publication are those of the author(s) and do not necessarily reflect the views of the organizations or agencies that provided support for the project.

International Standard Book Number-13: 978-0-309-16030-8
 International Standard Book Number-10: 0-309-16030-8
 Library of Congress Control Number: 2011933643


Additional copies of this report are available from the National Academies Press, 500 Fifth Street, N.W., Lockbox 285, Washington, DC 20055; (800) 624-6242 or (202) 334-3313 (in the Washington metropolitan area); Internet, http://www.nap.edu

Printed in the United States of America

# THE NATIONAL ACADEMIES
*Advisers to the Nation on Science, Engineering, and Medicine*

The National Academy of Sciences is a private, nonprofit, self-perpetuating society of distinguished scholars engaged in scientific and engineering research, dedicated to the furtherance of science and technology and to their use for the general welfare. Upon the authority of the charter granted to it by the Congress in 1863, the Academy has a mandate that requires it to advise the federal government on scientific and technical matters. Dr. Ralph J. Cicerone is president of the National Academy of Sciences.

The National Academy of Engineering was established in 1964, under the charter of the National Academy of Sciences, as a parallel organization of outstanding engineers. It is autonomous in its administration and in the selection of its members, sharing with the National Academy of Sciences the responsibility for advising the federal government. The National Academy of Engineering also sponsors engineering programs aimed at meeting national needs, encourages education and research, and recognizes the superior achievements of engineers. Dr. Charles M. Vest is president of the National Academy of Engineering.

The Institute of Medicine was established in 1970 by the National Academy of Sciences to secure the services of eminent members of appropriate professions in the examination of policy matters pertaining to the health of the public. The Institute acts under the responsibility given to the National Academy of Sciences by its congressional charter to be an adviser to the federal government and, upon its own initiative, to identify issues of medical care, research, and education. Dr. Harvey V. Fineberg is president of the Institute of Medicine.

The NRC was organized by the National Academy of Sciences in 1916 to associate the broad community of science and technology with the Academy's purposes of furthering knowledge and advising the federal government. Functioning in accordance with general policies determined by the Academy, the Council has become the principal operating agency of both the National Academy of Sciences and the National Academy of Engineering in providing services to the government, the public, and the scientific and engineering communities. The Council is administered jointly by both Academies and the Institute of Medicine. Dr. Ralph J. Cicerone and Dr. Charles M. Vest are chair and vice chair, respectively, of the NRC.

*www.national-academies.org*

# Committee on an Assessment of Research-Doctorate Programs

**Jeremiah P. Ostriker,** *Committee Chair,* Charles A. Young Professor of Astronomy and Provost Emeritus, Princeton University

**Virginia S. Hinshaw,** *Vice Chair,* Chancellor, University of Hawai'i at Mānoa

**Elton D. Aberle,** Dean Emeritus of the College of Agricultural and Life Sciences, University of Wisconsin–Madison

**Norman Bradburn,** Tiffany and Margaret Blake Distinguished Service Professor Emeritus, University of Chicago

**John I. Brauman,** J. G. Jackson–C. J. Wood Professor of Chemistry, Emeritus, Stanford University

**Jonathan R. Cole,** John Mitchell Mason Professor of the University, Columbia University (resigned June 2010)

**Paul W. Holland,** Frederic M. Lord Chair in Measurement and Statistics (retired), Educational Testing Service

**Eric W. Kaler,** Provost and Senior Vice President for Academic Affairs, Stony Brook University

**Earl Lewis,** Provost and Executive Vice President for Academic Affairs and Asa Griggs Candler Professor of History and African American Studies, Emory University

**Joan F. Lorden,** Provost and Vice Chancellor for Academic Affairs, University of North Carolina at Charlotte

**Carol B. Lynch**, Dean Emerita of the Graduate School, University of Colorado, Boulder

**Robert M. Nerem,** Parker H. Petit Distinguished Chair for Engineering in Medicine, and former director, Parker H. Petit Institute for Bioengineering and Bioscience, Georgia Institute of Technology

**Suzanne Ortega,** Provost and Executive Vice President for Academic Affairs, University of New Mexico

**Robert J. Spinrad,** Vice President (retired), Technology Strategy, Xerox Corporation (resigned January 2008; deceased September 2009)

**Catharine R. Stimpson,** Dean, Graduate School of Arts and Science, and University Professor, New York University

**Richard P. Wheeler,** Vice Provost, University of Illinois at Urbana-Champaign

*Staff*
Charlotte V. Kuh, Study Director
Peter H. Henderson, Senior Program Officer
James A. Voytuk, Senior Program Officer
John Sislin, Program Officer
Michelle Crosby-Nagy, Research Assistant
Kara Murphy, Research Assistant
Rae E. Allen, Administrative Coordinator
Sabrina E. Hall, Program Associate

## Data Panel for the Assessment of Research-Doctorate Programs

**Norman M. Bradburn, Ph.D.,** *(Chair),* Tiffany and Margaret Black Distinguished Service Professor and Provost *Emeritus*, University of Chicago

**Richard Attiyeh, Ph.D.,** Vice Chancellor for Research, Dean of Graduate Studies, and Professor of Economics *Emeritus,* University of California, San Diego

**Scott Bass, Ph.D.,** Provost, The American University

**Julie Carpenter-Hubin, M.A.,** Director of Institutional Research and Planning, The Ohio State University

**Janet L. Greger, Ph.D.,** Vice Provost for Strategic Planning, University of Connecticut (retired)

**Dianne Horgan, Ph.D.,** Associate Dean of the Graduate School, University of Arizona

**Marsha Kelman, M.B.A.,** Associate Vice President, Policy and Analysis, Office of the President, University of California

**Karen Klomparens, Ph.D.,** Dean of the Graduate School, Michigan State University

**Bernard F. Lentz, Ph.D.,** Vice Provost for Institutional Research, Drexel University

**Harvey Waterman, Ph.D.,** Associate Dean for Academic Affairs, Graduate School-New Brunswick, Rutgers, The State University of New Jersey

**Ami Zusman, Ph.D.,** Coordinator, Graduate Education Planning & Analysis, Office of the President, University of California (retired)

# BOARD ON HIGHER EDUCATION AND WORKFORCE

Emory University

**Paula Stephan**
Professor of Economics
Andrew Young School for Policy Studies
Georgia State University

Staff
Charlotte Kuh, Deputy Executive Director, Policy and Global Affairs
Peter Henderson, Director, Board on Higher Education and Workforce
James Voytuk, Senior Program Officer
Mark Regets, Senior Program Officer
Christopher Verhoff, Financial Associate
Michelle Crosby-Nagy, Research Associate
Sabrina E. Hall, Program Associate

# FOREWORD

This report and its large collection of quantitative data will become in our view an important and transparent instrument for strengthening doctoral education in the United States. The report follows in the tradition of assessments conducted by the National Research Council for almost 30 years, but with important changes. Beyond the traditional, printed document, the data that inform and grow out of this report are being made available electronically to promote widespread use and analysis of many characteristics of doctoral programs. The unparalleled data set covers twenty important variables for an enormous number of programs in 62 major fields. It enables university faculty, administrators, and funders to compare, evaluate and improve programs; it permits students to find those programs best suited to their needs; and it allows for updating important information on a regular basis to permit continuous improvement.

Much has been learned from this study, which turned out to be more challenging and to take longer than we originally expected. An enormous effort was contributed by universities to collect and recheck the data, demonstrating their desire to identify comparative strengths and weaknesses and to show accountability. The study committee had to refine and revise its methodology as it sought to provide tools for evaluating and comparing programs. Although the data are based on the 2005-2006 academic year, they permit many useful comparisons of programs across many dimensions. All those interested in graduate education can learn much from studying the data, comparing programs, and drawing lessons for how programs can be improved. The data for many variables can be updated and made current on a regular basis by universities.

In order to identify variables most valued by doctoral faculty as well as to avoid using exclusively reputational rankings as was done in earlier graduate doctorate assessments, the committee employed two alternative ranking methods. The first method asked faculty in each field to assign a weight to each of the quantitative variables in the institutional surveys, and the weighted variables could then be used to determine ratings and rankings of programs. The second method was to survey a subset of faculty to ask them to rank a sample of programs in their field, and then to use principal components and regression analyses to obtain the implied weights for the institutional variables that would most closely reproduce the results. The committee initially envisioned combining the results of these two methods into a unified set of rankings. The production of rankings from measures of quantitative data turned out to be more complicated and to have greater uncertainty than originally thought. The committee ultimately concluded that it should present the results of the two approaches separately as illustrations of how individuals can use the data to apply their own values to the quantitative measures to obtain rankings suitable for their own specific purposes. The illustrative rankings, which are provided with ranges to show some of the statistical uncertainties, should not be interpreted as definitive conclusions about the relative quality of doctoral programs. Doctoral programs are valued for a variety of reasons, and their characteristics are valued in different ways by stakeholders; there is no single universal criterion or set of criteria.

The illustrative rankings and their ranges do provide important insights on how programs can be ranked according to different criteria and what variables are most important to faculty, which typically are variables that measure per capita scholarly output. Faculty generally do not assign great importance to program size when assigning weights directly—but when they rank programs, program size appears to implicitly carry large weight.  It is our view that strengthening graduate education will require paying attention to all of the variables in the dataset, not just those most important to faculty.  Three additional metrics were presented in the report for each program; these focused separately on research activity, student support and outcomes, and diversity of the academic environment.  A major value of the study is that this data set allows all stakeholders to assign weights which they believe to be important and then compare the programs on that basis.

If a process of continuous improvement is to result from this exercise, all of the stakeholders interested in graduate education will need to focus upon steps to improve performance across the board.  A major commitment by universities will be needed to update the data set on a regular basis, so that programs can continue to be compared and evaluated.  If this is done with the updated dataset as an important new tool, and we strive to improve what is already the world's strongest system of higher education, we believe that American doctoral education can continue to bring enormous benefits to our citizens and remain the envy of the world.


Ralph J. Cicerone, President, National Academy of Sciences
Charles M. Vest, President, National Academy of Engineering
Harvey V. Fineberg, President, Institute of Medicine

# Preface and Acknowledgments

Doctoral education, a key component of higher education in the United States, is performing well. It educates future professors, researchers, innovators and entrepreneurs. It attracts students and scholars from all over the world and is being emulated globally. This success, however, should not engender complacency. It was the intent of this study to measure characteristics of doctoral programs that are of importance to students, faculty, administrators, and others who care about the quality and effectiveness of doctoral programs in order to permit comparisons among programs in a field of study and to provide a basis for self-improvement within the disciplines. To this end, the Committee on an Assessment of Research-Doctorate Programs collected a large amount of data relating to research productivity, student support and outcomes and program diversity from over 5000 doctoral programs in 62 fields at 212 U.S. universities. Some of these data, such as the percent of entering students who complete in a given time period, the percent of students funded in the first year, and the diversity of program faculty and students have not been collected in earlier studies. These data appear in the online spreadsheets that accompany this report and can easily be selected, downloaded, and compared. The most important benefits of this study will flow from examination and analysis of the data that were collected.

In addition to making new data available, the committee addressed the issue of program rankings from an illustrative standpoint. Rankings based on faculty opinions of program quality had been produced in earlier NRC reports in 1982 and 1995. In these studies, the ratings and rankings were derived from surveys in which faculty members were asked to assess the scholarly quality and effectiveness in education of individual doctoral programs in their own fields, i.e. they were based on reputation. There was a widespread reaction, after the completion of the 1995 study, that the one, reputation based, measure was inadequate to represent the many important characteristics that are needed to describe and assess the full range of US doctoral programs.

The present NRC study, *A Data-Based Assessment of Research-Doctorate Programs*, differs significantly from these earlier studies in that it uses objective data to estimate overall quality of doctoral programs using values important to faculty, and does so in two different ways as illustrations. It also creates measures of program strength along three separate dimensions, that is, five separate measures have been developed. Using a much broader range of collected data and information from new surveys, this data-based assessment obtains faculty importance weights for 20 program characteristics, and designs two specific techniques to obtain weights that relate these characteristics to perceived program quality. It has also incorporated the uncertainty that comes from differences in faculty views, variability in program data, and statistical variation to produce ranges of rankings for each program in 59 disciplines. The committee considers these ranges of rankings to be illustrative. Other ranges could have been obtained with different weights. One example of alternative ranges of rankings with weights obtained from the surveys are ranges of rankings along the separate dimensions of 1)research activity, 2)student support and outcomes, and 3)diversity of the academic environment. These dimensional measures are all examples of ways that the data and weights can be combined. Users are encouraged to develop additional measures employing weights that reflect their values.  None of these ranges of rankings should be considered NRC-endorsed.

The committee believes that the concept of a precise ranking of doctoral programs is mistaken.  How doctoral programs are ranked will depend on what raters are chosen, on year-to-year variability in program characteristics, and on the statistical error involved in any estimation.  These sources of uncertainty imply that rankings of programs are intrinsically imprecise.  The committee has tried to take into account these sources of variation in its illustrative rankings and, in order to convey that variation, has presented ranges of rankings.  The two overall measures illustrate that data-based rankings may vary, depending on the weights applied to program characteristics, and that these may vary depending on which raters are chosen and the techniques used to obtain their rankings.

As noted earlier, it is the comparison of the program characteristics that will, in the end, be more valuable than any range of rankings.  The analysis of these characteristics will help direct faculty in academic programs to areas of potential improvement and will expand what students understand about the programs that interest them.

Because some of the data collected for this study had not been collected previously, time had to be spent on data validation and assurance.  The statistical techniques also required time to develop and test.  As a result, much of the data presented here come from 2005-2006.  Programs and faculty may have changed in the intervening period.  In the on-line spreadsheets, each program has a url.  Users are encouraged to go to these program websites to obtain the latest information about programs of interest.  Now that the statistical machinery and the data structure are in place, it should be easier to replicate this study with current data in the near future.

## ACKNOWLEDGMENT OF REVIEWERS AND SPONSORS

This report has been reviewed in draft form by individuals chosen for their diverse perspectives and technical expertise, in accordance with procedures approved by the National Academies' Report Review Committee.  The purpose of this independent review is to provide candid and critical comments that will assist the institution in making its published report as sound as possible and to ensure that the report meets institutional standards for objectivity, evidence, and responsiveness to the study charge. The review comments and draft manuscript remain confidential to protect the integrity of the process.

We wish to thank the following individuals for their review of this report and the accompanying data: John Bailar, University of Chicago; Diane Birt, Iowa State University; Craig Calhoun, New York University; Alicia Carriquiry, Iowa State University; Joseph Cerny, University of California, Berkeley; Gill Clarke, University of Bristol; David Donoho, Stanford University; Ronald Ehrenberg, Cornell University; Daniel Fogel, University of Vermont; George Langford, Syracuse University; Risa Palm, The State University of New York; William Press, University of Texas, Austin; Raul Ramos, University of Houston; Lydia Snover, Massachusetts Institute of Technology; Stephen Stigler, University of Chicago; Patrick Stover, Cornell University; Andrew Wachtel, Northwestern University; and John Wiley, University of Wisconsin-Madison.

The review of this report was overseen by Lyle Jones, University of North Carolina, Chapel Hill and Stephen Fienberg, Carnegie Mellon University.

Although the reviewers listed above have provided many constructive comments and suggestions, they were not asked to endorse the conclusions or recommendations, nor did they see the final draft of the report before its release. Responsibility for the final content of this report rests entirely with the authoring committee and the institution.

In addition to the reviewers, the sponsors of this study deserve both recognition and thanks for their patience and resources. First, thanks to the 212 universities that provided not only significant financial support but also staff time to obtain and validate high quality data. Second, our thanks to the foundations and agencies that provided support to this project: the Andrew W. Mellon Foundation, the Alfred P. Sloan Foundation, the U.S. Department of Energy, the National Institutes of Health, the National Science Foundation, and the National Research Council. As the case with the reviewers, responsibility for the final content of this report rests entirely with the authoring committee and the institution.

I would also like to thank our data and statistical contractor, Mathematica Policy Research, and particularly David Edson, who oversaw countless runs and data revisions with calm and good sense. I am also grateful to the Council of Graduate Schools, the American Council of Learned Societies, and the Association of Graduate Schools of the Association of American Universities, which heard progress reports at various stages of the project and offered suggestions that, we hope, have resulted in a better report. Thanks also to the scholarly societies and councils of department chairs who have helped us shape both the data for this report and its presentation. Finally, I would like to thank the staff of the project--Charlotte Kuh, James Voytuk, Michelle Crosby-Nagy, Sabrina Hall, Rae Allen, and Kara Murphy-- for their tireless efforts to bring to completion what has been a lengthy but rewarding project.

Jeremiah P. Ostriker, Chair
Committee to Assess Research-Doctorate Programs

# Contents

# Boxes, Figures, and Tables

## BOXES

## FIGURES

## TABLES

# Summary

*A Data-Based Assessment of Research-Doctorate Programs in the United States* provides an unparalleled dataset collected from doctoral institutions, doctoral programs, doctoral faculty and public sources that can be used to assess the quality and effectiveness of doctoral programs based on measures important to faculty, students, administrators, funders, and other stakeholders. The committee collected 20 measures that include characteristics of the faculty, such as their publications, citations, grants, and diversity; characteristics of the students, such as their GRE scores, financial support, publications, and diversity; and characteristics of the program, such as number of Ph.D. 's granted over five years, time to degree, percentage of student completion, and placement of students after graduation. The data were collected for the academic year 2005-2006 from more than 5,000 doctoral programs at 212 universities. These observations span 62 fields, and the research productivity data are based typically on a five-year interval. Some datasets (such as publications and citations) go as far back as 1981. Information on enrollments and faculty size were also collected for 14 emerging fields.

The program-level data, collected using questionnaires, reflect the size, scope, and other components of each program, as well as, financial aid and training practices. In addition, data were collected about time to degree and completion rates and whether the program followed the progress of its students after completion. The faculty questionnaire, which was sent to all faculty identified as doctoral faculty by their institutions, collected data on funding, work history, and publications, as well as on demographic characteristics. One section of the questionnaire asked the respondent to rate the relative importance of program, faculty productivity, and demographic characteristics in assessing program quality, and then to rate the relative importance of components within these larger categories. The student questionnaire asked about student educational background and demographic characteristics, as well as research experiences in the program, scholarly productivity, career objectives, and satisfaction with a variety of aspects of the program.

This report also includes illustrations of how the dataset can be used to produce rankings of doctoral programs, based on the importance of individual measures to various users. Two of the approaches provided in the report are intended to be illustrative of constructing data-based ranges of rankings that reflect values to assess program quality determined by the faculty who teach in these programs. Other ranges of rankings can also be produced reflecting the values of the users. The production of rankings from measures of quantitative data turned out to be more complicated and to have greater uncertainty than originally thought. As a consequence, the illustrative rankings are neither endorsed nor recommended by the National Research Council (NRC) as an authoritative conclusion about the relative quality of doctoral programs. Nevertheless, the undertaking did produce important insights that are useful as stakeholders use the dataset and the illustrations to draw conclusions for their own purposes. The illustrative approaches illuminate the interplay between program characteristics and the weights based on values of users that go into constructing rankings. The ranges of rankings that are shown convey some, but not all, of the uncertainties that can be estimated in producing rankings based on assigning importance weights to quantitative measures.

The reader who seeks a single, authoritative declaration of the "best programs" in given fields will not find it in this report. The reason for this outcome is that no single such ranking can be produced in an unambiguous and rigorous way. To create illustrative rankings, the committee explored several approaches to evaluate and rate programs, with the subsequent rankings reflecting an ordered list of ratings from high to low. Program ratings depend on two things, namely the characteristics of the program (e.g., number of faculty, number of publications, citations, and other quantifiable measures) and the weighting, or value, that faculty assigned to each characteristic. The committee determined the weights to apply to important characteristics by two different methods based on faculty inputs. One method involved asking direct questions about what characteristics are important and how they should be weighed, while the second used an implicit method to determine the weights based on evaluations of programs by faculty raters. The results of these two approaches are different, and are presented separately in the report.

The committee also developed three other rankings based on separate dimensions of the doctoral programs. All five approaches, which are explained in more detail in the following paragraphs, have strengths and deficiencies. The committee is not endorsing any one approach or any one measure or combination of measures as best. Rather, the user is asked to consider the reason a ranking is needed and what measures would be important to that ranking. The different measures should then be examined by the user and given appropriate weights, and the user should choose an approach that weights most heavily what is important for that user's purpose. As the committee has stressed repeatedly, the user may take the data that the study provides and construct a set of rankings based on the values that the specific user places on the measures.

The faculty survey on the relative importance of various measures yielded weights that are used to develop one illustrative ranking, the S-ranking (for survey-based), for which we present ranges of rankings for each program. On a separate questionnaire, smaller groups of randomly selected faculty in each field were asked to rate programs from a sample of doctoral programs. The results of the regression of these ratings on the measures of program characteristics are used to develop another range of illustrative rankings, the R-rankings (for regression based). The ranges and weights for these two ways of calculating rankings—one direct (S-ranking) and one indirect (R ranking)—are reported separately and provided in an online spreadsheet (*http://www.nap.edu/rdp*) that includes a guide for the user.

The ranking methodology utilized by the committee in these illustrative approaches has been chosen to be based on faculty values. This decision was made because perceived quality of the graduate doctoral program in a field is typically based on the knowledge and views of scholars in that field. Dimensional measures in three areas—research activity, student support and outcomes, and diversity of the academic environment—are also provided to give additional illustrative ranges of rankings of separate aspects of doctoral programs.

An earlier version of the methodology is described in the Methodology Guide. [1] The primary change made since the Guide was prepared was the decision to provide separate R and S rankings as illustrations rather than combining them into one overall ranking. This methodology is now described in technical terms in Appendix J. Although the relative importance of measures varies in different fields, per capita measures for publications, citations, grants, and awards are strongly preferred by faculty as key measures of program quality. One interesting and important difference between the weights that result in the R and S rankings is that the one measure of program size — the average number of Ph.D.'s granted over the previous five years—is often the largest weight in the R rankings and relatively small in the S rankings. Faculty appear not to assign as much importance to program size when assigning weights directly compared to the importance of program size in weights assigned indirectly based on their rating of programs. Program size, while not likely to be a direct cause of higher program quality, may serve as a surrogate for other program features that do exert positive influences on perceived quality.

The illustrative ranges of rankings are instructive for several reasons. Most importantly, they allow for comparison of programs in a field in a way that recognizes some—but not all—of the uncertainties and variability inherent in any ranking process. This uncertainty and variability come partially from variability in rater opinions, variability in data from year to year, and the error that accompanies the estimation of any statistical model. The ranges that are provided cover a broad interval of 90 percent, which is another change from the original methodology report. There are other sources of uncertainty that are not captured in the ranges presented in the illustrative rankings. These additional sources include uncertainty in the model for assessing quality based on quantitative measures as well as the uncertainty that the 20 measures capture the most relevant factors that are needed to assess quality in a particular field.

The current approach does have the advantage of collecting exactly the same categories of data from all programs being assessed, and uses those data to calculate ratings based on the relative importance of measures as established by doctoral faculty. This approach, however, entails a key vulnerability. In the current methodology, when program measures in a field are similar, program differences in the range of rankings can depend strongly on the precise values of the input data, and so are quite sensitive to errors in those data. We have worked to assure the quality of the measures used to generate rankings and have tried to minimize such errors in the data collection. But errors can arise from clerical mistakes and possible misfit between the measures and the data. They can be caused by misunderstandings by our respondents concerning the nature of the data requested from them, or they may be embedded in the public data-bases that we have used. Some of the key publication sources in a field or subfield may not be included in the public database that was used.[2] Despite our efforts we are certain that mistakes,

---

[1] National Research Council. *A Revised Guide to the Methodology of the Data-Based Assessment of Research-Doctorate Programs in the United States (2010).* Washington, D.C. : National Academies Press, 2010, which has been incorporated as Appendix J in this volume.

[2] For example, for the field of computer science, refereed conference papers are an important form of scholarship. For the humanities fields, books are important. Publications for all these fields were compiled directly from faculty résumés.

misunderstandings and errors in input data remain, and these will propagate through to any rankings.

We believe, however, that careful error-checking both by the NRC and by the doctoral programs being assessed has produced a collection of data of great usefulness in understanding doctoral education, both by providing a means for users to assess the quality of doctoral programs and for what the detailed analyses of the data themselves can tell us. The data permit comparisons of programs on the basis of several program characteristics, each of which provides an important vantage point on doctoral education. The ranges of illustrative rankings, because of the values expressed in the faculty questionnaires, emphasize measures of faculty productivity. But the data enable comparisons using any of the categories in which data were collected. Doctoral programs can readily be compared, not only on measures of research activity in a program, but, for example, on measures of student support, degree completion, time to degree, and diversity of both students and faculty. These data will become even more valuable if they are updated periodically and made current, which the committee strongly encourages.[3]

The work that has gone into producing this assessment of doctoral programs has raised the level of data collection vital to understanding the broad dimensions of doctoral education in the United States. It would be difficult to overstate the efforts required of universities and doctoral programs to produce, check, and recheck the data collected for this assessment. The extensive reliance on data in this assessment called for the collection of an enormous amount of information that has not been routinely or systematically collected by doctoral programs in the past. Graduate schools, institutional researchers, program administrators, and individual doctoral faculty all contributed countless hours to compiling, clarifying, and substantiating the information on which this assessment is based. As a result, we believe that this focus on data collection in and of itself by participating universities and their programs has created new standards, and improved practices, for recording quantitatively information on which qualitative assessments of doctoral programs can be based.

With the abundance of data included in this assessment comes a great deal of freedom in determining which information is most useful to individual users. We are particularly hopeful that the wealth of data collected for this assessment will encourage potential applicants to doctoral programs to decide what characteristics are important to them and will enable them to compare programs with respect to those characteristics. Potential doctoral applicants, and, indeed, all users of this assessment, are invited to create customized assessment tables that reflect their own preferences.[4]

---

[3] Recommendation 4 of the 2003 Methodology Study was "Data for quantitative measures should be collected regularly and made accessible in a Web-readable format. These measures should be reported whenever significantly updated are available." (p. 3 and 63) and the study also says "More frequent updating of these data would provide more timely and objective assessments." (p. 64)

[4] The NRC is supplying the data from this study to *www.PhDs.org*, which will allow users to construct their own rankings with their own weights.

# SOME FINDINGS

## Changes between 1993 and 2006

Because the biological science fields have been extensively reorganized since 1993, when the last NRC assessment was carried out, it is difficult to make comparisons in these areas over time. Other programs that were not included in 1993 are included in this assessment, including many programs in the field of agricultural sciences.

For fields in engineering, physical sciences, humanities, and social sciences, where comparisons between the previous study and this one are possible, we find that:

- Since the last NRC study was published in 1995 (based on data collected in 1993), the numbers of students enrolled in the programs that participated in both studies have increased in some broad fields (in engineering by 4 percentage points, and in the physical sciences by 9 percentage points) and declined in others (down 5 percentage points in the social sciences and down 12 percentage points in the humanities).[5]

- The numbers of Ph.D.' s produced per program across these common programs has grown by 11 percent.

- All the common programs have experienced a growth in the percentage of female students with the smallest growth (3.4 percentage points) in the humanities fields, which were already heavily female, and the greatest growth in the engineering fields (9 percentage points, increasing to 22 percent overall).

- For all doctoral programs in fields covered by the study, there has been an increase in the percentage of Ph.D.'s from underrepresented minority groups[6] (a growth of 2.3 percentage points to 9.6 percent in the agricultural sciences, 3.7 percentage points to 9.8 percent in the biological sciences, 1.7 percentage points to 6.4 percent in the physical sciences, 5.2 percentage points to 10.1 percent in engineering, 5.0 percentage points to 14.4 percent in the social sciences and 3.5 percentage points to 10.9 percent in the humanities).[7]

- Because of differences between the definition of faculty in 1993 and 2006, we cannot strictly compare faculty sizes, but it appears that the number of faculty involved in doctoral education has also grown in most programs.

Users are warned that, because of fundamental changes in the methodology, comparisons between 1993 rankings and ranges of rankings from the current study may be misleading. They are encouraged to understand the derivation of the current ranges of rankings and to examine the weights and variable values that led to them.

---

[5] The current study contains six broad fields: agricultural sciences, biological and health sciences, physical sciences, engineering, social and behavioral science, and humanities. This aggregation of fields is a convenient way to summarize data for the 62 individual fields.

[6] These are based on data reported by the National Science Foundation, because the 1995 NRC Study did not collect data on minority Ph.D.'s.

[7] By underrepresented minorities we mean: African-Americans, Hispanics, and American Indians.

## Program Characteristics

*Institutions*

We found that doctoral education in the United States is dominated by programs in public universities in terms of numbers of doctorates produced. Seventy-two percent of the doctoral programs in the study are in public universities. Of the 37 universities that produced the most Ph.D.'s from 2002-2006 (making up 50 percent of the total Ph.D.'s granted during this time), only 12 were private universities. The health of research and doctoral education in the United States depends strongly on the health of public education.

*Size*

As was found in the 1982 and 1995 reports, program size continues to be positively related to program ranking. This result holds despite our reliance in the current study on *per capita* measures of scholarly productivity. In most broad fields, the programs with the largest number of Ph.D.'s publish more per faculty member, have more citations per publication, and receive more awards per faculty member than the average program.

*Students*

There is very little difference among fields in the percent of students who receive full support in their first year. For all fields, this percentage is somewhere between 80 percent (social and behavioral sciences) and 92 percent (physical sciences). The larger programs have significantly longer median times to degree in all fields except the biological sciences, and this is particularly true in the humanities (7.4 years as compared to 6.1 years for the broad field as a whole). There is no significant difference based on size in the percentage of students who have definite plans for an academic position upon graduation. There are, however, differences by field, ranging from a high of 46 percent for the humanities, to a low of 15 percent for engineering. In terms of completion, over 50 percent of students complete in six years or less in the agricultural sciences and in engineering, but a smaller percentage does so in the other broad fields. In the social sciences the percentage is 37 percent, which is the same percentage completion for the humanities after eight years. In the physical sciences, the six-year completion percentage is 44 percent.

*Diversity*

The faculty of doctoral programs is not diverse with respect to underrepresented minorities —5 percent or less in all broad fields except the social sciences (7 percent) and the humanities (11 percent). Student diversity is greater—10 percent or above in programs in all broad fields except the physical sciences (8 percent). The faculty is more diverse in terms of gender, with women making up over 30 percent of the doctoral faculty in the biological sciences (32 percent), social sciences (32 percent), and humanities (39 percent). Engineering (11 percent) and the physical sciences (14 percent) lag with the agricultural sciences falling in between (24 percent). Women make up nearly 50 percent or more of students in the agricultural, biological and social sciences and the humanities. Again, the physical sciences (14 percent) and engineering (11 percent) lag despite a decade of growth in the production of female Ph.D.'s. International students are well over 40 percent of students in the agricultural sciences (42 percent), the physical sciences (44 percent), and engineering (58 percent), and less in the other broad fields.

## Faculty Characteristics

Over 87,000 faculty involved in doctoral education answered our faculty questionnaire, and the committee focused its attention on obtaining the weights that showed what faculty thought mattered to program quality and that were then used in the rankings. We found that the majority of faculty are middle-aged (between the ages of 40 and 60), and over 70 percent have been at their current university for 8 years or more. The effect of pervasive postdoctoral study is apparent in the biological and agricultural sciences, where only 6 percent of the faculty in doctoral programs are under the age of 40 as compared to more than double that percentage in the social and physical sciences and engineering. In the humanities 9 percent of the faculty are under the age of 40, but the humanities also have the highest percentage (27 percent) over the age of 60.

## Student Characteristics

Questionnaires were sent to advanced[8] doctoral students in programs in five fields—chemical engineering, physics, neuroscience, economics, and English. Sixty-four percent of these programs had more than 10 students responding, which was the cutoff used by the committee for reporting the results for individual programs. These reportable programs made up 85 percent to 90 percent of the programs surveyed. In total, complete questionnaires were received from 70 percent of the students who had been asked to respond. This database should prove to be of great interest to researchers on doctoral education.[9]

Generally speaking, a majority of students were "very satisfied" or "somewhat satisfied" with the quality of their program in all fields. English stood out as a field where fewer than 40 percent of the students reported that their research facilities and their workspaces were "excellent" or "good," which may reflect a difference among fields over what constitutes quality research facilities and work spaces. Only 40 percent or less of students in all the fields were satisfied with the program-sponsored social interaction. Over 60 percent in most fields, however, felt they benefited from the program's intellectual environment. Programs do well in supporting students to attend professional and scholarly meetings and, in the science and engineering fields, over 35 percent have published articles in refereed journals while still enrolled in their doctoral program.

---

[8] By advanced, we mean that they have been admitted to candidacy.

[9] Because of confidentiality concerns, these and the faculty data will not be publicly available, but will be made available to researchers who sign a confidentiality agreement with the NRC.

Students were also asked about their career objectives recalled from when they entered the program and when they answered the questionnaire. There was a decline in the percentage who said they had "research and development" as a career objective in all fields and a decline in those interested in teaching in all fields but neuroscience. The percent of students who had management and administration as a career objective grew, but was still below 10 percent in all fields. Research and development was still the predominant career goal, except in English, where teaching (52 percent) dominated.

In summary, doctoral education in the United States is a vast undertaking comprising many programs in many fields with, overall, very high standards and intellectual reputation. For a long time, North American institutions of higher education have been the world's standard for the research doctorate. As universities across the globe compete with increasing intensity for the faculty and students who will advance the knowledge economy of the future, it is important that we take stock of the enormous value represented by the United States research doctorate programs. Taken together, these programs will produce the future thinkers and researchers for all kinds of employment as well as the faculty who nurture the next generation of scholars and the researchers. All are essential to scientific discovery, technological innovation, and cultural understanding in the United States and across the globe.

This study cannot, of course, provide a comprehensive understanding of these research doctorate programs. The data collected for this study represent an unprecedented wealth of information, and the committee hopes that they will be updated and used for further analysis.[10] These data have been used to produce illustrative ranges of rankings of research doctorate programs aimed at reflecting the values of the faculty who teach in these programs. The intent is to illustrate how individuals can use the data and apply their own values to the quantitative measures to obtain rankings suitable for their specific purposes. But the data themselves, even more so than the weighted summary measures and the illustrative ranges of rankings, can lead to analyses that throw revealing light on the state of doctoral education in the United States, can help university faculty and administrators to improve their programs, and can help students to find the most appropriate graduate programs to meet their needs.

---

[10] Some of these analyses will be reported as part of this study at a workshop to be held after the data are released.

# 1

# Introduction

This assessment of research doctorate programs conducted by the National Research Council (NRC) presents data that provide, for the first time in one place, basic information about many aspects of doctoral education in the United States. The data were compiled on a uniform basis[1] and collected from the universities themselves. Data from the assessment will allow comparisons of similar doctoral programs, with the goal of informing efforts to improve current practices in doctoral education, and will help matriculating students pick the graduate programs best suited to their individual needs.[2]

The assessment, which covers doctoral programs in 62 fields[3] at 221 institutions,[4] offers accessible data about program characteristics that will be of interest to policy makers, researchers, university administrators, and faculty, as well as to students who are considering doctoral study. Furthermore, in an illustrative manner, the assessment analyzes and combines these data to create two ranges of rankings based on overall measures of program quality that were derived from faculty perceptions of program quality approached in two different ways.

The National Research Council has a tradition of conducting careful assessments of doctoral education in the United States. The first NRC assessment, published in 1982,[5] was a rich source of data for educational planners and policy makers, as well as a source of reputational ratings of perceived program quality obtained from raters who were acquainted with the programs in the discipline.[6] The next NRC study, published in 1995, expanded the coverage of

---

[1] The data were collected on a uniform basis in the sense that the universities were given careful definitions of the data elements and, if these definitions were adhered to, the data would be uniform. Data were checked and validated for internal consistency, but differences may still exist in university definitions of what a doctoral program is.

[2] The study covers Ph.D. programs, some of which are offered in professional schools. It does not cover doctoral programs in professional fields.

[3] In addition to the 59 fields with program rankings, a full set of data was collected for three fields: (1) languages, societies, and cultures, for which rankings could not be calculated because of the heterogeneity of subfields, which made the calculation of rankings for the field as a whole impractical; (2) computer engineering, which was initially identified as a field separate from electrical engineering and computer engineering, but had only 20 programs, fewer than the 25 required for the application of the ranking methodology; and (3) "Engineering Science and Materials (not elsewhere classified)," which also was not ranked when it turned out to have only 16 eligible programs. Data on size of faculty and enrollment were also collected for 14 emerging fields that did not have enough programs to qualify for inclusion in the ranking study.

[4] The institutions include 212 universities and nine combinations of universities that offer joint programs.

[5] The 1982 study and the 1995 study were both conducted under the auspices of the Conference Board of Associated Research Councils of which the NRC is a member. The current study members initially consulted closely with the Conference Board, but this study was conducted primarily by the NRC.

[6] National Research Council, *An Assessment of Research-Doctorate Programs in the United States*. 5 vols.(Washington, D.C.: National Academy Press, 1982).

fields and types of data.[7] The current study continues that tradition but uses a methodology that directly relates a measure of perceived reputation to quantified variables.  Earlier studies relied on a program questionnaire and a faculty "rating" questionnaire. In addition to these, the current study fielded an institutional questionnaire, a student questionnaire in five fields, and an extensive faculty questionnaire. These numbers refer only to the program measures. The questionnaires appear in Appendix D.  The expansion of field coverage over time is shown in Table 1-1.

| TABLE 1-1 Coverage of NRC Studies, 1982–2006 | | |
|---|---|---|
| Study Year | Number of Fields Covered | Measures Collected |
| 1982 | 32 | 16 (except for the humanities for which publication measures were not collected) |
| 1993 | 41 | 14 |
| 2006 | 59 ranked, 3 unranked but with complete data, and 14 unranked emerging fields with partial data | 20 (for rankings including the reputational measures) plus expanded coverage of completion, student service in teaching and research, support services provided, student costs and financial support, interdisciplinarity, and postdoctoral study. |

Distinct from the earlier studies, the primary purpose of the current study, as outlined in the study's statement of task, was the following: "(1) the collection of quantitative data through questionnaires administered to institutions, programs, faculty, and 'admitted to candidacy' students (in selected fields); (2) collection of program data on publications, citations, and dissertation keywords;[8] and (3) the design and construction of program ratings using the collected data including quantitatively based estimates of program quality."

## WHO WILL FIND THESE DATA USEFUL?

These data will be useful to administrators, faculty, students considering doctoral study, and to those concerned with governance and policy related to doctoral education, as well as to the employers of Ph.D.'s outside of academia. In addition to comparisons of specific characteristics of interest, users will be able to understand the calculation of ranges of rankings of doctoral programs in each field through a spreadsheet downloadable from the National Academies Press Web site, *http://www.nap.edu/rdp*. Details of the illustrative rankings can be obtained by clicking on links provided in this spreadsheet. This study uses a methodology that permits users interested in rankings to understand the sources of those rankings. It also enables programs and individuals to benchmark themselves against peer or nearby programs using criteria that seem to them most appropriate. Examples are discussed in Chapter 5.

## DESIGN OF THE STUDY

[7]National Research Council, *Research Doctorate Programs in the United States: Continuity and Change* (Washington, D.C.: National Academy Press, 1995). This report refers to data from this study as the *1993 data*, but it refers to the study itself as the *1995 study*.

[8] As the study proceeded, the collection of dissertation keywords proved too complex, and this effort was dropped.

This study was designed with two objectives in mind: first, to collect comparable data across doctoral programs that would permit benchmarking for faculty and administrators, and second, to relate these data to measures of overall program quality and measures of particular aspects of doctoral programs. How the study was designed to achieve these objectives is described briefly in Chapter 2.

Briefly, to characterize doctoral programs, data were collected from universities, their programs, and faculty in 62 fields, as well as from students in five fields.[9] The data reported by the programs reflected the size, scope, and practices of each program, as well as financial aid and training practices that affect students. In addition, data were collected about time to degree and completion rates and whether the program tracked its students after completion.

Because interdisciplinarity is an issue of increasing importance for doctoral programs, the program questionnaire gathered data to address this issue by counting faculty from outside the program who were engaged in supervising dissertations and by asking directly whether the program was considered to be interdisciplinary.

The faculty questionnaire collected data on funding, work history, and publications, as well as on demographic characteristics. One section of the questionnaire asked the respondent to rate the relative importance of program, faculty, and demographic characteristics to program quality. It also asked whether the faculty member would be willing to respond to a questionnaire asking for ratings of programs. Nonrespondents were replaced in the rating study until approximately 50 raters were obtained for each sampled program in each discipline. See Appendix H for details by discipline.

The student questionnaire, administered to advanced[10] students in physics, chemical engineering, neuroscience, economics, and English, asked about student educational background and demographic characteristics, as well as research experiences in the program, scholarly productivity, career objectives, and satisfaction with a variety of aspects of the program. The size of the sample for each questionnaire and response rates are shown in Table 1-2.

---

[9] The five fields were chemical engineering, physics, neuroscience, economics, and English. These fields were chosen because they are large, represented all but one of the broad fields, and were viewed by the committee as appropriate for a pilot study to understand whether such a questionnaire could provide useful information.

[10] "Advanced" means students who have been admitted to candidacy.

| TABLE 1-2 Study Questionnaires and Response Rates | | |
|---|---|---|
| Questionnaire | Total Responses | Response Rate (%) |
| Institution and program | 221 institutions and combinations of institutions; 4,838 rated programs | 100 |
| Faculty | 87,515 | 88 |
| Student (five fields) | 11,888 | 73 |
| Rating | 7,932 | a |

a Nonrespondents were replaced in the rating study until approximately 50 raters were obtained or each sampled program in each discipline. See Appendix H for details by discipline.

The importance of the measured variables to perceived quality was ascertained in two ways: (1) from the relative importance of weights calculated from answers to the faculty questionnaire, and (2) from taking a sample of programs and faculty in each field and statistically deriving weights for each variable from the faculty's response to a rating questionnaire.[11] Both of these approaches reflect faculty values, which are discussed in Chapter 5. The method of obtaining rankings through two separate ways of calculating ranges of overall rankings is discussed briefly in Chapter 4 and in far more detail in the methodology guide. Chapter 3 also compares the current methodology to that of the 1995 study and explains some sources of noncomparability. Chapter 5 discusses the ways in which the study ascertains faculty values, which are key to understanding the rankings in the study. In Chapter 6 users learn how different groups may wish to approach and use these data. And Chapter 7 discusses some general patterns of the data and presents the principal characteristics of the programs in the study. It contrasts the methodology and results from the 1995 study with the current study and then presents a description of important findings about doctoral education in 2006–2007.[12] It also presents selected findings from the faculty and student questionnaires. The concluding Chapter 8 provides the committee's views of how the data from the study might be the subject of future work.

## WHAT THIS STUDY HAS REVEALED

Doctoral education in the United States is a far-flung and varied enterprise. Every field has its highly ranked and renowned programs, which are typically characterized by a large size and the high research productivity of faculty. To be sure, there are also many smaller programs with high rates of completion and times to degree similar to highly ranked programs. However, doctoral education is in fact concentrated in relatively few institutions whose programs have many students and faculty. Of the 221 institutions and combinations of institutions that participated in the study, half of the Ph.D.'s were granted by 37 universities, or 17 percent of the total participating in the study. Because most of these programs are in public institutions, the health of

---

[11] Each faculty member was asked to rate 15 programs, and these faculty ratings were then related to the variables for each sampled program. Data on numbers of program, raters, and raters per program for each field are shown in Appendix H.

[12] Much more data are available than will be reported in the spreadsheet for this report. This report focuses on 20 program characteristics, but many more questions were asked. The committee plans to make the full database for all questionnaires except the rating questionnaire available to interested parties, unless particular items would violate individual confidentiality restrictions. Items whose answers would violate individual confidentiality restrictions will be masked for this dataset. Researchers who wish to use the full dataset with unmasked values must apply to the NRC and agree to comply with confidentiality restrictions in their published data.

these institutions and the nation's ability to produce highly trained researchers and the next generation of professors are inextricably linked.

As an illustration of the kinds of data-based rankings that can be produced, the committee explains and reports rankings based on two measures. One measure, the S ranking, is based on a survey of the importance to faculty in a given field of the general characteristics of doctoral programs. The other, the R ranking, is based on values reflected in ratings given to a sample of programs by a sample of faculty in a field. These latter measures are then related, through a regression, to the same measures used in the S ranking for the sampled programs, and the coefficients[13] from that regression are used as weights to calculate these rankings for all programs in the field.[14] The uncertainty in all rankings is measured in part by calculating the ranking 500 times, with a different half sample of raters taken each time, so that all rankings are presented as *ranges* of rankings. In addition to these overall rankings, the study provides ranges of program rankings, based on the weights obtained for subsets of the S measure in each field. These rankings address three specific dimensions of doctoral education: (1) research activity, (2) student support and outcomes, and (3) diversity of the educational environment. For all measures, attention is given to the presentation of statistical uncertainties in the reported results.

The ranking methodology is based on faculty values, expressed either explicitly through the questionnaire results that are used to calculate S rankings or implicitly through the ratings of a sample of programs that are used to calculate the R rankings. The measures viewed as most important to the quality of a doctoral program are related primarily to faculty research productivity. According to faculty, publications, citations, grants, and awards matter more than other metrics.

In some cases the ranges of R rankings and S rankings do not overlap. One interesting and important difference between the weights that result in the R and S rankings is that the one measure of program size—the average number of Ph.D.'s granted over the previous five years—often receives the largest weight in the R rankings but relatively small in the S rankings. Faculty appear to not assign as much importance to program size when assigning weights directly as when assigning them indirectly based on their rating of programs. Program size, while not likely to be a direct cause of higher program quality, may serve as a surrogate for other program features that do exert positive influences on quality.

Another possible cause of these differences between the R and S measures is heterogeneity in the modes of scholarship in the field so that the statistical model does not fit very well.[15] A table showing the correlation of the medians of the two measures for programs in each discipline appears in Appendix G. Meanwhile, measures other than the range of R rankings and S rankings may be important to others engaged in doctoral education, such as granting agencies and the students themselves, and as such should not be ignored. The committee

---

[13] The coefficient expresses the relation between the rating and a particular characteristic when all the other characteristics are taken into account—that is, through a multivariate regression. The committee interprets them as weights that express the contribution of the particular characteristic to the variation in the rating.

[14] The sample was designed to reflect the national population of faculty in each field with respect to faculty rank, program size, and geographic distribution.

[15] Heterogeneity would create problems if two subfields in the same discipline had different modes of scholarship, so that the relationship between number of publications per faculty member and rating was different for each subfield. For example, if the rate of publication was much lower for programs in one subfield, highly rated programs dominated by this subfield would appear to be anomalous when combined with the subfield with a higher rate of publication. This problem could be solved by dividing the field and estimating the coefficients separately for the R ranking.

approached comparisons in three distinct areas through the dimensional measures. These measures summarize the program characteristics of research activity, student treatment and outcomes, and diversity of the academic environment. Student treatment and outcomes is related to research activity, because programs with a high level of research activity have the resources to treat students better. Programs with a high level of research activity have more faculty with research funding, and they typically exist in research universities with higher levels of available support. Many such programs have high rates of student funding in the first year and relatively high completion rates. They often do not, however, have shorter median times to degree. Based on data from the National Science Foundation Survey of Doctorate Recipients, the committee found that less than 50 percent of Ph.D.'s in each broad field has definite plans to seek an academic position or postdoctoral study in academia. Thus the findings of this study are important to employers of Ph.D.'s in the nonacademic sectors, as well as to academia. Furthermore, many Ph.D.'s are now employers in research-intensive businesses, and the characteristics of the programs from which they hire Ph.D.'s may be useful to them.

Diversity among the faculty has improved impressively since the 1995 NRC study. Gender diversity has increased substantially in all fields, and the percentage of new Ph.D.'s who are female has risen from 38 percent to 45 percent overall, although the percentages are still low in the physical and mathematical sciences (30 percent) and engineering (20 percent). The racial diversity of Ph.D.'s has also grown markedly, at an average annual rate of 4.6 percent, whereas the number of nonminority Ph.D.'s has declined by 1.7 percent. Underrepresented minorities were 7.4 percent of Ph.D.'s overall in 1993 and were 13.5 percent in 2006, but their proportion remains low, especially in the more highly ranked programs in science and engineering.[16] Overall, the number of Ph.D.'s granted annually to white males declined from 12,867 in 1993 to 7,297 in 2006.[17]

The ratio of faculty to students has changed since the 1995 NRC study. The ratio of faculty to Ph.D.'s graduated increased in most broad fields from 1993 to 2006, the years in which the data were collected. This finding may reflect a deeper faculty involvement in doctoral education, or it may be partially a result of definitional changes between the two studies.[18]

Finally and most importantly, this study is a tool that can be useful to administrators, faculty, students, and others with an interest in the characteristics of doctoral programs. Users can pick programs of interest and measures of interest and make customized comparisons. For students, these comparisons may be along the lines of funding and completion rates, or characteristics of programs near their homes.

---

[16] "Underrepresented minorities" refers to African Americans, Hispanics, and American Indians.

[17] Source: National Science Foundation.

[18] In the 1995 study, programs were asked for the "names and ranks of all faculty members who participate significantly in education toward the research doctorate." In the 2006 questionnaire, programs were given a far more specific definition of faculty, who were divided into three categories: core, new, and associated. The definitions are as follows:

*Core Faculty.* Faculty who
    (1) have served as a chair or member of a program dissertation committee in the past five academic years (2001-2002 through 2005-2006), *or*
    (2) are serving as a member of the graduate admissions or curriculum committee.
    The faculty member must be currently (2006-2007) and formally designated as faculty in the program, and not be an outside reader who reads the dissertation but does not contribute substantially to its development. Include emeritus faculty only if the faculty member has, within the past three years, either chaired a dissertation committee or been the primary instructor for a regular Ph.D. course.

*New Faculty.* Faculty who are not core *and*
    (1) do not meet the criteria for core faculty, but who have been hired in tenured or tenure-track positions within the past three academic years (2003-2004 through 2005-2006) *and*
    (2) are currently employed at your university and are expected to become involved in doctoral education in your program.

*Associated Faculty.* Faculty who are neither core nor new, but
    (1) have chaired or served on program dissertation committees in the past five years (2001-2002 through 2005-2006), *and*
    (2) have a current (2006-2007) appointment at your institution, but who are not designated faculty in the program.
    They should not be outside readers, or faculty currently employed at other universities, unless they are on leave from the faculty at your institution. Include emeritus faculty only if the faculty member has, within the past three years, either chaired a dissertation committee or been the primary instructor for a regular Ph.D. course.

Administrators may find comparisons with peer programs nationwide or regionally. With that in mind, six months after the release of this report and the accompanying data, the National Research Council will hold a workshop at which researchers and others who have used the data will report on the uses they have made of them. The proceedings of this workshop will be published as a workshop report and will expand on the descriptive summary discussion provided in this report. Whatever their interest, all users will find that they have access to information about doctoral programs that was not available in the past.

# 2

# Context and Motivation

Doctoral education is at the heart of the U.S. system of innovation. It is the process that generates highly educated scholars and researchers, significant research results, and avenues for innovation, thereby creating the leaders needed to produce the research advances that will create new careers and economic vitality for the nation.[1] Doctoral education trains the professors of the future—it inculcates the habits of mind necessary for productive research and scholarship. Doctoral education is intimately involved in the creation of scholars whose ideas will shape both future innovations and how Americans use and understand innovation as it changes their lives. American graduate education draws students from across the United States and around the globe, particularly in the science, technology, engineering, and mathematics (STEM) fields, and has been the envy of the world since World War II. Now, however, the U.S. position is facing substantial challenges, from a growing emphasis on doctoral education in other countries to financial constraints stemming both from the economic downturn of 2008–2009 and from the continuation of declining trends in state support for higher education.[2]

Several reports have highlighted the threats to U.S. leadership in innovation, including recently from the National Research Council, *Rising Above the Gathering Storm: Energizing and Employing America for a Brighter Economic Future*, which focuses especially on the need to improve U.S. graduate programs in STEM fields in order to improve U.S. economic competitiveness. The need for enhanced performance and accessibility is also highlighted in the recent report from the Council of Graduate Schools *Graduate Education: The Backbone of American Competitiveness and Innovation.*[3] These and other reports lay out clear frameworks for a focused commitment to improving graduate education. As additional resources are being considered for graduate programs, it becomes increasingly important to have structures in place to continually assess these investments.

In addition to international competitive forces, strong drivers in the United States are underlying efforts to improve the quality and efficiency of graduate programs. For

---

[1] See, for example, National Research Council, *Rising Above the Gathering Storm: Energizing and Employing America for a Brighter Economic Future* (Washington, D.C.: National Academies Press, 2007), chap. 1.

[2] A report issued in May 2010 by the Commission on the Future of Graduate Education, *The Path Forward: The Future of Graduate Education in the United States,* May 2010, eloquently lays out the importance of graduate education. To read the report, visit *www.fgereport.org/rsc/pdf/CFGE_report.pdf.* Accessed July 9, 2010.

[3] Council of Graduate Schools, *Graduate Education: The Backbone of American Competitiveness and Innovation* (Washington, D.C.: Council of Graduate Schools, 2007).

one thing, public universities are experiencing a sustained decline in state support that is forcing institutions to increase tuition and raise funds privately, thereby mirroring some of the features of private universities. For both public and private universities, doctoral education is expensive in the commitment of time and dollars both by those engaged in the enterprise and by its funders. Thus an assessment of program effectiveness to weigh the justification of that investment is always necessary.

Finally, efforts to determine whether doctoral education is living up to its promise call for an evaluation of whether it has done so by expanding domestic sources of talent, improving time to degree, and raising rates of completion. These are just some of the challenges that this study has attempted to address in view of the fact that few previous studies have been able to investigate these challenges as thoroughly.

## WHY ASSESS DOCTORAL PROGRAMS?

The assessment of doctoral programs dates back to 1925, when Raymond M. Hughes first conducted a survey to gauge faculty opinion of "the esteem at the present time for graduate work in your subject."[4] His survey, which appeared in a report to the Association of American Colleges, was aimed at constructing rankings of doctoral programs. The results were greeted with both interest and criticism. Since then, however, reputational measures have been repeatedly used to assess the quality of doctoral programs.

In the more than 80 years since the Hughes report, doctoral education has changed tremendously in size, number of fields, and the nature of employment destinations of Ph.D. recipients. The nature of assessing doctoral programs has changed as well, from reputational rankings provided by department chairs to studies that have increasingly included objective measures of aspects of doctoral programs.[5]

Today, a similar kind of reappraisal, but with a different motivation, may be warranted. With the enormous importance of and investment in doctoral education comes the need for accountability, because many different sectors of the U.S. economy rely heavily on the quality of knowledge produced by the nation's Ph.D.'s. Colleges and universities across the United States and around the world rely on American doctoral programs to educate the next generation of faculty and professional researchers. Corporations depend on highly trained doctoral students ready to bring cutting-edge technology and science to their labs and offices. Federal agencies also invest considerable sums of money to support doctoral students as fellows, trainees, and research assistants,

---

[4] Quoted in National Research Council, *Research Doctorate Programs in the United States,* 10.

[5] For this discussion it is important to recognize the distinction between reputational measures and those called "objective measures" in this report. Reputations of program quality are derived, here and in the past NRC studies, from respondents' ranking of Ph.D. programs on a six-point scale from distinguished to poor, which includes one category that indicates that a respondent does not have enough knowledge of the program to rate it. These data are quantitative, objective, and measurable, just like the Likert-type scales that have been used in the social and behavioral sciences for decades. Objective measures, as used here, refer to measurements based on data derived from sources that yield faculty publication counts, citations of their work, and honorific awards, as well as measures of student support and outcomes and program diversity. These kinds of measured data may partially predict the reputational standing of a program. But reputations, as a composite subjective assessment translated into a score on a scale, may capture other elements of program quality that cannot be obtained by means of the objective measures used here.

as do private foundations. The provision of information for benchmarking and improvement is salient in all these sectors.

For students considering a doctorate, the importance of accountability is no less striking. The decision to enroll in a doctoral program represents an enormous personal commitment. And the selection of a doctoral program is a life choice of great importance. How effective is a particular program in graduating its students in a timely way? What is the reputation of the program? What are its particular strengths and weaknesses? What kind of financial support will be available? What benefits are available for students with families? What kind of record does the program have in attracting, supporting, and graduating underrepresented students? Is the program successful in recruiting and supporting women in traditionally male-dominated fields? How do its graduates fare in the world? It is important that students considering doctoral education pose such questions and that there be places where they can find reliable answers to them. The availability of data that are comparable across similar programs can serve as a guide to areas that need action and thus the collection of such data was a goal of this study.

Still in use today, the traditional measures for assessment of doctoral education have been time to degree and completion rates.[6] The shift toward including student opinion in perceived learning outcomes did occur until recently.[7] Additional measures used include race and gender diversity, test scores, financial support of students, percentage completing, relationship with mentor, and overall socialization. These measures were addressed in the student questionnaire.

No one source, of course, can answer all questions about all doctoral programs for all prospective doctoral students, funding agencies, or university administrators. But one important purpose of this NRC study is to make a very large amount of information—arranged in as manageable a form as possible—available to those with a variety of interests: to students facing such choices and asking such questions, to agencies and government bodies and foundations that invest heavily in doctoral education, and to universities that must manage their own doctoral programs effectively. Even when the NRC study findings cannot answer all the important questions that the many constituencies of doctoral education will bring to it, the study will put them in a better position to know the questions that they then need to pose to the programs they are considering.

As this committee understands, not only must an enterprise of this significance be operated effectively, but also constituencies crucial to the support of doctoral education must have access to the information that can help provide reliable assessments of its effectiveness. Likewise, using such information, policy makers must be sensitive to the changing characteristics, or evolution, of doctoral education, because such changes are

---

[6] William G. Bowen and Neil L. Rudenstine, *In Pursuit of the PhD* (Princeton, N.J.: Princeton University Press, 1992); J. Gravois, In humanities, 10 years may not be enough to get a Ph.D., *Chronicle of Higher Education,* July 27, 2007.

[7] Council of Graduate Schools, *PhD Completion and Attrition: Analysis of Baseline Program Data from the PhD Completion Project* (Washington, D.C.: Council of Graduate Schools, 2008); B. E. Lovitts, *Leaving the Ivory Tower: The Causes and Consequences of Departure from Doctoral Study* (New York: Rowman and Littlefield, 2001).

likely to be a consequence of the prominence of doctoral education in the national system of innovation. These changes include the increasing interdisciplinarity of U.S doctoral programs. As a result, the committee went to great lengths to try to capture this complex variable.

## DIVERSITY OF FACULTY AND STUDENTS IN DOCTORAL PROGRAMS

An area of importance in assessing doctoral programs is the demographic characteristics of doctoral students. These characteristics include their international diversity, as well as their race, ethnicity, and gender. U.S. doctoral programs have attracted students from around the world for many years. These programs are also striving to become more diverse in race, ethnicity, and gender, and to some extent they are succeeding.

### International Students

The number of international students pursuing doctoral programs in the United States has grown significantly since the 1990s. According to the Institute for International Education, the absolute numbers of enrollments of international doctoral students increased from 100,092 in 2003–2004 (academic year) to 108,976 in 2007–2008.[8] Graduate applications overall, however, moved in the opposite direction. International graduate applications for the 2003–2004 academic year dropped suddenly and sharply. Although this brief downward trend now appears to have slowed or stopped, the decline was sharp enough that graduate applications and new enrollments have not yet returned to pre-2003 levels.[9]

One cause of this reversal in growth was the sensitivity of the international graduate application process to perturbations in visa policy and practices. Measures put in place after the terrorists attacks of September 11, 2001, not only made entry into the United States for study more difficult, but may also have had a chilling effect on the interest of international students in pursuing graduate study in the U.S. universities. Compounding the issue was an escalation in the level of competition worldwide for the best international doctoral students. For example, the European Union nations have recognized how important the knowledge and skills developed through doctoral education are to building a twenty-first century economy, and so those nations have given high priority to strengthening the doctoral education they offer. And China, which has provided large numbers of superb doctoral students for U.S. universities for the last half-century, has introduced ambitious programs to expand and strengthen doctoral education in its own universities. Furthermore, countries that provide doctoral study in English, such as Great Britain, Canada, and Australia, capitalized on the situation in the United States by moving rapidly to recruit more international students.

Students from other countries enrolled in the entire range of doctoral programs were surveyed for this study. These students come from all over the world, but the

---

[8] Institute for International Education, *Open Doors* (Washington, D.C.: IIE, 2003–2007).

[9] N. Bell, *Findings from 2009 CGS Graduate Admissions Survey, Phase III: Final Offer of Admissions and Enrollment* (Washington, D.C.: Council of Graduate Schools, 2009).

number of students from India, China, and South Korea are particularly high. International enrollments are especially high in doctoral programs in engineering and the physical and mathematical sciences. Indeed, it is not unusual for major Ph.D. programs in engineering to award half or more of their doctorates to students from other countries.

U.S. research universities have benefited greatly from the influx of doctoral students from other nations. While enrolled, these students characteristically show higher than average completion rates and shorter than average times to degree.[10] Their contribution to laboratory research in the STEM fields is enormous. In fact, the research productivity of U.S. universities is closely tied to their ability to recruit and retain talented students who come to this country to pursue doctoral study.

Many successful international doctoral students stay in the United States. By becoming university faculty, by establishing start-up companies, and by contributing to the research enterprise of corporate America, these international Ph.D.'s are a powerful component of the research engine that fuels the American economy.

When international graduates return to their country of origin, they take back with them an understanding of American culture and values that is important in clarifying and stabilizing the place of the United States in the global political and economic culture. Similarly, domestic students gain a more global perspective and benefit from collaborations with graduate students from other countries and are thus better prepared for the global workplace they will encounter after graduation. Overall, international recipients of American doctorates play important roles in the educational, social, political, economic, and cultural infrastructures of many countries. In the increasingly global arena of high-level research, the U.S. capacity to develop international research partnerships is greatly strengthened by the presence of former students from American universities in key positions in laboratories and universities around the world.

In short, the appeal of the U.S. doctorate to students in other countries is one of its great, essential strengths. That importance is borne out by the data collected for this study. The continued success of the United States in this increasingly competitive arena, which is crucial to sustaining the excellence of U.S. doctoral education, is the responsibility of research universities, of state and federal government policy makers, of powerful funding agencies and foundations, and of all other stakeholders in the American doctorate and the vast research enterprise that depends on it.

## Race, Ethnicity, and Gender of American Doctoral Students

Doctoral programs across the nation have recognized the implications of powerful demographic trends in the general growth of the population and in college graduation rates that shape the educated workforce in an increasingly knowledge-based economy. Growth rates in the underrepresented minority population outstrip those of the majority, and more women now are awarded bachelor's degrees each year than men. Both of these trends point to a change in the composition of participants in doctoral education in the United States.

---

[10] Council of Graduate Schools, *PhD Completion and Attrition*.

Through the 1970s doctoral education in almost all fields was largely a man's enterprise, and the number of underrepresented minorities pursuing Ph.D.'s was very small. It became clear, however, that if doctoral education was to serve the population equitably, and if domestic doctoral production was to adequately meet the research and professorial needs of the nation, universities must increase the participation in doctoral education of underrepresented minorities and women. But success in this effort would require effective strategies that would address a range of cultural and historical forces that had long distributed educational opportunities unevenly across the population.

In response to this situation, many universities have introduced programs to emphasize the importance of recruiting and supporting underrepresented minorities in virtually all fields, as well as the need to increase the presence of women in many of them. Such programs are a high priority of most graduate schools, which have developed procedures and funding mechanisms to encourage minority and female undergraduates to consider doctoral education and to provide support for women and minorities who enroll in doctoral programs. Indeed, government funding agencies—among them the National Institutes of Health (NIH) and the National Science Foundation (NSF) —have developed targeted programs to stimulate the recruitment, retention, and success of women and minorities in doctoral programs. Meanwhile, the significant gains in minority and female enrollments in undergraduate education are broadening the base from which these students may be recruited.

Some of the results are encouraging. The data gathered for this study show considerable progress in these areas since the 1995 NRC study was conducted. The percentage of underrepresented minorities produced by doctoral programs overall has increased somewhat, and increases are apparent in all the fields surveyed in this study. Far more women are in doctoral education now than in the 1980s and 1990s, and in some fields once dominated by males, women doctoral candidates now are the majority.

Despite these significant gains, underrepresented minorities are still a small proportion of students in many areas of doctoral study—a percentage that remains considerably lower in fact than at earlier levels of education. Women have made striking gains in some biological science and social science fields, but they remain underrepresented in many areas, especially in engineering and the physical and mathematical sciences. And the number of faculty who are women or minorities in many fields remains small.[11]

Areas in which increases in underrepresented minorities and women have been most prominent include some fields not included in this study. A 2009 article in the *Chronicle of Higher Education* by Marc Goulden et al. noted that selection of disciplines represented in this study does not capture many of the fields in which the minority population is relatively high—for example, programs in education or social work.[12] For the fields surveyed in this study, NSF data indicate that the largest gains in underrepresented minorities have been in the humanities and the biological sciences.[13]

---

[11] National Research Council, *From Scarcity to Visibility* (Washington, D.C.: National Academies Press, 2001); S. Cole and E. Barber, *Increasing Faculty Diversity: The Occupational Choice of High-Achieving Minority Students* (Cambridge, Mass.: Harvard University Press, 2003).

[12] M. Goulden, A. Stacey, and M. A. Mason, Assessment denied: The NRC's sins of omission. *Chronicle of Higher Education,* August 31, 2009, A184.

[13] Nation Science Foundation, *Survey of Earned Doctorates* (Washington, D.C.: NSF, various years).

The rate of growth from 1993 to 2006 for the humanities was 6.4 percent and 5.2 percent for biological sciences, compared with only 0.4 percent growth rate in the agricultural sciences for the same period. Nevertheless, the gains in minority and female representation in doctoral programs are one of the most notable trends in doctoral education since the 1995 NRC study was conducted.

More broadly, since the 1995 study doctoral education has benefited greatly from dramatic increases in enrollments of international students and of domestic minorities and women. These gains demonstrate the ongoing desirability of American doctoral education in an educational world increasingly shaped by intense global competition for exceptional students. They also demonstrate the capacity to bring into doctoral education vital components of the national citizenry historically underrepresented in Ph.D. programs. The demographic group that has not shown gains during this period is the group that was long dominant in doctoral education—nonminority American males. Indeed, the domestic nonminority male population in doctoral education has decreased in both numbers and as a percentage of total doctoral enrollments. According to *Science and Engineering Indicators,* from 1996 to 2004 the percentage of doctoral degrees awarded to white, non-Hispanic U.S. citizens or permanent resident males decreased from 34.6 percent to 25.2 percent (Table 2-1). In absolute numbers, in the broad fields in this study the total number of doctoral degrees awarded to white, non-Hispanic U.S. citizens or permanent resident males decreased from 9,619 in 1993 to 8,392 in 2006. The largest decrease was in the social sciences and psychology: from 2,501 to 2,048.

TABLE 2-1 Ph.D.'s Awarded to White, Non-Hispanic U.S. Citizens or Permanent Resident Males, in Selected Broad Fields, 1993 and 2006

| Broad Field | 1993 | 2006 |
|---|---|---|
| Engineering | 1,608 | 1,269 |
| Physical sciences, math and computer sciences, and geosciences | 2,512 | 2,072 |
| Life sciences | 1,290 | 1,416 |
| Social sciences and psychology | 2,501 | 2,048 |
| Humanities | 1,193 | 1,183 |
| Total | 9,619 | 8,392 |

Source: NSF Special Tabulation

## THE DATA

All kinds of anecdotal evidence contribute to the reputations of doctoral programs, and all of them provide interesting, often useful information. Examples are stories of a long heritage of powerful research findings in a distinguished department; recollections of the accomplishments of famous graduates of years past; recounts of new faculty appointments made to strengthen particular areas of studies; lists of faculty publications that have shaped, changed, or even brought into existence whole fields of scholarship; recitations of the high hopes and aspirations engendered by the development of a new Ph.D. program; or reminders of the traditional high regard for the university in which a program is housed. These reputational dimensions can make a program look very attractive to prospective students, to prospective donors, and to funding agencies.

But there are limits to the reliability of a picture of graduate program quality and opportunity that is based on reputation alone. A program's reputation may reflect renowned professors long retired or the contributions of a handful of faculty in a large program. Doctoral programs that do not have storied histories may find it difficult to demonstrate their current strengths. Others may be more narrowly focused but excel in their areas of specialization. Some programs with excellent reputations but a narrow focus may not match the preferences of all students. Even when reputations for high quality are soundly based and current, they may not help guide prospective students to the best fit for the needs and ambitions they bring to doctoral study.

Several important dimensions of doctoral programs become much clearer when viewed from the vantage point of reliable data. How long does it typically take for a student to earn a Ph.D. in chemistry at University A? How much financial support will likely be available for a doctoral student in history at University B, and for how long and in what form? How many students enroll for each one accepted for doctoral study in electrical engineering at University C, and what range of Graduate Record Examination (GRE) scores were likely expected for admission? Of the students who initially enroll for a doctorate in anthropology at University D, what percentage completes that degree within a six-year period? Which universities provide adequate health insurance programs and child care services for their doctoral students?

Most universities now produce compelling statements in support of diversity in graduate education, but which doctoral programs demonstrate strong records in recruiting, retaining, and graduating underrepresented students? Will newly enrolled doctoral students be expected to join a graduate employees union if they attend University X? How much teaching, and of what sort, is expected of teaching assistants? Are funds available to doctoral students for travel to conferences or for research?

Other questions might be: what is the record of research productivity as determined by objective measures among the faculty in any given doctoral program? Do the faculty fully understand their own disciplinary and cross-disciplinary academic interests? Are fields of study supported by enough faculty to make research in that area a viable doctoral option? What does the university do to facilitate interdisciplinary study, how fully are the faculty engaged in it, and how is such work across disciplinary lines reflected in the degree structure?

Good, well-organized data in such areas provide ways to begin answering these questions and many more. The program questionnaire collected data relevant to many of these questions. The answers to some of them can be found in the full dataset, which is larger than the amount of data in the spreadsheet that accompanies the report. The data in the spreadsheet are being made easily accessible because they bear directly on the rankings or they had high response rates or both. The full dataset contains all the responses to all the questions on the program questionnaire, but response rates to some questions may be lower.

This NRC study has engaged the surveyed universities in an unprecedented effort to identify the most appropriate data categories and the most effective ways to collect and organize data within them. The universities have responded in kind. An active group of institutional representatives, institutional researchers, and staff from the NRC and Mathematica Policy Research (MPR), the survey research firm engaged for data collection, spent many months refining the questionnaires that organized the information collected from universities. Once the data were collected, they were checked and rechecked via continued correspondence with the participating universities. The data are useful for comparative purposes only insofar as they are generated using definitions and collection procedures that are consistent across all programs and universities. Reaching a shared understanding of the kind of questions that would produce the best data in the most pertinent categories was a challenge of significant dimensions.

On each campus enormous efforts went into collecting data consistent with the NRC definitions and methodology. Because this is the first study to make such extensive demands on programs to provide so much comparable data, nearly all programs had to adapt existing practices, or devise new ones, to produce the information required by the questionnaires. Individual doctoral programs, whether they were expected to organize their own records or check the data supplied from central sources, or, as in most cases, both, put much time and effort into the data collection process. Faculty asked to fill out questionnaires providing information about their scholarly records responded at an exceptionally high rate, as did doctoral students in the five disciplines selected for an experimental student survey. Graduate schools, or other institutional units asked to submit the data to the NRC, mobilized exceptional efforts to complete the forms. A productive side benefit of this study is that in many institutions the effort required by the NRC survey has contributed to better internal practices and improved understanding, both centrally and in individual doctoral programs, of data collection and self-assessment.

Even though the data collected in 2006 for this NRC study are already dated, they will increase in usefulness as long as they are regularly updated. Updatable data in the key dimensions of doctoral study will enable programs to, for example, measure the success of their own reforms, identify possible slippage in quality, learn extensively from other universities that have introduced changes into their doctoral programs, and gauge program solidity through performance over a more extended period of time.

Identifying the procedures needed to ensure that the data collected by this NRC study will be systematically updated at intervals timed to enable doctoral programs to assess their achievements and efforts to improve practices will pose a new set of challenges both for the NRC and for universities. But developing such procedures will be crucial to realizing the maximum benefit of the process begun with the extensive collection of data for this study.

# 3

# Study Design

The National Research Council's Committee on an Assessment of Research Doctorate Programs directed its research at fulfilling the following task:

> An assessment of the quality and characteristics of research-doctorate programs in the United States will be conducted. The study will consist of (1) the collection of quantitative data through questionnaires administered to institutions, programs, faculty, and admitted to candidacy students (in selected fields), (2) collection of program data on publications, citations, and dissertation keywords, and (3) the design and construction of program ratings using the collected data including quantitatively based estimates of program quality. These data will be released through a web-based, periodically updatable database and accompanied by an analytic summary report. Following this release, further analyses will be conducted by the committee and other researchers and discussed at a workshop focusing on doctoral education in the United States. The methodology for the study will be a refinement of that described by the Committee to Examine the Methodology for the Assessment of Research-Doctorate Programs, which recommended that a new assessment be conducted.

This chapter describes how the study was organized for that purpose.

## PH.D. PROGRAMS AS THE UNIT OF ANALYSIS

Like all large organizations, research universities in the United States consist of many related parts. These parts include the central administration, which oversees and coordinates the parts; the school or division, which has a faculty, admits students, and focuses on a large academic area such as engineering or arts and science; and the department, which tends to represent a discipline—that is, a field of teaching and learning within that large area. The faculty of a department specialize in the discipline and offer a curriculum that organizes and transmits disciplinary knowledge.

For doctoral education another administrative unit is of central importance: the graduate program. In most graduate schools the program admits doctoral students, works with the graduate school to fund them, designs their course of study and advisement, establishes the partnerships between mentoring faculty members and students that are the

27

bedrock of doctoral education, and recommends a successful student for a degree. The program best represents the site on which students do their studies and associate with other students and faculty. As a result, most of the data in this study are related to doctoral programs and their faculty. The committee's decision was logical, but it also presents some complex problems for the most accurate possible representation of doctoral education. Perhaps the most vexing issue the committee faced was how to reconcile the various ways that universities structure their graduate educational experiences. Universities do not follow one standard method of organizing graduate education. As a result, in many fields there is substantial variability in the names of programs and in their content.

The years since 1993 have been characterized by the increasing interdisciplinarity in doctoral programs and the blurring of the boundaries across fields, which has been manifested in a variety of ways. An example would be a neuroscience Ph.D. program that involves faculty from several departments and literally "cuts across" departmental lines. Even when a Ph.D. program is offered by a single department, however, it may include faculty from other departments, called "associated faculty" here, and thus it will have an interdepartmental or interdisciplinary character. A major challenge faced by this study was to find measures that do justice to the growth of interdisciplinarity in doctoral education. In the end, the questions asked and the measures constructed to gauge interdisciplinarity met with limited success. One measure tried was to measure the proportion of faculty from outside the program who helped to supervise dissertations. This measure, however, underestimates interdisciplinarity that is internal to the program. The committee also asked programs whether they were interdisciplinary. A large proportion answered yes, suggesting more extensive interdisciplinarity than that measured by the share of associated faculty.

In contrast to classifying graduate programs, classifying academic disciplines is comparatively straightforward because of the reasonably high level of consensus within a field about its general boundaries and its major subspecialties and subcategories. Some fields have relatively few subspecialties, and the basic predissertation years of doctoral education are similar for all students in the program. However, disciplines and specialties that have grown out of other disciplines—such as biochemistry—or that have emerged from earlier interdisciplinary work present knotty problems with program classification and with the variety of ways in which different universities organize doctoral education.

The biological and health sciences, a broad field that proved difficult to address in prior assessments, again proved the most problematic in this assessment. The swift growth of knowledge in the biological and health sciences—revolutionary changes in only a few decades or less—has produced rapidly evolving and highly differentiated ways of organizing graduate education in this field. The increasingly interdisciplinary character of the biological and health sciences is both a cause and a consequence of these academic and institutional changes. Interdisciplinarity means that a plethora of faculty members from several disciplines and programs have multiple responsibilities for training graduate students and identify with several of the programs offered at the university.

As a result, obtaining agreement on the classification of core programs within disciplines in this field proved a difficult task. The committee recognized that it had to disaggregate the unit of analysis beyond the general disciplinary name. It could not lump all biological and health science programs together and get an accurate representation of the experiences of students in various parts of the biological and health sciences at a university. Unfortunately, there was no consensus about the nomenclature for programs within the biological and health sciences, because different universities classify their biological programs differently. The committee thus worked closely with leaders in the disciplines before arriving at broadly acceptable names for the various programs that would be assessed.

In asking about the student experience within these programs, the committee had to remember that students at some universities are admitted to biological and health sciences programs without having to choose an area of specialization until the second or third year of study. In principle, such an approach allows students to "find" their interest before choosing a special area of interest in which they will do their doctoral research. These programs often call themselves "Biological Sciences" or "Integrated Biological Science." If the Ph.D. was offered in a program with this name, it was reported as such. If the Ph.D. was offered in a more specialized area, then the program was given the name of that area. Even as the committee sought to find reasonable patterns in the names of programs, it realized that increasingly "the laboratory" might be becoming the meaningful unit of analysis in some disciplines. Although this development is more often true at the postdoctoral level than at the Ph.D. level, the committee found evidence of graduate students identifying their own intellectual roots or heritage with the laboratory supported by their graduate thesis adviser or the professor who organizes a laboratory.

In short, even the "program" as the unit of analysis may not fully capture the source of research training received by graduate students. And it seems increasingly true that faculty sponsors of doctoral students have a greater influence on the next steps in their careers than the program faculty as a whole. Yet on balance the committee believes that the core educational experience of doctoral students takes place within a program that embraces both the course work that they experience with multiple members of the faculty and the concentrated research experience within the laboratory of one or several faculty members or in seminars or in individual discussion with faculty.

Outside of the biological and health sciences, the program as the unit of analysis also does some injustice to new, interdisciplinary programs that have not been sufficiently filtered into a standard curriculum and a standard method of organizing the educational experience. These programs transcend traditional boundaries and include experts from several existing disciplines. The names of these interdisciplinary programs often vary, and it is not altogether evident that what is being taught in the new programs is in fact comparable. For example, at the graduate level what are the academic relations between women's studies and gender studies? Thus admittedly, interdisciplinary programs, even though they are becoming increasingly important at universities, are shortchanged in the evaluation of more standard scholarly and scientific programs. Moreover, they may not be sufficiently numerous on the national scene to make comparative ratings possible.

Interdisciplinary studies and collaborations may give rise to new programs of study that evolve over time into fields distinct from their origins. Examples of recently emerged, but now established and recognized, fields fully surveyed here are biomedical engineering and American studies. These fields reflect the maturation of research areas that originally were interdisciplinary. Other fields may emerge from a single discipline, just as aerospace engineering has arisen from mechanical engineering. Some of the currently emerging fields identified by the committee are nanoscience, systems biology, urban studies and planning, and film studies. For these emerging fields the committee collected data only on the number of faculty (core, new, and associated) and the number of students overall and in candidacy.

This information should be useful for future benchmarking studies and may assist prospective students in the identification of these programs.

A final challenge inherent in making the program the unit of analysis was how to measure the workload of faculty members, whose appointment generally lies in a single department but who participate in more than one graduate program. Programs draw on faculty from within the discipline and to some extent on colleagues in related disciplines. For example, a nanoscientist may offer instruction and research guidance in the fields of physics, applied physics, and chemistry. A neuroscientist may work with students in programs ranging from biochemistry to cognitive psychology. A history professor may work in history, African American studies, and American studies.

Thus how were professors assigned to programs? The committee spent a lot of time discussing this question. It largely agreed on one principle: it should not allow double counting and should try to prevent universities from assigning their most prolific and distinguished faculty to multiple programs unless they actually expended "effort" within them. Faculty members would demonstrate the effort they put into each program primarily by stating the number of doctoral students whose dissertations they advised or on whose doctoral committees they served. The total amount of time spent by faculty members in all the programs in which they are involved could not exceed 100 percent.

The committee was aware that allocations of faculty time are sometimes not easily determined. Moreover, some faculty members have huge responsibilities in multiple programs—many graduate students and many sponsored dissertations—while others do far less in training and mentoring students. In actual time and energy spent, 50 percent of effort by some faculty members in a program may in fact be greater than 100 percent effort by others. Of course, this observation also applies to human activity outside of research universities. Faced with the practical question of whether the allocations of faculty time were realistic, the committee counted the dissertations that faculty members were directing and allocated their time among the programs in which they served. It then asked institutional coordinators to consult with the programs to judge whether this numerical allocation adequately reflected how a faculty member's time should be allocated across several programs. In a few cases it did not, and the committee accepted the allocation provided by the institution. This decision was important because the total publications of faculty in a program were adjusted by the allocation of the faculty member to the program.

Despite these problems of classification and assignment, the committee believes that the program continues to represent the unit that most accurately defines the range of experiences of the graduate student once admitted to a specific department or program. In this assessment, quantitative data on 4,839 programs have been assembled (see Table 3-1). These programs correspond to six broad fields and 59 different academic disciplines. Each of these programs was subjected to an overall, primary assessment represented by a range of rankings. In addition, assessments were conducted of three separate dimensions of doctoral education: (1) research activity; (2) student support and outcomes, a measure that reflects program characteristics that are specifically relevant to the student experience; and (3) diversity of the academic environment, a measure that includes the gender, racial, and ethnic diversity of the faculty and of the student body, as well as a measure of the percentage of international students. [1] Taken together, these individual assessments represent a comprehensive assessment of Ph.D. education in the United States.

---

[1] The components of these measures are shown in Table 5-2A–C.

TABLE 3-1 Numbers of Programs and Institutions in Each Broad Field

| Broad Field | Programs in the Broad Field | Institutions with Programs in the Field |
|---|---|---|
| Agricultural sciences | 312 | 70 |
| Biological and health sciences | 1,168 | 191 |
| Physical and mathematical sciences | 911 | 182 |
| Engineering | 759 | 151 |
| Social and behavioral sciences | 924 | 180 |
| Humanities | 764 | 146 |
| Total | 4,838 | 221 |

## FIELD COVERAGE

The studies by the NRC in 1982 and 1995 focused primarily on fields in the arts and sciences and engineering. However, the committee recognizes that research doctorate programs have grown and diversified since 1993 and that research doctorates are not limited to the arts and sciences. Therefore, the taxonomy for this study has been expanded from the 41 fields in 1993 to the current 62 fields of which 59 have program rankings. In addition, it has placed more emphasis on studies that extend beyond a single field, and so 14 emerging fields are included to recognize the growth of multi-, cross- and interdisciplinary study. It is anticipated that many of these fields could become established areas of scholarship and eligible for inclusion in future studies. Finally, when the committee developed the taxonomy it expected that each field would have enough programs to be ranked, but after it administered the program questionnaires it found that three fields could not be ranked: languages, societies, and cultures (LSC), engineering science and materials (not elsewhere classified), and computer engineering. LSC could not be ranked because the subfields were too heterogeneous for raters to provide informed rankings across them, and no subfield was large enough that rankings could be calculated for it alone. Computer engineering was put forward as a field that was separate from electrical engineering, but the universities in the study reported only 20 computer engineering programs. Similarly, engineering science and materials (not elsewhere classified) did not have enough programs to be included in the rankings. Although rankings are not provided for these fields, full data are provided in the online data that accompany this study.

## DEVELOPMENT OF THE TAXONOMY

Immediately after the release of the 1995 study, some institutions and users expressed their concerns about the scope of fields covered and the taxonomy. During the period leading up to the current study, some fields, such as communications, kinesiology, and theater research, matured and established themselves. Other areas, such as doctoral education in nursing, public health, and public administration, convinced the committee that they had emerged from predominantly master's fields to established areas of doctoral research. The 1995 study report specifically mentioned the difficulty encountered in defining fields in the biological and health sciences. Furthermore, the taxonomy did not cover fields in the agricultural sciences. Coverage of Ph.D. programs in the basic biomedical sciences that were housed in medical schools was spotty.

In establishing the taxonomy of fields to be included in the current study, the committee used as a starting point *Assessing Research-Doctorate Programs: A Methodology Study,* the 2003 report of the Committee to Examine the Methodology for the Assessment of Research-Doctorate Programs.[2] On the one hand, it recognized that the taxonomy should build on previous taxonomies in order to maintain continuity with earlier studies, that it should correspond as much as possible to the actual programmatic organization of doctoral studies, and that it should capture the development of new and diversifying activities. On the other hand, it recognized that there was no "right" way of organizing academic fields. The organization used by one university as opposed to another is often an outcome of historical circumstances rather than some universal organizing principle. In general, faced with this variability, the committee adopted whatever seemed to be the most commonly used current taxonomic divisions.

To go back to the example of biology, the changes in biology that were evident in the 1995 study have transformed the discipline. Biology is now a complex field that appears under the umbrella of the biological and health sciences, a grouping with 19 fields and 3 emerging fields. The impact of new technology, the digital revolution, and the explosion of knowledge at the molecular level have moved the biological sciences from fields defined by levels of organization to problem-based, interdisciplinary fields. The inclusion of immunology and infectious disease as a field exemplifies this change, as does the modification of pharmacology to include toxicology and environmental health. The growing importance of computation to biology is evident in the subfields of genetics and genomics and neuroscience and neurobiology, as well as in the presence of bioinformatics as an emerging field.

All the biological science fields represented in the 1995 study are retained in this study with several noteworthy changes. Biochemistry now appears as biochemistry, biophysics, and structural biology rather than biochemistry and molecular biology. Biophysics and structural biology are new to this study, and the committee relegated

---

[2] National Research Council, *Assessing Research-Doctorate Programs: A Methodology Study* (Washington, D.C.: National Academies Press, 2003).

molecular biology to subfield status after discussion of whether molecular biology has become more of a technique integrated into many areas rather than a separate field.

Commonalities in research methodology along with research problems that increasingly merge traditional disciplines have resulted in greater integration across the life sciences. In the biomedical sciences in particular, newly developed programs offer students a common port of entry to a wide range of disciplines or, alternatively, degrees are offered in integrated programs without further differentiation. Programs draw on faculty from across the campus, making the assignment of faculty to programs more complex. These changes to traditional disciplinary structures have blurred the boundaries of research fields and departments and challenged the committee to define what was being rated. The inclusion of biology/integrated biomedical science accommodated these programs. The fields covered in the two studies are shown in Table 3-2.

| TABLE 3-2 Fields in 1993 and 2006 Data Collection | | |
|---|---|---|
| Broad Field | 1993 | 2006 |
| Agricultural sciences | ** | *Animal sciences*<br>*Entomology*<br>*Food science*<br>*Forestry and forest sciences*<br>*Nutrition*<br>*Plant sciences* |
| Biological and health sciences | Biochemistry and molecular Biology<br><br>Cell and developmental biology<br>Ecology and evolutionary biology<br>Molecular and general genetics<br>Neurosciences<br>Pharmacology<br>Physiology | Biochemistry, biophysics, and structural biology<br><br>Cell and developmental biology<br>Ecology and evolutionary biology<br>Genetics and genomics<br>Neuroscience and neurobiology<br>Pharmacology, toxicology, and environmental health<br>Physiology<br>*Biology/integrated biomedical sciences (Note: Use this field only if the degree field is not specialized.)*<br>*Immunology and infectious disease*<br>*Kinesiology*<br>*Microbiology*<br>*Nursing*<br>*Public health* |
| Engineering | Aerospace engineering<br>Biomedical engineering<br>Chemical engineering<br>Civil engineering<br>Electrical engineering<br>Materials science<br>Mechanical engineering<br>Industrial engineering | Aerospace engineering<br>Biomedical engineering and bioengineering<br>Chemical engineering<br>Civil and environmental engineering<br>Electrical and computer engineering<br>Materials science and engineering<br>Mechanical engineering<br>Operations research, systems engineering, and industrial engineering<br><br><br><br>*Computer engineering*[a]<br>*Engineering science and materials (not elsewhere classified)*[b] |
| Broad Field | 1993 | *2006* |
| Physical and mathematical sciences | Astrophysics and astronomy | *Astrophysics and astronomy* |
| | Chemistry | *Chemistry* |
| | Computer sciences | *Computer sciences* |
| | Geosciences | *Earth sciences* |
| | Mathematics | *Mathematics* |
| | Oceanography | *Oceanography, atmospheric sciences, and meteorology* |
| | Physics | *Physics* |
| | Statistics and biostatistics | *Statistics and probability* |
| | | *Applied mathematics* |
| Social and behavioral sciences | Anthropology | *Anthropology* |
| | Economics | *Economics* |
| | Geography | *Geography* |
| | Political science | *Political science* |
| | Psychology | *Psychology* |
| | Sociology | *Sociology* |
| | | *Agricultural and resource economics*<br>*Communication* |
| | | *Linguistics (moved from humanities)* |

| | | *Public affairs, public policy, and public administration* |
|---|---|---|
| | | |
| | History (moved to Humanities) | |
| Humanities | Classics | *Classics* |
| | Comparative literature | *Comparative literature* |
| | English language and literature | *English language and literature* |
| | French and Francophone language and literature | *French and Francophone language and literature* |
| | German language and literature | *German language and literature* |
| | Art history | *History of art, architecture, and archeology* |
| | Music | *Music* |
| | Philosophy | *Philosophy* |
| | Religion | *Religion* |
| | Spanish and Portuguese language and literature | *Spanish and Portuguese language and literature* |
| | | *American studies* |
| | | *History (moved from social sciences)* |
| | | *Languages, societies, and culture (no rankings)* |
| | | *Theater and performance studies* |
| | | |
| | | |
| | Linguistics (moved to social sciences) | |
| Total | 41 | *62 (3 unranked)* |
| Emerging | | *Bioinformatics* |
| fields | | *Biotechnology* |
| | | *Computational engineering* |
| | | *Criminology and criminal justice* |
| | | *Feminist, gender, and sexuality studies* |
| | | *Film studies* |
| | | *Information science* |
| | | *Nanoscience and nanotechnology* |
| | | *Nuclear engineering* |
| | | *Race, ethnicity, and post-colonial studies* |
| | | *Rhetoric and composition* |
| | | *Science and technology studies* |
| | | *Systems biology* |
| | | *Urban studies and planning* |

Note: Italics indicates a new or reclassified field.

[a] Computer engineering was not ranked because relatively few universities provided data about computer engineering as a field distinct from electrical and computer engineering.

[b] Engineering science and materials (not elsewhere classified) was not ranked because relatively few universities provided data.

As early as 1996 a planning meeting was held to consider a separate study of the agricultural sciences, because they were not included in the 1995 study. That study did not go forward, however, because of funding considerations, and the decision was made to wait until a more comprehensive study was conducted to include these fields. Thus this study includes six agricultural fields in the agricultural sciences category and one agricultural field (agricultural and resource economics) in the social and behavioral sciences category. Most of these programs are located in colleges or schools of agriculture in the land grant universities or other public universities. Some of these fields include groupings of programs that may be separate entities as some institutions. For example, the plant sciences include programs that may be named agronomy, horticulture, plant pathology, or crop sciences at different institutions; the animal sciences include programs that might be named dairy science, animal science, or poultry sciences at different institutions.

Many excellent research doctorate programs in the basic biomedical sciences are located in colleges or schools of medicine. The biological and health sciences taxonomy recognizes this fact and provides for the inclusion of such programs among the basic biological research doctorate programs. It also recognizes the maturation of several interdisciplinary programs, such as neuroscience, into established independent fields.

The treatment of psychology as a field has changed from its treatment in the 1995 study, which included a number of programs in clinical psychology. During the late 1990s, some universities with established programs in clinical psychology awarded a Psy.D. degree, as opposed to a Ph.D. In its data collection, the committee asked universities to exclude their clinical programs even if they awarded a Ph.D. and their faculty from the study, but this request was not heeded in all cases.[3]

## ELIGIBILITY CRITERIA FOR FIELDS AND PROGRAMS

The committee chose to preserve the criteria from the 1995 study for the selection of fields to be included in the current study. To be included, a field as a whole had to have (1) granted at least 500 doctorates in the last five years (2001–2002 to 2005–2006); and (2) be represented in at least 25 institutions.

Taken together, these criteria ensure that the field is a significant presence in doctoral education and that there are enough programs nationwide to make comparison meaningful. Fifty-nine fields met these criteria.

The unit of observation in this study is the doctoral program. A program is a unit of graduate study that is defined by its performance of at least three of the following four activities:

1. Enrolls students in doctoral study
2. Designates its own faculty
3. Develops its own curriculum
4. Recommends students for doctoral degrees.

To be included in the study, a doctoral program meeting these criteria must also have produced at least five doctorates between 2001–2002 and 2005–2006. This quantitative criterion is designed to ensure that doctoral education and research are a central part or a mission of any included program. Given these ground rules, institutions were asked to name the programs they wished to see included in the study. They named 4,839 for which the committee calculated illustrative ranges of rankings.

## PARTICIPATION IN THE STUDY

In September 2005 Ralph J. Cicerone, chair of the National Research Council, wrote the presidents of all universities offering doctoral programs to invite them to participate in the study. The invitation explained the purpose, organization, and time line of the study and encouraged the institutions to contribute funding to it. Contribution guidelines were determined by the number of Ph.D.'s granted in the fields in the NRC taxonomy over the

---

[3] Four out of 146 psychology programs were called "clinical psychology." It is not clear how many other programs were primarily clinical in their focus.

period 2001–2002 to 2003–2004. Copies of the letter were sent to the provost and graduate dean. Although universities were asked to contribute to the study, and most did, a financial contribution was not a requirement for participation. Indeed, the financial contributions of U.S. institutions of higher education, while vital to the study, were small compared with the value of very significant efforts by senior staff at the participating institutions to gather, check, collate, and communicate the data requested from their schools. In many cases such data had not been collected in the past, and the efforts initiated in response to the questionnaires were far from trivial.

## QUESTIONNAIRE DEVELOPMENT AND DATA COLLECTION

A Panel on Data Collection composed of graduate deans and institutional researchers was tasked with drafting questionnaires for this study. Starting from survey instruments drafted originally by the 2003 study committee that developed a methodology for the assessment, the panel drafted questionnaires for four groups of respondents: institutions, programs, faculty, and students.

After approval by the committee, the questionnaires were posted on the project web site and participating institutions were asked to comment on them. The e-mail list created was open to anyone from participating institutions who was working on the study. Through the list, the NRC received hundreds of comments and suggestions. Answers were posted by both NRC staff and the survey contractor, Mathematica Policy Research. The comment and response processes were open and iterative and, as such, resulted in decisions that were acceptable to most institutions and programs, but did not fit all (see Appendix D for copies of the questionnaires). Each of the four questionnaires was also reviewed by the Nation Research Council's Institutional Review Board (IRB). And many institutions required that they be reviewed by their own IRBs. The introductory section of the questionnaires was revised to comply with their recommendations when needed.

In designing the questionnaires the committee had to make many choices. In some cases the choices were obvious; in others they were less so and therefore engendered considerable debate among the committee members. These issues included definitions and choices of what information to collect.

The program was chosen as the primary unit for the study because programs admit students, offer degrees, and are the obvious target of student interest. The treatment of faculty presented a more difficult problem. In many institutions emeritus faculty play an important role in teaching and research, as do adjunct faculty. For this study the committee chose to define faculty as those who had directed doctoral research dissertations within the last five years. It recognizes that many individuals whom it is not "counting" as faculty make valuable contributions, but for uniformity and consistency it chose this definition. There is also inconsistency across programs in the definition of a *doctoral student*. In most programs students apply directly for admission to the doctoral program without having first obtained a master's degree. Other programs, however, do not admit students to the doctoral program until they have satisfactorily completed a master's degree and shown they are capable of carrying out work in a doctoral program. The committee asked programs which definition they used and, under that definition, how many students they enrolled.

The proliferation of multidisciplinary or cross-disciplinary programs presents a problem in how to "allocate" faculty. To ensure that the total number of faculty members across programs equaled the total number of faculty in the study, the committee had to allocate faculty to programs. A self-allocation procedure in which faculty assigned themselves or were assigned by their institutions was deemed unacceptable by most of the committee, because that procedure allowed allocations that did not accurately reflect the strength of programs. The formula eventually developed related allocation to the number of dissertations chaired by individual faculty members.[4] The resulting allocations were, however, reviewed by the institutions, which in a small number of cases revised the allocations if they felt they were unreasonable or not representative of a faculty member's scholarly efforts.

Finally, the committee had to decide which kinds of data to collect. Two factors were important. First, the data had to be useful to the readers of the report, especially to potential students. Second, the data had to be consistent and available in an accessible form. Some data, such as publications in the scholarly literature and citation indices, can be obtained from commercial databases, and information about federal grants is available as well. By contrast, institutional data such as time to degree, levels of student support, and infrastructure investment are not uniform and not always available or as easily compared.

---

[4] Faculty productivity (citations and publications) was allocated by the following formulas. For faculty members who are core in one or more programs that fall within the NRC taxonomy (regardless of the number of programs with which they may be associated),

$$A_i = \frac{\left(5\,P_i + n_i + 5\left(\frac{d_i}{m}\right)\right)}{\sum_i \left(5\,P_i + n_i + 5\left(\frac{d_i}{m}\right)\right)},$$

where $A_i$ is the share of publications and citations allocated to the faculty member in program $i$; $P_i$ is the number of committees in program $i$ for which the faculty member serves as chair or principal adviser; $n_i$ is the number of committees in program $i$ on which the faculty member serves in a capacity other than chair or principal adviser; $d_i$ is a variable that takes on the value of 1 if the faculty member is a core faculty member in program $i$ and 0 otherwise; and $m$ is the total number of programs in which the faculty member is a core faculty member.

For faculty members who are core in a program in a nonincluded field but are listed as associate faculty in an included one,

$$A_i = \frac{\left(5\,P_i + n_i\right)}{2\sum_i \left(5\,P_i + n_i\right)},$$

where $P_i$ and $n_i$ are defined as above.

The factor of 2 in the denominator was included to reduce the overallocation of associate faculty members when information is not available on their core programs. The +5 that was there previously would have become proportionally smaller as these faculty sit on more and more committees outside their core program, making the allocation closer to 100 percent. To remedy this situation, the committee multiplied the denominator by 2 to effectively reduce the allocation to a reasonable fraction. With this modification, the allocation for associate faculty members (who are core in a nonincluded field or program) will never be greater than 50 percent.

For new faculty members, all their publications and citations were allocated to their core program(s), because they will not yet have a record of dissertation committee service. For new faculty who are listed in more than one program (such as a joint appointment), their allocations were split evenly among their programs.

These allocations were calculated directly by MPR from the faculty lists.

The characteristics for which data appear for each program in the online data tables, and how they are measured, are shown in Table 3-3.

**TABLE 3-3 Characteristics Listed in the Online Data Table**

| CATEGORY | COLUMN | DESCRIPTION |
|---|---|---|
| **General Information** | **A: Program ID** | |
| | **B: Broad Field** | |
| | **C: Field** | |
| | **D: Institution Name** | |
| | **E: Program Name** | |
| | **F: Program Website** | |
| | **G: Control** | Public or private institution |
| | **H: Regional Code** | 1=Northeast; 2=Midwest; 3=South Atlantic; 4=South Central;5=West: |
| | **I: Program Size Quartile** | 1 is smallest; 4 is largest. Quartiles based on Number of Students Enrolled, Fall 2005 (see Column AT). |
| **R Rankings** | **J: R Rankings: 5th Percentile** | 5th percentile value of the program's R ranking |
| | **K: R Rankings: 95th Percentile** | 95th percentile value of the program's R ranking |
| **S Rankings** | **L: S Rankings: 5th Percentile** | 5th percentile value of the program's S ranking |
| | **M: S Rankings: 95th Percentile** | 95th percentile value of the program's S ranking |
| **Dimensional Rankings** | **N: Research Activity: 5th Percentile** | 5th percentile value of the program's ranking for faculty research activity in 2006 |
| | **O: Research Activity: 95th Percentile** | 95th percentile value of the program's ranking for faculty research activity in 2006 |
| | **P: Student Support & Outcomes: 5th Percentile** | 5th percentile value of the program's ranking for student support and outcomes in 2006 |
| | **Q: Student Support & Outcomes: 95th Percentile** | 95th percentile value of the program's ranking for student support and outcomes in 2006 |
| | **R: Diversity: 5th Percentile** | 5th percentile value of the program's ranking for diversity in 2006 |
| | **S: Diversity: 95th Percentile** | 95th percentile value of the program's ranking for diversity in 2006 |
| **Data: Research Activity** | **T: Average Number of Publications (2000-2006) per Allocated Faculty, 2006** | This variable is the total over seven years, 2000-2006, of the number of articles for each faculty member divided by the total number of faculty allocated to the program. Data were obtained by matching faculty lists supplied by the programs to the |

| | | Thomson-Reuters list of publications. The list of journals included in the ISI database can be found here, *http://science.thomsonreuters.com/mjl/*. To find journal coverage for 2005-2006, contact Thomson Reuters. Books were not counted for the non-humanities. |
|---|---|---|
| | **U: Average Citations per Publication (Non-Humanities)** | The annual average of the number of allocated citations in the years 2000-2006 to papers published during the period 1981-2006 by program faculty divided by the allocated publications that could contribute to the citations. For example, the number of allocated citations for a faculty member in 2003 is found by taking the 2003 citations to that faculty member's publications between 1981 and 2003. These counts are summed over the total faculty in the program and divided by the sum of the allocated publications to the program in 2003. Citations were not calculated for the humanities. |
| | **V: Percent of Faculty with Grants, 2006** | The faculty questionnaire asks whether a faculty member's work is currently supported by an extramural grant or contract. The total of faculty who answered affirmatively was divided by the total respondents in the program and the percentage was calculated. |
| | **W: Awards per Allocated Faculty Member, 2006** | Data from a review of 1,393 awards and honors from various scholarly organizations were used for this variable. The awards were identified by the committee as "Highly Prestigious" or "Prestigious," with the former given a weight five times that of the latter. The award recipients were matched to the faculty in all programs and the total awards for a faculty member in a program was the sum of the weighted awards times the faculty member's allocation to that program. These awards were added across the faculty in a program and divided by the total allocation of the faculty in the program. |
| **Data: Student Support & Outcomes** | **X: Percent of First Year Students with Full Financial Support, Fall 2005** | For each program, question E5 reported the number of full-time first-year graduate students who received full financial support during the fall 2005 term. This number was divided by the total number of full-time, first-year doctoral students enrolled fall |

|  |  | 2005. When there was zero first-year students enrolled, this value was imputed (average over the field). |
|---|---|---|
|  | **Y: Average Completion Ratio, 6 Years or Less** | Questions C16 and C17 reported for males and females separately the number of graduate students who entered in different cohorts from 1996-1997 to 2005-2006 and the number in each cohort who completed in 3 years or less, in their 4th, 5th, 6th, 7th, 8th, 9th years, and in 10 or more years. To compute the completion rate, the number of doctoral students for a given entering cohort who completed their doctorate in 3 years or less and in their 4th, 5th, 6th years were totaled and the total was divided by the entering students in that cohort. This computation was made for each cohort that entered from 1996-1997 to 1998-1999 for the humanities and 1996-1997 to 2000-2001 for the other fields. Cohorts beyond these years were not considered, since the students could complete in a year that was after the final year 2005-2006 for which data were collected. To compute the average completion rate, an average was taken over 3 cohorts for the humanities and over 5 cohorts for other fields. |
|  | **Z: Median Time to Degree (Full- and Part-time Graduates), 2006** | Question C2 reported the median time to degree for full-time and part-time students. That reported number was used for this variable. The median was calculated from graduates who received doctoral degrees in the period 2003-2004 through 2005-2006. |
|  | **AA: Percent with Academic Plans** | A crosswalk was generated between the NSF Doctorate Record File Specialty Fields of Study and the fields in the study taxonomy. Data from the DRF for 5 years (2001-2005) were matched by field and institution to the programs in the research-doctorate study. The percentage was computed by taking the number of individuals who have a signed contract or are negotiating a contract for a position at an educational institution and dividing by the number of survey responses. Positions included employment and postdoctoral fellowships. |

| | AB: Collects Data About Post-graduation Employment (1=Yes; 0=No) | This variable takes the value of 1 if the program collects data about the post-graduation employment of its graduates. A zero is given if otherwise. |
|---|---|---|
| **Data: Diversity** | **AC: Non-Asian Minority Faculty as a Percent of Total Core and New Faculty, 2006** | For each program the data reported for question B7, the race/ethnicity of core and new faculty in the program, was used to compute the ratio of non-Hispanic Blacks, Hispanic, and American Indians or Alaska Natives to that of all faculty with known race/ethnicity. "Core" faculty are those whose primary appointment is in the doctoral program. "New" faculty are those with tenure track appointments who were appointed in 2003-2006. |
| | **AD: Female Faculty as a Percent of Total Core and New Faculty, 2006** | For each program the data reported for question B5, the gender of core and new faculty in the program, was used to compute the ratio of core or new female faculty to the total of core and new faculty. Allocations were not used in the construction of this variable. |
| | **AE: Non-Asian Minority Students as a Percent of Total Students, Fall 2005** | Question C9c reported the race/ethnicity of graduate students in the program. This was used to compute the ratio of non-Hispanic Blacks, Hispanics, and American Indians or Alaska Natives to that of the total of students with known race/ethnicity. |
| | **AF: Female Students as a Percent of Total Students, Fall 2005** | Question C9 reported the gender of graduate students in the program. This was used to compute the percentage by taking the number of female graduate students divided by the total number of graduate students. |
| | **AG: International Students as a Percent of Total Students, Fall 2005** | Question C9b reported the citizenship of graduate students in the program. These data were used to compute the percentage of international graduate students by taking the number with temporary visas and dividing it by the number of graduate students with known citizenship status. |

| Data: Other Overall Ranking Measures | AH: Average Number Ph.D.s Graduated, 2002-2006 | Question C1 reported the number of doctoral degrees awarded each academic year from 2001-2002 to 2005-2006. The average of these numbers was used for this variable. If no data were provided for a particular year, the average was taken over the years for which there were data. |
|---|---|---|
| | AI: Percent of Interdisciplinary Faculty, 2006 | Faculty were identified as either core, new, or associated. Percent interdisciplinary is the ratio of associated to the sum of core, new, and associated faculty. Allocations were not used in the construction of this variable. |
| | AJ: Average GRE Scores, 2004-2006 | For each program, question D4 reported the average GRE verbal and quantitative scores for the 2003-2004, 2004-2005, and 2005-2006 academic years and the number of individuals who reported their scores. A weighted average was used to compute the average GRE, which was calculated by multiplying the number of individuals reporting scores by the reported average GRE score for each year, adding these three quantities and dividing by the sum of the individuals reporting scores. |
| | AK: Percent of First-Year Students with External Fellowships, 2005 | For each program question E8 reported the type of support full-time graduate students received during fall term each year of enrollment. For this variable the data for the first year were added for support by externally funded fellowships and combinations of external fellowships and other internal support and then divided by the total number of students. |
| | AL: Is Student Work Space Provided to All Students? (1=Yes; 0=No) | Question D12 reported the percentage of graduate students who have work space for their exclusive use. |
| | AM: Is Health Insurance Provided by the Institution? (1=Yes; 0=No) | Question A1 reported whether or not the institution provided health care insurance for its graduate students. At some institutions, the program might provide support when the institution does not. |

|  | **AN: Number of Student Activities (Max=18)** | Question D8 listed 18 different kinds of support activities for doctoral students or doctoral education. This variable is a count of the number of student support activities provided by the program or the institution. |
|---|---|---|
| **Data Not Used in Ranking** | **AO: Total Faculty, 2006** | Questions B1, B2 and B3, total responses. |
|  | **AP: Number of Allocated Faculty, 2006** | Calculated as the number of program faculty corrected for association with multiple programs. For more detail on how these data were calculated, refer to footnote 46 in A Data-Based Assessment of Research-Doctorate Programs in the United States (2010), Chapter 3, "Study Design." |
|  | **AQ: Assistant Professors as a Percent of Total Faculty, 2006** | Of those faculty who reported any rank, the percentage of assistant faculty were calculated as the number of assistant professors divided by the number of total faculty. |
|  | **AR: Tenured Faculty as a Percent of Total Faculty, 2006** | Number of tenured faculty divided by the number of total faculty. |
|  | **AS: Number of Core and New Faculty, 2006** | Total number of core and new faculty. |
|  | **AT: Number of Students Enrolled, Fall 2005** | Question C9 reported the total number of students enrolled in the fall of 2005. |
|  | **AU: Average Annual First Year Enrollment, 2002-2006** | Question C3 reflects the number of first-time enrolled for 2001-2002, 2002-2003, 2003-2004, 2004-2005, and 2005-2006. An average was taken over 5 years. |
|  | **AV: Percent of Students with Research Assistantships, Fall 2005** | Question E8 reported the number of students who received support as a research assistant in the fall of 2005. A percentage was calculated over the total number of students. |
|  | **AW: Percent of Students with Teaching Assistantships, Fall 2005** | Question E8 reported the number of students who received support as a teaching assistant in the fall of 2005. A percentage was calculated over the total number of students. |

| Student Activities | AX through BP | Question D8 reports whether the institution and/or program provides support for doctoral students or doctoral education. Key: 1= provided for by institution; 2= program support only; 3= both institutional and program support; 4= neither institutional nor program support |
|---|---|---|

Note: Unless otherwise noted, all data refer to the 2005-2006 academic year. Further details are provided in Appendix E.

Data collection was administered by the project's survey contractor, Mathematica Policy Research. Responses at the institutional and program levels relied heavily on the institutional coordinator at each institution, who, depending on the administrative structure of the university, was either the graduate dean or the director of institutional research. This person knew how to find data about doctoral programs and made sure that the questionnaires were answered by knowledgeable respondents. Some institutions have highly centralized and automated data systems, and the institutional research office was able to provide many of the answers to the program and institutional questionnaires. Other universities relied on program and departmental administrators to provide the data. In addition, the universities provided MPR with faculty and student e-mail and student lists in order to administer their respective questionnaires. To preserve confidentiality, replies were sent directly to MPR.

## DATA VALIDATION AND CLEANING

Once the data were collected from the universities, they had to be checked. The first data cleaning and accuracy check was conducted in 2007, after institutions had submitted program data for the study. This step involved returning the data for all programs, with a request that the data be checked for accuracy and missing data be supplied. To ensure that eligible programs that submitted data to the NRC could be included in the ratings, the NRC took several steps beyond the initial checking to "clean" the data.

Second, in February 2008 the NRC contacted institutions to inquire about programs that were either missing too much data or for which it had identified some data as "outliers." This process involved 107 institutions and 387 programs. To determine which programs required cleaning, the 2 sigma (outlier) test was performed for 14 key variables (see Box 3-

---

**BOX 3-1** Variables Used in Data Cleaning

Percent Female Faculty (Program questionnaire question B5)
Percent Minority Faculty (B7)
Average Number of Graduates 2001-2006 (C1)
Median Time to Degree, Full-time and Part-time Students (C2)
Percent Female Doctoral Students in 2005 (C9)
Percent Minority Students (C9c)
6-Year Completion Rate, Males (C16)
6-Year Completion Rate, Females (C17)
8-Year Completion Rate, Males (C16)
8-Year Completion Rate, Females (C17)
Percent Students with Individual Workspace (D12)
Percent Full-time 1st-Year Students with Full Support (E5)
1st-Year External Fellowship (E8)
1st-Year External Traineeship (E8)

1). In an e-mail to the institutional coordinators, NRC staff explained that the check was necessary to calculate ratings for the programs. Institutional coordinators received spreadsheets and were asked to fill in blanks and make sure the outlier values of variables for the programs were correct, changing them if necessary. During this process, 298 programs submitted new data or confirmed their existing data. Twenty-three programs requested to be removed from the ratings or the study or both. Sixty-six programs did not respond to requests or did not have the data available. An additional 95 programs (not in the original 387) submitted cleaned data. Following this process, NRC staff identified 70 programs that had left the health insurance or student outcomes variable, or both, blank. Most of the programs, though not all, responded with data.

Third, in January 2009 members of the committee identified 27 programs that appeared to have been assigned to the wrong field. To check, NRC staff contacted 23 institutions to ask about one or more programs. Institutional coordinators responded, and, as a result, seven programs were moved to a different field. Another 20 programs did not move because the institutional coordinator explained why the school had placed the program in that field.

Aside from external checks with the institutions, NRC staff and the committee performed repeated ongoing internal checks on the data. These checks included looking at grants, awards and honors, GRE scores, completion rates, and the like. In most cases anomalies in the ratings did not appear to be the result of data errors—that is, careful review by the committee did not find data from the anomalous program very different from that for similar programs. However, in one case there did appear to be an error. The calculated rating for one particular program was very low because of its GRE scores. After these data were questioned, the institutional coordinator submitted new data that reflected the scores of *admitted* students, as had been instructed, rather than applicants. Publication and citation data were obtained from Thomson Reuters (formerly ISI, the Institute for Scientific Information) and matched to faculty lists. Matching was checked both by examining outliers and by checking and eliminating attribution to faculty with similar names.

Finally, no matter how careful the committee was in collecting data and designing measures, sources of error remain. Here are some examples:

- *Classification errors.* The taxonomy of fields may not adequately reflect distinctions that the field itself considers to be important. For example, in anthropology physical anthropology is a different scholarly undertaking from cultural anthropology, and each subfield has different patterns of publication. By lumping together these subfields into one overall field, the committee is implying comparability. Were they separate, different weights might be given to publications or citations. Anthropology is not alone in this problem. Other fields are public health, communications, psychology, and integrated biological science. Although this study presents ranges of rankings across these fields, the committee encourages users to choose comparable programs and use the data, but apply their own weights or examine ranges of rankings only within their peer group.
- *Data collection errors.* The committee provided detailed definitions of important data elements used in the study, such as doctoral program faculty, but not every program that responded paid careful attention to these definitions. The committee

carried out broad statistical tests, examined outliers, and got back to the institutions when it had questions, but that does not mean it caught every mistake. In fields outside the humanities it counted publications by matching faculty names to Thomson Reuters data and tried to limit mistaken attribution of publications to people with similar names. Despite these efforts, some errors may remain.

- *Omission of field-specific measures of scholarly productivity.* The measures of scholarly productivity used were journal articles and, in the humanities, books and articles. Some fields have additional important measures of scholarly productivity. These were included in only one field, the computer sciences. In that field peer-reviewed conference papers are very important. A discussion of data from the computer sciences with its professional society led to further work on counting publications for the entire field.[5] In the humanities the committee omitted curated exhibition volumes for art history. It also omitted books for the science fields and edited volumes and articles in edited volumes for all fields, since these were not indexed by Thomson Reuters. All of these omissions result in an undercounting of scholarly productivity. The committee regrets them, but it was limited by the available sources. In the future it might be possible to obtain data on these kinds of publication from résumés, but that is expensive and time-consuming.

---

[5] The computer sciences count as publications articles that are presented at refereed conferences, but until recently few of these papers were indexed by Thomson Reuters. To deal with this practice, the committee compiled a list of such conferences that were not indexed and counted these publications from faculty résumés, as it did in the humanities.

# 4

# The Methodologies Used to Derive

# Two Illustrative Rankings

Ranking programs based on quantitatively based estimates of program quality is a highly complex task. Rankings should be based both on data that reflect the relative importance to the user of the available measures and on the uncertainty inherent in them. Users of rankings should clearly understand the basis of the ranking, the choice of measures, and the source and extent of uncertainty in them. It is highly unlikely that rankings calculated from composite measures will serve all or even most purposes in comparing the quality of doctoral programs.

The committee has worked for more than three years on arriving at a satisfactory methodology for generating rankings for doctoral programs. This work was pursuant to the portion of the charge, which states:

> The study will consist of . . . 3) the design and construction of program ratings using the collected data including quantitatively based estimates of program quality.

It is this portion of the charge that called for constructing program ratings and deriving rankings from them that reflect program quality. Were it not in the committee's charge, it would be a useful exercise in itself simply to collect program data under comparable definitions and share them widely. This chapter describes how the committee decided what kinds of data to collect and how to use those data to approach the task of providing ratings and rankings for programs. In pursuing this task, it was guided by some motivating ideas that reflected concerns in the higher education community about rankings and their uses and that were described in considerable detail in the 2003 study already noted, *Assessing Research-Doctorate Programs: A Methodology Study*. These concerns about the 1995 rankings and rankings from other sources were that they do the following:

- *Encourage spurious inferences of precision.* As the committee describes in this report, there are many sources of uncertainty in any ranking, ranging from the philosophical—any ranking implies comparability of what may not be comparable—to the statistical—sources of variation are present in any aggregation of measures.
- *Overly rely on reputation.* Reputation, although it has the advantage of reflecting dimensions of program quality that are difficult to quantify, may also be dated and include halo effects—that is, visibility effects that obscure the quality of smaller programs or good programs in less well-known universities.

- *Lack transparency.* Even when it is based on explicit measures, the weighting of these measures in the ranking may not be discernable or may change from year to year in ways that are not made clear.

In addressing these weaknesses in rankings, the committee sought to design a methodology that would result in rankings with the following characteristics:

- *Data-based.* The rankings were constructed from observable measures derived from variables that reflected academic values.
- *A reflection of the prevailing values of faculty in each program area.* The rankings were calculated using the opinions of faculty in each program area of both what was important to program quality in the abstract and, separately, how experts implicitly valued the same measures when asked to rate the quality of specific programs.
- *Transparent.* Users of the rankings could understand the weights applied to the different measures that underlay the rankings and, if they wished, calculate rankings under alternative weighting assumptions.

Achieving these seemingly simple objectives in a scientifically defensible way was not a simple undertaking. The committee had to undertake the following tasks:

- *Determine what kinds of measures to include.* To be included, a measure had to be one that the participating universities either collected in the course of regular institutional research and management, such as enrollment counts, or that the committee felt should be known by a responsible doctoral program, such as the percentage of entering students who complete a degree in a given amount of time.
- *Ascertain faculty values.* Faculty were asked, on the one hand, to identify the measures that were important to program quality and then asked, on the other, to rate a stratified sample of programs in their fields.
- *Reflect variation among faculty and faculty raters.* Because faculty may not be in complete agreement on the importance of the different measures or the rating of sampled programs, differences in views were reflected by repeatedly resampling the ratings and, for each resampling, calculating the resulting weights or overall program ratings. This approach leads naturally to presenting a range of rankings on any measure for a given program.
- *Design specific measures along separate dimensions of program quality.* Although overall measures are useful, some users may be particularly interested in measures that focus on specific aspects of a graduate program. The committee calculated ranges of rankings for three of these aspects: research activity, student support and outcomes, and diversity of the academic environment.

That said, the two approaches provided in this report are intended to be illustrative of the process of constructing data-based ranges of rankings that reflect the values of the faculty who teach in these programs. It is also possible to produce ranges of rankings that reflect the values of the users. Production of the rankings turned out to be more complicated and to be accompanied by more uncertainty than originally thought. *As a consequence, the illustrative rankings described in this chapter are neither endorsed nor recommended by the National Research Council as an authoritative conclusion about the relative quality of doctoral programs.*

In summary, the committee urges users of these rankings and data to examine them very carefully, as the committee has. It also apologizes for any errors that might be uncovered. It does expect that, as a result of this data collection effort, updating will be easier next time for the respondents and will result in fewer errors.

## USE OF RANKINGS

In attempts to rank doctoral programs, sports analogies are especially inappropriate. There are no doctoral programs that, after a long regular season of competition followed by a month or more of elimination playoffs, survive to claim "We're Number 1!" Perceptions of the quality of doctoral programs are built over many years of making agonizing tenure decisions and making choices about areas of specialization and the resolution of competing views about the most fruitful direction of a field of study. The evidence of excellence is not easily summarized in runs batted in, earned run averages, or percentage of games won. Instead, it is the result of hundreds of judgments by peer reviewers for journals and presses, as well as citations that accumulate as an area of study develops and grows. The answer, then, to "What is the best doctoral program in biochemistry?" should not be the name of a university, but a follow-up question to the interlocutor about what he or she means by "best" and in what respects.

The committee was keenly aware of the complexity of assessing quality in doctoral programs and chose to approach it in two separate ways. The first, the general survey (S) approach, was to present faculty in a field with characteristics of doctoral programs and ask them to identify the ones they felt were the most important to doctoral program quality. The second, the rating or regression (R) approach, was to ask a sample of faculty to provide ratings (on a scale of 1 to 5) for a representative sample of programs and then to ascertain how, statistically, those ratings were related to the measurable program characteristics. In many cases the rankings that could be inferred from the S approach and the R approach were very similar, but in some cases they were not. Thus the committee decided to publish both the S-based and R-based rankings and encourage users to look beyond the range of rankings on both measures. Appendix G shows the correlations of the medians of the two overall measures for programs in each field. The fields for which the agreement between the R and S medians is poorest are shown in Box 4-1.

---

BOX 4-1 Fields for Which the Correlation of the Median R  and S
Ranking Is Less than 0.75

---

Animal Sciences
Civil and Environmental Engineering
Comparative Literature
French and Francophone Language and Literature
Geography
German Language and Literature
Linguistics
Mechanical Engineering
Pharmacology, Toxicology and Environmental Health
Philosophy
Religion
Sociology
Spanish and Portuguese Language and Literature

---

The online tables that accompany this study present ranges of rankings for two overall measures for all ranked programs and additional ranges of rankings for three dimensional measures. Those who view rankings as a competition may find this abundance of rankings confusing, but those who care about informative indicators of the quality of doctoral programs will likely be pleased to have access to data that will help them to improve their doctoral programs.

## SUMMARY OF THE METHODOLOGY OF THE ILLUSTRATIVE PROGRAM RANKINGS

Figure 4-1 shows the steps involved in calculating the two types of overall program rankings (R and S).

| Faculty | Students | Institutions and Programs | Existing |
|---|---|---|---|

**1. DATA**
- Answers to questions provided by 4,838 doctoral programs at 221 institutions and combinations of institutions in 59 fields across the sciences, engineering, social sciences, arts, and humanities covering institutional practices, program characteristics, and faculty and student demographics obtained through a combination of original surveys and existing data sources (NSF surveys and Thompson-Reuters publication and citation data).

**2. WEIGHTS**
- In two surveys shown in Appendix D, program faculty provided the NRC with information on what they value most in Ph.D. programs:
  1. Faculty were asked *directly* how important they felt 21 items in a list of program
  2. characteristics were (for S weights).
  2. A sample of faculty rated a sample of programs in their fields. These ratings were then related through regressions to the same items as appeared in (1) using a principal components transformation to correct for colinearity (for R weights).

**3. ANALYSIS**
- "Survey (S)" and "regression-based (R)" weights provided by faculty were used to calculate separate ratings, reflecting the multidimensional views faculty hold about factors contributing to the quality of doctoral programs.

**4. RANGES OF RANKINGS**
- Each program's rating was calculated 500 times by randomly selecting half of the raters from the faculty sample in step 2 and also incorporating statistical and measurement variability. Similarly, 500 samples of survey based weights were selected.
- The R weights and the S weights were then applied to 500 randomly selected sets of program data to produce two sets of ratings for each program.
- These ratings for each of the 500 samples determined the R and S rank orderings of the programs.
- A "range of rankings" was then constructed showing the *middle 90 percent* range of calculated rankings. What may be compared, among programs in a field, is this range of rankings.

Faculty were surveyed to obtain their views on the importance of different characteristics of programs as measures of quality.[1] Ratings were then constructed based on these faculty views of how those measures related to criteria of program quality, as discussed in the section on dimensional measures. The views were related to program quality using two distinct methods: (1) asking faculty directly to rank the importance of characteristics in a survey (S); and (2) asking faculty raters[2] to provide reputational program ratings (R) for a sample of programs in a field and then relating these ratings, through a regression model that corrected for correlation among the characteristics, to data on the program characteristics. The two methods approach the ratings from different perspectives. The direct, or survey-based, approach is a bottom-up approach that builds up the ratings from the importance that faculty members give to specific program characteristics independent of reference to any actual program. The regression-based method is a top-down approach that begins with ratings of actual programs and uses statistical techniques to infer the weights given by the raters to specific program characteristics. The survey-based approach is idealized. It asks about the characteristics that faculty feel contribute to quality of doctoral programs without reference to any particular program. The second approach presents the respondent with 15 programs in his or her field and information about them[3] and asks for ratings of program quality,[4] but the responders are not explicitly queried about the basis of their ratings.

The weights derived from each approach were then applied to the value of the 20 measures for each program to yield two sets of ratings for each program. Each rating was then recalculated 500 times using different samples of raters and varying the data values within a range.[5] The program ratings obtained from all these calculations could then be arranged in rank order and, in conjunction with all the ratings from all the other programs in the field, used to determine a range of possible rankings.

Because of the various sources of uncertainty, each ranking is expressed as a range of values. These ranges were obtained by taking into account the different sources of uncertainty in these ratings (statistical variability from the estimation, program data variability, and variability among raters). The measure of uncertainty is expressed by reporting the endpoints of the 90

---

[1] All questionnaires, including that for faculty, appear in Appendix D.

[2] The raters were chosen through a sampling process that was representative of the distribution in each field of faculty by rank, size of program, and region of the country.

[3] The following data were given to the raters: the program URL, the list of program faculty, the average number of Ph.D.'s (2001–2006), the percentage of new Ph.D.'s planning academic positions, the percentage of the entering cohort completing their degree in six years or less (fields outside the humanities fields) or eight years or less (humanities), the median time to degree (2004–2006), the percentage of female faculty, and the percentage of faculty from underrepresented minorities. All data were for 2005–2006 unless otherwise indicated.

[4] The question given raters about program quality was as follows:

On a scale from 1 to 6, where 1 equals not adequate for doctoral education and 6 equals a distinguished program, how would you rate this program?

| Not Adequate for Doctoral Education | Marginal | Adequate | Good | Strong | Distinguished | Don't Know Well Enough |
|---|---|---|---|---|---|---|
| 1 | 2 | 3 | 4 | 5 | 6 | 9 |

[5] The range of data values was either plus or minus 10 percent or the actual range of variation if multiyear data were collected on the questionnaire. A Monte Carlo selection was used to vary the selection of raters and of data.

percent range of rankings[6] for each program—that is, the range that contains the middle 90 percent of a large number of ratings calculations that take uncertainty into account.[7]

In summary, the committee obtained a range of rankings for each program in a given field by first devising two sets of weights through two different methods, direct, or survey-based, and regression-based. It then standardized all the measures to put them on the same scale and obtain ratings by multiplying the value of each standardized measure by its weights and adding them together. It acquired both the direct weights and the coefficients from regressions through calculations carried out 500 times, each time with a different set of faculty, to generate a distribution of ratings that reflects their variability. The range of rankings for each program was obtained by trimming the bottom 5 percent and the top 5 percent of the 500 rankings to obtain the 90 percent range. This method of calculating ratings and rankings takes into account variability in rater assessment of the things that contribute to program quality within a field, variability in the values of the measures for a particular program, and the range of error in the statistical estimation.

It is important that these techniques yield a *range* of rankings for most programs. The committee does not know the exact ranking for each program, and to try to obtain one—by averaging, for example—would be misleading because it has not assumed any particular distribution of the range of rankings.[8] Thus within the 90 percent range, a program's rankings could be clustered at one endpoint or the other, so that averaging the two endpoints could be misleading. The datasheet that presents the range of rankings for each program lists the programs alphabetically and gives the range for each program. Users are encouraged to look at groups of programs that are in the same range as their own programs, as well as programs whose ranges are above or below, in trying to answer the question "Where do we stand?" A similar technique was used to calculate the range of rankings for each of the dimensional measures for each field.

Some possible ways of using the ranges of rankings and the data tables are discussed in Chapter 6. The rankings for the overall R and S measures and for the dimensional measures for each of the programs in each of the 59 fields with ranges of rankings are available on the Web site (*www.nap.edu/rdp*) and should be taken as illustrative of the different approaches.[9] The 2009 *Guide to the Methodology* described a methodology that assumed that the R-based coefficients could be combined with the S-based coefficients using a formula that appears on page 48 of the Technical Appendix to the pre-publication version of the guide. This formula relied on the variances of the samples used to calculate each set of coefficients. Upon looking at every field, however, the committee found that for some fields these variances could be very large, especially for those fields in which either the field was heterogeneous in the sense that the same field encompassed very different forms of scholarly productivity or there were relatively few raters. This situation resulted in R and S medians that did not correlate well, and so the committee abandoned its plan to combine the coefficients that were calculated in the two ways. Instead of one overall range of rankings the committee presents these two measures separately. The fields for which the correlation of the two measures at the median was below 0.75 were listed earlier in Box 4-1 with details shown in Appendix G.

---

[6] The committee calls these endpoint values the 95th percentile and the 5th percentile.

[7] The 90 percent range eliminates the top and bottom 25 ratings calculated from 500 regressions and 500 samples of direct weights from faculty. The range contains 90 percent of all the rankings for a program. In the *Guide to the Methodology*, the range chosen was 50 percent, but the committee later decided that this range was overly restrictive.

[8] Two programs with the same 90 percent range could have very different means and medians.

[9] The 24,190 rankings (one range for each of the 5 measures for 4,838 programs) are too numerous to present in this written report.

## DIFFERENCES FROM THE 1995 REPORT

The summary in Table 4-1 makes it immediately clear that there are significant differences in the methodology for the two studies. *These differences alone can have an effect on the relative ranking of a program.* Here are some of the more obvious sources of difference:

TABLE 4-1 Summary of Differences Between 1995 and 2006 Studies

| 1995 Study | 2006 Study |
|---|---|
| *University Participation* | |
| 274 universities (including schools of professional psychology) | 221 universities and combinations of universities |
| *Field Coverage* | |
| 41 fields, all of which were ranked | 59 ranked fields, 3 fields not ranked but with full data collection, 14 emerging fields |
| *Program Inclusion* | |
| Nominated by institutional coordinators | Based on NSF Ph.D. production data and the nominations of institutional coordinators |
| *Number of Programs* | |
| 3,634 ranked | 4,838 ranked, 166 unrated |
| *Faculty Definition* | |
| 78,000 total, 16,738 nominated as raters (faculty could be counted in more than one program) | Of the 104,600 total, 7,932 faculty were chosen through a stratified sample for each field to participate in the rating study. Faculty could be counted in more than one program, but were usually counted as "core" in only one. Faculty members were allocated fractionally among programs according to dissertation service so that, over all programs, he or she was counted no more than once. |
| 1995 Study | 2010 Study |
| *Ratings and Rankings* | |
| Raters nominated by the institutional coordinators were sent the *National Survey of Graduate Faculty,* which contained a faculty list for up to 50 programs in the field. Raters were asked to indicate familiarity with program faculty, scholarly quality of program faculty (scale 1–6), familiarity with graduates of program (scale 1–3), effectiveness of program in educating research scholars (scale 1–4), and change in program quality in the last five years (scale 1–3). | 1. All faculty were given a questionnaire and asked to identify the program characteristics in three categories that they felt were most important, and then identify the categories that were most important. This technique provided the *survey-based (S)* weights for each field.<br><br>2. A stratified sample of faculty in each field were given a stratified sample of 15 or fewer sampled programs to rate them on a scale of from 1 to 6. Included in the data for raters was a faculty list and program characteristics. These ratings were regressed on the program characteristics to determine the *regression-based (R)* weights. These weights were then assumed to hold for all programs in the field so that all programs could receive a rating based on these weights. |
| Rankings were determined for each program by calculating the average rating for a program and arranging all the programs from lowest to highest based on average ranking. | 3. The S weights and the R weights, calculated as just described, were used to calculate S rankings and R rankings.<br><br>4. Uncertainty was taken into account by |

introducing variation into the values of the measures and by repeatedly estimating the ratings obtained by taking repeated halves of the raters chosen at random. Ratings were calculated 500 times.

5.  The ratings in step 4 were ordered from lowest to highest. The ratings of all programs in a field were pooled and arranged in rank order. The range covering 90 percent of rankings was then calculated for each program.[a]

[a] This is a simplified description. The exact process is more complex and is described in detail in Appendix J.

## Measurement of Quality

The 1995 measure of program quality is known as a "reputational measure"—that is, raters judged the "scholarly quality of program faculty." The 1995 study noted that this measure is highly correlated with program size and, quite possibly, with visible faculty.[10] Reputation may also be "dated" and not reflect recent changes in faculty composition. Finally, the reputation of program faculty may not be closely related to faculty performance in mentoring students or encouraging a high proportion to complete their degrees within a reasonable period of time.[11]

By contrast, in its rating exercise the committee for the current study asked respondents for their familiarity with each program, and presented data on size, completion, time to degree, and faculty diversity. It also provided a Web site for the program, in addition to a faculty list. The task was to rate the program rather than the scholarly quality of program faculty. A rater had to rate at most 15 programs, not 50. Once the ratings were obtained, they were then related to the 20 measures through a modified regression technique.[12]

## Specification of the Measures

In addition to the reputational measures the 1995 study provided a few program characteristics: faculty size, percentage of full professors, and percentage of faculty with research support. In addition, awards and honors received in the previous five years and the percentage of program faculty who had received at least one honor or award in that period were given for the arts and humanities. For engineering and the sciences, the percentage of program faculty who published in the previous five years and the ratio of these citations to total faculty, as well as the Gini coefficients for these measures (a measure of dispersion), were shown. Data were also presented on students: the total number of students, the percentage of students who were female, and the number of Ph.D.'s produced in the previous seven years. Finally, information was provided on doctoral recipients: the percentage who were female, minority, and U.S. citizens; the percentage

---

[10] "Visible faculty" refers to faculty who are highly productive and visible in the scholarly literature, but also faculty who may have been highly productive in the past, are less productive in the present, and are often called upon for public comment.

[11] For a more detailed discussion of the strengths and weaknesses of reputational measures, see the 1995 study (National Research Council, *Research Doctorate Programs in the United States,* 22–23) and the section in this chapter "Cautionary Words."

[12] For details of the statistical techniques, see Appendix J.

who reported research assistants and teaching assistants as their primary form of support; and the median time to degree. But even though all of these "objective measures" were reported, they played no explicit part in determining program ranking. By contrast, the current study explicitly includes most of these measures and many more, and attempts to relate them directly to the rating that goes into the program ranking.

## Overall Comparability

*If the "quality" of a program is unchanged, will any of the present ranges of rankings be the same as the 1995 ranking?* Although an excellent program is an excellent program by any measure, there is no reason to expect the 1995 rankings to match the present range of rankings on either the S-based or the R-based measure. As this description of the two studies makes clear, the studies used different methodologies for all three calculations. Some important sources of variability are as follows:

- The current study is highly data-dependent. Although the data submitted by the universities were checked and verified repeatedly, errors may remain. And large errors could skew the rankings. Nonreputational data were not explicitly a part of the 1995 rankings, although they were reported in tables in the appendixes.
- The research strength of the faculty as measured by publications and citations was an important determinant of quality in both studies, but the method of counting differed between the studies in two important respects:
  In the current study, publications for the previous 10 years for humanities faculty, which were not counted in 1995, were collected from faculty résumés. Books were given a weight of 5, and humanities articles were given a weight of 1.
  Second, in non-humanities fields, the 1995 study counted citations for articles published by faculty that had appeared in the previous five years. In the current study, citations that appeared in 2001–2006 were traced to articles that had been published as far back as 1981. This method of counting had the advantage of including "classic" long-lived articles. Again, the committee was unable to collect citation data for the humanities.
- The committee for the current study asked the institutional coordinators to name the programs they wished to include, but it did define a program as an academic unit that fits at least three of these four criteria:
  — Enrolls doctoral students
  — Has a designated faculty
  — Develops a curriculum for doctoral study
  — Makes recommendations for the award of degrees.[13]
Because separate programs were being housed in different academic units, a few institutions used this definition to split what would normally be considered a program into smaller units that still met the criteria—that is, what is normally perceived as a unified program was ranked as separate programs. In the rating sample, however, only the one program judged to be the major program in the field at that institution was included.

---

[13]These were the criteria listed on the NRC program questionnaire.

- Dimensional measures were not included in the 1995 study. In the planning meetings that preceded the study, the point was repeatedly raised that earlier rankings had not explicitly taken into account measures that reflected on graduate education[14] or the diversity of the educational environment.

In summary, the current study differs in methodology and conception from the 1995 study. Both studies do provide rankings, however, the current study provides ranges of rankings, reflecting a variety of sources of uncertainty. In addition, are illustrative of two different approaches. There are other approaches and weighting of characteristics that reflect alternative user values. It is possible to try to compare the sets of rankings from the two studies, but the definition of faculty, methods of enumerating publications and citations, and the inclusion of additional characteristics in this have all changed, as well as the methodology.


## CAUTIONARY WORDS


*A Guide to the Methodology of the National Research Council Assessment of Doctoral Programs* (2009) details the methodology used to create the rankings in the current study. As noted in the previous section, the methodology adopted in the current work is substantially different from that used to obtain the rankings described in the 1995 National Research Council report *An Assessment of Research-Doctorate Programs: Continuity and Change*, although it is very similar to that proposed in the 2003 NRC report *Assessing Research-Doctorate Programs: A Methodology Study*.

Under the current methodology, when program measures in a field are similar, program differences in the range of rankings can be highly dependent on the precise values of the input data and very sensitive to errors in those data. The committee and the staff have worked diligently in recent years to ensure the quality of the measures used to generate ratings and rankings and have tried to reduce measurement errors as much as possible. Such errors can arise from clerical mistakes, from misunderstandings by respondents about the nature of the data requested from them, or from problems within the public databases used. That said, even though the input data underwent numerous consistency checks and the participating respondent institutions were given the opportunity to provide additional quality assurance, the committee is certain that errors in input data remain, and that these errors will propagate through to the final posted rankings. Its hope is that after all of the input data are made public, any significant errors will be found and reported so they can be rectified in a timely fashion before the ranking and rating exercise is repeated.

Some readers may be surprised about the degree to which program rankings will have changed from the 1995 report. These changes may stem from three factors: (1) real changes in the quality of the programs over time; (2) changes in the principles behind the ranking methods; and (3) simple error, either statistical or from faulty data. The reader should keep in mind that the charge to the committee and the consequent decisions of the committee may have increased the sensitivity of the results to the third factor, and it would now like to spell out some of these issues in greater detail

---

[14] In the 1995 study "93E" was a reputational measure of the effectiveness of the program in graduate education, but was very closely correlated with "93Q," the reputational measure of scholarly quality. The committee felt it needed a separate measure based on data.

## Reputational Measures

From the outset the committee, responsive to the statement of task, favored producing a large variety of measures that correlate with the quality of Ph.D. programs. Those measures included publications and citations, peer recognition in the form of honorific awards, and indicators of the resources necessary to create new knowledge. One measure rejected was the direct use of perceived quality, or reputational standing, of these programs, even though this measure was the principal one used in the 1995 study. At present there is widespread distaste in the academic community for the use of reputational measures. On the one hand, reputational measures are generally recognized to have many strengths, including subtlety and breadth of assessment and the widespread use of such markers. On the other hand, reputational measures may reflect outdated perceptions of program strength as well as the well-known halo effect by which some weak programs at a strong institution may be overrated.[15] On balance, recognition of these shortcomings resulted in the committee's decision to reject the direct use of these perceived quality measures. But the committee was divided: some members did not want to collect data on perceived quality at all, while others favored the direct use of reputation. The policy finally adopted was an intermediate one—to collect direct data on the perceived quality of Ph.D. programs only for a sample of programs in each field and from a sample of faculty members who had responded to the faculty survey that produced the "direct measures" of quality. The ratings that resulted were then correlated with the measured variables (such as citations, honors, and awards), and "weights" were obtained for the latter to best "predict" the reputational measures. The idea here was to benchmark objective measures against a reputational measure, but not to use the reputational measure itself. This was the procedure recommended in the 2003 NRC report, and it had numerous consequences, foreseen and unforeseen.

Perceived quality, or reputation, is, of course, real, and it is real in its consequences. Reputation affects students' and professors' perceptions and their actions related to graduate Ph.D. education. Because it is an important element in the measurement of program quality, the methodology was designed to utilize its virtues but avoid some of the attendant defects (such as time lag). And yet this decision, while required by the statement of task, remained controversial, with some committee members still preferring the direct use of reputational measures. As several committee members noted, some of the other "quantitative" measures used, such as honors and awards, were in fact very closely related to and reflected perceived quality—that is, reputation.

## Weights and Measures

The committee collected an unprecedented amount of useful data on Ph.D. programs. But to turn this set of discrete measures into an overall set of rankings, it had to combine the various measures into a summary measure, which required, in turn, decisions about how much weight to give to each of the measures. One obvious way to weight the different quality measures was to use faculty ratings of the importance of the measures in assessing overall program quality, and this method was one of the two(the S measure) used to derive the criteria for quality. However, because faculty were not asked to evaluate reputation as a quality, it was excluded from the summary measure constructed from the weighted average of strictly objective measures.

---

[15] However, weak programs at strong institutions may benefit from the presence of the stronger programs in an increasingly interdisciplinary environment.

An attempt to model reputation was made by conducting a rating exercise for a sample of programs and then relating these ratings to the same characteristics as were included in the "S" measure. The result was a measure of quality (the R measure) based on statistical modeling of the quality evaluations (the regression-based model) but made up of the same components as the direct measures. The measures of importance to the faculty were correlated with the perceived quality measure, suggesting that these two parameters describe valid measures of real program quality. The R ranking, then, reflects the relation of the subjective ratings to the data, but by relying entirely on objective data, even this measure, in effect, eliminated any subjective adjustments raters might make in the way they perceived the quality of specific programs, as contrasted with the application of rules they might apply to evaluate programs in general.

Reliance solely on data-based objective measures rather than the explicit use of direct measures of reputation sometimes resulted in ratings that appeared to some committee members to lack face validity. To take one example of what may be lost when using only the objective data, faculty members in almost all fields in the sciences give a high weight to citations. Citations, however, are a complex indicator of impact or quality, and, of course, they are indirect measures of reputation. Their complexity arises from the equally complex pattern of behavior of scholars and scientists when referencing works in their published writings. The pattern of citations varies considerably by field, by specialty, by the use of books versus journals as the principal mode of scholarly communication, by self-citation practices, and by the decay of citation frequency over time, among many other patterned differences. Take, for example, two equally distinguished statistics departments: one heavily emphasizes statistical theory, the other, biostatistics. Every member of these departments is honored in a variety of ways. And yet it is almost certain that the average number of citations will be far greater in the department that emphasizes biostatistics, because it is a much larger field with a far larger publishing audience than statistical theory. Thus the score on citations as a measure of quality will differ greatly between the two departments and will lead to very different ratings. A reputational measure would have confirmed the point that both of these departments are truly distinguished.

The ranges of rankings based on S measures and R measures differ in the degree to which subjective considerations enter. The ratings on which the R measures are based may depend on the subjective assessment of omitted variables for which there may be no quantitative measures. The omission of subjective considerations in the regression-based measure is treated as an error term in the regression equation and does not appear in the model values reported in the rankings. The result is ranges of rankings for some programs that deviate markedly from what many experts in the fields might find convincing when they take subjective considerations into account. By contrast, the S measures may be subject to variations resulting from incorrect or misunderstood reports of data. Users of these ranges of rankings need to be aware of the consequences of using purely objective measures and interpret the range of rankings in light of the major methodological differences between what was done in this study and what has been done previously.

## Principles of Academic Organization

The interpretation of ranking ranges is further complicated by two other decisions that the committee made in designing the study. It decided to accept the respondent institution's principles of academic organization and to thus include multiple programs from the same university in the same program category if they met the criteria for a separate program and the university submitted the data for assessment. Each of these programs was rated separately, but they were all included in computation of the range of rankings. For example, Harvard has three doctoral programs under "Economics," and Princeton has two doctoral programs under "History."[16] Because the assessed quality of these programs tends to be similar, multiple programs from the same university could occupy multiple slots in a similar position in the range of rankings, thereby "crowding out" or reducing the rankings of other programs entering higher-ranking ranges and thus distorting the reported results. Another factor is that the committee's definition of a program to be rated did not always produce uniform definitions of comparable program areas, leading in some cases to results that are difficult to interpret in terms of ranges of rankings. For example, some mathematics programs include statistics and applied math, whereas others do not. Some anthropology departments include physical anthropology, while others do not. Perhaps at the extreme is the broad field of public health. Different subfields, such as biostatistics and epidemiology, are included as if they are the same program area, when clearly they are different in kind. This situation produces results that are difficult to interpret. When these differences were known, they are noted, but the reader should be alert when comparing specific programs to the possibility that they are not completely comparable.

## Counting Citations and Publications

The committee initially chose to collect citation data for relatively recent publications produced by core and new faculty in each of the Ph.D. programs. This decision, however, tended to bias the data against Ph.D. programs with more senior scholars, particularly in the social and behavioral sciences and humanities, where the pattern of publication over a career differs considerably from those patterns in the physical and biological sciences and engineering. After this bias was noted, the committee decided to collect citations over a much longer timescale. Thus publications going back roughly 20 years, to 1981, in the science, social sciences, and engineering fields are considered in the citation count. This set of procedures can lead to a bias either for or against senior scholars, and without further research even the sign of the effect is uncertain. The situation is inherently complex.

## Summary of Cautions

The cautions mentioned here are intended to alert readers to aspects of the methods used in this study that differ from those used in other studies, including ones conducted by the National Research Council. These innovations may produce ranges of rankings that surprise knowledgeable people in a field and contradict their views of the actual quality of specific programs. An examination of the data on individual variables for a program, together with the weights assigned to the different objective measures for each program should help to clarify the reasons for the specific rankings. The subtle, nonquantifiable variables that might make reputation more than the weighted sum of objective variables are not captured by the method adopted by the committee. In view of these limitations to the methods for obtaining ranges of rankings, some members of the committee remained skeptical that these results capture fully the relative quality

---

[16] At Harvard each one is in a different administrative unit; Princeton has both a history program and a history of science program.

of the doctoral programs in certain fields. For this reason, they should be used as illustrative. *In general, the range of rankings captures well the relative standing of most Ph.D. programs.* Some outliers, however, cannot be explained by the data in hand, and it may be that had more robust measures of reputational standing, or perceived quality, been used, these anomalies might be better understood or might have disappeared. Therefore, the committee suggests that anyone making strong comparisons with the 1995 rankings using either the R or S measure be cautious. Such comparisons can lead to a misinterpretation of the "actual" rankings of programs, however they might be defined. It would be especially misleading to overstate the significance of changes in rankings from the 1995 NRC report in view of the differences in adopted methodologies.

Finally, it is useful at this point to return to the topic of simple errors in the input data, because this is the most serious problem with which the staff and the committee wrestled. At a very late stage in its work the committee undertook a final set of "sanity checks"; the fields were divided up, and groups of academic fields were assigned to individual committee members to see if they could identify any anomalies in areas with which they were familiar. Many anomalies were found and were addressed, but surely some must have escaped notice. The committee thus urges readers to use the illustrative ranges of rankings with caution. Small differences in the variables can result in major differences in the range of rankings, especially when a program is very similar on other measures to other programs in its field. But individual instances of programs that should have been ranked considerably lower or significantly higher than the tables indicate may emerge, and so it is strongly recommended that the rankings of individual programs be treated with circumspection and caution and analyzed carefully.

# 5

# Faculty Values as Reflected in the Two Illustrative Rankings

This study is valuable for both the comparative data it makes available and the importance it attaches to some of the collected data by conducting a survey of faculty and relating program ratings to measured characteristics. The values used throughout this report, for the two overall rankings and, taken separately, for the dimensional rankings, derive in part from faculty members' answers to questions designed to measure faculty perceptions of the relative importance of program characteristics to the quality of doctoral programs.

The 21 characteristics identified by the committee and in the literature as important were divided into three categories are shown in Box 5-1.

| BOX 5-1 Characteristics Included in the Faculty Weighting Process |
|---|
| *CATEGORY I—Program Faculty Quality* |
| a. Number of publications (books, articles, etc.) per faculty member |
| b. Number of citations per faculty member |
| c. Receipt of extramural grants for research |
| d. Involvement in interdisciplinary work |
| e. Racial and ethnic diversity of the program faculty |
| f. Gender diversity of the program faculty |
| g. Reception by peers of a faculty member's work, as measured by honors and awards |
| *CATEGORY II—Student Characteristics* |
| a. Median GRE scores of entering students |
| b. Percentage of students receiving full financial support |
| c. Percentage of students with portable fellowships |
| d. Number of student publications and presentations[a] |
| e. Racial and ethnic diversity of the student population |
| f. Gender diversity of the student population |
| g. A high percentage of international students |

| | *CATEGORY III—Program Characteristics* |
|---|---|
| a. | Average number of Ph.D.'s granted over the previous five years |
| b. | Percentage of entering students who complete a doctoral degree |
| c. | Time to degree |
| d. | Placement of students after graduation |
| e. | Percentage of students with individual work space |
| f. | Percentage of health insurance premiums covered by the institution or program |
| g. | Number of student support activities provided at either the institutional or program level[b] |

[a] The committee initially believed this variable should be included, but later found no data to support it. It was eliminated from the calculation of weights, and the data tables in this report include 20, not 21, variables.

[b] This variable is a tally of whether the following services are provided to graduate students at either the institutional or program level: orientation for new students, prizes or awards to doctoral students for teaching or research, formal training in academic integrity/ethics, travel funds to attend professional meetings, grievance and dispute resolution procedures, annual review of all enrolled doctoral students, training to improve teaching skills, institutionally supported graduate student association, information about employment outcomes of graduates, and on-campus graduate student research conference.

Faculty respondents were asked to choose up to four characteristics in each category that they thought were important. They were then asked to indicate which one or two of the four they found the most important. The final task was to assign an importance score of from 0–100 to each category; the sum of the importance scores over all categories was to equal 100.[1]

The five characteristics given the highest rating on each measure are shown in Table 5-1. Specifically, it shows the average ranking of the characteristic in the field across all 20 measures.[2] This table makes the differences in the two rating methods clear. On the general survey (S measure) in all fields, the publication measure was very important. It was less important in the regression-based R measure, where for all fields size, as measured by the average number of Ph.D.'s was important. The percentage of faculty with grants was highly ranked on the S measure in all fields but the humanities. Awards per allocated faculty, a measure that may reflect reputation, was important in all fields but the agricultural sciences, and it was highly ranked for both the R and S measures in three of the five broad fields. None of the diversity measures appeared to be important in either methodology. GRE scores were important for R measures, but not for S measures, while placement of students in academic positions was important for S measures, but not for R measures.

---

[1] This was a forced choice. Faculty could not enter a characteristic beyond the ones given.

[2] To calculate the ranking of the importance weight of a characteristic, the rank order (1–20, with 1 being the highest) of the median weight was calculated for each characteristic, and this rank was averaged across all the fields in the each broad field.

TABLE 5-1 Most Highly Rated Characteristics of Doctoral Programs on R and S Measures

| Characteristic | Measure Type | Agricultural Sciences | Biological and Health Sciences | Engineering | Physical and Mathematical Sciences | Social and Behavioral Sciences | Humanities |
|---|---|---|---|---|---|---|---|
| Publications per allocated faculty | R | 2.67 | 6.23 | 3.00 | --- | --- | --- |
| | S | 1.17 | 1.85 | 1.38 | 1.67 | 1.00 | 1.00 |
| Cites per publication | R | --- | 4.31 | --- | 4.88 | 6.60 | n.a. |
| | S | 4.00 | 3.77 | 3.00 | 2.63 | 2.40 | n.a. |
| Percentage of faculty with grants | R | --- | --- | --- | --- | 8.30 | --- |
| | S | 1.83 | 1.15 | 1.63 | 1.67 | 3.20 | --- |
| Percentage of interdisciplinary faculty | R | --- | --- | --- | --- | --- | --- |
| | S | 5.67 | --- | --- | --- | --- | 4.77 |
| Awards per allocated faculty | R | 5.17 | 5.31 | 3.63 | 4.11 | 3.10 | 4.54 |
| | S | 1.83 | 1.15 | 1.63 | 1.67 | 3.20 | --- |
| Average GRE (GRE-V for the humanities, GRE-Q otherwise) | R | 5.50 | 5.69 | 5.63 | 7.33 | 4.20 | 3.62 |
| | S | --- | 5.00 | --- | --- | --- | --- |
| Percentage of first-year students with full support | R | --- | --- | --- | --- | --- | 8.08 |
| | S | --- | --- | --- | --- | --- | 4.77 |
| Average number of Ph.D.'s, 2002–2006 | R | 1.00 | 3.46 | 1.00 | 1.44 | 4.20 | 3.85 |
| | S | --- | --- | --- | --- | --- | --- |
| Percentage of students in academic positions | R | --- | --- | --- | 6.78 | --- | 4.77 |
| | S | 3.17 | 4.23 | 5.25 | 4.78 | 4.20 | 2.92 |
| Health insurance | R | --- | --- | --- | --- | --- | --- |
| | S | --- | --- | --- | --- | --- | --- |
| Number of student activities offered | R | 5.33 | --- | 7.63 | --- | --- | --- |
| | S | --- | --- | --- | --- | --- | --- |

Note: Number shown is average rank of the characteristic taken across the disciplines in the broad field. The five categories given
the highest rankings are shown for each field. "---" indicates the characteristic was not one of the top five for the field. "n.a."
indicates not collected; GRE-Q = GRE-Quantitative Reasoning; GRE-V = GRE-Verbal.

Faculty values are also reflected in the relative importance of each category measured on the faculty questionnaire. For all fields the importance score for the faculty productivity variables was highest, followed by the student support and outcomes category, with program demographic characteristics coming in last. These category importance values are shown in Table 5-2. One interesting observation is that although these weights are different from one another in a statistical sense, they are remarkably similar regardless of the field of the respondents.

TABLE 5-2  Faculty Importance Weights by Broad Field

|  | Faculty Productivity and Associated Characteristics (%) | Student Support and Outcome Characteristics (%) | Program Diversity Characteristics (%) |
|---|---|---|---|
| Agricultural sciences | 45.2 | 30.5 | 25.1 |
| Biological and health sciences | 45.1 | 31.9 | 23.7 |
| Physical and mathematical sciences | 48.9 | 29.7 | 22.2 |
| Engineering | 46.5 | 31.8 | 22.5 |
| Social and behavioral sciences | 49.1 | 28.2 | 23.6 |
| Humanities | 46.4 | 28.9 | 25.6 |

## DIMENSIONAL MEASURES

Despite the relatively moderate importance that faculty placed on the student treatment and program diversity dimensions of doctoral education, the committee felt it was very important to measure and discuss these dimensions, in part because they have figured prominently in national discussions of doctoral education.[3] The dimensional measures were obtained by means of the faculty responses to Section G (see Table 5-1).[4] These measures take a subset of all the characteristics and recalculate the weights so that the total of the weights for the subset adds up to 1. The dimensional measures used in this study—research activity, student support and outcomes, and diversity of the academic environment—are described in the sections that follow.

### Research Activity

This dimensional measure relates to the various ways in which to gauge the contribution of research: publications, citations (except for the humanities), the percentage of the faculty holding research grants, and recognition of scholarship as evidenced by honors and awards. The importance weights are shown in Table 5-2a. Specifically, the components of the research activity dimensional measure are average publications per

---

[3] See, for example, Ronald G. Ehrenberg, Harriet Zuckerman, Jeffrey A. Groen, and Sharon M. Brucker, *Educating Scholars: Doctoral Education in the Humanities* (Princeton, N.J.: Princeton University Press, 2010).

[4] These dimensional weights are different from the S weights, which take *all* 20 variables into account.

| Broad Field | Publications per Allocated Faculty[a] | Cites per Publication | Percentage of Allocated Faculty Holding Grants | Awards per Allocated Faculty |
|---|---|---|---|---|
| Agricultural sciences | 0.349 | 0.175 | 0.348 | 0.128 |
| Biological and health sciences | 0.314 | 0.192 | 0.377 | 0.118 |
| Physical and mathematical sciences | 0.281 | 0.258 | 0.294 | 0.167 |
| Engineering | 0.291 | 0.238 | 0.304 | 0.167 |
| Social and behavioral sciences | 0.376 | 0.250 | 0.216 | 0.158 |
| Humanities | 0.591 | [a] | 0.124 | 0.284 |

TABLE 5-2A Average Faculty Importance Weights on Components of Research Activity Dimensional Measure

[a] For the humanities, publications are measured by books and articles per allocated faculty member. There are no data for citations.

allocated faculty member,[5] average citations per publication, percentage of core and new doctoral faculty respondents holding grants, and awards per allocated faculty member.[6] Publishing patterns and the availability of research funding and awards for scholarship vary by field, but the weight placed on publications per faculty member is remarkably consistent—about 30 percent—across fields. Research activity is the dimensional measure that most closely tracks the overall measure of program quality, because in all fields both the S measure—based on abstract faculty preferences—and the R measure place high weights on these characteristics.

For the research activity measures, faculty in the sciences and engineering place the greatest weight on grants per faculty member. In some fields research funding is common, and grants are an important source of support for faculty and doctoral students. In the social and behavioral sciences and the humanities, the greatest weight is placed on publications. In one social science discipline, economics, the weight placed on citations is almost equal to that placed on publications, but in all other fields publication is more highly valued. Grants are a less important source of funding in the humanities, and for those fields publications and awards are the most important visible signs of research activity. The values evinced in the broad fields are, with the exception of the humanities, very similar.

## Student Support and Outcomes

This measure combines data on the percentage of students fully funded in the first year, the percentage of students completing their degrees in a given time period, time to degree, and placement in academic positions (including academic postdoctoral positions).

---

[5] Because many faculty members supervise dissertations in more than one program, faculty members were allocated across these programs so that the total, taken across all programs, equaled 1 or less (when the faculty member was in a professional school).

[6] In constructing this measure, a distinction was made between "highly prestigious" and "prestigious" awards, with the former given a weight of 5 and the latter given a weight of 1. The committee reviewed 1,393 awards and honors from various scholarly organizations. Highly prestigious awards were identified by the committee.

The committee found that faculty typically placed a larger weight on student support and completion rates than on median time to degree or academic placement.[7]

Surprising uniformity appears across broad fields on the weights, which are shown in Table 5-2B.

| TABLE 5-2B Average Faculty Importance Weights on Components of the Student Support and Outcomes Dimensional Measure | | | | |
|---|---|---|---|---|
| Broad Field | First-Year Students with Full Support | Percentage Completing Degree Within Six  or Eight Years[a] | Time to Degree, Full- and Part-Time[b] | Percentage of Graduates in Academic Positions |
| Agricultural sciences | 0.304 | 0.231 | −0.109 | 0.357 |
| Biological and health sciences | 0.259 | 0.264 | −0.135 | 0.342 |
| Physical and mathematical sciences | 0.306 | 0.221 | −0.114 | 0.359 |
| Engineering | 0.346 | 0.200 | −0.099 | 0.356 |
| Social and behavioral sciences | 0.291 | 0.229 | −0.110 | 0.370 |
| Humanities | 0.316 | 0.245 | −0.102 | 0.337 |

[a] For the humanities, eight years are used in the completion measure. This completion measure is measured as the fraction of the entering cohort that has received a Ph.D. within six or eight years.  [b] Time to degree has a negative weight reflecting that a shorter time is better.  The sum of the absolute values of the weights is 1.

The percentage of graduates obtaining academic positions dominates these measures, and, interestingly, the weight given to this variable (0.34 –0.37) is essentially the same in all of the broad academic fields. The negative sign on time to degree indicates that the shorter the time to degree, the better.  Student support in the first year is also an important variable in all fields. Percentage of completion and time to degree are less important, and although these variables have been discussed within the community of graduate deans, they are not variables that faculty feel are important in determining the quality of a doctoral program.

## Diversity of the Academic Environment

The diversity measures—percentage of faculty and of students from underrepresented minority groups, percentage of faculty and of students who are female, and percentage of students who are international (that is, in the United States on a temporary visa)—did not appear to be major factors in determining the overall perceived quality of doctoral programs.[8] When these measures are taken separately, definite patterns emerge for variables that faculty thought were more important, and these patterns vary by field. Most fields place the highest weight on the percentage of students from underrepresented

---

[7] Ideally, the committee would have used a measure such as employment in one's field five years after receipt of a Ph.D., but many programs did not collect such data. The committee hoped that including this measure would encourage more programs to pay attention to postdegree outcomes for their graduates.

[8] In other words, the weights on these characteristics were small relative to other characteristics in the R and S measures.

minority groups. In the biological and health sciences, social and behavioral sciences, and humanities, relatively high weights are also placed on the percentage of faculty who are underrepresented minorities. The percentage of international students was not highly weighted relative to the other diversity weights, except for the physical and mathematical sciences. These weights, by broad field, are shown in Table 5-2C.

| Broad Field | Non-Asian Minority Faculty | Female Faculty | Non-Asian Minority Students | Female Students | International Students |
|---|---|---|---|---|---|
| Agricultural sciences | 0.101 | 0.124 | 0.348 | 0.231 | 0.196 |
| Biological and health sciences | 0.115 | 0.173 | 0.362 | 0.235 | 0.115 |
| Physical and mathematical sciences | 0.059 | 0.144 | 0.200 | 0.318 | 0.279 |
| Engineering | 0.083 | 0.107 | 0.281 | 0.295 | 0.234 |
| Social and behavioral sciences | 0.156 | 0.150 | 0.298 | 0.166 | 0.230 |
| Humanities | 0.172 | 0.212 | 0.212 | 0.192 | 0.213 |

TABLE 5-2C Average Faculty Importance Weights on Components of the Diversity Dimensional Measure

The preferences of faculty in the broad fields are very similar across fields. The physical and mathematical sciences place a greater weight on the percentage of students who are female than the percentage of students who from a underrepresented minority. This weighting is reversed for the other fields. None of the fields places a large weight on faculty diversity, although generally a slightly higher weight is placed on the percentage of faculty who are female. The physical sciences and engineering and, to some extent, the social sciences faculty indicate that a higher percentage of international students is beneficial and important to program quality. The relatively high weight for this measure for the humanities reflects high weighting in the foreign language fields and comparative literature.

## SUMMARY OF THE FINDINGS

The findings of the committee fall into three areas:

1. Indicators of research activity are of the greatest importance to faculty in determining program quality by means of the S measures, which are based on the program characteristics that faculty say explicitly are important. In many cases program size is very important when quality is measured by the regression-based, or R measures.
2. Of the student support and outcome characteristics, placement in an academic position and support in the first year are highly weighted. Completion rates and time to degree are not.
3. Faculty view student diversity as important, when considered with other diversity measures, but not as a direct predictor of overall program quality.

# 6

# Some Uses of the Data

Students and their families, faculty members, administrators, boards of higher education, trustees, and departments of education, both state and federal, as well as private sector employers and policy analysts and scholars, among others, should find the data in this study of interest. This chapter provides examples of some uses of the study data.

## POTENTIAL USERS

### Students

Once students know the discipline in which they want to pursue doctoral study, they usually take the next step of discussing with their adviser or a professor in that field what that doctoral study would involve. Here are some examples of the questions that might be asked:

- Do I know what I want to specialize in?
- Do I want a program in a particular region—for example, near my home?
- Do I want a large program or a small program?
- Do I want a program in which a high proportion of the faculty has grants?
- Are my GRE scores competitive with those of other students in programs that interest me?
- Do I want a program in which a high proportion of students complete their degrees in a reasonable period of time?
- Do I want a program in which I am likely to find other students and faculty like myself
  (e.g., who are female or from underrepresented minority groups)?
- Do I want a program that funds most of its students in their first year?
- Do I want a program that is interdisciplinary?
- Do I want a program whose faculty are highly cited?

After choosing among the doctoral programs suggested by their adviser, students can then create a spreadsheet of those programs from the online data available from this study, which will allow them compare the programs on the various measures of interest. For example, Table 6-1 shows the rankings and data for 5 of the 34 chemistry programs in universities in the mid-Atlantic area.

| TABLE 6-1 Ranges of Rankings and Data for Five Mid-Atlantic Chemistry Programs | | | | | |
|---|---|---|---|---|---|
| | Institution A | Institution B | Institution C | Institution D | Institution E |
| *Overall measures at 5th and 95th percentile points* | | | | | |
| R5 | 6 | 6 | 17 | 53 | 32 |
| R95 | 29 | 24 | 49 | 112 | 83 |
| S5 | 5 | 10 | 9 | 88 | 33 |
| S95 | 18 | 38 | 31 | 155 | 89 |
| *Dimensional measures at 5th and 95th percentile points[a]* | | | | | |
| RA5 | 5 | 8 | 10 | 62 | 20 |
| RA95 | 21 | 37 | 53 | 146 | 91 |
| SS5 | 17 | 35 | 5 | 75 | 25 |
| SS95 | 113 | 134 | 66 | 156 | 114 |
| D5 | 87 | 103 | 109 | 81 | 44 |
| D95 | 141 | 158 | 162 | 138 | 103 |
| *Characteristic* | | | | | |
| Publications per allocated faculty | 4.413 | 4.601 | 4.136 | 1.891 | 2.896 |
| Cites per publication | 2.971 | 2.933 | 2.504 | 1.578 | 2.513 |
| Faculty with grants (%)[b] | 100.0% | 88.6% | 95.4% | 85.9% | 90.5% |
| Interdisciplinary faculty (%) | 0.0% | 71.4% | 38.1% | 6.3% | 18.8% |
| Non-Asian minority faculty (%) | 5.0% | 0.0% | 0.0% | 3.7% | 2.9% |
| Female faculty (%) | 13.6% | 16.2% | 8.0% | 13.8% | 17.9% |
| Awards per allocated faculty | 13.837 | 6.475 | 3.802 | 0.067 | 1.907 |
| Average GRE-Q | 772 | 712 | 769 | 700 | 703 |
| First-year students with full support (%) | 100.0% | 100.0% | 100.0% | 100.0% | 100.0% |
| First-year students with external funding (%) | 0.0% | 0.0% | 22.2% | 0.0% | 0.0% |
| Non-Asian minority students (%) | 1.9% | 2.8% | 3.2% | 5.4% | 8.0% |
| Female students (%) | 39.1% | 39.3% | 39.8% | 39.7% | 42.2% |
| International students (%) | 42.7% | 23.0% | 37.2% | 35.8% | 45.1% |
| Average Ph.D.'s, 2002–2006 | 17.4 | 31.6 | 20.2 | 12.8 | 11.4 |
| Completing within six years (%), | 77.8% | 49.3% | 67.6% | 43.3% | 41.6% |

| | | | | | |
|---|---|---|---|---|---|
| Time to degree, full- and part-time  (years) | 5 | 5.7 | 4.9 | 6 | 4.3 |
| Students in academic positions (%) | 57.0% | 44.7% | 54.3% | 37.8% | 48.7% |
| Student work space | 1 | 1 | 1 | 1 | 1 |
| Health insurance | 1 | 1 | 1 | 1 | 1 |
| Number of student activities offered. | 16 | 18 | 16 | 16 | 18 |

[a] RA = research activity; SS = student support and outcomes; D = diversity of academic environment.

[b] All percentages are the percentage of total in the relevant group (faculty, students, or Ph.D.'s).

The data reveal clearly that these programs are different. The chemistry program in Institution B is large—it graduates almost 32 students a year compared with 20 or fewer for the remaining four programs. In terms of research activity, the first three programs are highly productive, and their range of rankings would likely place them among the top 20 programs in the field. One of the institutions has a prestigious (and likely older) faculty, as measured by awards. With one exception, all of the programs support all of their first-year students. All of the institutions have a time to degree of between four and six years, but in institutions A, D, and E less than 50 percent of their students complete their degrees within six years. Institution A places almost a third of its graduates in academic positions. The comparisons based on the diversity variables are mixed. Women make up more than one-third of the students at all the programs, but the gender diversity of faculty varies. In all of the programs more than 20 percent of the students are international, but none of the programs have more than 10 percent of students from racial or ethnic minorities, and two programs have no minorities in their teaching faculty.

This example illustrates that for many uses the data themselves may be more useful than any range of rankings. The temptation, however, will be to use the ranges of rankings.

### Faculty and Administrators

It is hoped faculty and administrators will look at the data, ask what characteristics are important to the purpose at hand, and rank programs accordingly. They may, however, want to look at the illustrative R and S ranges, which are after all constructed from faculty opinions, and try to understand where their programs fall in these illustrative rankings. A detailed understanding of the generation of the rankings of a single program in biochemistry can be obtained in part through Table 6-2, which shows the overall and dimensional rankings for a program in that field of study.

| TABLE 6-2  An Example of Selected Ranges of Rankings for a Doctoral Program in Biochemistry | | | | | |
|---|---|---|---|---|---|
| | Range of Overall Rankings | | Dimensional Rankings | | |
| | R Rankings | S Rankings | Research Activity | Student Support and Outcomes | Diversity of the Educational Environment |

| | R5 | R95 | S5 | S95 | RA5 | RA95 | SS5 | SS95 | D5 | D95 |
|---|---|---|---|---|---|---|---|---|---|---|
| Program name | 11 | 19 | 7 | 31 | 5 | 29 | 7 | 107 | 89 | 134 |

It is natural to ask at this point: where did these rankings come from? Table 6-3 provides the details for this program, which can be obtained by clicking on the link in the online spreadsheet.

| Characteristic | Standardized Values of the Variables, for the Program[a] | | | | R Coefficients | | S Coefficients | |
|---|---|---|---|---|---|---|---|---|
| | R5 | R95 | S5 | S95 | R5 | R95 | S5 | R5 |
| Publications per allocated faculty | 1.807 | 1.619 | 1.755 | 1.668 | 0.059 | 0.111 | 0.144 | 0.139 |
| Cites per publication | 1.222 | 1.221 | 1.274 | 1.216 | 0.102 | 0.118 | 0.102 | 0.103 |
| Faculty with grants (%) | -0.437 | -1.204 | 2.071 | -1.068 | 0.018 | 0.024 | 0.171 | 0.172 |
| Interdisciplinary faculty (%) | -0.387 | -0.425 | -0.457 | -0.280 | 0.027 | -0.016 | 0.042 | 0.039 |
| Non-Asian minority faculty (%) | -0.837 | -0.818 | -0.461 | -0.275 | -0.059 | -0.015 | 0.009 | 0.010 |
| Female faculty (%) | 0.315 | 0.675 | 0.379 | 1.042 | -0.002 | 0.045 | 0.015 | 0.015 |
| Awards per allocated faculty | 3.249 | 3.064 | 2.973 | 2.686 | 0.093 | 0.140 | 0.062 | 0.062 |
| Average GRE-Q | 0.015 | 0.261 | 0.031 | 0.390 | 0.101 | 0.092 | 0.081 | 0.079 |
| First-year students with full support (%) | 0.433 | -0.233 | 0.158 | 0.779 | 0.027 | -0.012 | 0.057 | 0.056 |
| First-year students with portable fellowships (%) | 0.846 | 1.044 | 0.696 | 1.006 | 0.064 | 0.037 | 0.047 | 0.046 |
| Non-Asian minority students (%) | -0.922 | -0.961 | -1.097 | -1.001 | 0.023 | 0.008 | 0.020 | 0.020 |
| Female students (%) | -0.242 | -0.266 | 0.080 | -0.368 | -0.051 | -0.064 | 0.017 | 0.017 |
| International students (%) | 0.196 | 0.630 | 0.194 | 0.070 | -0.022 | -0.008 | 0.008 | 0.009 |
| Average Ph.D.'s, 2002–2006 | -0.494 | -0.967 | -0.552 | -0.405 | 0.117 | 0.121 | 0.026 | 0.027 |
| Completing degree within six years (%) | -0.387 | 2.088 | -0.381 | -0.362 | 0.035 | -0.035 | 0.055 | 0.056 |
| Time to degree, full- and part-time | -0.764 | -1.145 | -0.636 | -0.260 | 0.016 | 0.018 | -0.031 | -0.030 |
| Students in academic positions (%) | -0.610 | -1.287 | -1.235 | -1.493 | -0.047 | 0.004 | 0.074 | 0.078 |
| Student work space | 1 | 1 | 1 | 1 | -0.025 | -0.067 | 0.004 | 0.005 |
| Health insurance | 1 | 1 | 1 | 1 | -0.028 | 0.003 | 0.005 | 0.005 |
| Number of student activities offered | 1.950 | 0.293 | 0.876 | 0.495 | 0.083 | 0.061 | 0.032 | 0.034 |
| R rating | 0.671 | 0.578 | S rating | 0.858 | 0.322 | | | |
| R ranking | 11 | 19 | S ranking | 7 | 31 | | | |

[a] Because of the Monte Carlo technique used to generate the ranking ranges, in some cases the R95 (or S95) standardized measure may be smaller than the R05 (or S05) measure for a particular variable.

Table 6-3 shows the standardized values of the variables for the particular estimation that resulted in the program's rank for the 5th percentile and the 95th percentile for each methodology. Uncertainty has been taken into account for the value of each variable, and 500 separate sets of half-samples of the raters have been selected for each measure. The values of the variables have been selected from a random distribution within which the variable values can vary by plus or minus 10 percent or by the extent of their actual variation, if data were collected on that variation.[1] It is apparent from Table 6-2 that the range of S rankings is larger than the range of R rankings for this program, and that it does especially well on the research activity dimensional measure and less well on the other two measures. Closer examination reveals that the coefficients on both measures place a high weight on the research characteristics, where this program is well above average.

Administrators with budget allocation responsibility will be particularly interested in an analysis of all the programs of one university or in one division of a university. Keeping in mind that each discipline is different, administrators may find the NRC data useful in making allocation decisions designed to shorten the time to degree, for example, or to improve completion rates in particular programs, or to enhance support for faculty research. But, again, the NRC data are just a start, and universities will want to supplement and update them.

Comparison of a given program with those in a higher echelon will likely indicate that ratings will improve if the research impact of the faculty improves. Although hiring "stars" is one obvious solution, another is to enable faculty to increase their research productivity by seeding new research programs or giving faculty more time to spend on research. These data provide some quantitative measures to inform decisions about the balance between research and teaching for a given program. But, again, the NRC dataset is only part of the information needed for budget allocations.

Indeed, the NRC data are only one way of measuring a doctoral program, and in all fields the ranges of rankings are heavily influenced by metrics about the research productivity of the faculty in terms of publications and citations as well as grants and awards. No effort has been devoted to assessing the outcomes of graduate education or to determining the effectiveness of the doctoral research experience in preparing students for a life of scholarly inquiry. Nor has effort been given to measuring or assessing the need for doctoral studies in any given area, or of the career outcomes of students who follow any particular course of study. These considerations also influence administrative decisions about resource allocations to graduate programs. Additional central university support may target not the highest-ranked programs or the lowest, but rather the units best equipped to use additional funding in a productive fashion.

## Boards of Higher Education and Trustees

As the ultimate authority on which doctoral programs should be offered by a university or universities in each state, boards of higher education and boards of trustees are ultimately responsible for the quality of doctoral programs. They are also aware of the full range of doctoral programs in a state or university. They may find that a program does not rank highly, but it plays an important role in producing Ph.D.'s who well serve an industry that

---

[1] The questionnaires in Appendix D reveal whether variable values for multiple years were collected.

is important to the state's economy. Some programs offered in the same field by various institutions may display a measurable quality differential that is supported by differences in one or more selected characteristics, thereby indicating that consolidation could be the answer. However, resolving such matters requires fine-grained study of the programs and more detailed analysis than can be provided by the NRC data alone.

## Private Sector Employers

Academia is no longer the majority employer of Ph.D.'s. They are employed by industry, nonprofit organizations, government, and consulting firms. Rather than just the programs with the highest rankings, these employers may wish to look for programs that tend to aim at the nonacademic sector, as well as programs that are more diverse and focused, as evidenced by higher completion rates and shorter times to degree.

## Policy Analysts and Scholars

The data from this study contain a wide selection of information needed for policy analysis of graduate education. Additional data from the program, student, and faculty questionnaires will be made available in a public-use dataset. How to obtain access to the dataset will be announced following release of this report. These data will contain tabulations of the answers to most questions on the questionnaires aggregated by program, provided that this aggregation preserves individual confidentiality. Upon publication of this report, the analytic tables showing the derivations of the rankings for each program, and the master tables for programs by discipline, will be available. If a researcher needs individual-level records, these will be made available to researchers who agree to respect the confidentiality of respondents and sign a confidentiality agreement with the NRC. Researchers are warned, however, that the data not shown in the master tables have spottier response rates.

# A WORKSHOP ON ANALYTIC USES OF THE DATA

A workshop on the ways in which universities and researchers have used the data was held after the release of the report and data tables. The committee believes it is very important that ways of analyzing the data become widely known throughout the graduate and higher education research community and to enhance their usefulness.

# 7

# The Data and Principal Findings

All doctoral programs have similarities. Typically, they admit students, maintain a curriculum of study, adhere to a "certification" requirement (preliminary or comprehensive examinations), and require completion of a piece of original work that demonstrates the ability of their students to conduct research that advances the state of knowledge. But that is where the similarities end. Depending on the discipline, a student may spend years perusing archival materials, or conducting fieldwork, or working closely on a problem as part of a research team based in a laboratory. Thus each discipline has its own ways of educating doctoral students. It makes sense, then, to examine doctoral education in each broad field or discipline separately. It does not make sense to compare time to degree in anthropology, with its years of fieldwork and close observation, with that for biochemistry, where a student typically works in a laboratory on a problem until it is solved.

Within broad fields, however, many programs may exhibit similar characteristics and faculty preferences. Thus because this study covers large numbers of programs, the committee chose to summarize the data for broad fields rather than for individual disciplines. The committee also found similarities in particular characteristics among programs in a discipline. For example, larger programs in a discipline may have more resources for research, but provide a more impersonal environment for students than the smaller ones. Across disciplines, there may be fewer resources available for student support at public universities than at some private ones and, as a result, students in programs in these institutions may take longer to complete their studies, even in the same field. This chapter examines the program data in each broad field in an attempt to discover commonalities and differences. The focus here is on the variables that can be affected by administrative decisions or changes in program practices.

To convey a sense of how the doctoral education enterprise has changed since the 1995 study (for which data were collected in 1993), this chapter presents data for programs in four broad fields[1] that were included in both the 1995 study and the current study (designated here as "common programs"). It then moves to a discussion of the 2006 data on characteristics of all programs in the study grouped by broad field and classified by the following broad groupings of variables: research and faculty productivity, student support and outcomes, and diversity. The chapter concludes with a description of findings from the faculty and student questionnaires.

---

[1] Agricultural sciences were not included in the 1995 study. The biological and health sciences field definitions changed too much to be strictly comparable. In the other broad fields, only the disciplines and programs included in both studies are included.

## CHANGES IN DOCTORAL PROGRAMS BETWEEN 1993 AND 2006[2]

As described in Chapter 3 of this report, the changes in the eligibility criteria and definition of doctoral faculty render comparisons between the two studies inexact. It is possible, however, to match programs that were in both studies and see how the characteristics that were measured in both have changed. Table 7-1 displays these results for engineering, the physical and mathematical sciences, the social and behavioral sciences, and the humanities.

| TABLE 7-1 Weighted Measures for Faculty and Students, 1993 and 2006 | | | | | | | |
|---|---|---|---|---|---|---|---|
| Broad Field | 1993 Programs | 2006 Programs | 1993 and 2006 Common Programs | Average Faculty per Program, 1993 | Average Faculty per Program, 2006 | Assistant Professors, 1993 (% of total faculty[a]) | Assistant Professors, 2006 (% of total faculty[a]) |
| Engineering | 588 | 747 | 457 | 21 | 40 | 20.3 | 20.0 |
| Physical and mathematical sciences | 786 | 876 | 552 | 26 | 37 | 17.8 | 20.1 |
| Social and behavioral sciences | 630 | 759 | 493 | 24 | 33 | 19.9 | 23.2 |
| Humanities | 656 | 716 | 498 | 23 | 31 | 17.2 | 19.6 |

[a] Average over all fields in the broad field.

The number of programs grew in all fields and in all disciplines common to the two studies.[3] Among the comparable broad fields, the greatest growth in number of programs was in engineering, with bioengineering a relatively new field in 1993, leading the way. The only field in which the number of programs declined was aerospace engineering. The social and behavioral sciences were next in growth of programs. Geography, a field revolutionized by the availability of satellite information, experienced the greatest percentage of growth in programs, and psychology experienced the greatest growth in number of programs. Although the humanities as a whole saw an increase of 60 programs, declines in the number of programs were most prevalent in the humanities, especially in English and the foreign language fields. The exception was Spanish language and literature. The number of programs in history grew. The physical and mathematical science expanded by 90 programs, and the greatest increase was in the earth sciences, which added 40 programs.

As for the programs common to both studies, the average number of faculty in the common programs increased in all broad fields, but by far the highest growth over the period was in engineering (82 percent). This growth was experienced to some extent by all the fields, but by biomedical engineering and chemical engineering in particular. The growth in interest and funding in bioscience has fueled much of this change. Faculty per program in all other broad fields grew by more than one-third. The only field in which average faculty declined was music (–13 percent).[4] Mathematics appears to have been a slow-growing field (9 percent), but this

---

[2] A note on dates.  The 1995 study collected data from the 1993 academic year.  This study used a survey administered in 2007 to collect data from the 2006 academic year.  Typically, the data in tables are identified by the academic year in which they were counted.

[3] The committee does not know how much of this growth stems from the  increased participation in the study between 1993 and 2006 and how much stems from the establishment of new programs.

[4] This decline may be attributable to the greater emphasis on excluding performance faculty in the 2007 survey.

finding may be stem from the committee's decision in the 2007 survey to treat applied mathematics as a separate field. Table 7-2 summarizes these data for common programs.

| Broad Field | Average Ph.D.'s, 1987–1991 | Average Ph.D.'s, 2002–2006 | Average Total Enrollment per Program, 1993 | Average Total Enrollment per Program, 2006 | Female Students, 1993 (average %) | Female Students, 2006 (average %) |
|---|---|---|---|---|---|---|
| TABLE 7-2 Changes in Ph.D.'s, Enrollment, and Gender Composition, Common Programs, 1993 and 2006 | | | | | | |
| Engineering | 7.4 | 8.6 | 64.2 | 68.2 | 14 | 23 |
| Physical and mathematical sciences | 7.9 | 8.2 | 67.4 | 74.9 | 24 | 30 |
| Social and behavioral sciences | 6.1 | 7.1 | 59.0 | 61.5 | 42 | 53 |
| Humanities | 4.8 | 5.8 | 59.0 | 53.0 | 50 | 50 |

The size of programs, as measured by Ph.D. production, generally displays a skewed distribution. A substantial fraction of Ph.D.'s is produced by a much smaller fraction of programs. Consequently, although the average sizes of programs as measured by either Ph.D.s or enrollments are interesting, their significance for changes in individual program size is not always clear. The changes in program size as measured by enrollment and by faculty are shown in Tables 7-3 and 7-4.

The changes in average measures of size for the common programs—Ph.D.'s per program and enrollment—are much smaller in magnitude than changes in the average number of faculty. The growth in the average number of Ph.D.'s per program in all broad fields was generally modest, less than 15 percent over 13 years for all the broad fields except the humanities. Notable field exceptions were music (–8 percent), earth sciences (–34 percent), physics (–6 percent), and linguistics (–9 percent). In all other fields the average number of Ph.D.'s per program increased. Such increases can be achieved in two ways: programs grow in size, or programs shorten the time to degree, thereby producing more Ph.D.'s in the same time period. Although good data are not available from the earlier study, there is no evidence that the time to degree has diminished significantly. It seems likely, then, that the existing programs increased enrollments. A more complete analysis of the faculty-to-student ratios in the institutions that produce most of the Ph.D.'s would be required to ascertain whether there has been much of a change for most students. It is possible that most of the growth in faculty has occurred in institutions that produce relatively few Ph.D.'s.[5]

---

[5] The difference in how the two studies defined *doctoral faculty* was discussed earlier. If anything, the definition in the 2007 survey was more restrictive than the definition used in 1993so we can be sure growth occurred but cannot be certain of its magnitude.

| TABLE 7-3 Average of Total Faculty, All Common Programs, 1993 and 2006, | | | |
|---|---|---|---|
| Broad Field | Number of Common Programs, 1995–2006 | Average Total Faculty per Program, 1993 | Average Total Faculty per Program, 2006 |
| Engineering | 457 | 21.88 | 39.75 |
| Physical and mathematical sciences | 552 | 26.40 | 37.22 |
| Social and behavioral sciences | 493 | 23.64 | 32.76 |
| Humanities | 498 | 23.35 | 30.97 |

The growth in the common programs is mirrored by the growth of doctoral recipients nationwide (see Table 7-4). The greatest percentage growth was in engineering.

| TABLE 7-4 Percentage Change in Number of Doctoral Recipients, Common Programs, 1993 and 2006 | | | | |
|---|---|---|---|---|
| | 1993 | 2006 | Difference | Percentage change |
| Engineering | 5,061 | 6,707 | 1,646 | 33 |
| Physical and mathematical sciences | 6,425 | 7,283 | 858 | 13 |
| Social and behavioral sciences | 7,538 | 8,326 | 788 | 10 |
| Humanities | 3,174 | 3,821 | 647 | 20 |

Source: NSF Survey of Doctoral Recipients, 2006 and 1993.

## Growth in Postdoctoral Scholars

One of the major changes in the academic research enterprise since the last study is the increase in the number of postdoctoral scholars, primarily in the sciences.[6] Data on postdocs were not collected in the 1995 study; however, it is now clear that, especially in the biological sciences, these young scholars play a major role both in research and in the mentoring of Ph.D. students. In many respects they share some of the roles of both advanced graduate students and faculty. Thus, because some faculty time is spent on the education of postdoctoral scholars and part of postdoctoral scholars' time is spent on the education of graduate students, any interpretation of the NRC data on student-to-faculty ratios, for example, should consider whether the increased number of faculty directly affects Ph.D. student mentoring. This study addresses doctoral education specifically, so it does not address the participation of postdoctoral scholars. However, the presence of substantial numbers of postdoctoral scholars changes the context of graduate education, especially the Ph.D. research experience. The number and therefore the impact of postdoctoral scholars differ significantly across disciplines and size of programs—being more prominent in the sciences and much less so in the humanities. Table 7-6 shows the number of postdocs by broad field in 2006. The greatest impact of postdocs is clearly in the biological and health sciences.

---

[6] This growth, through 1997, was documented in National Research Council, *Enhancing the Postdoctoral Experience for Scientists and Engineers: A Guide for Postdoctoral Scholars, Advisers, Institutions, Funding Organizations, and Disciplinary Societies,* Committee on Science, Engineering, and Public Policy (COSEPUP). (Washington, D.C.: National Academies Press, 2000), 5.

| TABLE 7-5 Number of Postdocs by Broad Field, 2006 | |
|---|---|
| Broad Field | Number of Postdocs |
| Agricultural sciences | 2,429 |
| Biological and health sciences | 24,084 |
| Physical and mathematical sciences | 9,952 |
| Engineering | 5,387 |
| Social and behavioral sciences | 1,430 |
| Humanities | 233 |

## Changes in the Diversity of Programs

For all the common programs, with the exception of classics (–5.2 percent) and linguistics (–2.5 percent), in all broad fields, the percentage of enrollment for women increased. For the broad fields the absolute numbers of women enrolled also grew. Increases of greater than 10 percentage points were found in several engineering fields (biomedical, chemical, civil, and mechanical), several fields in the physical sciences (astrophysics, earth sciences, oceanography, and statistics), and one field in the social sciences (economics). All these fields had relatively low levels of female enrollment in 1993. Data on racial and ethnic diversity were not collected in 1993, but the NSF data shown in Figure 7-1 reveal a considerable increase in minority Ph.D.'s across the board. However, in some fields, especially engineering, the social and behavioral sciences, and the physical and mathematical sciences, the numbers of non-underrepresented minorities (Asian Americans and whites) have been declining.

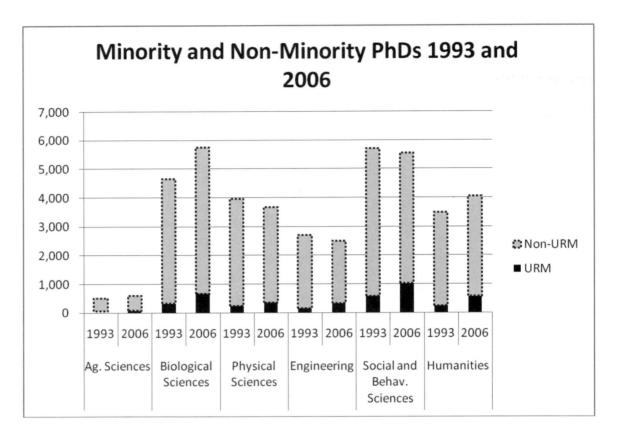

FIGURE 7-1 Minority and Nonminority Ph.D.'s, 1993 and 2006
Note: Non-URM = non-underrepresented minorities; URM = underrepresented minorities.
Source: National Science Foundation, Division of Science Resources Statistics.


In summary, the 13 years from 1993 to 2006 saw an increase in the number of doctoral programs in the common broad fields and disciplines, growth in the numbers of faculty and students per program, expanded production of Ph.D.'s per program, and an increase in the gender and ethnic diversity of programs. These quantitative changes were accompanied by changes in the average faculty-to-student ratios, which increased significantly over this period. This chapter now turns to a more detailed description of doctoral education in 2005–2006.

## U.S. DOCTORAL PROGRAMS IN 2006: A DESCRIPTION

Although this study does not include all doctoral programs or all fields, it does cover the vast majority of research doctorate programs in the United States.[7] This section begins by describing the characteristics of the programs in the study. Of particular interest is the size of programs in these fields and the type of control (public or private). The section then moves to comparing and contrasting the fields along these dimensions.

### Coverage

The programs with rankings in this study account for approximately 90 percent of the doctorates in the fields included in the study taxonomy in 2006. A comparison with NSF's Doctorate Record File (DRF) by broad field is shown in Table 7-6. In view of these high rates of coverage, the generalizations drawn from the study sample can, in all likelihood, be applied to U. S. doctoral education as a whole.

TABLE 7-6 Number of Ph.D.'s in 2006 NRC Study Compared with Ph.D.'s in NSF Doctorate Record File

| Broad Field | DRF 2006 | 2006 NRC Study | % in Study |
|---|---|---|---|
| Agricultural sciences | 1,470 | 1,147 | 78 |
| Biological and health sciences[a] | 5,737 | 5,543 | 97 |
| Physical and mathematical sciences | 7,283 | 7,092 | 97 |
| Engineering | 6,707 | 6,716 | 100 |
| Social and behavioral sciences[b] | 7,783 | 5,997 | 77 |
| Humanities | 4,624 | 3,754 | 81 |
| Total | 33,604 | 30,249 | 90 |
| Total minus psychology | 30,346 | 28,283 | 93 |

Note: The DRF responses are from a questionnaire administered to students at the time of graduation. The NRC data are from responses to the program questionnaire. The timing of the answers to the two questionnaires may account for discrepancies. The NRC questionnaire was answered in 2007, for 2005–2006 graduates, whereas the NSF questionnaire covered Ph.D.'s awarded in 2005–2006.
[a] Integrated biological science, which appears in the NRC biological and health sciences taxonomy (Appendix B), is not a DRF field. The 867 Ph.D.'s from these programs were probably spread across the NSF biological sciences taxonomy.
[b] Universities were asked to exclude programs in clinical and counseling psychology. The exclusion of these programs accounts for the low rate of coverage in the social and behavioral sciences. The coverage rate for all social science fields, excluding psychology, is 89 percent.

Excluded from the NRC study are Ph.D.'s in professional fields as well as small fields and programs. The professional fields are excluded for historical reasons. The study originally included programs in the liberal arts and sciences. The committee then expanded this coverage to include fields outside the arts and sciences and Ph.D. programs in schools of medicine that award a research Ph.D., but professional fields with a substantial practice component were still

---

[7] From this point on, to the term *doctoral programs* refers to the fields and programs included in the ranking study. This group does not include small doctoral programs that produced less than one Ph.D. per year during 2002–2006, nor does it include fields that were not ranked in the study. It also does not include the programs and universities that, for a variety of reasons, did not participate in the study. All told, the study covers the programs that produced about 90 percent of Ph.D.'s in the ranked fields during that period.

excluded from the study on the grounds that publications in scholarly journals are not an adequate metric of the quality of these programs.[8] Small fields and small programs in the humanities were excluded because they provide too few observations for reliable statistical analysis.

## Size and Control

For all fields, most doctoral programs, most enrolled doctoral students, and most Ph.D.'s are found in public universities. Programs in public universities are typically larger than those in private universities, and there are far more of them. Seventy-one percent of the programs ranked in the NRC study are in public universities. The proportion of programs in the universities with the largest programs is similar (70 percent). Among the 37 universities that produced 50 percent of Ph.D.'s from 2002 to 2006, 70 percent were public (see Table 7-7). Although public universities rely increasingly on nonpublic sources of funding, cutbacks in public funding for universities has a powerful effect on doctoral education simply because of how many large Ph.D. programs exist in public universities. These cutbacks will, of course, affect public higher education in general.

---

[8] A different view can be found in M. Goulden, et al.

TABLE 7-7 Institutions with 50 Percent of Ph.D.'s in Ranked Programs, by Control (Public or Private), 2002–2006 (average number of Ph.D.'s)

| Institution | Private | Public | Cumulative Total |
|---|---|---|---|
| University of California, Berkeley | | 623 | 623 |
| University of Texas at Austin | | 533 | 1,158 |
| University of Michigan–Ann Arbor | | 523 | 1,681 |
| University of California, Los Angeles | | 518 | 2,198 |
| University of Wisconsin–Madison | | 513 | 2,712 |
| Stanford University | 505 | | 3,217 |
| University of Minnesota–Twin Cities | | 455 | 3,672 |
| University of Illinois at Urbana-Champaign | | 455 | 4,128 |
| Massachusetts Institute of Technology | 448 | | 4,576 |
| Ohio State University Main Campus | | 439 | 5,015 |
| Harvard University | 436 | | 5,450 |
| Pennsylvania State University | | 431 | 5,882 |
| University of Washington | | 429 | 6,311 |
| University of Florida | | 412 | 6,723 |
| Purdue University Main Campus | | 389 | 7,112 |
| University of Maryland, College Park | | 378 | 7,490 |
| Cornell University | 373 | | 7,863 |
| Texas A&M University | | 347 | 8,210 |
| Columbia University in the City of New York | 344 | | 8,554 |
| University of California, Davis | | 341 | 8,895 |
| Michigan State University | | 325 | 9,220 |
| University of Pennsylvania | 312 | | 9,533 |
| Johns Hopkins University | 312 | | 9,845 |
| Georgia Institute of Technology | | 297 | 10,142 |
| University of North Carolina at Chapel Hill | | 294 | 10,435 |
| Yale University | 293 | | 10,729 |
| University of Chicago | 292 | | 11,021 |
| University of Southern California | 287 | | 11,308 |
| University of California, San Diego | | 266 | 11,573 |
| North Carolina State University | | 264 | 11,837 |
| Princeton University | 260 | | 12,097 |
| University of Arizona | | 259 | 12,356 |
| University of Colorado at Boulder | | 257 | 12,613 |
| City University of New York Graduate Center | | 255 | 12,868 |
| Rutgers, the State University of New Jersey, New Brunswick Campus | | 254 | 13,122 |
| University of Georgia | | 244 | 13,366 |
| Northwestern University | 244 | | 13,610 |
| | | | |
| Grand total of average number of Ph.D.'s—all universities | 8,236 | 19,382 | 27,618 |

*Importance of Program Size*

After release of the 1995 study, some readers, and the report itself, commented on how important program size was to the ranking of a program.[9] As mentioned in Chapters 5 and 6, the coefficient on size is especially large in most fields in the regression-based ranking (R ranking), and generally far less prominent in the survey-based ranking (S ranking). One example of an analytic use of the data is an investigation of the characteristics of programs as they relate to size as measured by number of Ph.D.'s. The committee divided programs in each field into size quartiles,[10] grouped the fields into broad ones, and investigated whether the quartile with the largest programs also ranked high on the 20 characteristics. It found that this quartile has the highest levels of publications per faculty member. Citations also follow this pattern, although the dominance of the largest quartile programs is not significant for engineering. In line with the findings for the other research variables, the largest programs also have a significantly higher average number of awards per faculty member. The greater research productivity in the largest quartile occurs even though our measures of research activity are on a per capita basis. These values are shown in Table 7-8.

TABLE 7-8 Research Measures and Program Size

| Row Labels | Number of Programs | Average of Average Number of Publications (2000-2006) per Allocated Faculty, 2006 | Average of Average Citations per Publication | Average of Percent of Faculty with Grants, | Average of Awards per Allocated Faculty Member, 2006 | Average of Tenured Faculty as a Percent of Total Faculty, 2006 |
|---|---|---|---|---|---|---|
| **Agricultural Sciences** | **312** | **1.32** | **1.66** | **81.8%** | **0.35** | **71.3%** |
| Largest Quartile by Program Size | 33 | 1.61[a] | 2.10[a] | 85.0%[a] | 0.50[a] | 68.7% |
| **Biological and Health Sciences** | **1168** | **1.54** | **3.48** | **82.3%** | **1.10** | **66.0%** |
| Largest Quartile by Program Size | 101 | 1.95[a] | 4.46[a] | 87.8%[a] | 2.43[a] | 64.3% |
| **Engineering** | **759** | **1.62** | **1.45** | **80.9%** | **0.61** | **72.2%** |
| Largest Quartile by Program Size | 39 | 2.42[a] | 1.54[a] | 86.4%[a] | 1.21[a] | 76.0%[a] |
| **Physical and Mathematical Sciences** | **911** | **2.05** | **2.05** | **75.2%** | **1.04** | **72.8%** |
| Largest Quartile by Program Size | 54 | 3.98[a] | 3.00[a] | 86.6%[a] | 4.54[a] | 73.8% |
| **Social and Behavioral Sciences** | **924** | **0.52** | **1.40** | **44.3%** | **0.62** | **72.9%** |
| Largest Quartile by Program Size | 83 | 0.81[a] | 2.10[a] | 54.7%[a] | 1.20[a] | 71.7% |
| **Humanities** | **764** | **11.62** | **n.a** | **14.5%** | **2.00** | **76.2%** |
| Largest Quartile by Program Size | 55 | 12.86[a] | n.a | 16.0%[a] | 3.42[a] | 77.8%[a] |

Note: "n.a." indicates not available

[a] The fourth quartile is different from the average at the p= 0.05 level.

[b] Publications in the humanities are measured by books and articles with books given a weight of 5 and articles a weight of 1. Humanities publications are not comparable to publications in other fields, which are measured by articles.

---

[9] This discussion appears on pages 22–23 of the 1995 NRC study.

[10] The programs were arrayed from highest to lowest by the number of Ph.D.s produced. The "Largest quartile" was defined as those programs that produced 25 percent of Ph.D.s at the top of this array. The number of programs in the Largest quartile is smaller than the number of programs divided by four because some of the programs in this Largest quartile are quite large.

*Student Variables and Program Size*

Findings for the student variables are shown in Table 7-9. Measures of interest to students include the annual average number of Ph.D.'s, GRE scores, completion rates, time to degree, employment destination upon graduation, and whether the program keeps track of its graduates after graduation. In the larger science and engineering programs students have higher GRE quantitative scores. The average humanities programs have lower GRE verbal scores and completion percentage within eight years than the programs in the largest quartile. Placement of Ph.D.'s in academic positions does not differ significantly by size quartile of programs, except in engineering where the placement in the largest quartile is lower.[11] This percentage is highest for the biological and health sciences, and this is expected, since postdoctoral appointments are counted in this measure. The next highest percentage is in the humanities. Time to degree is significantly longer in the larger programs, except for the social and behavioral sciences, although completion rates do not seem to vary significantly with size. Finally, the largest physical science, biological and health sciences and engineering fields have a higher percentage of programs that collect placement data for their students.

Among broad fields overall, GRE-Quantitative Reasoning scores are higher, as expected, in engineering and the physical and mathematical sciences than in other fields. The percentage of students with first-year support is greater than 80 percent in all fields and is over 90 percent in the physical and mathematical sciences.

The data on completion rates and average time to degree raise important questions about the proportion of students entering doctoral programs who actually complete a degree. The completion rate in six years ranges from nearly 60 percent (agricultural sciences) to 37 percent (social and behavioral sciences and yet the median time to degree, only for those who complete their degrees, has a narrower range (4.8–6.2 years). In the humanities, where 43 percent of enrolled students complete their degree in eight years and the median time to degree is 7.1 years, it can be inferred that a very high proportion of humanities students who enter doctoral programs never complete a Ph.D. degree. The factors that influence attrition rates and student success in research doctorate programs are certainly worthy of ongoing attention.

---

[11] Academic placement includes postdoctoral study in academic institutions.

TABLE 7-9 Student Characteristics by Broad Field Average and for the Largest Quartile

| Row Labels | Number of Programs | Average of Average GRE Scores, | Average of Percent of First Year Students with Full Financial Support, | Average of Avg. Completion Percentage: | Average of Median Time to Degree (Full- and Part-Time Graduates), | Average of Percent with Academic Plans | Average of Collects Data About Post-Graduation Employment |
|---|---|---|---|---|---|---|---|
| **Agricultural Sciences** | **312** | **656** | **88.0%** | **58.0%** | **4.81** | **56.0%** | **47.0%** |
| Largest Quartile by Program Size | 33 | 680[b] | 83.0% | 58.0% | 5.12[b] | 54.0% | 41.0% |
| **Biological and Health Sciences** | **1168** | **686** | **91.0%** | **49.0%** | **5.50** | **69.0%** | **55.0%** |
| Largest Quartile by Program Size | 101 | 708[b] | 92.0% | 50.0% | 5.63[b] | 69.0% | 62.0%[b] |
| **Engineering** | **759** | **760** | **83.0%** | **51.0%** | **4.88** | **35.0%** | **25.0%** |
| Largest Quartile by Program Size | 39 | 789[b] | 77.0% | 55.0%[b] | 5.13[b] | 27.0% | 44.0%[b] |
| **Physical and Mathematical Sciences** | **911** | **745** | **92.0%** | **43.0%** | **5.47** | **56.0%** | **56.0%** |
| Largest Quartile by Program Size | 54 | 755[b] | 98.0%[b] | 49.0%[b] | 5.51 | 54.0% | 59.0% |
| **Social and Behavioral Sciences** | **924** | **662** | **81.0%** | **37.0%** | **6.16** | **57.0%** | **67.0%** |
| Largest Quartile by Program Size | 83 | 700[b] | 84.0%[b] | 45.0%[b] | 6.07 | 55.0% | 61.0% |
| **Humanities** | **764** | **610** | **83.0%** | **43.0%** | **7.11** | **59.0%** | **67.0%** |
| Largest Quartile by Program Size | 55 | 653[b] | 77.0% | 46.0%[b] | 7.38[b] | 59.0% | 66.0% |

[a] For the humanities, the time to completion is eight years and the GRE score is for GRE-V.
[b] Indicates that the largest quartile value differs from the average at the p = 0.05 level.

**Diversity**

Average measures of various kinds of diversity are shown in Table 7-10. It also shows the results of tests to determine whether the largest quartile is different from the average.

TABLE 7-10 Diversity Measures

| Row Labels | Number of Programs | Average of Non-Asian Minority Faculty as a Percent of Total Core and New Domestic Faculty, 2006 | Average of Non-Asian Minority Students as a Percent of Total Domestic Students, Fall 2005 | Average of Female Faculty as a Percent of Total Core and New Faculty, 2006 | Average of Female Students as a Percent of Total Students, | Average of International Students as a Percent of Total Students, |
|---|---|---|---|---|---|---|
| Agricultural Sciences | 312 | 4.3% | 9.1% | 9.3% | 47.8% | 42.2% |
| Largest Quartile by Program Size | 33 | 3.6% | 8.5% | 3.0% | 49.5% | 34.3% |
| Biological and Health Sciences | 1168 | 3.9% | 11.5% | 8.9% | 55.0% | 29.1% |
| Largest Quartile by Program Size | 101 | 3.9% | 12.7%[a] | 7.9% | 54.7% | 24.0% |
| Engineering | 759 | 5.2% | 12.6% | 0.5% | 23.9% | 61.0% |
| Largest Quartile by Program Size | 39 | 4.4% | 11.5% | 0.0% | 18.4% | 58.6% |
| Physical and Mathematical Sciences | 911 | 3.3% | 8.4% | 0.5% | 32.2% | 45.3% |
| Largest Quartile by Program Size | 54 | 2.7% | 7.4% | 0.0% | 30.3% | 35.8% |
| Social and Behavioral Sciences | 924 | 7.6% | 13.3% | 15.7% | 55.0% | 27.2% |
| Largest Quartile by Program Size | 83 | 7.2% | 13.5% | 10.8% | 58.3%[a] | 23.9% |
| Humanities | 764 | 10.8% | 13.0% | 23.3% | 53.1% | 17.5% |
| Largest Quartile by Program Size | 55 | 9.7% | 12.6% | 10.9% | 53.3% | 13.5% |

[a] The largest quartile value is different from the average at the $p = 0.05$ level.

Increasing gender and racial and ethnic diversity has been a goal of the graduate community for many years. Although substantial progress has been made, that goal is far from achieved. The percentage of underrepresented minorities by broad field for students and faculty is shown in Figure 7-2.

With the exception of the humanities, in no field is more than 10 percent of the faculty from underrepresented minorities, and the sciences are at or less than 5 percent. Because larger percentages of doctoral students are from underrepresented minorities, it is likely there will be larger pools of Ph.D.'s from which to draw from in the future. However, the underrepresented minority enrollments in the agricultural and physical and mathematical sciences and engineering are still less than 10 percent. The percentage of minority students and faculty in all broad fields is less than 15 percent. Nevertheless, in some individual fields, listed in Table 7-11, more than 10 percent of enrollments are from underrepresented minority groups.

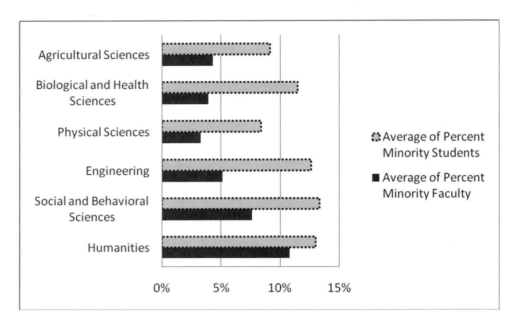

FIGURE 7-2 Percentage of Underrepresented Minority Faculty and Students by broad field, 2006.

| TABLE 7-11 Fields with More than 10 Percent of Enrolled Students from Underrepresented Minority (URM) Groups | | |
|---|---|---|
| Broad Field | Field | Percentage URM |
| Agricultural sciences | Food science | 13.2 |
| | Nutrition | 15.0 |
| Agricultural sciences total | | 9.1 |
| Biological and health sciences | Biochemistry, biophysics, and structural biology | 10.4 |
| | Cell and developmental biology | 11.0 |
| | Genetics and genomics | 10.3 |
| | Immunology and infectious disease | 13.3 |
| | Microbiology | 12.8 |
| | Neuroscience and neurobiology | 11.1 |
| | Nursing | 12.4 |
| | Pharmacology, toxicology, and environmental health | 13.9 |
| | Physiology | 14.3 |
| | Public health | 14.9 |
| Biological and health sciences total | | 11.5 |
| Physical and mathematical sciences | Applied mathematics | 11.5 |
| | Chemistry | 11.0 |
| Physical and mathematical sciences total | | 8.4 |
| Engineering | Biomedical engineering and bioengineering | 11.3 |
| | Chemical engineering | 11.0 |
| | Civil and environmental engineering | 12.3 |
| | Electrical and computer engineering | 12.6 |
| | Engineering science and materials (not elsewhere classified) | 20.7 |
| | Materials science and engineering | 12.1 |
| | Mechanical engineering | 14.6 |
| | Operations research, systems engineering, and industrial engineering | 17.0 |
| Engineering total | | 12.6 |
| Social and behavioral sciences | Anthropology | 14.7 |
| | Communication | 13.3 |
| | Linguistics | 10.6 |
| | Political science | 12.8 |
| | Psychology | 13.0 |
| | Public affairs, public policy, and public administration | 20.0 |
| | Sociology | 19.0 |
| Social and behavioral sciences total | | 13.3 |
| Humanities | American studies | 28.0 |
| | Comparative literature | 14.0 |
| | English language and literature | 10.0 |
| | History | 12.0 |
| | Religion | 10.0 |
| | Spanish and Portuguese language and literature | 46.0 |
| | Theater and performance studies | 13.0 |
| Humanities total | | 13.0 |

Some of these fields are training students who will work with underrepresented minority populations or specialize in studies related to the history and culture of underrepresented minorities, but all have focused on increasing minority participation and have, to some extent, succeeded.

The increased participation of women, as both faculty and students, is even more of a success story (see Figure 7-3).

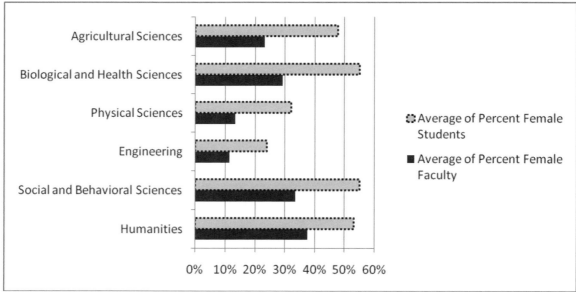

FIGURE 7-3 Percentage of Faculty and Students Female by broad field, 2006.

Enrollments in a few broad fields (humanities, social and behavioral sciences, and biological and health sciences) are more than 50 percent female, but the representation of women in the faculty has yet to reach even 40 percent. In none of the broad fields in science or engineering is more than 30 percent of the faculty female. The disciplines in the science, technology, engineering, and mathematics (STEM) fields in which more than 15 percent of the doctoral faculty is female are shown in Table 7-12.

TABLE 7-12 Science and Engineering Fields with More than 15 Percent of Doctoral Faculty Female

| Broad Field | Field | Total % |
|---|---|---|
| Agricultural sciences | Entomology | 15.4 |
| | Food science | 27.1 |
| | Nutrition | 50.6 |
| | Plant sciences | 20.4 |
| Agricultural sciences total | | 23.2 |
| Biological and health sciences | All fields | |
| Biological and health sciences Total | | 29.2 |
| Engineering | Biomedical engineering and bioengineering | 15.2 |
| | Operations research, systems engineering, and industrial engineering | 15.8 |
| Engineering total | | 11.4 |
| Physical and mathematical sciences | Earth sciences | 15.8 |
| | Oceanography, atmospheric sciences, and meteorology | 16.1 |
| | Statistics and probability | 19.1 |
| Physical and mathematical sciences total | | 13.3 |
| Social and behavioral sciences | All programs | |
| Social and behavioral sciences total | | 33.5 |
| Humanities | All programs | |
| Humanities total | | 37.7 |

One other aspect of diversity is the percentage of students who are from outside the United States. The variation in percentages of enrolled international students across the broad fields is considerable: engineering as a whole, 60 percent; the humanities, slightly more than 15 percent; the physical and mathematical sciences, 45 percent; the biological and health sciences and the social and behavioral sciences, less than 30 percent. Within the broad fields, some disciplines differ noticeably from the average. In economics, for example, 63 percent of its students are international.

## FINDINGS

The spreadsheet online at *http://www.nap.edu/rdp* contain a vast amount of data that could be characterized, mined, and modeled. With the previous discussion, the committee offers only a glimpse into the descriptive richness possible from analyzing the data available for many of the programs in 59 fields[12].

To illustrate one possible analysis, it looked at the characteristics associated with program size. Program size is positively associated with most measures of the research productivity of doctoral programs, even when productivity is measured on a per capita basis.[13] As for student characteristics, the larger programs are also more likely to have higher average GRE scores, except in the humanities. There is a size difference for median time to degree; students in the larger programs take about half a year longer to complete their degrees. In the physical and social sciences a significantly greater percentage of large programs collect outcomes data for their students. Interestingly, size, analyzed within broad fields, does not appear to be associated systematically with the percentage of students with support in their first year, which is high across the board, or completion rates, or the percentage of students who plan on a position in academia (including postdoctoral study) after graduation. Readers should note that the committee has been careful to discuss association, not causation.

The committee also looked at racial and ethnic and gender diversity. It found that much less diversity is found in the physical and mathematical sciences than in other broad fields. Although some fields have succeeded in becoming more diverse, most programs still have percentages of underrepresented minority students that are far under 10 percent. That said, although the percentages remain very low, they are in all cases significantly higher than were indicated by the NSF data from 1993 and discussed in the previous section. Thus doctoral programs have achieved far greater diversity with gender.

This completes the discussion of examples of simple analyses that can be conducted using the program data. We now discuss a few findings from data obtained from the faculty questionnaire and the student questionnaire. Data from these questionnaires will be made available with the public use data set.

## CHARACTERISTICS OF THE FACULTY OF THE DOCTORAL PROGRAMS

This report has focused primarily on information from the doctoral program questionnaire, but two other questionnaires—those directed at faculty and at students—also provide interesting insights into doctoral education. Although in the faculty questionnaire there were variations in the response rates by field, the overall response rate was 88 percent, and so it is likely that generalizations to doctoral faculty can be made from the survey responses. This section focuses on three areas: (1) the age profile of the faculty, (2) the length of time at their current institution, and (2) their demographic composition. Age is important because younger faculty are typically very active in research, although this activity may not yet translate into large numbers of

---

[12] Actually, 62 fields, since data, but not ranges of rankings, are shown for computer engineering, engineering science and materials, and languages societies and cultures.

[13] Of course, one would expect larger programs to have greater total levels of research production.

publications or citations. Time at the current institution is a reflection of faculty turnover—the longer faculty stay in place, the less the turnover. The importance of demographic composition was discussed earlier. Selected data on faculty are shown in Table 7-13.

TABLE 7-13 Faculty Data: Selected Measures, 2006

| Variable | Agricultural Sciences | Biological and Health Sciences | Engineering | Physical and Mathematical Sciences | Social and Behavioral Sciences | Humanities |
|---|---|---|---|---|---|---|
| Number of responses | 5,761 | 28,952 | 15,428 | 21,614 | 18,460 | 14,376 |
| Time at current institution (% of total faculty) | | | | | | |
| < 8 years | 22 | 25 | 24 | 23 | 26 | 24 |
| 8–20 years | 40 | 44 | 39 | 37 | 38 | 39 |
| > 20 years | 38 | 28 | 33 | 37 | 33 | 33 |
| Nonresponse | 0 | 3 | 4 | 3 | 3 | 4 |
| Employment before current employment (%) | | | | | | |
| Student | 18 | 5 | 21 | 13 | 27 | 26 |
| Postdoc | 30 | 42 | 21 | 36 | 13 | 6 |
| Faculty—associate or full professor | 12 | 16 | 15 | 15 | 21 | 22 |
| Faculty—assistant professor | 11 | 12 | 10 | 12 | 20 | 23 |
| Other | 20 | 15 | 24 | 18 | 13 | 15 |
| Nonresponse | 9 | 9 | 7 | 7 | 6 | 8 |
| Age in 2007 (%) | | | | | | |
| < 40 years old | 6 | 6 | 14 | 13 | 14 | 9 |
| 40–60 years old | 58 | 59 | 53 | 51 | 50 | 49 |
| > 60 years old | 20 | 19 | 19 | 24 | 24 | 27 |
| Nonresponse | 16 | 17 | 14 | 12 | 11 | 14 |
| Citizenship (%) | | | | | | |
| U.S. citizen or permanent resident | 84 | 83 | 83 | 84 | 87 | 85 |
| Temporary visa holder | 2 | 1 | 4 | 4 | 3 | 2 |
| Nonresponse | 14 | 15 | 13 | 11 | 10 | 12 |
| Race and Ethnicity (%) | | | | | | |
| White | 76 | 72 | 63 | 72 | 78 | 77 |
| Asian | 8 | 10 | 21 | 14 | 6 | 4 |
| Underrepresented Minority | 5 | 4 | 5 | 4 | 8 | 10 |
| Nonresponse | 11 | 13 | 11 | 10 | 8 | 9 |
| Gender (%) | | | | | | |
| Male | 66 | 59 | 77 | 76 | 59 | 53 |
| Female | 19 | 25 | 10 | 12 | 30 | 34 |
| Nonresponse | 16 | 16 | 13 | 12 | 11 | 13 |

The agricultural and the biological and health sciences appear to have fewer doctoral faculty under the age of 40 than the other broad fields. This is a result of different hiring patterns in the broad fields, as evidenced by the answers to the question about previous employment. About one-third of respondents in the agricultural, physical, and biological and health sciences have one or more postdocs before becoming doctoral faculty. By contrast, in the humanities, engineering, and social and behavioral sciences more than 20 percent of the faculty came to a faculty position directly from receiving their Ph.D. Engineering, which draws many of its faculty from industry brings in almost a quarter of its faculty from "other," which includes nonacademic employment. Movement from within academia is about 25 percent in the sciences and engineering. The pattern is different for the humanities and social sciences, where more than 40 percent of respondents were employed in academia before moving to their current employer. The humanities distinguish themselves by the age of their doctoral faculty. More than 27 percent are over the age of 60, in contrast with 20 percent or less in the agricultural sciences, engineering, and the biological and health sciences. As for mobility, doctoral faculty tend to stay at one institution. About three-quarters of them, in all fields, have been at their current institution for 8 years or more, and more than one-third have been in one place for more than 20 years. The one exception is the biological and health sciences.

The composition of the faculty by racial and ethnic diversity and gender was discussed earlier in this chapter, and is confirmed here. Only the humanities draw more than 10 percent of its faculty from underrepresented minorities. As for gender, in the social sciences, humanities, and biological and health sciences, one-quarter or more of the doctoral faculty is female.

## DATA FROM STUDENT QUESTIONNAIRES

The 4,838 ranked programs in the study include 236,417 students. Despite the high cost of sending questionnaires to all these students, the committee believed that the voices of the students should be heard. It surveyed students in disciplines in five of the broad fields: engineering, the physical and mathematical sciences, the biological and health sciences, the social sciences, and the humanities. The specific fields chosen were chemical engineering, physics, neuroscience, economics, and English. Each of the programs in these fields was asked for the names and e-mail addresses of their students who had been advanced to candidacy but had not yet completed their degrees. This group was chosen because the committee believed these students would have experienced many of the program practices and would have formed views of their doctoral programs. Confidentiality concerns prevent the committee from reporting results by program for the smaller programs. However, more than 90 percent of the responding students were in programs in which more than 10 students responded and thus could be reported on a program-by-program basis. In all, the responses that were reportable at the program level represented about 64 percent of all the programs in the five fields, and for the participating programs the student response rates were high. The response rates and other details of the student survey are reported in Table 7-14.

| TABLE 7-14 Response Rates: Student Survey, Five Fields, 2006 | Chemical Engineering | Physics | Neuroscience | Economics | English | Overall |
|---|---|---|---|---|---|---|
| Total students surveyed | 2,411 | 5,250 | 1,997 | 2,903 | 3,878 | 16,439 |
| Total students responding | 1,820 | 3,596 | 1,562 | 2,067 | 2,544 | 11,589 |
| Overall response rate (%) | 75.5 | 68.5 | 78.2 | 71.2 | 65.6 | 70 |
| Number of students in programs with more than 10 responses | 1,538 | 3,322 | 1,373 | 1,829 | 2,354 | 10,416 |
| Total programs | 108 | 153 | 94 | 116 | 122 | 593 |
| Programs with more than 10 responses | 55 | 106 | 61 | 69 | 89 | 380 |
| Percentage of responding students in programs with more than 10 responses | 84.5 | 92.3 | 87.9 | 88.4 | 92.5 | 90 |
| Percentage of programs with more than 10 responses | 50.9 | 69.2 | 64.8 | 59.4 | 72.9 | 64 |

## Student Satisfaction

Table 7-15, which summarizes the results for each of the surveyed fields, reveals that most students are satisfied with their program. In all fields the percentages of programs whose students are not satisfied are less than 10 percent. On the whole, students value the intellectual environment provided by their programs. The main characteristic that receives a low rating from students is "quality of (program-sponsored) social interaction." In the sciences and engineering, students report being highly satisfied with the quality of the research facilities available to them. Computing facilities are satisfactory in all fields, but students in programs in English and economics appear more critical of the research facilities and work space available to them. Investigators should look into the programs in these two fields in which students failed to say that research facilities were excellent or good. In fact, for the programs with more than 10 respondents, the questionnaire results may point to a follow-up agenda. The relatively low ratings in English and economics may indicate inadequate library facilities or inadequate support of other scholarly infrastructure. However, the survey did not collect data at this level of detail.

| TABLE 7-15 Student Satisfaction: Programs with More Than 10 Students Responding, 2006 | | | | | | | |
|---|---|---|---|---|---|---|---|
| | Overall Quality | | | Intellectual Environment | Social Interaction | Computer Resources | Research Facilities | Work Space |
| Field | Very Satisfied | Somewhat Satisfied | Not Satisfied | Benefiting a lot from program's intellectual environment | Very satisfied with the [program-sponsored] social interaction in the program | Rating computer resources as excellent or good | Rating research facilities as excellent or good | Rating work space as excellent or good |
| | % | | | % | % | % | % | % |
| Chemical engineering | 51 | 44 | 5 | 63 | 38 | 89 | 80 | 82 |
| Economics | 44 | 47 | 9 | 58 | 25 | 76 | 41 | 57 |
| English | 50 | 39 | 7 | 63 | 28 | 74 | 38 | 39 |
| Neuroscience | 54 | 41 | 5 | 67 | 37 | 89 | 91 | 86 |
| Physics | 46 | 47 | 7 | 60 | 26 | 85 | 70 | 76 |

## Student Productivity

Generally, the programs in all fields seem to be performing well in encouraging students to become productive scholars. As shown in Table 7-16, well more than half the students in all fields have presented papers at conferences on campus, and a similarly high proportion has presented papers at national or regional meetings, even if only a smaller proportion found funds for their travel. A high proportion of students in the science and engineering programs also report that they have published articles in refereed journals, but less so in economics and English. In all fields the percentage of students who have published either articles or book chapters has risen since they enrolled in doctoral study.

It is clear from Table 7-16 that students produce papers in refereed journals while studying in their doctoral programs. The data for individual programs (not shown) reveal that in more than 90 percent of the individual programs in all five fields at least one student had published in a refereed journal.

| TABLE 7-16 Student Productivity: Programs with More Than 10 Student Responses | | | | | | | | |
|---|---|---|---|---|---|---|---|---|
| | Making Research Presentations on Campus | Making Research Presentations at Meetings (Regional, National, or International) | Securing Travel Funds to Present Research at Meetings | Publications Before Graduate Study | | Publications During Graduate Study | | Number of Programs | Average Program Response Rate |
| | | | | Refereed Articles | Book Chapters | Refereed Articles | Book Chapters | | |
| | % | | | % | | % | | % | |
| Chemical engineering | 78 | 85 | 73 | 39 | 1 | 72 | 9 | 56 | 81.5 |
| Economics | 67 | 51 | 43 | 13 | 4 | 23 | 7 | 70 | 76.1 |
| English | 63 | 83 | 69 | 10 | 3 | 34 | 17 | 89 | 71.0 |
| Neuroscience | 88 | 86 | 74 | 48 | 2 | 69 | 10 | 63 | 83.7 |
| Physics | 61 | 76 | 69 | 37 | 1 | 69 | 4 | 106 | 72.2 |

## Advising and Academic Support

Assessment of student academic progress appears to be the norm in neuroscience. In all but nine programs surveyed, more than 75 percent of the students responding indicated that their programs provided an assessment of students' academic progress. Although not all fields reported this level of assessment, a high proportion of students in all fields indicated that they valued the assessments they did receive. A high proportion of students in virtually all programs also indicated that they received timely and helpful feedback on their dissertations.

Doctoral education is characterized by the apprenticeship of students to mentors and advisers. For this reason a students' evaluations of their relationship with the faculty is both interesting and important. Across the five fields surveyed, about 50 percent of the students in all fields reported that they had highly interactive and supportive mentors and advisers. This uniformity is striking considering that students in the sciences and engineering might be expected to have more sustained interaction with faculty in laboratory settings. Interaction with other faculty members appears very limited. This finding was also consistent across the fields surveyed (see Table 7-17 for the results).

TABLE 7-17 Students: Advising and Academic Support (percent)

| Field | Mentor in Program | Program Provides Assessment of Academic Progress | Assessment of Academic Progress Is Helpful | Timely Feedback on Dissertation Research | Dissertation Feedback is Helpful | Highly Supportive Adviser | Highly Supportive Other Faculty |
|---|---|---|---|---|---|---|---|
| Chemical engineering | 80 | 50 | 90 | 90 | 90 | 50 | 20 |
| Economics | 80 | 60 | 80 | 90 | 90 | 50 | 20 |
| English | 90 | 50 | 80 | 80 | 80 | 50 | 20 |
| Neuroscience | 92 | 87 | 90 | 87 | 86 | 51 | 24 |
| Physics | 83 | 52 | 81 | 81 | 79 | 50 | 19 |

Doctoral students enter programs with career goals in mind, but in most fields that were queried these goals undergo modification during the course of graduate study. Doctoral students learn what kind of scholarly work they enjoy, and they also learn how good they are at it. With the exception of chemical engineering students, who were most likely to select careers in the private sector, most students anticipated a career in the education sector as they began doctoral study. But this interest tended to wane during graduate school, as students appeared to explore options in government or the private sector. Advisers and mentors are students' principal sources of career advice. Only students in chemical engineering reported making much use of university career centers. Students generally indicated that their advisers supported their career plans.

## Career Goals

Yet another measure is what students want to do when they graduate (Table 7-18).

| TABLE 7-18 Student Career Objectives at Program Entry and at Time of Response (percent) | | | | | |
|---|---|---|---|---|---|
| | At Program Entry | | | At Time of Response | | |
| | Research and Development | Teaching | Management and Administration | Research and Development | Teaching | Management and Administration |
| Chemical engineering | 76.5 | 11.6 | 6.2 | 74.9 | 8.0 | 9.1 |
| Economics | 68.1 | 20.4 | 3.4 | 64.6 | 16.6 | 5.4 |
| English | 34.2 | 58.2 | 1.0 | 34.3 | 52.0 | 3.9 |
| Neuroscience | 80.5 | 10.8 | 1.2 | 67.5 | 12.4 | 4.3 |
| Physics | 82.6 | 14.1 | 1.0 | 76.2 | 13.9 | 2.8 |

Note: Omitted choices are "professional services" and "other," and so the percentage across a row for a particular point in time does not add to 100 percent

Overall, only 38.2 percent of programs showed an increase in student interest in research and development. Eighteen percent of programs saw an increase in students wanting to go into teaching, and 47.1 percent of programs saw an increase in student interest in management and administration. These findings suggest that as students learn what is actually involved in research and teaching, they become more interested in other, untried undertakings.

To summarize, the student questionnaire reveals that students are generally pleased with their doctoral programs and that the programs are successful at improving student research productivity, but that by the time students are working at an advanced level at least some of them have shifted their career objectives away from research. This effect is not large, but it may explain in part the lower completion rates observed by the committee. Although it is likely that the decline in interest in research careers is the result of students learning more about what such a career entails, programs may wish to look at their individual results to determine the steps that might be taken to address this falloff in student interest in research.

## SUMMARY

This chapter has provided a glimpse into the large amount of data about doctoral programs available in the study's online database. By matching programs, the committee was able to compare the 2006 and the 1993 data and see that the number of enrollments and the number of Ph.D.'s produced by the common doctoral programs have grown in most fields, with the exception of the humanities. Using NSF data, it also saw that the gender and racial and ethnic diversity of these programs has increased as well since the last study.

The committee used the most current data to conduct an illustrative analysis in which it looked at program characteristics and size of program as measured by Ph.D. production. Although some smaller programs certainly have high research activity, generally the larger programs are associated with higher values for characteristics related to research. This association does not carry over to student support and outcome variables. The most consistent finding is that the larger programs have somewhat longer times to the completion of a degree. Size is not consistently related to differences in diversity.

The great deal of data to be made available from the faculty and student questionnaires can be used to explore relationships among program characteristics and the characteristics of faculty and of students in the five fields studied.

# 8

# Looking Ahead

The charge to the committee for this study was the following:

> An assessment of the quality and characteristics of research-doctorate programs in the United States will be conducted. The study will consist of (1) the collection of quantitative data through questionnaires administered to institutions, programs, faculty, and admitted to candidacy students (in selected fields), (2) collection of program data on publications, citations, and dissertation keywords, and (3) the design and construction of program ratings using the collected data including quantitatively based estimates of program quality. These data will be released through a Web-based, periodically updatable database and accompanied by an analytic summary report. Following this release, further analyses will be conducted by the committee and other researchers and discussed at a workshop focusing on doctoral education in the United States. The methodology for the study will be a refinement of that described by the Committee to Examine the Methodology for the Assessment of Research-Doctorate Programs, which recommended that a new assessment be conducted.

This study has completed the tasks specified in the charge, but they proved far more difficult and, as a result, took much more time than the committee initially anticipated. In this concluding chapter the committee looks at a few lessons learned from the conduct of the study and at other areas it has not fully explored and encourages researchers to use the study data to go farther.

## LESSONS LEARNED

While conducting this study, and creating an unparalleled database on doctoral programs in 2005-2006, the committee learned many lessons about the data-based approach to describing doctoral education in the United States. These lessons are in the areas of taxonomy and multidisciplinarity, measurement, and the data-based construction of measures of perceived quality. In addition, the committee has areas that would be of great interest—such as the dimensional measures and the relation between postdoctoral scholars and doctoral study— that it did not have the time to investigate and on which it recommends further work.

### Taxonomy and Multidisciplinarity

Although most doctoral work is still organized in disciplines, scholarly work in doctoral programs increasingly crosses disciplinary boundaries in both content and methods. The committee tried to identify measures of multi- and interdisciplinarity, but it believes it did not address the issue in the depth deserved, nor did the committee discover the kind of relation, if any, between multidisciplinarity and the perceived quality of doctoral programs. It therefore recommends that greater attention be paid to the relationship between multidisciplinarity and program quality the next time this study is undertaken.

## Measurement

The validation of program data was a time-consuming process. The committee hopes that, based on the collection of data for this study, programs will better understand and have an easier time providing data for a future study. In particular, there should be greater clarity about what is meant by core faculty for a doctoral program and associated faculty. This distinction was made to prevent overcounting the productivity of faculty who are involved with multiple programs. In any case, techniques to check data are now in place and it is essential that they be further developed before the next survey is initiated and that instructions to the data providers be clear. Such steps could shorten the data validation process substantially.

## Data-Based Construction of Measures of Perceived Quality

*Ranking Programs*

Initially the committee was deeply divided on whether an effort to rank programs should be undertaken at all. However, there was universal agreement within the committee that efforts that relied entirely on reputation or on single measures of scholarly productivity could be misleading to potential applicants and others. The quality of reputational measures depends critically on who is asked and how knowledgeable they are about scholarship in a discipline. Thus the committee focused on doctoral program faculty, who are presumably engaged both in scholarship and in hiring decisions that involve judgments of the scholarly quality of programs other than their own. The committee surveyed these faculty members about the factors they thought were important, ideally, to the quality of a doctoral program. A sample of them was then asked to rate actual programs, as described in Chapter 4. This "anchoring" rating study was a compromise. The committee sampled programs to ensure that a broad range of programs was included in the rating sample, but raters were more informed about program characteristics than in the 1995 study. The committee did not compare rating results from the two studies because the methodological differences were too great and the committee could not justify using the 1995 study as a benchmark.

The committee also wanted to convey the degree of uncertainty in rankings. Very early in the study process the committee agreed that presentation of ranges of rankings would best convey the uncertainty inherent in any ranking study. It felt that a technique that combined the regression results with the survey results would give a more accurate estimate of program quality. The anchoring study, however, was based on relatively small samples of programs, and the committee found that the estimates of the ranges of rankings based on regression (R rankings) and general survey (S rankings) were not well correlated for some programs in some fields. This finding applied especially to fields with relatively few programs or to programs within a taxonomy that encompassed a diversity of scholarly practices. In any attempt to determine the values of faculty members as they relate to program ratings (R rankings), it is extremely important that the questions be tested for clarity and that the sample sizes be large enough to minimize statistical error. Thus, although the methodology for combining the coefficients, which lessens the weight on the coefficients with a larger standard error, could lead to better estimates of program quality in most cases, the committee agreed it would be better to show the regression-based and general survey-based results separately as additional information is conveyed. Further work that focuses on differences in the R's and S's and the circumstances under which coefficients could be validly combined would be helpful.

## TWO AREAS FOR FURTHER STUDY

### Dimensional Measures

As described in Chapters 3 and 4, the committee's reliance on faculty views of program quality and its determinants resulted in some variables that the committee strongly believed were important to doctoral program quality showing up with very low weights in the overall rankings. Perhaps scholarly activity is clearly of paramount importance to most faculty members and thus to the quality of doctoral programs that produce future faculty members. And yet additional aspects of the doctoral experience and environment may prove important to students, many of whom will not take academic positions, and to the faculty who prepare them. The committee took this factor into account in its data-based ranking methodology by constructing dimensional measures that maintained the relative weighting of the included characteristics, but only included the characteristics relevant to a particular dimension of doctoral education. A look at these measures reveals that many of the programs that rank high on the research dimension may not rank as well on the student support and outcomes dimension, or on the diversity dimension. Such an outcome might be expected because the committee was trying to capture separate aspects of doctoral education, but saw no reason why a program could not rank highly on all three dimensional measures. However, in general this failed to be the case. In the future a larger student survey and an effort to incorporate student values could enhance the study findings.

### The Connection Between Postdoctoral Study and Doctoral Education

The connection between postdoctoral study and doctoral education was not explored in any depth in this study, although the committee did collect data about the number of postdoctoral scholars associated with each program. Especially in the biosciences, postdocs are part of a continuum of research training. Whether the characteristics of doctoral programs with many postdocs differ greatly from those with few should be studied. The difference may be in the nature of research being undertaken, or it may be that the nature of the doctoral education experience differs, depending on the number of postdocs associated with a doctoral program.

## CONCLUSION

This study developed a methodology based on relating data about doctoral programs to the reputational ratings of particular programs and also to idealized preferences about program characteristics. For many fields it found that the separate approaches resulted in different characteristics appearing as important as determinants of rankings, depending on the measure. Program size was very important for the R, or regression-based, approach, and various measures of research activity were very important for the S, or survey, approach. If there is an overall lesson to be learned, it is that people who use rankings should be cautious before relying on them. The production of rankings from quantitative measures of program characteristics turned out to be more complicated and to be associated with greater uncertainty than originally thought. Any set of evaluations rests on the core values given to program characteristics. In many other efforts of this type, the investigators have not been explicit about the basis for the values adopted. Users of this and other studies need to understand what goes into them—assumptions, weights, surveys, and uncertainty. In this study, if users relied on ranges of rankings alone, they would find a few programs at the top and the bottom with a narrow range of rankings. Most programs have a wide range of rankings and fall somewhere in the middle. This finding struck the committee as corresponding well to the way the world really is. Users need to go beyond rankings and examine the characteristics that are important for their purposes and concerns.

# Appendixes

# Appendix A

# Committee Biographies

**JEREMIAH P. OSTRIKER**, Ph.D. (NAS), *Committee Chair*, is a professor of astrophysical sciences at Princeton University and Plumian Professor of Astronomy and Experimental Philosophy, Emeritus, at the University of Cambridge. He received his B.A. in physics and chemistry from Harvard University and his Ph.D. in astrophysics from the University of Chicago. After a postdoctoral fellowship at Cambridge University, Dr. Ostriker served on the faculty at Princeton University as a professor (1966–present); as department chair, and as university provost. During his tenure as provost, Princeton received a major grant from the Mellon Foundation to improve doctoral education in the humanities. He is a renowned astrophysicist and has received many awards and honors, including membership in the National Academy of Sciences (NAS) and the U.S. National Medal of Science in 2001. He has served on several National Research Council (NRC) and National Academies committees, including the NAS Council and the NRC Governing Board. Dr. Ostriker also served as the chair of the Panel on Quantitative Measures. Currently, he is treasurer of the National Academy of Sciences.

**VIRGINIA S. HINSHAW**, Ph.D., *Committee Vice Chair*, is the chancellor of the University of Hawaiʻi at Mānoa and professor of virology in the John A. Burns School of Medicine at UH Mānoa. Dr. Hinshaw earned her B.S. in laboratory technology and her M.S. and Ph.D. in microbiology from Auburn University. For over 25 years, her research focused on influenza viruses in humans, lower mammals, and birds, investigating such aspects as: important hosts in nature; transmission among species; genetic changes related to disease severity; the molecular basis of cell killing; and new approaches to vaccines. She conducted research at various hospitals and universities, including the Medical College of Virginia, UC Berkeley, St. Jude Children's Research Hospital, Harvard Medical School and University of Wisconsin-Madison. She has been recognized for her innovative and energetic teaching style and her continual advocacy for research and education, particularly related to increased participation by women and minorities. She has served on numerous national and international committees associated with the American Society of Virology, Committee on Institutional Cooperation, World Health Organization, Association of American Universities (AAU) and Association of Public and Land-grant Universities (APLU, formerly NASULGC) and she currently serves as Co-Chair for the Energy Advisory Committee for APLU and as a member of the American Council on Education (ACE) Commission for Effective Leadership. Prior to joining UH Mānoa, Dr. Hinshaw served as the provost and executive vice chancellor at the University of California Davis and as dean of the graduate school and vice chancellor for research at the University of Wisconsin–Madison.

**ELTON D. ABERLE**, Ph.D., is dean emeritus and professor emeritus of the College of Agricultural and Life Sciences at the University of Wisconsin–Madison. He received his B.S. from Kansas State University, his M.S. from Michigan State University, and his Ph.D. from Michigan State University in food sciences. Dr. Aberle has held administrative positions at the University of Nebraska–Lincoln's Institute of Agriculture and Natural Resources and a faculty position at Purdue University. His research and teaching background is in muscle biology and the animal and food sciences. Dr. Aberle has received teaching and research awards from the American Society of Animal Sciences and the American Meat Science Association, and he is a fellow of the American Association for the Advancement of Science and the American Society of Animal Science. He also served on the Panel of Taxonomy and Interdisciplinarity.

**NORMAN M. BRADBURN**, Ph.D., is Tiffany and Margaret Blake Distinguished Service Professor Emeritus at the University of Chicago and senior fellow at the National Opinion Research Center at the University of Chicago. He has served three terms as director of the center, from 1967 to 1992. From 2000 to 2004 he was assistant director for social, behavioral and economic sciences at the National Science Foundation (NSF). He also served as provost of the University of Chicago from 1984 to 1989. He received his Ph.D. degree in social psychology from Harvard University. He has been a member of the research and advisory panel of the U.S. General Accounting Office; a member and former chair of the Committee on National Statistics, NRC/NAS; and a member of the Panel to Review the Statistical Procedures for the Decennial Census. He also is an elected member of the International Statistical Institute and a fellow of the American Academy of Arts and Sciences and the American Statistical Association. His research has focused on psychological well-being and assessing the quality of life; nonsampling errors in sample surveys; and research on cognitive processes in responses to sample surveys. He is currently working on developing a humanities indicator system and a large scale study of the cultural infrastructure. His book, *Thinking About Answers: The Application of Cognitive Process to Survey Methodology* (co-authored with Seymour Sudman and Norbert Schwarz; Jossey-Bass, 1996), follows three other publications on the methodology of designing and constructing questionnaires: *Polls and Surveys: Understanding What They Tell Us* (with Seymour Sudman; Jossey-Bass, 1988); *Asking Questions: A Practical Guide to Questionnaire Construction* (with Seymour Sudman; Jossey-Bass, 1982; 2nd edition with Brian Wansink, 2004) and *Improving Interviewing Method and Questionnaire Design* (Jossey-Bass, 1979).

**JOHN I. BRAUMAN**, Ph.D. (NAS), is J. G. Jackson–C. J. Wood Professor of Chemistry, Emeritus, at Stanford University. Dr. Brauman received his S.B from MIT and his Ph.D. from the University of California, Berkeley. He was an NSF postdoctoral fellow at the University of California, Los Angeles, and then he took the position at Stanford University, where he served as department chair, associate dean for natural sciences, and associate dean of research (since 2005). He also currently serves as the home secretary of the National Academy of Sciences. Dr. Brauman has received a number of awards, including the American Chemical Society Award in Pure Chemistry, Harrison Howe Award, Guggenheim Fellowship, R. C. Fuson Award, Arthur C. Cope Scholar Award, James Flack Norris Award in Physical Organic Chemistry, the National Academy of Sciences Award in Chemical Sciences, Linus Pauling Medal, Willard Gibbs Medal, and National Medal of Science. He also received the Dean's Award for Distinguished Teaching from Stanford University. Dr. Brauman is a member of the National Academy of Sciences, American Academy of Arts and Sciences, and American Philosophical Society, and a fellow of the AAAS and an honorary fellow of the

California Academy of Sciences. He has served as well on many national committees and advisory boards. He was deputy editor for physical sciences for SCIENCE from 1985 to 2000 and is currently chair of the Senior Editorial Board. Dr. Brauman's research has centered on structure and reactivity.

**JONATHAN R. COLE**, Ph.D., is at Columbia University. He is currently the John Mitchell Mason Professor of the University, and was provost and dean of faculties at Columbia from 1989 to 2003. He received his B.A. and Ph.D. from Columbia. At Columbia he was the Adolphe Quetelet Professor of Social Science (1989–2001); professor of sociology (1976–present; vice president of arts and sciences, 1987–1989); and director, Center for the Social Sciences (1979–1987). His awards and memberships include the following: fellow, Center for Advanced Study in the Behavioral Sciences, Stanford, California, 1975–1976; John Simon Guggenheim Foundation Fellowship recipient, 1975–1976; elected fellow, American Academy of Arts and Sciences, 1992; "National Associate," U.S. National Academies of Sciences, 2003; elected member, Council on Foreign Relations, 2003; elected member, American Philosophical Society, 2005; Cavaliere Ufficiale in the Order of Merit of the Republic of Italy, 1996; and Commendatore in the Order of Merit of the Republic of Italy, 2003. Some publications in the sociology of science, science policy, and higher education, include: *Social Stratification in Science* (with Stephen Cole) (1973); *Peer Review in the National Science Foundation: Phase One* (1978) and *Phase Two* (1981) *of a Study* (co-authored); *Fair Science: Women in the Scientific Community* (1979); *The Wages of Writing: Per Word, Per Piece, or Perhaps* (1986) (co-authored); *The Outer Circle: Women in the Scientific Community* (1991) (co-edited and author); *The Research University in a Time of Discontent* (co-edited and author)(1994); multiple journal publications on similar topics. His book, *The Great American University: Its Rise to Preeminence, Its Threatened Future*, published by Public Affairs in the fall of 2009.*Resigned June 2010.*

**PAUL W. HOLLAND**, Ph.D., holds the Frederic M. Lord Chair in Measurement and Statistics (retired) in the Research & Development Division at the Educational Testing Service (ETS) in Princeton, New Jersey. He received a B.A. in mathematics from the University of Michigan and a M.A. and Ph.D. in statistics from Stanford University. His association with ETS began in 1975. In 1979 he became director of the Research Statistics Group. In 1986 Dr. Holland was appointed ETS's first distinguished research scientist. He left ETS in 1993 to join the faculty at University of California, Berkeley, as a professor in the Graduate School of Education and the Department of Statistics, but returned in 2000 to his current position at ETS. He has made significant contributions to the following applications of statistics to social science research, categorical data analysis, social networks, test equating, differential item functioning, test security issues, causal inference in nonexperimental research, and the foundations of item response theory. His current research interests include kernel equating methods, population invariance of test linking, software for item response theory, and causal inference in program evaluation and policy research.

**ERIC W. KALER**, Ph.D. (NAE), became the provost and senior vice president for academic affairs at Stony Brook University in 2007. Prior to that, he was the Elizabeth

Inez Kelley Professor in the Department of Chemical Engineering and the dean of the College of Engineering at the University of Delaware. He holds a B.S. from the California Institute of Technology and a Ph.D. from the University of Minnesota, both in chemical engineering. He has served on several NRC panels, including the subpanel for the National Institute of Standards and Technology's Center for Neutron Research, which he chaired, and the Panel for Materials Science and Engineering. He was one of the first scientists to receive a Presidential Young Investigator Award from the National Science Foundation in 1984. In 2001 he was named an AAAS fellow. Among other awards are the Curtis W. McGraw Research Award from the American Society of Engineering Education in 1995 and the 1998 American Chemical Society Award in Colloid or Surface Chemistry. Dr. Kaler was elected to the National Academy of Engineering in 2010 and is co-editor-in-chief of *Current Opinion in Colloid & Interface Science*. He is known for his distinguished study of the science and application of complex fluids.

**EARL LEWIS**, Ph.D., is provost and executive vice president for academic affairs and the Asa Griggs Candler Professor of History and African American Studies at Emory University. Before joining the Emory faculty in July 2004, Dr. Lewis served as dean of the Horace H. Rackham School of Graduate Studies and vice provost for academic affairs/graduate studies at the University of Michigan. At Michigan, he was the Elsa Barkley Brown and Robin D. G. Kelley Collegiate Professor of History and African American and African Studies and served as director of the Center for Afro-American and African Studies. From 1984 to 1989 he was on the faculty of the Department of African American Studies at the University of California, Berkeley. Dr. Lewis, who holds degrees in history and psychology, is author and co-editor of seven books, among them *In Their Own Interests: Race, Class and Power in 20th Century Norfolk* (University of California Press, 1993) and the award-*winning To Make Our World Anew: A History of African Americans* (Oxford University Press, 2000). Between 1997 and 2000 he co-edited the eleven-volume *The Young Oxford History of African Americans*. Lewis co-authored the widely acclaimed *Love on Trial: An American Scandal in Black and White*, published in 2001 by WW Norton. His most recent books are *The African American Urban Experience: Perspectives from the Colonial Period to the Present*, co-edited and published with Palgrave (2004), and the co-written *Defending Diversity: Affirmative Action at the University of Michigan*, published by the University of Michigan Press (2004). He is co-editor of the award-winning book series *American Crossroads* (University of California Press). Dr. Lewis is a current or past member of a number of editorial boards and boards of directors. In 2001 he received the University of Minnesota's Outstanding Achievement Award, which is given to a distinguished graduate. Concordia College, whose board of regents he joined in 2008, awarded him an honorary degree in 2002. He was named a fellow of the American Academy of Arts and Sciences in 2008.

**JOAN F. LORDEN**, Ph.D., is provost and vice chancellor for academic affairs at the University of North Carolina at Charlotte. She received a B.A. from the City College of New York and a Ph.D. from Yale University. For over eight years Dr. Lorden served as dean of the graduate school and associate provost for research at the University of Alabama at Birmingham (UAB). From 2002 to 2003, she was the dean-in-residence of the Council of Graduate Schools (CGS) at the Division of Graduate Education at the National Science Foundation, and she chaired the CGS board. She also has chaired the board of Oak Ridge Associated Universities and was president of the Conference of Southern Graduate Schools. Dr. Lorden has been a member of the Executive Committee of the Council on Academic Affairs, and she chaired the Executive Committee of the Council on Research Policy and Graduate Education of the National Association of State Universities and Land Grant Colleges (NASULGC, now the Association of Public and Land-Grant Universities). She was awarded the Ireland Prize for Scholarly Distinction by UAB. She has served on review panels and study sections at NSF, the National Institutes of Health, the Department of Defense, and private agencies. At UAB she organized the doctoral program in behavioral neuroscience and was a founding member and director of the university-wide interdisciplinary Graduate Training Program in Neuroscience. As graduate dean, Dr. Lorden fostered programs that would increase the breadth of training among graduate students, served as the program director for an interdisciplinary biological sciences training grant, and established one of the first offices for postdoctoral support. She is actively involved in programs designed to improve the success of women and minorities in graduate education and faculty careers in science and engineering, and has received several grants to advance these goals. Dr. Lorden's research focuses on brain-behavior relationships.

**CAROL B. LYNCH**, Ph.D., is a senior scholar at the Council of Graduate Schools, where she directs the professional master's initiatives. She is also dean emerita at the University of Colorado at Boulder where she was dean of the graduate school and vice chancellor for research from 1992 to 2004. She was professor of ecological and evolutionary biology, and is a fellow of the Institute for Behavioral Genetics. She received her B.A. from Mount Holyoke College, her M.A. from the University of Michigan, and her Ph.D. from the University of Iowa. She held a National Science Foundation Postdoctoral Fellowship in the Institute for Behavioral Genetics at the University of Colorado. Much of her professional career was spent at Wesleyan University in Middletown, Connecticut, where she served as a professor of biology and dean of the sciences. She has received a Research Career Development Award from the National Institutes of Health, is a fellow of the AAAS, and was president of the Behavior Genetics Association. Prior to coming to the University of Colorado, Dr. Lynch was the program director in population biology and physiological ecology at the NSF. She was president of the Western Association of Graduate Schools and has served on the board of directors of the Council of Graduate Schools and on the executive committee of the Council on Research Policy and Graduate Education at NASULGC (now APLU). She is currently a member of the Graduate Record Examination Board and was the chair of the TOEFL Board (Educational Testing Service, ETS). Dr. Lynch has authored numerous publications in evolutionary and behavioral genetics.

**ROBERT M. NEREM,** Ph. D., joined Georgia Tech in 1987 as the Parker H. Petit Distinguished Chair for Engineering in Medicine. He is an Institute Professor and Parker H. Petit Distinguished Chair Emeritus. He currently serves as the Director of the Georgia Tech/Emory Center (GTEC) for Regenerative Medicine, a center established with an NSF- Engineering Research award. He also is a part-time Distinguished Visiting Professor at Chonbuk National University in Korea. He received his Ph.D. in 1964 from

Ohio State University and is the author of more than 200 publications. He is a Fellow and was the founding President of the American Institute of Medical and Biological Engineering (1992-1994), and he is past President of the Tissue Engineering Society International, the forerunner of the Tissue Engineering and Regenerative medicine International Society (TERMIS). In addition, he was the part-time Senior Advisor for Bioengineering in the new National Institute for Biomedical Imaging and Bioengineering at the National Institutes of Health (2003-2006). In 1988 Professor Nerem was elected to the National Academy of Engineering (NAE), and he served on the NAE Council (1998-2004). In 1992 he was elected to the Institute of Medicine of the National Academy of Sciences and in 1998 a Fellow of the American Academy of Arts and Sciences. 1994 he was elected a Foreign Member of the Polish Academy of Sciences, and in 1998 he was made an Honorary Fellow of the Institution of Mechanical Engineers in the United Kingdom. In 2004 he was elected an honorary foreign member of the Japan Society for Medical and Biological Engineering and in 2006 a Foreign Member of the Swedish Royal Academy of Engineering Sciences. Professor Nerem holds honorary doctorates from the University of Paris, Imperial College London, and Illinois Institute of Technology. In 2008 he was selected by NAE for the Founders Award.

**SUZANNE ORTEGA**, Ph.D., assumed the position of provost and executive vice president for academic affairs at the University of New Mexico on August 1, 2008. From 2005 to 2008 she served as dean and vice provost of the graduate school at the University of Washington and from 2000 to 2005 as vice provost for advanced studies and dean of the graduate school at the University of Missouri–Columbia (MU). She received a bachelor's degree in sociology from Austin Peay State University in Clarksville, Tennessee, and a master's and doctorate in sociology from Vanderbilt University. Dr. Ortega was at the University of Nebraska–Lincoln from 1980 to 2000, rising from assistant professor to associate dean of graduate studies and professor. Her most important administrative accomplishments include securing funding for the Ronald E. McNair Postbaccalaureate Degree, Preparing Future Faculty, Diversity Enhancement, and Ph.D. Completion programs. Dr. Ortega has served as chair of the board of the Council of Graduate Schools, chair of the Graduate Record Examination Board, and chair of the Midwestern Association of Graduate Schools. She has served on the executive committee of the Council on Research Policy and Graduate Education of NASULGC. She has also served on the American Sociological Association (ASA) Advisory Board for Preparing Future Faculty, the ASA Executive Office and Budget Committee, and NSF's Human Resources Expert Panel. She is the author of numerous articles and an introductory sociology textbook, now in its seventh edition.

**ROBERT SPINRAD**, Ph.D. (NAE), now deceased, served as Vice President, Technology Strategy for Xerox. He joined Xerox in 1968, and over the years held a variety of research and technology management positions, including that of Director of Xerox PARC (Palo Alto Research Center). Prior to that, Dr. Spinrad worked as a Senior Scientist at Brookhaven National Laboratory. He received a Ph.D. in Electrical Engineering from the Massachusetts Institute of Technology (MIT) and an M.S. in Electrical Engineering and a B.S. in Engineering from Columbia University. He was a Bridgham Fellow at Columbia and a Whitney Fellow at MIT. He was  also a licensed

Professional Engineer (New York). Dr. Spinrad was a member of the National Academy of Engineering. He served on the Boards of the California Council on Science and Technology and the Pardee RAND Graduate School. He was also a member of the NASA Ames Executive Forum and the National Research Council's Committee on An Assessment of Research-Doctorate Programs. Dr. Spinrad served in various advisory and contributing roles for Harvard, Stanford, MIT, the University of California, the Council on Foreign Relations, the American Association for the Advancement of Science, the Library of Congress, the National Research Council, the National Science Foundation, DARPA, the Jet Propulsion Laboratory, Livermore National Laboratory, EDUCOM, Bell Laboratories and the Encyclopedia of Science & Technology.

**CATHARINE R. STIMPSON**, Ph.D., is University Professor and Dean Emerita of the Graduate School of Arts and Sciences at New York University. She earned an A.B. from Bryn Mawr College; a B.A. and M.A. from Newnham College, Cambridge University; and a Ph.D. from Columbia University. Dr. Stimpson was a member of the English Department of Barnard College from 1963 to 1980, where she was the first director of the Women's Center and the founding editor of *Signs: Journal of Women in Culture and Society* for the University of Chicago Press. In 1981 she became professor of English at Rutgers University, then dean of the graduate school, vice provost for graduate education, and university professor. She was also the first director of the Institute for Research on Women. While at Rutgers, Dr. Stimpson continued to teach while she served as director of the MacArthur Foundation Fellows Program (1994–1997). She is a former chair of the New York State Humanities Council and the National Council for Research on Women as well as past president of the Modern Language Association. Dr. Stimpson also served as president of the Association of Graduate Schools in 2000–2001. She holds honorary degrees from several universities and colleges, including Upsala, Bates, Hamilton, and the University of Arizona. Dr. Stimpson's publications include the book *Where the Meanings Are: Feminism and Cultural Spaces*, and a novel, *Class Notes*. She has edited seven books, has served as co-editor of *the Library of America's Gertrude Stein: Writings 1903–1932* and *Gertrude Stein: Writings 1932–1946*, and has published over 150 monographs, essays, stories, and reviews.

**RICHARD P. WHEELER**, Ph.D., is interim vice chancellor for academic affairs and vice provost at the University of Illinois, Urbana-Champaign. He received his Ph.D. in English from the State University of Buffalo in 1970. He joined the Department of English at the University of Illinois at Urbana-Champaign in 1969 and has been on the Illinois faculty ever since. From 1987 to 1997 he headed the Department of English, and in 1999–2000 he was acting head of the Department of Anthropology. From 2000 to 2009 he served as dean of the graduate college. He has chaired the executive committee of the Midwest Association of Graduate Schools, the Graduate Deans Group of the Committee on Institutional Cooperation, and the executive committee of the board of the Council of Graduate Schools. His scholarly publications include *Shakespeare's Development and the Problem Comedies: Turn and Counter-Turn* (U of California P, 1981), *The Whole Journey: Shakespeare's Power of Development* (co-authored, U of California P, 1986), *Creating Elizabethan Tragedy* (ed., U of Chicago P, 1988), *Critical Essays on Shakespeare's Measure for Measure* (ed., G.K. Hall, 1999), and articles on

Shakespeare, renaissance drama, and modern British literature. His scholarship has been largely directed toward identifying key psychological patterns that shape the development of Shakespeare's work and, more recently, plausible links between the plays and the life of their author.

# Appendix B

# Taxonomy of Fields

**AGRICULTURAL SCIENCES**
Animal Sciences
Entomology
Food Science
Forestry and Forest Sciences
Nutrition
Plant Sciences

**BIOLOGICAL AND HEALTH SCIENCES**
Biochemistry, Biophysics, and Structural Biology
Cell and Developmental Biology
Ecology and Evolutionary Biology
Public Health
Genetics and Genomics
Immunology and Infectious Disease
Biology/Integrated Biomedical Sciences (Note: Use this field only if the degree field is not specialized.)
Kinesiology
Microbiology
Neuroscience and Neurobiology
Nursing
Pharmacology, Toxicology and Environmental Health
Physiology

*Emerging Fields:*
Bioinformatics
Biotechnology
Systems Biology

**ENGINEERING**
Aerospace Engineering
Biomedical Engineering and Bioengineering
Chemical Engineering
Civil and Environmental Engineering
Computer Engineering
Electrical and Computer Engineering
Engineering Science and Materials (not elsewhere classified)
Materials Science and Engineering
Mechanical Engineering
Operations Research, Systems Engineering and Industrial Engineering

119

*Emerging Fields:*
Computational Engineering
Information Science
Nanoscience and Nanotechnology
Nuclear Engineering

## PHYSICAL & MATHEMATICAL SCIENCES
Applied Mathematics
Astrophysics and Astronomy
Chemistry
Computer Sciences
Earth Sciences
Mathematics
Oceanography, Atmospheric Sciences and Meteorology
Physics
Statistics and Probability

*Emerging Fields:*
None

## SOCIAL AND BEHAVIORAL SCIENCES
Agricultural and Resource Economics
Anthropology
Communication
Economics
Geography
Linguistics
Political Science
Public Affairs, Public Policy and Public Administration
Psychology
Sociology

*Emerging Fields:*
Criminology and Criminal Justice
Science and Technology Studies
Urban Studies and Planning

**HUMANITIES**
American Studies
Classics
Comparative Literature
English Language and Literature
French and Francophone Language and Literature
German Language and Literature
Language, Societies, and Cultures
History
History of Art, Architecture and Archaeology
Music (except performance)
Philosophy
Religion
Spanish and Portuguese Language and Literature
Theatre and Performance Studies

*Emerging Fields:*
Feminist, Gender, and Sexuality Studies
Film Studies
Race, Ethnicity and post-Colonial Studies
Rhetoric and Composition

# Appendix C

# Participating Institutions

ADELPHI UNIVERSITY

AMERICAN UNIVERSITY

ARIZONA STATE UNIVERSITY

AUBURN UNIVERSITY

BAYLOR COLLEGE OF MEDICINE

BAYLOR UNIVERSITY

BOSTON COLLEGE

BOSTON UNIVERSITY

BOWLING GREEN STATE UNIVERSITY

BRANDEIS UNIVERSITY

BRIGHAM YOUNG UNIVERSITY

BROWN UNIVERSITY

BRYN MAWR COLLEGE

CALIFORNIA INSTITUTE OF TECHNOLOGY

CARNEGIE MELLON UNIVERSITY

CASE WESTERN RESERVE UNIVERSITY

CATHOLIC UNIVERSITY OF AMERICA

CITY UNIVERSITY OF NEW YORK GRAD. CENTER

CLAREMONT GRADUATE UNIVERSITY

CLARK UNIVERSITY

CLARKSON UNIVERSITY

CLEMSON UNIVERSITY

CLEVELAND STATE UNIVERSITY

COLD SPRING HARBOR

COLLEGE OF WILLIAM AND MARY

COLORADO STATE UNIVERSITY

COLUMBIA UNIVERSITY IN THE CITY OF NEW YORK

CORNELL UNIVERSITY

DARTMOUTH COLLEGE

DREW UNIVERSITY

DREXEL UNIVERSITY

DUKE UNIVERSITY

DUQUESNE UNIVERSITY

EMORY UNIVERSITY

FLORIDA ATLANTIC UNIVERSITY

FLORIDA INSTITUTE OF TECHNOLOGY

FLORIDA INTERNATIONAL UNIVERSITY

FLORIDA STATE UNIVERSITY

FORDHAM UNIVERSITY

GEORGE WASHINGTON UNIVERSITY

GEORGETOWN UNIVERSITY

GEORGIA INSTITUTE OF TECHNOLOGY

GEORGIA INSTITUTE OF TECHNOLOGY - EMORY UNIVERSITY

GEORGIA STATE UNIVERSITY

GEORGIA STATE UNIVERSITY / GEORGIA TECH

GRADUATE THEOLOGICAL UNION

HARVARD UNIVERSITY

HEBREW UNION COLLEGE-JEWISH INSTITUTE OF RELIGION

HOWARD UNIVERSITY

ILLINOIS INSTITUTE OF TECHNOLOGY

INDIANA UNIVERSITY AT BLOOMINGTON

INDIANA UNIVERSITY PURDUE UNIVERSITY INDIANAPOLIS

IOWA STATE UNIVERSITY

JOHNS HOPKINS UNIVERSITY

KANSAS STATE UNIVERSITY

KENT STATE UNIVERSITY MAIN CAMPUS

LEHIGH UNIVERSITY

LOMA LINDA UNIVERSITY

LOUISIANA STATE UNIVERSITY AND AGRICULTURAL AND MECHANICAL COLLEGE

LOYOLA UNIVERSITY CHICAGO

MARQUETTE UNIVERSITY

MASSACHUSETTS INSTITUTE OF TECHNOLOGY

MIAMI UNIVERSITY

MICHIGAN STATE UNIVERSITY

MICHIGAN TECHNOLOGICAL UNIVERSITY

MISSISSIPPI STATE UNIVERSITY

MONTANA STATE UNIVERSITY - BOZEMAN

MT. SINAI SCHOOL OF MEDICINE

NEW JERSEY INSTITUTE OF TECHNOLOGY

NEW MEXICO STATE UNIVERSITY MAIN CAMPUS

NEW YORK MEDICAL COLLEGE

NEW YORK UNIVERSITY

NORTH CAROLINA STATE UNIVERSITY

NORTH DAKOTA STATE UNIVERSITY MAIN CAMPUS

NORTHEASTERN UNIVERSITY

NORTHERN ILLINOIS UNIVERSITY

NORTHWESTERN UNIVERSITY

OHIO STATE UNIVERSITY MAIN CAMPUS

OHIO UNIVERSITY MAIN CAMPUS

OKLAHOMA STATE UNIVERSITY MAIN CAMPUS

OLD DOMINION UNIVERSITY

OREGON HEALTH AND SCIENCE UNIVERSITY

OREGON STATE UNIVERSITY

PENNSYLVANIA STATE UNIVERSITY

PRINCETON UNIVERSITY

PURDUE UNIVERSITY MAIN CAMPUS

RENSSELAER POLYTECHNIC INSTITUTE

RICE UNIVERSITY

ROCKEFELLER UNIVERSITY

RUTGERS THE STATE UNIVERSITY OF NEW JERSEY NEW BRUNSWICK CAMPUS

RUTGERS THE STATE UNIVERSITY OF NEW JERSEY NEWARK CAMPUS

RUTGERS-NEW BRUNSWICK AND UNIVERSITY OF MEDICINE AND DENTISTRY OF NEW
JERSEY-PISCATAWAY

SAN DIEGO STATE UNIVERSITY-UNIVERSITY OF CALIFORNIA DAVIS

SAN DIEGO STATE UNIVERSITY-UNIVERSITY OF CALIFORNIA SAN DIEGO

SAN DIEGO STATE UNIVERSITY-UNIVERSITY OF CALIFORNIA SANTA BARBARA

SETON HALL UNIVERSITY

SOUTHERN ILLINOIS UNIVERSITY CARBONDALE

SOUTHERN METHODIST UNIVERSITY

STANFORD UNIVERSITY

STATE UNIVERSITY OF NEW YORK AT ALBANY

STATE UNIVERSITY OF NEW YORK AT BINGHAMTON

STATE UNIVERSITY OF NEW YORK AT BUFFALO

STATE UNIVERSITY OF NEW YORK AT STONY BROOK

STATE UNIVERSITY OF NEW YORK HEALTH SCIENCE CENTER AT BROOKLYN

STATE UNIVERSITY OF NEW YORK UPSTATE MEDICAL UNIVERSITY

STEVENS INSTITUTE OF TECHNOLOGY

SYRACUSE UNIVERSITY MAIN CAMPUS

TEMPLE UNIVERSITY

TENNESSEE TECHNOLOGICAL UNIVERSITY

TEXAS A & M UNIVERSITY

TEXAS CHRISTIAN UNIVERSITY

TEXAS TECH UNIVERSITY

THE UNIVERSITY OF ALABAMA AT BIRMINGHAM (UAB)/THE UNIVERSITY OF ALABAMA IN HUNTSVILLE (UAH)

THOMAS JEFFERSON UNIVERSITY

TUFTS UNIVERSITY

TULANE UNIVERSITY

UNIFORMED SERVICES UNIVERSITY OF THE HEALTH SCIENCES

UNIVERSITY OF MARYLAND BALTIMORE COUNTY/UNIVERSITY OF MARYLAND BALTIMORE

UNIVERSITY OF MARYLAND BALTIMORE COUNTY/UNIV. MD BALTIMORE/UNIV. MD EASTERN SHORE/UNIV. MD COLLEGE PARK

UNIVERSITY OF ALABAMA-BIRMINGHAM (UAB)/UNIV. OF ALABAMA-HUNTSVILLE (UAH)/UNIV. OF ALABAMA (UA)

UNIVERSITY OF TEXAS HLTH SCI CNTR. AT HOUSTON\UNIV. OF TEXAS M.D. ANDERSON CANCER CNTR.(UTHSCH\UTMDACC)

UNIVERSITY OF AKRON

UNIVERSITY OF ALABAMA

UNIVERSITY OF ALABAMA AT BIRMINGHAM

UNIVERSITY OF ALABAMA IN HUNTSVILLE

UNIVERSITY OF ALABAMA-UAB-UAH

UNIVERSITY OF ALASKA FAIRBANKS

UNIVERSITY OF ARIZONA

UNIVERSITY OF ARKANSAS MAIN CAMPUS

UNIVERSITY OF CALIFORNIA BERKELEY/UNIVERSITY OF CALIFORNIA SAN FRANCISCO

UNIVERSITY OF CALFORNIA IRVINE - UC RIVERSIDE - UC SAN DIEGO

UNIVERSITY CALIFORNIA IRVINE - UNIVERSITY OF CALIFORNIA SAN DIEGO

UNIVERSITY OF CALIFORNIA-BERKELEY

UNIVERSITY OF CALIFORNIA-DAVIS

UNIVERSITY OF CALIFORNIA-IRVINE

UNIVERSITY OF CALIFORNIA-LOS ANGELES

UNIVERSITY OF CALIFORNIA-RIVERSIDE

UNIVERSITY OF CALIFORNIA-SAN DIEGO

UNIVERSITY OF CALIFORNIA-SAN FRANCISCO

UNIVERSITY OF CALIFORNIA-SANTA BARBARA

UNIVERSITY OF CALIFORNIA-SANTA CRUZ

UNIVERSITY OF CENTRAL FLORIDA

UNIVERSITY OF CHICAGO

UNIVERSITY OF CINCINNATI MAIN CAMPUS

UNIVERSITY OF COLORADO AT BOULDER

UNIVERSITY OF COLORADO AT DENVER AND HEALTH SCIENCES CENTER

UNIVERSITY OF CONNECTICUT

UNIVERSITY OF DALLAS

UNIVERSITY OF DAYTON

UNIVERSITY OF DELAWARE

UNIVERSITY OF FLORIDA

UNIVERSITY OF GEORGIA

UNIVERSITY OF HAWAII AT MANOA

UNIVERSITY OF HOUSTON

UNIVERSITY OF IDAHO

UNIVERSITY OF ILLINOIS AT CHICAGO

UNIVERSITY OF ILLINOIS AT URBANA-CHAMPAIGN

UNIVERSITY OF IOWA

UNIVERSITY OF KANSAS

UNIVERSITY OF KENTUCKY

UNIVERSITY OF LOUISIANA AT LAFAYETTE

UNIVERSITY OF LOUISVILLE

UNIVERSITY OF MARYLAND BALTIMORE COUNTY

UNIVERSITY OF MARYLAND COLLEGE PARK

UNIVERSITY OF MASSACHUSETTS AMHERST

UNIVERSITY OF MASSACHUSETTS AT WORCESTER

UNIVERSITY OF MEMPHIS

UNIVERSITY OF MIAMI

UNIVERSITY OF MICHIGAN-ANN ARBOR

UNIVERSITY OF MINNESOTA-TWIN CITIES

UNIVERSITY OF MISSISSIPPI

UNIVERSITY OF MISSOURI - COLUMBIA

UNIVERSITY OF MISSOURI - KANSAS CITY

UNIVERSITY OF MISSOURI - ROLLA

UNIVERSITY OF MISSOURI - SAINT LOUIS

UNIVERSITY OF MONTANA - MISSOULA

UNIVERSITY OF NEBRASKA - LINCOLN

UNIVERSITY OF NEVADA RENO

UNIVERSITY OF NEW HAMPSHIRE

UNIVERSITY OF NEW MEXICO MAIN CAMPUS

UNIVERSITY OF NEW ORLEANS

UNIVERSITY OF NORTH CAROLINA AT CHAPEL HILL

UNIVERSITY OF NORTH CAROLINA AT CHARLOTTE

UNIVERSITY OF NORTH CAROLINA AT GREENSBORO

UNIVERSITY OF NORTH DAKOTA MAIN CAMPUS

UNIVERSITY OF NORTH TEXAS

UNIVERSITY OF NORTH TEXAS HEALTH SCIENCE CENTER

UNIVERSITY OF NOTRE DAME

UNIVERSITY OF OKLAHOMA NORMAN CAMPUS

UNIVERSITY OF OREGON

UNIVERSITY OF PENNSYLVANIA

UNIVERSITY OF PITTSBURGH PITTSBURGH CAMPUS

UNIVERSITY OF RHODE ISLAND

UNIVERSITY OF ROCHESTER

UNIVERSITY OF SOUTH CAROLINA COLUMBIA

UNIVERSITY OF SOUTH FLORIDA

UNIVERSITY OF SOUTHERN CALIFORNIA

UNIVERSITY OF SOUTHERN MISSISSIPPI

UNIVERSITY OF TENNESSEE

UNIVERSITY OF TEXAS AT AUSTIN

UNIVERSITY OF TEXAS AT DALLAS

UNIVERSITY OF TEXAS HEALTH SCIENCE CENTER AT HOUSTON

UNIVERSITY OF TEXAS SOUTHWESTERN MEDICAL CENTER AT DALLAS

UNIVERSITY OF TOLEDO

UNIVERSITY OF UTAH

UNIVERSITY OF VERMONT

UNIVERSITY OF VIRGINIA

UNIVERSITY OF WASHINGTON

UNIVERSITY OF WISCONSIN-MADISON

UNIVERSITY OF WISCONSIN-MILWAUKEE

UNIVERSITY OF WYOMING

UTAH STATE UNIVERSITY

VANDERBILT UNIVERSITY

VIRGINIA COMMONWEALTH UNIVERSITY

VIRGINIA POLYTECHNIC INSTITUTE AND STATE UNIVERSITY

WAKE FOREST UNIVERSITY

WASHINGTON STATE UNIVERSITY

WASHINGTON UNIVERSITY IN ST. LOUIS

WAYNE STATE UNIVERSITY

WESTERN MICHIGAN UNIVERSITY

WRIGHT STATE UNIVERSITY MAIN CAMPUS

YALE UNIVERSITY

# APPENDIX D

# Questionnaires

## National Research Council

## Assessment of Research Doctorate Programs

## 2006

## Institutional Questionnaire

Every 10 or so years, the National Research Council conducts a study of national importance regarding the quality and characteristics of doctoral programs in the United States. This comparative assessment is designed to assist prospective doctoral students with selecting programs that best fit their interests and to permit programs to benchmark themselves against similar programs.

The 2006 Assessment of Research Doctorate Programs collects data about the doctoral programs in over 60 areas of study in American universities. This Institutional Questionnaire is designed to collect data about institution-wide policies and practices.

**A.      Health Benefits and Services**

**A1. Is university-supported health care insurance part of the financial support provided to enrolled doctoral students?**

☐  Yes
☐  No      *If no, skip to question A3*

**A2. Does the university-supported health insurance for doctoral students cover mental health services?**

☐  Yes
☐  No

NOTE: For questions that follow about postdoctoral scholars, please use this definition of a postdoctoral scholar developed by the Association of American Universities:

- The appointee was recently awarded a Ph.D. or equivalent doctorate (e.g., Sc.D., M.D.) in an appropriate field; and
- the appointment is temporary; and
- the appointment involves substantially full-time research or scholarship; and
- the appointment is viewed as preparatory for a full-time academic and/or research career; and

- the appointment is not part of a clinical training program; and
- the appointee works under the supervision of a senior scholar or a department in a university or similar research institution (e.g., national laboratory, NIH, etc.); and
- the appointee has the freedom, and is expected, to publish the results of his or her research or scholarship during the period of the appointment.

(See: *http://www.aau.edu/reports/PostDocRpt.html*.  Accessed 6/27/06)

**A3.  Is university-supported health care insurance part of the financial support provided to postdoctoral scholars?**

☐  Yes
☐  No     *If no, skip to question B1*

**A4. Does the university-supported health insurance for postdoctoral scholars cover mental health services?**

☐  Yes
☐  No

**B.          Collective Bargaining**
**B1.  Is there a collective bargaining agreement for <u>teaching assistants</u> on your campus?**

☐  Yes
☐  No     *If no, skip to question B2*

**B1a.  Does the collective bargaining agreement for teaching assistants cover:**

☐  Some teaching assistants
☐  All teaching assistants

**B2.  Is there a collective bargaining agreement for <u>research assistants</u> on your campus?**

☐  Yes
☐  No     *If no, skip to Question C1*

**B2a.  Does the collective bargaining agreement for research assistants cover:**

☐  Some research assistants
☐  All research assistants

**C.   New Ph.D. Programs**

**C1 . What <u>new</u> Ph.D. programs have been added to the university since 1995?**

*Please list all programs added since 1995, even if not included in this study*

**D.  Research Location**

**D1.  Please list all of the zip code(s) that your institution or faculty members use when submitting proposals to potential sponsors.**

a.
b.
c.
d.

[Note: The web version of the questionnaire will allow the respondent to add as many zip codes as needed.]

**E.  Academic Year**
**E1.  How is an academic year defined at this institution?**

☐ From July 1st to June 30th
☐ Other, please specify:_____

**F. Doctoral Student Representation in 5 Selected Fields**

**This section collects outcomes by race/ethnicity on the full-time doctoral students who are <u>U.S. citizens or permanent residents</u> in each of five broad fields 1) Life Sciences, 2) Physical Sciences and Mathematics, 3) Engineering, 4) Social and Behavioral Sciences, and 5) Arts and Humanities.**

- If the numbers in these tables are too small to release for reasons of confidentiality, please provide the raw data to the NRC and we will aggregate over cohorts so that the size of any cell is always greater than or equal to 5.

- For purposes of this question only, "Physical Sciences, Mathematics, and Engineering" in the taxonomy have been disaggregated into two separate broad fields: "Physical Sciences and Mathematics" and "Engineering."

- <u>Do not include</u> Emerging Fields unless they are also included as part of a program in an established field within the taxonomy

- <u>Include</u> doctoral students enrolled in your doctoral programs, whether or not they have been admitted to candidacy.

- <u>Do not include</u> doctoral students who have declared that they only intend to earn a master's degree.

- Doctoral students who "left the program" are those who are no longer enrolled at this time.

- Doctoral students who "stopped out" (left but later enrolled again) should not be counted as students who left if they are currently enrolled or completed the doctoral degree.

## Native Americans/Alaska Natives in the Life Sciences

**F1a. Please record the number of Native American/Alaskan Natives who entered the Life Sciences programs included in this study between 1996 and 2005.**

|  | Number of entering doctoral students If none: enter zero | Number of students who left the program without a master's or doctoral degree | Number of students who left the program after receiving a master's degree | Number of students admitted to doctoral candidacy |
|---|---|---|---|---|
| 1996-1997 |  |  |  |  |
| 1997-1998 |  |  |  |  |
| 1998-1999 |  |  |  |  |
| 1999-2000 |  |  |  |  |
| 2000-2001 |  |  |  |  |
| 2001-2002 |  |  |  |  |
| 2002-2003 |  |  |  |  |
| 2003-2004 |  |  |  |  |
| 2004-2005 |  |  |  |  |
| 2005-2006 |  |  |  |  |

**F1b. Of the Native American/Alaska Natives admitted to candidacy in the Life Sciences, record the number of students from each cohort listed below who completed degrees within the given number of years after enrolling.**

|  | 3 years or less | 4 years | 5 years | 6 years | 7 years | 8 years | 9 years | 10 years | Number still enrolled after 10 years |
|---|---|---|---|---|---|---|---|---|---|
| 1996-1997 |  |  |  |  |  |  |  |  |  |
| 1997-1998 |  |  |  |  |  |  |  |  |  |
| 1998-1999 |  |  |  |  |  |  |  |  |  |
| 1999-2000 |  |  |  |  |  |  |  |  |  |
| 2000-2001 |  |  |  |  |  |  |  |  |  |
| 2001-2002 |  |  |  |  |  |  |  |  |  |
| 2002-2003 |  |  |  |  |  |  |  |  |  |

| | | | | | | | | |
|---|---|---|---|---|---|---|---|---|
| **2003-2004** | | | | | | | | |
| **2004-2005** | | | | | | | | |
| **2005-2006** | | | | | | | | |

## Non-Hispanic Blacks in the Life Sciences

**F2a. Please record the number of Non-Hispanic Blacks who entered the Life Sciences programs included in this study between 1996 and 2005.**

| | **Number of entering doctoral students If none: enter zero** | **Number of students who left the program without a master's or doctoral degree** | **Number of students who left the program after receiving a master's degree** | **Number of students admitted to doctoral candidacy** |
|---|---|---|---|---|
| **1996-1997** | | | | |
| **1997-1998** | | | | |
| **1998-1999** | | | | |
| **1999-2000** | | | | |
| **2000-2001** | | | | |
| **2001-2002** | | | | |
| **2002-2003** | | | | |
| **2003-2004** | | | | |
| **2004-2005** | | | | |
| **2005-2006** | | | | |

**F2b. Of the Non-Hispanic Blacks admitted to candidacy in the Life Sciences, record the number of students from each cohort listed below who completed degrees within the given number of years after enrolling.**

| | **3 years or less** | **4 years** | **5 years** | **6 years** | **7 years** | **8 years** | **9 years** | **10 years** | **Number still enrolled after 10 years** |
|---|---|---|---|---|---|---|---|---|---|
| **1996-1997** | | | | | | | | | |
| **1997-1998** | | | | | | | | | |
| **1998-1999** | | | | | | | | | |
| **1999-2000** | | | | | | | | | |
| **2000-2001** | | | | | | | | | |
| **2001-2002** | | | | | | | | | |
| **2002-** | | | | | | | | | |

| | | | | | | | | | |
|---|---|---|---|---|---|---|---|---|---|
| **2003** | | | | | | | | | |
| **2003-2004** | | | | | | | | | |
| **2004-2005** | | | | | | | | | |
| **2005-2006** | | | | | | | | | |

## Non-Hispanic Whites in the Life Sciences

**F3a. Please record the number of Non-Hispanic Whites who entered the Life Sciences programs included in this study between 1996 and 2005.**

| | Number of entering doctoral students If none: enter zero | Number of students who left the program without a master's or doctoral degree | Number of students who left the program after receiving a master's degree | Number of students admitted to doctoral candidacy |
|---|---|---|---|---|
| **1996-1997** | | | | |
| **1997-1998** | | | | |
| **1998-1999** | | | | |
| **1999-2000** | | | | |
| **2000-2001** | | | | |
| **2001-2002** | | | | |
| **2002-2003** | | | | |
| **2003-2004** | | | | |
| **2004-2005** | | | | |
| **2005-2006** | | | | |

**F3b. Of the Non-Hispanic Whites admitted to candidacy in the Life Sciences, record the number of students from each cohort listed below who completed degrees within the given number of years after enrolling.**

| | 3 years or less | 4 years | 5 years | 6 years | 7 years | 8 years | 9 years | 10 years | Number still enrolled after 10 years |
|---|---|---|---|---|---|---|---|---|---|
| **1996-1997** | | | | | | | | | |
| **1997-1998** | | | | | | | | | |
| **1998-1999** | | | | | | | | | |
| **1999-2000** | | | | | | | | | |
| **2000-2001** | | | | | | | | | |
| **2001-2002** | | | | | | | | | |

| | | | | | | | | | |
|---|---|---|---|---|---|---|---|---|---|
| **2002-2003** | | | | | | | | | |
| **2003-2004** | | | | | | | | | |
| **2004-2005** | | | | | | | | | |
| **2005-2006** | | | | | | | | | |

## Hispanics in the Life Sciences

**F4a. Please record the number of Hispanics who entered the Life Sciences programs included in this study between 1996 and 2005.**

| | Number of entering doctoral students If none: enter zero | Number of students who left the program without a master's or doctoral degree | Number of students who left the program after receiving a master's degree | Number of students admitted to doctoral candidacy |
|---|---|---|---|---|
| **1996-1997** | | | | |
| **1997-1998** | | | | |
| **1998-1999** | | | | |
| **1999-2000** | | | | |
| **2000-2001** | | | | |
| **2001-2002** | | | | |
| **2002-2003** | | | | |
| **2003-2004** | | | | |
| **2004-2005** | | | | |
| **2005-2006** | | | | |

**F4b. Of the Hispanics admitted to candidacy in the Life Sciences, record the number of students from each cohort listed below who completed degrees within the given number of years after enrolling.**

| | 3 years or less | 4 years | 5 years | 6 years | 7 years | 8 years | 9 years | 10 years | Number still enrolled after 10 years |
|---|---|---|---|---|---|---|---|---|---|
| **1996-1997** | | | | | | | | | |
| **1997-1998** | | | | | | | | | |
| **1998-1999** | | | | | | | | | |
| **1999-2000** | | | | | | | | | |
| **2000-2001** | | | | | | | | | |
| **2001-** | | | | | | | | | |

| | | | | | | | | | |
|---|---|---|---|---|---|---|---|---|---|
| **2002** | | | | | | | | | |
| **2002-2003** | | | | | | | | | |
| **2003-2004** | | | | | | | | | |
| **2004-2005** | | | | | | | | | |
| **2005-2006** | | | | | | | | | |

## Asians and Pacific Islanders in the Life Sciences

**F5a. Please record the number of Asians and Pacific Islanders who entered the Life Sciences programs included in this study between 1996 and 2005.**

| | **Number of entering doctoral students If none: enter zero** | **Number of students who left the program without a master's or doctoral degree** | **Number of students who left the program after receiving a master's degree** | **Number of students admitted to doctoral candidacy** |
|---|---|---|---|---|
| **1996-1997** | | | | |
| **1997-1998** | | | | |
| **1998-1999** | | | | |
| **1999-2000** | | | | |
| **2000-2001** | | | | |
| **2001-2002** | | | | |
| **2002-2003** | | | | |
| **2003-2004** | | | | |
| **2004-2005** | | | | |
| **2005-2006** | | | | |

**F5b. Of the Asians and Pacific Islanders admitted to candidacy in the Life Sciences, record the number of students from each cohort listed below who completed degrees within the given number of years after enrolling.**

| | 3 years or less | 4 years | 5 years | 6 years | 7 years | 8 years | 9 years | 10 years | Number still enrolled after 10 years |
|---|---|---|---|---|---|---|---|---|---|
| 1996-1997 | | | | | | | | | |
| 1997-1998 | | | | | | | | | |
| 1998-1999 | | | | | | | | | |
| 1999-2000 | | | | | | | | | |
| 2000-2001 | | | | | | | | | |
| 2001-2002 | | | | | | | | | |
| 2002-2003 | | | | | | | | | |
| 2003-2004 | | | | | | | | | |
| 2004-2005 | | | | | | | | | |
| 2005-2006 | | | | | | | | | |

## Native Americans/Alaska Natives in the Physical Sciences and Mathematics

**F6a. Please record the number of Native Americans and Alaska Natives who entered the Physical Sciences and Mathematics programs included in this study between 1996 and 2005.**

| | Number of entering doctoral students If none: enter zero | Number of students who left the program without a master's or doctoral degree | Number of students who left the program after receiving a master's degree | Number of students admitted to doctoral candidacy |
|---|---|---|---|---|
| 1996-1997 | | | | |
| 1997-1998 | | | | |
| 1998-1999 | | | | |
| 1999-2000 | | | | |
| 2000-2001 | | | | |
| 2001-2002 | | | | |
| 2002-2003 | | | | |
| 2003-2004 | | | | |
| 2004-2005 | | | | |

| 2005-2006 | | | | |
|-----------|--|--|--|--|

**F6b. Of the Native Americans and Alaskan Natives admitted to candidacy in the Physical Sciences and Mathematics, record the number of students from each cohort listed below who completed degrees within the given number of years after enrolling.**

| | 3 years or less | 4 years | 5 years | 6 years | 7 years | 8 years | 9 years | 10 years | Number still enrolled after 10 years |
|--|--|--|--|--|--|--|--|--|--|
| 1996-1997 | | | | | | | | | |
| 1997-1998 | | | | | | | | | |
| 1998-1999 | | | | | | | | | |
| 1999-2000 | | | | | | | | | |
| 2000-2001 | | | | | | | | | |
| 2001-2002 | | | | | | | | | |
| 2002-2003 | | | | | | | | | |
| 2003-2004 | | | | | | | | | |
| 2004-2005 | | | | | | | | | |
| 2005-2006 | | | | | | | | | |

## Non-Hispanic Blacks in the Physical Sciences and Mathematics

**F7a. Please record the number of Non-Hispanic Blacks who entered the Physical Sciences and Mathematics programs included in this study between 1996 and 2005.**

| | Number of entering doctoral students If none: enter zero | Number of students who left the program without a master's or doctoral degree | Number of students who left the program after receiving a master's degree | Number of students admitted to doctoral candidacy |
|--|--|--|--|--|
| 1996-1997 | | | | |
| 1997-1998 | | | | |
| 1998-1999 | | | | |
| 1999-2000 | | | | |
| 2000-2001 | | | | |
| 2001-2002 | | | | |
| 2002-2003 | | | | |
| 2003-2004 | | | | |

| | | | | |
|---|---|---|---|---|
| **2004-2005** | | | | |
| **2005-2006** | | | | |

**F7b. Of the Non-Hispanic Blacks admitted to candidacy in the Physical Sciences and Mathematics, record the number of students from each cohort listed below who completed degrees within the given number of years after enrolling.**

| | 3 years or less | 4 years | 5 years | 6 years | 7 years | 8 years | 9 years | 10 years | Number still enrolled after 10 years |
|---|---|---|---|---|---|---|---|---|---|
| **1996-1997** | | | | | | | | | |
| **1997-1998** | | | | | | | | | |
| **1998-1999** | | | | | | | | | |
| **1999-2000** | | | | | | | | | |
| **2000-2001** | | | | | | | | | |
| **2001-2002** | | | | | | | | | |
| **2002-2003** | | | | | | | | | |
| **2003-2004** | | | | | | | | | |
| **2004-2005** | | | | | | | | | |
| **2005-2006** | | | | | | | | | |

## Non-Hispanic Whites in the Physical Sciences and Mathematics

**F8a. Please record the number of Non-Hispanic Whites who entered the Physical Sciences and Mathematics programs included in this study between 1996 and 2005.**

| | Number of entering doctoral students If none: enter zero | Number of students who left the program without a master's or doctoral degree | Number of students who left the program after receiving a master's degree | Number of students admitted to doctoral candidacy |
|---|---|---|---|---|
| **1996-1997** | | | | |
| **1997-1998** | | | | |
| **1998-1999** | | | | |
| **1999-2000** | | | | |
| **2000-2001** | | | | |
| **2001-2002** | | | | |
| **2002-2003** | | | | |

| | | | | |
|---|---|---|---|---|
| **2003-2004** | | | | |
| **2004-2005** | | | | |
| **2005-2006** | | | | |

**F8b. Of the Non-Hispanic Whites admitted to candidacy in the Physical Sciences and Mathematics, record the number of students from each cohort listed below who completed degrees within the given number of years after enrolling.**

| | 3 years or less | 4 years | 5 years | 6 years | 7 years | 8 years | 9 years | 10 years | Number still enrolled after 10 years |
|---|---|---|---|---|---|---|---|---|---|
| **1996-1997** | | | | | | | | | |
| **1997-1998** | | | | | | | | | |
| **1998-1999** | | | | | | | | | |
| **1999-2000** | | | | | | | | | |
| **2000-2001** | | | | | | | | | |
| **2001-2002** | | | | | | | | | |
| **2002-2003** | | | | | | | | | |
| **2003-2004** | | | | | | | | | |
| **2004-2005** | | | | | | | | | |
| **2005-2006** | | | | | | | | | |

# Hispanics in the Physical Sciences and Mathematics

**F9a. Please record the number of Hispanics who entered the Physical Sciences and Mathematics programs included in this study between 1996 and 2005.**

|  | Number of entering doctoral students If none: enter zero | Number of students who left the program without a master's or doctoral degree | Number of students who left the program after receiving a master's degree | Number of students admitted to doctoral candidacy |
|---|---|---|---|---|
| 1996-1997 | | | | |
| 1997-1998 | | | | |
| 1998-1999 | | | | |
| 1999-2000 | | | | |
| 2000-2001 | | | | |
| 2001-2002 | | | | |
| 2002-2003 | | | | |
| 2003-2004 | | | | |
| 2004-2005 | | | | |
| 2005-2006 | | | | |

**F9b. Of the Hispanics admitted to candidacy in the Physical Sciences and Mathematics, record the number of students from each cohort listed below who completed degrees within the given number of years after enrolling.**

|  | 3 years or less | 4 years | 5 years | 6 years | 7 years | 8 years | 9 years | 10 years | Number still enrolled after 10 years |
|---|---|---|---|---|---|---|---|---|---|
| 1996-1997 | | | | | | | | | |
| 1997-1998 | | | | | | | | | |
| 1998-1999 | | | | | | | | | |
| 1999-2000 | | | | | | | | | |
| 2000-2001 | | | | | | | | | |
| 2001-2002 | | | | | | | | | |
| 2002-2003 | | | | | | | | | |
| 2003-2004 | | | | | | | | | |
| 2004-2005 | | | | | | | | | |
| 2005-2006 | | | | | | | | | |

## Asians and Pacific Islanders in the Physical Sciences and Mathematics

**F10a.** Please record the number of Asians and Pacific Islanders who entered the Physical Sciences and Mathematics programs included in this study between 1996 and 2005.

| | Number of entering doctoral students If none: enter zero | Number of students who left the program without a master's or doctoral degree | Number of students who left the program after receiving a master's degree | Number of students admitted to doctoral candidacy |
|---|---|---|---|---|
| 1996-1997 | | | | |
| 1997-1998 | | | | |
| 1998-1999 | | | | |
| 1999-2000 | | | | |
| 2000-2001 | | | | |
| 2001-2002 | | | | |
| 2002-2003 | | | | |
| 2003-2004 | | | | |
| 2004-2005 | | | | |
| 2005-2006 | | | | |

**F10b.** Of the Asians and Pacific Islanders admitted to candidacy in the Physical Sciences and Mathematics, record the number of students from each cohort listed below who completed degrees within the given number of years after enrolling.

| | 3 years or less | 4 years | 5 years | 6 years | 7 years | 8 years | 9 years | 10 years | Number still enrolled after 10 years |
|---|---|---|---|---|---|---|---|---|---|
| 1996-1997 | | | | | | | | | |
| 1997-1998 | | | | | | | | | |
| 1998-1999 | | | | | | | | | |
| 1999-2000 | | | | | | | | | |
| 2000-2001 | | | | | | | | | |
| 2001-2002 | | | | | | | | | |
| 2002-2003 | | | | | | | | | |
| 2003-2004 | | | | | | | | | |
| 2004-2005 | | | | | | | | | |
| 2005- | | | | | | | | | |

| 2006 | | | | | | | | | |
|---|---|---|---|---|---|---|---|---|---|

## Native Americans and Alaska Natives in Engineering

**F11. Please record the number of Native Americans and Alaska Natives who entered the Engineering programs included in this study between 1996 and 2005.**

| | Number of entering doctoral students If none: enter zero | Number of students who left the program without a master's or doctoral degree | Number of students who left the program after receiving a master's degree | Number of students admitted to doctoral candidacy |
|---|---|---|---|---|
| 1996-1997 | | | | |
| 1997-1998 | | | | |
| 1998-1999 | | | | |
| 1999-2000 | | | | |
| 2000-2001 | | | | |
| 2001-2002 | | | | |
| 2002-2003 | | | | |
| 2003-2004 | | | | |
| 2004-2005 | | | | |
| 2005-2006 | | | | |

**F11b. Of the Native Americans and Alaskan Natives admitted to candidacy in Engineering, record the number of students from each cohort listed below who completed degrees within the given number of years after enrolling.**

| | 3 years or less | 4 years | 5 years | 6 years | 7 years | 8 years | 9 years | 10 years | Number still enrolled after 10 years |
|---|---|---|---|---|---|---|---|---|---|
| 1996-1997 | | | | | | | | | |
| 1997-1998 | | | | | | | | | |
| 1998-1999 | | | | | | | | | |
| 1999-2000 | | | | | | | | | |
| 2000-2001 | | | | | | | | | |
| 2001-2002 | | | | | | | | | |
| 2002-2003 | | | | | | | | | |
| 2003-2004 | | | | | | | | | |
| 2004-2005 | | | | | | | | | |

| 2005-2006 | | | | | | | | | |
|---|---|---|---|---|---|---|---|---|---|
| | | | | | | | | | |

## Non-Hispanic Blacks in Engineering

**F12a. Please record the number of Non-Hispanic Blacks who entered the Engineering programs included in this study between 1996 and 2005.**

| | Number of entering doctoral students If none: enter zero | Number of students who left the program without a master's or doctoral degree | Number of students who left the program after receiving a master's degree | Number of students admitted to doctoral candidacy |
|---|---|---|---|---|
| 1996-1997 | | | | |
| 1997-1998 | | | | |
| 1998-1999 | | | | |
| 1999-2000 | | | | |
| 2000-2001 | | | | |
| 2001-2002 | | | | |
| 2002-2003 | | | | |
| 2003-2004 | | | | |
| 2004-2005 | | | | |
| 2005-2006 | | | | |

**F12b. Of the Non-Hispanic Blacks admitted to candidacy in Engineering, record the number of students from each cohort listed below who completed degrees within the given number of years after enrolling.**

| | 3 years or less | 4 years | 5 years | 6 years | 7 years | 8 years | 9 years | 10 years | Number still enrolled after 10 years |
|---|---|---|---|---|---|---|---|---|---|
| 1996-1997 | | | | | | | | | |
| 1997-1998 | | | | | | | | | |
| 1998-1999 | | | | | | | | | |
| 1999-2000 | | | | | | | | | |
| 2000-2001 | | | | | | | | | |
| 2001-2002 | | | | | | | | | |
| 2002-2003 | | | | | | | | | |
| 2003-2004 | | | | | | | | | |
| 2004-2005 | | | | | | | | | |

| 2005-2006 | | | | | | | | | |
|---|---|---|---|---|---|---|---|---|---|

## Non-Hispanic Whites in Engineering

**F13a. Please record the number of Non-Hispanic Whites who entered the Engineering programs included in this study between 1996 and 2005.**

| | Number of entering doctoral students If none: enter zero | Number of students who left the program without a master's or doctoral degree | Number of students who left the program after receiving a master's degree | Number of students admitted to doctoral candidacy |
|---|---|---|---|---|
| 1996-1997 | | | | |
| 1997-1998 | | | | |
| 1998-1999 | | | | |
| 1999-2000 | | | | |
| 2000-2001 | | | | |
| 2001-2002 | | | | |
| 2002-2003 | | | | |
| 2003-2004 | | | | |
| 2004-2005 | | | | |
| 2005-2006 | | | | |

**F13b. Of the Non-Hispanic Whites admitted to candidacy in Engineering, record the number of students from each cohort listed below who completed degrees within the given number of years after enrolling.**

| | 3 years or less | 4 years | 5 years | 6 years | 7 years | 8 years | 9 years | 10 years | Number still enrolled after 10 years |
|---|---|---|---|---|---|---|---|---|---|
| 1996-1997 | | | | | | | | | |
| 1997-1998 | | | | | | | | | |
| 1998-1999 | | | | | | | | | |
| 1999-2000 | | | | | | | | | |
| 2000-2001 | | | | | | | | | |
| 2001-2002 | | | | | | | | | |
| 2002-2003 | | | | | | | | | |
| 2003-2004 | | | | | | | | | |
| 2004- | | | | | | | | | |

| | | | | | | | | |
|---|---|---|---|---|---|---|---|---|
| **2005** | | | | | | | | |
| **2005-2006** | | | | | | | | |

## Hispanics in Engineering

**F14a. Please record the number of Hispanics who entered the Engineering programs included in this study between 1996 and 2005.**

| | Number of entering doctoral students If none: enter zero | Number of students who left the program without a master's or doctoral degree | Number of students who left the program after receiving a master's degree | Number of students admitted to doctoral candidacy |
|---|---|---|---|---|
| **1996-1997** | | | | |
| **1997-1998** | | | | |
| **1998-1999** | | | | |
| **1999-2000** | | | | |
| **2000-2001** | | | | |
| **2001-2002** | | | | |
| **2002-2003** | | | | |
| **2003-2004** | | | | |
| **2004-2005** | | | | |
| **2005-2006** | | | | |

**F14b. Of the Hispanics admitted to candidacy in Engineering, record the number of students from each cohort listed below who completed degrees within the given number of years after enrolling.**

| | 3 years or less | 4 years | 5 years | 6 years | 7 years | 8 years | 9 years | 10 years | Number still enrolled after 10 years |
|---|---|---|---|---|---|---|---|---|---|
| **1996-1997** | | | | | | | | | |
| **1997-1998** | | | | | | | | | |
| **1998-1999** | | | | | | | | | |
| **1999-2000** | | | | | | | | | |
| **2000-2001** | | | | | | | | | |
| **2001-2002** | | | | | | | | | |
| **2002-2003** | | | | | | | | | |
| **2003-2004** | | | | | | | | | |

| | | | | | | | |
|---|---|---|---|---|---|---|---|
| 2004-2005 | | | | | | | |
| 2005-2006 | | | | | | | |

## Asians and Pacific Islanders in Engineering

**F15a.** Please record the number of Asians and Pacific Islanders who entered the Engineering programs included in this study between 1996 and 2005.

| | Number of entering doctoral students If none: enter zero | Number of students who left the program without a master's or doctoral degree | Number of students who left the program after receiving a master's degree | Number of students admitted to doctoral candidacy |
|---|---|---|---|---|
| 1996-1997 | | | | |
| 1997-1998 | | | | |
| 1998-1999 | | | | |
| 1999-2000 | | | | |
| 2000-2001 | | | | |
| 2001-2002 | | | | |
| 2002-2003 | | | | |
| 2003-2004 | | | | |
| 2004-2005 | | | | |
| 2005-2006 | | | | |

**F15b.** Of the Asians and Pacific Islanders admitted to candidacy in Engineering, record the number of students from each cohort listed below who completed degrees within the given number of years after enrolling.

| | 3 years or less | 4 years | 5 years | 6 years | 7 years | 8 years | 9 years | 10 years | Number still enrolled after 10 years |
|---|---|---|---|---|---|---|---|---|---|
| 1996-1997 | | | | | | | | | |
| 1997-1998 | | | | | | | | | |
| 1998-1999 | | | | | | | | | |
| 1999-2000 | | | | | | | | | |
| 2000-2001 | | | | | | | | | |
| 2001-2002 | | | | | | | | | |
| 2002-2003 | | | | | | | | | |
| 2003- | | | | | | | | | |

| | | | | | | | | | |
|---|---|---|---|---|---|---|---|---|---|
| **2004** | | | | | | | | | |
| **2004-2005** | | | | | | | | | |
| **2005-2006** | | | | | | | | | |

## Native Americans/Alaska Natives in the Social Sciences

**F16a. Please record the number of Native American/Alaska Natives who entered the Social Sciences programs included in this study between 1996 and 2005.**

| | Number of entering doctoral students If none: enter zero | Number of students who left the program without a master's or doctoral degree | Number of students who left the program after receiving a master's degree | Number of students admitted to doctoral candidacy |
|---|---|---|---|---|
| **1996-1997** | | | | |
| **1997-1998** | | | | |
| **1998-1999** | | | | |
| **1999-2000** | | | | |
| **2000-2001** | | | | |
| **2001-2002** | | | | |
| **2002-2003** | | | | |
| **2003-2004** | | | | |
| **2004-2005** | | | | |
| **2005-2006** | | | | |

**F16b. Of the Native American/Alaskan Natives admitted to candidacy in the Social Sciences, record the number of students from each cohort listed below who completed degrees within the given number of years after enrolling.**

| | 3 years or less | 4 years | 5 years | 6 years | 7 years | 8 years | 9 years | 10 years | Number still enrolled after 10 years |
|---|---|---|---|---|---|---|---|---|---|
| **1996-1997** | | | | | | | | | |
| **1997-1998** | | | | | | | | | |
| **1998-1999** | | | | | | | | | |
| **1999-2000** | | | | | | | | | |
| **2000-2001** | | | | | | | | | |
| **2001-2002** | | | | | | | | | |
| **2002-2003** | | | | | | | | | |

| | | | | | | | |
|---|---|---|---|---|---|---|---|
| 2003-2004 | | | | | | | |
| 2004-2005 | | | | | | | |
| 2005-2006 | | | | | | | |

## Non-Hispanic Blacks in the Social Sciences

**F17a. Please record the number of Non-Hispanic Blacks who entered the Social Sciences programs included in this study between 1996 and 2005.**

| | Number of entering doctoral students If none: enter zero | Number of students who left the program without a master's or doctoral degree | Number of students who left the program after receiving a master's degree | Number of students admitted to doctoral candidacy |
|---|---|---|---|---|
| 1996-1997 | | | | |
| 1997-1998 | | | | |
| 1998-1999 | | | | |
| 1999-2000 | | | | |
| 2000-2001 | | | | |
| 2001-2002 | | | | |
| 2002-2003 | | | | |
| 2003-2004 | | | | |
| 2004-2005 | | | | |
| 2005-2006 | | | | |

**F17b. Of the Non-Hispanic Blacks admitted to candidacy in the Social Sciences, record the number of students from each cohort listed below who completed degrees within the given number of years after enrolling.**

| | 3 years or less | 4 years | 5 years | 6 years | 7 years | 8 years | 9 years | 10 years | Number still enrolled after 10 years |
|---|---|---|---|---|---|---|---|---|---|
| 1996-1997 | | | | | | | | | |
| 1997-1998 | | | | | | | | | |
| 1998-1999 | | | | | | | | | |
| 1999-2000 | | | | | | | | | |
| 2000-2001 | | | | | | | | | |
| 2001-2002 | | | | | | | | | |
| 2002- | | | | | | | | | |

| 2003 | | | | | | | | | |
|------|--|--|--|--|--|--|--|--|--|
| 2003-2004 | | | | | | | | | |
| 2004-2005 | | | | | | | | | |
| 2005-2006 | | | | | | | | | |

## Non-Hispanic Whites in the Social Sciences

**F18a.** Please record the number of Non-Hispanic Whites who entered the Social Sciences programs included in this study between 1996 and 2005.

| | Number of entering doctoral students If none: enter zero | Number of students who left the program without a master's or doctoral degree | Number of students who left the program after receiving a master's degree | Number of students admitted to doctoral candidacy |
|--|--|--|--|--|
| 1996-1997 | | | | |
| 1997-1998 | | | | |
| 1998-1999 | | | | |
| 1999-2000 | | | | |
| 2000-2001 | | | | |
| 2001-2002 | | | | |
| 2002-2003 | | | | |
| 2003-2004 | | | | |
| 2004-2005 | | | | |
| 2005-2006 | | | | |

**F18b.** Of the Non-Hispanic Whites admitted to candidacy in the Social Sciences, record the number of students from each cohort listed below who completed degrees within the given number of years after enrolling.

| | 3 years or less | 4 years | 5 years | 6 years | 7 years | 8 years | 9 years | 10 years | Number still enrolled after 10 years |
|--|--|--|--|--|--|--|--|--|--|
| 1996-1997 | | | | | | | | | |
| 1997-1998 | | | | | | | | | |
| 1998-1999 | | | | | | | | | |
| 1999-2000 | | | | | | | | | |
| 2000-2001 | | | | | | | | | |
| 2001-2002 | | | | | | | | | |

| | | | | | | | | | |
|---|---|---|---|---|---|---|---|---|---|
| 2002-2003 | | | | | | | | | |
| 2003-2004 | | | | | | | | | |
| 2004-2005 | | | | | | | | | |
| 2005-2006 | | | | | | | | | |

## Hispanics in the Social Sciences

**F19a. Please record the number of Hispanics who entered the Social Sciences programs included in this study between 1996 and 2005.**

| | Number of entering doctoral students If none: enter zero | Number of students who left the program without a master's or doctoral degree | Number of students who left the program after receiving a master's degree | Number of students admitted to doctoral candidacy |
|---|---|---|---|---|
| 1996-1997 | | | | |
| 1997-1998 | | | | |
| 1998-1999 | | | | |
| 1999-2000 | | | | |
| 2000-2001 | | | | |
| 2001-2002 | | | | |
| 2002-2003 | | | | |
| 2003-2004 | | | | |
| 2004-2005 | | | | |
| 2005-2006 | | | | |

**F19b. Of the Hispanics admitted to candidacy in the Social Sciences, record the number of students from each cohort listed below who completed degrees within the given number of years after enrolling.**

| | 3 years or less | 4 years | 5 years | 6 years | 7 years | 8 years | 9 years | 10 years | Number still enrolled after 10 years |
|---|---|---|---|---|---|---|---|---|---|
| 1996-1997 | | | | | | | | | |
| 1997-1998 | | | | | | | | | |
| 1998-1999 | | | | | | | | | |
| 1999-2000 | | | | | | | | | |
| 2000-2001 | | | | | | | | | |
| 2001-2002 | | | | | | | | | |
| 2002-2003 | | | | | | | | | |
| 2003-2004 | | | | | | | | | |
| 2004-2005 | | | | | | | | | |
| 2005-2006 | | | | | | | | | |

## Asians and Pacific Islanders in the Social Sciences

**F20a. Please record the number of Asians and Pacific Islanders who entered the Social Sciences programs included in this study between 1996 and 2005.**

| | Number of entering doctoral students If none: enter zero | Number of students who left the program without a master's or doctoral degree | Number of students who left the program after receiving a master's degree | Number of students admitted to doctoral candidacy |
|---|---|---|---|---|
| 1996-1997 | | | | |
| 1997-1998 | | | | |
| 1998-1999 | | | | |
| 1999-2000 | | | | |
| 2000-2001 | | | | |
| 2001-2002 | | | | |
| 2002-2003 | | | | |
| 2003-2004 | | | | |
| 2004-2005 | | | | |
| 2005-2006 | | | | |

**F20b. Of the Asians and Pacific Islanders admitted to candidacy in the Social Sciences, record the number of students from each cohort listed below who completed degrees within the given number of years after enrolling.**

|  | 3 years or less | 4 years | 5 years | 6 years | 7 years | 8 years | 9 years | 10 years | Number still enrolled after 10 years |
|---|---|---|---|---|---|---|---|---|---|
| 1996-1997 | | | | | | | | | |
| 1997-1998 | | | | | | | | | |
| 1998-1999 | | | | | | | | | |
| 1999-2000 | | | | | | | | | |
| 2000-2001 | | | | | | | | | |
| 2001-2002 | | | | | | | | | |
| 2002-2003 | | | | | | | | | |
| 2003-2004 | | | | | | | | | |
| 2004-2005 | | | | | | | | | |
| 2005-2006 | | | | | | | | | |

## Native Americans/Alaska Natives in the Arts and Humanities

**F21a. Please record the number of Native American/Alaska Natives who entered the Arts and Humanities programs included in this study between 1996 and 2005.**

|  | Number of entering doctoral students If none: enter zero | Number of students who left the program without a master's or doctoral degree | Number of students who left the program after receiving a master's degree | Number of students admitted to doctoral candidacy |
|---|---|---|---|---|
| 1996-1997 | | | | |
| 1997-1998 | | | | |
| 1998-1999 | | | | |
| 1999-2000 | | | | |
| 2000-2001 | | | | |
| 2001-2002 | | | | |
| 2002-2003 | | | | |
| 2003-2004 | | | | |
| 2004-2005 | | | | |

| 2005-2006 |  |  |  |  |
|---|---|---|---|---|

**F21b. Of the Native American/Alaskan Natives admitted to candidacy in the Arts and Humanities, record the number of students from each cohort listed below who completed degrees within the given number of years after enrolling.**

|  | 3 years or less | 4 years | 5 years | 6 years | 7 years | 8 years | 9 years | 10 years | Number still enrolled after 10 years |
|---|---|---|---|---|---|---|---|---|---|
| 1996-1997 |  |  |  |  |  |  |  |  |  |
| 1997-1998 |  |  |  |  |  |  |  |  |  |
| 1998-1999 |  |  |  |  |  |  |  |  |  |
| 1999-2000 |  |  |  |  |  |  |  |  |  |
| 2000-2001 |  |  |  |  |  |  |  |  |  |
| 2001-2002 |  |  |  |  |  |  |  |  |  |
| 2002-2003 |  |  |  |  |  |  |  |  |  |
| 2003-2004 |  |  |  |  |  |  |  |  |  |
| 2004-2005 |  |  |  |  |  |  |  |  |  |
| 2005-2006 |  |  |  |  |  |  |  |  |  |

## Non-Hispanic Blacks in the Arts and Humanities

**F22a. Please record the number of Non-Hispanic Blacks who entered the Arts and Humanities programs included in this study between 1996 and 2005.**

|  | Number of entering doctoral students If none: enter zero | Number of students who left the program without a master's or doctoral degree | Number of students who left the program after receiving a master's degree | Number of students admitted to doctoral candidacy |
|---|---|---|---|---|
| 1996-1997 |  |  |  |  |
| 1997-1998 |  |  |  |  |
| 1998-1999 |  |  |  |  |
| 1999-2000 |  |  |  |  |
| 2000-2001 |  |  |  |  |
| 2001-2002 |  |  |  |  |
| 2002-2003 |  |  |  |  |
| 2003-2004 |  |  |  |  |

| | | | | |
|---|---|---|---|---|
| **2004-2005** | | | | |
| **2005-2006** | | | | |

**F22b. Of the Non-Hispanic Blacks admitted to candidacy in the Arts and Humanities, record the number of students from each cohort listed below who completed degrees within the given number of years after enrolling.**

| | 3 years or less | 4 years | 5 years | 6 years | 7 years | 8 years | 9 years | 10 years | Number still enrolled after 10 years |
|---|---|---|---|---|---|---|---|---|---|
| **1996-1997** | | | | | | | | | |
| **1997-1998** | | | | | | | | | |
| **1998-1999** | | | | | | | | | |
| **1999-2000** | | | | | | | | | |
| **2000-2001** | | | | | | | | | |
| **2001-2002** | | | | | | | | | |
| **2002-2003** | | | | | | | | | |
| **2003-2004** | | | | | | | | | |
| **2004-2005** | | | | | | | | | |
| **2005-2006** | | | | | | | | | |

## Non-Hispanic Whites in the Arts and Humanities

**F23a. Please record the number of Non-Hispanic Whites who entered the Arts and Humanities programs included in this study between 1996 and 2005.**

| | Number of entering doctoral students If none: enter zero | Number of students who left the program without a master's or doctoral degree | Number of students who left the program after receiving a master's degree | Number of students admitted to doctoral candidacy |
|---|---|---|---|---|
| **1996-1997** | | | | |
| **1997-1998** | | | | |
| **1998-1999** | | | | |
| **1999-2000** | | | | |
| **2000-2001** | | | | |
| **2001-2002** | | | | |
| **2002-2003** | | | | |

| | | | | |
|---|---|---|---|---|
| **2003-2004** | | | | |
| **2004-2005** | | | | |
| **2005-2006** | | | | |

**F23b. Of the Non-Hispanic Whites admitted to candidacy in the Arts and Humanities, record the number of students from each cohort listed below who completed degrees within the given number of years after enrolling.**

| | 3 years or less | 4 years | 5 years | 6 years | 7 years | 8 years | 9 years | 10 years | Number still enrolled after 10 years |
|---|---|---|---|---|---|---|---|---|---|
| **1996-1997** | | | | | | | | | |
| **1997-1998** | | | | | | | | | |
| **1998-1999** | | | | | | | | | |
| **1999-2000** | | | | | | | | | |
| **2000-2001** | | | | | | | | | |
| **2001-2002** | | | | | | | | | |
| **2002-2003** | | | | | | | | | |
| **2003-2004** | | | | | | | | | |
| **2004-2005** | | | | | | | | | |
| **2005-2006** | | | | | | | | | |

## Hispanics in the Arts and Humanities

**F24a. Please record the number of Hispanics who entered the Arts and Humanities programs included in this study between 1996 and 2005.**

| | Number of entering doctoral students If none: enter zero | Number of students who left the program without a master's or doctoral degree | Number of students who left the program after receiving a master's degree | Number of students admitted to doctoral candidacy |
|---|---|---|---|---|
| **1996-1997** | | | | |
| **1997-1998** | | | | |
| **1998-1999** | | | | |
| **1999-2000** | | | | |
| **2000-2001** | | | | |
| **2001-2002** | | | | |

| 2002-2003 | | | | |
|---|---|---|---|---|
| 2003-2004 | | | | |
| 2004-2005 | | | | |
| 2005-2006 | | | | |

**F24b. Of the Hispanics admitted to candidacy in the Arts and Humanities, record the number of students from each cohort listed below who completed degrees within the given number of years after enrolling.**

| | 3 years or less | 4 years | 5 years | 6 years | 7 years | 8 years | 9 years | 10 years | Number still enrolled after 10 years |
|---|---|---|---|---|---|---|---|---|---|
| 1996-1997 | | | | | | | | | |
| 1997-1998 | | | | | | | | | |
| 1998-1999 | | | | | | | | | |
| 1999-2000 | | | | | | | | | |
| 2000-2001 | | | | | | | | | |
| 2001-2002 | | | | | | | | | |
| 2002-2003 | | | | | | | | | |
| 2003-2004 | | | | | | | | | |
| 2004-2005 | | | | | | | | | |
| 2005-2006 | | | | | | | | | |

## Asians and Pacific Islanders in the Arts and Humanities

**F25a. Please record the number of Asians and Pacific Islanders who entered the Arts and Humanities programs included in this study between 1996 and 2005.**

| | Number of entering doctoral students If none: enter zero | Number of students who left the program without a master's or doctoral degree | Number of students who left the program after receiving a master's degree | Number of students admitted to doctoral candidacy |
|---|---|---|---|---|
| 1996-1997 | | | | |
| 1997-1998 | | | | |
| 1998-1999 | | | | |
| 1999-2000 | | | | |
| 2000-2001 | | | | |
| 2001-2002 | | | | |
| 2002-2003 | | | | |
| 2003-2004 | | | | |
| 2004-2005 | | | | |
| 2005-2006 | | | | |

**F25b. Of the Asians and Pacific Islanders admitted to candidacy in the Arts and Humanities, record the number of students from each cohort listed below who completed degrees within the given number of years after enrolling.**

| | 3 years or less | 4 years | 5 years | 6 years | 7 years | 8 years | 9 years | 10 years | Number still enrolled after 10 years |
|---|---|---|---|---|---|---|---|---|---|
| 1996-1997 | | | | | | | | | |
| 1997-1998 | | | | | | | | | |
| 1998-1999 | | | | | | | | | |
| 1999-2000 | | | | | | | | | |
| 2000-2001 | | | | | | | | | |
| 2001-2002 | | | | | | | | | |
| 2002-2003 | | | | | | | | | |
| 2003-2004 | | | | | | | | | |
| 2004-2005 | | | | | | | | | |
| 2005-2006 | | | | | | | | | |

# National Research Council

# 2006 Assessment of Research Doctorate Programs

# Program Questionnaire

Every ten or so years, the National Research Council conducts a study of national importance regarding the quality and characteristics of doctoral programs in the United States. This comparative assessment is designed to assist prospective doctoral students with selecting programs that best fit their interests and to permit programs to benchmark themselves against similar programs.

The 2006 Assessment of Research Doctorate Programs collects data about the doctoral programs in over 60 areas of study in American universities.

The information from your responses to this questionnaire will be compiled by Mathematica Policy Research and provided to the National Research Council for their analyses. The National Research Council staff who analyze the data will sign non-disclosure confidentiality agreements to protect the identity of individuals participating in this survey. Any information, including race/ethnicity and gender, that is not currently available to the public, will be <u>treated as confidential</u> and only reported in aggregated form so that it cannot be used to discern the identity of any survey participant in any report or presentation concerning the survey or in the public use file that will be made available to the public at the conclusion of this study.

**Your institution has identified your program in:**


\_\_\_\_(Name of program that was identified by the institution)_____


as an area of doctoral study that corresponds to the following field in the NRC taxonomy:


\_\_\_\_(Name of field in the NRC taxonomy)_____



1)  **Your program was selected because it satisfies at least three of the following four criteria for a doctoral program:**

    1. Enrolls doctoral students
    2. Has a designated faculty
    3. Develops a curriculum for doctoral study
    4. Makes recommendations for the award of degrees.

    In addition, the program must have awarded 5 Ph.D.s during the period 2001/2 to 2005/6.

    a.      **I believe my program may be ineligible** ☐ *(go to IN1)*

2)  **The following other program(s) at your institution will also be part of the study in the field of\_(Name of field in the NRC taxonomy):**

    \_\_\_\_(Name of program that was identified by the institution)_____
    \_\_\_\_(Name of program that was identified by the institution)_____ etc.


3)  **If other doctoral degree-granting programs in this field exist at your institution (see above),**
    **data and faculty lists for those programs will be provided to the NRC separately.**
    *Consequently, please do not include faculty members in those programs here, unless they actively participate in your program.*

## Part A. Program Fields and Research Specialties

*In this section of the questionnaire, we collect information on the fields your program is associated with and the research specialties of your faculty.*

**\*A0. Please enter the website address (URL) for this program. (e.g. www.myuniversity.edu/my program)**

_____

**A1. Is this program interdisciplinary in nature, drawing significantly on knowledge and techniques in two or more fields?**

☐ *Yes*
☐ *No*

*If not an engineering field, skip to Part B*

**A2. Although students accepted into this program may specialize in areas within engineering, does this program confer. . .**

☐ *A general (or nonspecific) doctoral degree in engineering*
☐ *A doctorate in a specific engineering field such as mechanical engineering or biomedical engineering*

## Part B.     Program Faculty

*Some institutions may find submitting this information easier in a spreadsheet format. If you would prefer using the Excel spreadsheet available from Mathematica, click on "Will use spreadsheet" below. You will be skipped to the next section in the questionnaire. Please submit the spreadsheet to Mathematica at your earliest convenience.*

- *SPREADSHEETS WILL NOT BE ACCEPTED AFTER CLOSE OF BUSINESS DECEMBER 15, 2006.*

☐ *Will use spreadsheet*
☐ *Continue to the faculty section of the web survey*

*In this section, we ask you to provide  information about your faculty in three categories—core, new, and associated.*

**B1.  Core Faculty.  Please complete the table below with the names of faculty members who:**

1)  have served as a chair or member of a program dissertation committee in the past 5 academic years (2001-2002 through 2005-2006), OR
2)  are serving as a member of the graduate admissions or curriculum committee

The faculty member must be currently (2006-2007) and formally designated as faculty in the program, and not be an outside reader who reads the dissertation but does not contribute substantially to its development. Include emeritus faculty only if the faculty member has, within the past three years, either chaired a dissertation committee or been the primary instructor for a regular PhD course.

| Information Collected | Answer Options |
|---|---|
| Name:<br>*First :<br>Middle Initial:<br>*Last : | |
| Fields of Specialization:<br>Primary :<br>Secondary: | |
| Faculty Rank: | Professor<br>Associate Professor<br>Assistant Professor<br>Emeritus<br>Other, specify |
| Tenure status: | Tenured<br>Nontenured, tenure-track<br>Nontenured, non tenure-track |
| Highest degree: | Doctorate (e.g. PhD DSc EdD etc.)<br>Other professional degree (e.g. JD LLB MD DDS DVM etc.)<br>Master's degree (e.g. MS MA MBA)<br>Other (specify) |
| Number of Dissertation Committees:<br>*Chaired in this Program in the last five years (acted on as primary dissertation advisor)<br>*Served on in this Program in the Last Five Years (include Committees Served on as a member or chair) | |

| Gender: | Male |
|---|---|
| | Female |
| Citizenship: | U.S. Citizen |
| | Permanent Resident |
| | Temporary Visa Holder |
| | Unknown |
| Race/Ethnicity: | White, Non-Hispanic |
| | Black, Non-Hispanic |
| | Hispanic |
| | Asian or Pacific Islander |
| | American Indian or Alaska Native |
| | Race/Ethnicity Unknown |
| University Address:<br>*Line 1:<br>Line 2:<br>*City<br>*State<br>*Zip Code | |
| *Telephone | |
| *Email | |

*=Required fields

**B2.    New Faculty. Please complete the table below with the names of faculty members not listed as core in the previous questions who:**

1) do not meet the criteria for core faculty, but who have been hired in tenured or tenure-track positions within the past three academic years  (2003-2004 through 2005-2006) AND

2) are currently employed at your university and are expected to become involved in doctoral education in your program.

| Information Collected | Answer Options |
|---|---|
| Name:<br>*First :<br>Middle Initial:<br>*Last : | |
| Fields of Specialization:<br>Primary :<br>Secondary: | |
| Faculty Rank: | Professor<br>Associate Professor<br>Assistant Professor<br>Emeritus<br>Other, specify |
| Tenure status: | Tenured<br>Nontenured, tenure-track<br>Nontenured, non tenure-track |
| Highest degree: | Doctorate (e.g. PhD DSc EdD etc.)<br>Other professional degree (e.g. JD LLB MD DDS DVM etc.)<br>Master's degree (e.g. MS MA MBA)<br>Other (specify) |
| Gender: | Male<br>Female |
| Citizenship: | U.S. Citizen<br>Permanent Resident<br>Temporary Visa Holder<br>Unknown |
| Race/Ethnicity: | White, Non-Hispanic<br>Black, Non-Hispanic<br>Hispanic<br>Asian or Pacific Islander<br>American Indian or Alaska Native<br>Race/Ethnicity Unknown |

| University Address: | |
|---|---|
| *Line 1:<br>Line 2:<br>*City<br>*State<br>*Zip Code | |
| *Telephone | |
| *Email | |

*=Required fields

**B3.**     <u>**Associated Faculty.**</u>  **Please complete the table below with the names of faculty members who:**

1) have chaired or served on program dissertation committees in the past five years (2001 2002 through 2005-2006), AND

2) have a current (2006-2007) appointment at your institution, but who are not designated faculty in the program.

They should not be outside readers, or faculty currently employed at other universities, unless they are on leave from the faculty at your institution.  Include emeritus faculty only if the faculty member has, within the past three years, either chaired a dissertation committee or been the primary instructor for a regular PhD course.

| Information Collected | Answer Options |
|---|---|
| Name:<br>*First :<br>Middle Initial:<br>*Last : | |
| Fields of Specialization:<br>Primary :<br>Secondary: | |
| Faculty Rank: | Professor<br>Associate Professor<br>Assistant Professor<br>Emeritus<br>Other, specify |
| Tenure status: | Tenured<br>Nontenured, tenure-track<br>Nontenured, non tenure-track |
| Highest degree: | Doctorate (e.g. PhD DSc EdD etc.)<br>Other professional degree (e.g. JD LLB MD DDS DVM etc.)<br>Master's degree (e.g. MS MA MBA)<br>Other (specify) |
| Number of Dissertation Committees:<br>*Chaired in this Program in the last five years (acted on as primary dissertation advisor)<br>*Served on in this Program in the Last Five Years (include Committees Served on as a member or chair) | |
| Gender: | Male<br>Female |
| Citizenship: | U.S. Citizen |

| | |
|---|---|
| | Permanent Resident<br>Temporary Visa Holder<br>Unknown |
| Race/Ethnicity: | White, Non-Hispanic<br>Black, Non-Hispanic<br>Hispanic<br>Asian or Pacific Islander<br>American Indian or Alaska Native<br>Race/Ethnicity Unknown |

*=Required fields

**B5.** The next question(s) collect aggregate information on faculty diversity. The total number of core and new faculty for this program was provided by this institution.

How many of the approximately *[number of faculty from spreadsheet]* **core and new faculty members in this program are . . .**

*If none, enter as 0*

☐ Male
☐ Female

**B6.** The next question(s) collect aggregate information on faculty diversity. The total number of core and new faculty for this program was provided by this institution.

How many of the approximately *[number of faculty from spreadsheet]* **core and new faculty members in this program are . . . .**

*If none, enter zero*

U.S. Citizens:
Permanent Residents:
Temporary Visa Holders:
Citizenship Unknown:

**\*B7.** The next question(s) collect aggregate information on faculty diversity. The total number of core and new faculty for this program was provided by this institution.

**Of the core and new faculty members in the program who are <u>U.S. citizens or permanent residents,</u> how many are:**

*If none, enter zero*

White, Non-Hispanic:           ☐
Black, Non-Hispanic:           ☐
Hispanic:                      ☐
Asian or Pacific Islander:     ☐
American Indian or Alaska Native: ☐
Race/Ethnicity Unknown:        ☐

*[Program will check to make sure the total of responses to this question equals the numbers entered for U.S. citizens and permanent residents in B6.]*

**B8. Is the dissertation committee chair typically the primary advisor of doctoral students in your program?**

☐ Yes
☐ No

**Part C. Doctoral Program: Enrollment and Degree Completion**

*In this section, we ask for information about your program's doctoral students and degree recipients, including demographic information, enrollments, and degrees awarded.*

**\*C1. For each academic year listed below, please indicate the number of doctoral degrees awarded in your program that year.**

Number of Doctoral
Degrees Awarded
If none: enter zero

| | |
|---|---|
| 2001-2002 | ☐☐☐ |
| 2002-2003 | ☐☐☐ |
| 2003-2004 | ☐☐☐ |
| 2004-2005 | ☐☐☐ |
| 2005-2006 | ☐☐☐ |

**\*C2. Of the doctoral graduates who received doctoral degrees in the period 2003-2004 through 2005-2006, what was the <u>median time to degree?</u>**

- The median is the mid-point measured from the date of first enrollment in the program to date of graduation—50 percent took a shorter time to complete their degrees and 50 percent took longer
- When entering a number that includes a decimal, please type the decimal
- If this program enrolls MD/PhD students and the time to degree for these students can be calculated separately, do NOT include these students below. You will be asked about the MD/PhD students later.

**Median Number
of Years**

a. All full-time and part-time doctoral students     |__| . |__|

b. Doctoral students who were full-time during
their entire time in the program     |__| . |__|

**C3. For each academic year listed below, please indicate:**

**1)  The number of doctoral students to whom your program <u>offered admission</u> AND**
**2) The number of doctoral students who then <u>enrolled</u> for the first time.**

| | **Number Offered Admission** *If none:  enter zero* | **Number First-Time Enrolled** *If none:  enter zero* |
|---|---|---|
| 2001-2002 | ☐☐☐ | ☐☐☐ |
| 2002-2003 | ☐☐☐ | ☐☐☐ |
| 2003-2004 | ☐☐☐ | ☐☐☐ |
| 2004-2005 | ☐☐☐ | ☐☐☐ |
| 2005-2006 | ☐☐☐ | ☐☐☐ |

*[The program will check that for each row, the number entered in col 1 must be larger that the number entered in col 2.]*

**C4.  What is your program's policy regarding whether a master's degree in the field is required prior to admission to this program:**

      *Mark one only*
      ☐ It is required prior to admission

      ☐ It is expected that students will earn it as a stage in their doctoral program
      ☐ Neither of the above

**C5.  Of the** *[program automatically calculates number from response to question C3]* **students who enrolled for the first-time in 2003-2004, 2004-2005, and 2005-2006, what number had a master's degree <u>in the field of your program</u> prior to enrollment?**

      *If not known: check this box:* ☐ *and continue*

                          *If none:  enter zero*
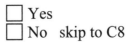

*[The program will check that the number entered must be equal to or smaller than the total number of students in col 2 for years 2003-2006 in C3.]*

**C6.  Does your doctoral program have a continuous enrollment policy?**
    *Continuous Enrollment* means that a person is considered to be a doctoral student only if he or she is enrolled and pays tuition or a fee.  Under this policy, a student who drops out must apply for reinstatement.

      ☐ Yes
      ☐ No   skip to C8

**C7.  To whom does this policy apply?**

*Mark one only*

☐ All Students
☐ Students Admitted to Candidacy
☐ Other (Specify _____ )

**C8.  How many doctoral students, whether or not they were yet admitted to candidacy, were enrolled in your program during fall of 2005?**

Number of Doctoral
Students Enrolled Fall 2005:   ☐☐☐

**C9.  Of the** *[program automatically enters the number from C8]* **doctoral students enrolled in your program during the fall of 2005, how many were …**

*If none:  enter zero*

Male:   ☐☐☐
Female:   ☐☐☐

*[Program will check to make sure the total of responses to this question equal the numbers entered for total in C8.]*

**a.  Of the** *[program automatically enters the number from C8]* **doctoral students enrolled in your program during the fall of 2005, how many were enrolled. . .**

*If none:  enter zero*

Full-Time:   ☐☐☐
Part-time:   ☐☐☐

*[Program will check to make sure the total of responses to this question equal the numbers entered for total in C8]*

**b.  Of the** *[program automatically enters the number from C8]* **doctoral students enrolled in your program during the fall of 2005, how many were …**

*If none:  enter zero*

U.S. Citizens:   ☐☐☐
Permanent Residents:   ☐☐☐
Temporary Visa Holders:   ☐☐☐
Citizenship Unknown:   ☐☐☐

*[Program will check to make sure the total of responses to this question equal the numbers entered for total in C8.]*

**\*c. Of the** *[program enters the number of US citizens and permanent residents from C9b]* **doctoral students who were <u>U.S. citizens or permanent residents</u>, how many were...**

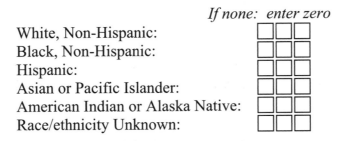

*If none:  enter zero*

White, Non-Hispanic:

Black, Non-Hispanic:

Hispanic:

Asian or Pacific Islander:

American Indian or Alaska Native:

Race/ethnicity Unknown:

*[Program will check to make sure the total of responses to this question equal the numbers entered for U.S. citizens and permanent residents in C9b.]*

**C10. Does this program enroll dual professional degree/PhD students?**
Dual professional degree/PhD students include students such as MD/PhD, DVM/PhD or ThD/PhD students.

☐ Yes
☐ No

If no, skip to C12

**a. How many dual professional degree /PhD students were enrolled in this program in Fall 2005?**
**Dual professional degree/PhD students include students such as MD/PhD, DVM/PhD or ThD/PhD students.**

*If none:  enter zero*

Number of **dual professional degree**/PhD Students            |_____|

**b. Does this program include <u>only</u> dual professional degree /PhD students?**

*Dual professional degree/PhD students include students such as MD/PhD, DVM/PhD or ThD/PhD students.*

☐ Yes *(skip to C12)*
☐ No *(go to C10c)*

c. **How will you be reporting the progress of the dual professional degree /PhD students enrolled in this program?**

*Dual professional degree/PhD students include students such as MD/PhD, DVM/PhD or ThD/PhD students.*

   Can report separately on the dual professional degree/PhD students

       Cannot report separately on the dual professional degree/PhD students *(skip to C12)*

**\*C11. What was the median time to degree for students enrolled in the dual professional degree/PhD segment of this program who graduated in the period 2003-2004 through 2005-2006?**

*Dual professional degree/PhD students include students such as MD/PhD, DVM/PhD or ThD/PhD students.*
*The median is the mid-point measured from the date of first enrollment in the program to date of graduation—50 percent took a shorter time to complete their degrees and 50 percent took longer*
*When entering a number that includes a decimal, please type the decimal.*

|  | **Median Number of Years** |
|---|---|
| All full-time and part-time dual professional degree/PhD graduates | \|__\| . \|__\| |
| dual professional degree/PhD graduates who were full-time during their entire time in the program | \|__\| . \|__\| |

**C12. Please describe how your program defines a full-time doctoral student:**

_____

_____

_____

**C13. Does your program have formal requirements for being admitted to candidacy?**

       Yes

       No   skip to C15

**C14. Please indicate the criteria your program uses to admit students to candidacy.**

*Mark all that apply*

☐ Successful Completion of Required Coursework
☐ Successful Completion of Written Examination(s)
☐ Successful Completion of Oral Examination(s)
☐ Award of the Master's Degree
☐ Defense of a Dissertation Prospectus
☐ Other Specify:_____

**C15.  During the 10 years between 1996 and 2005, did your program distinguish between students seeking a master's and those seeking a doctorate?**

*Mark one only*

☐ Yes, distinguished between seeking a master's and seeking a
   doctorate during that entire time period   →     skip to C16

☐ Began that period making the distinction but later changed

☐  Began that period making no distinction but later changed

☐ No, made no such distinction during that entire period   →     skip to C16

**C15a.  In what year did the policy change?**

Year:☐☐☐☐

**C16.    The next series of questions collects information on how many of the full-time students in your program complete doctoral study by gender.**

[*FILL if C10c = "can report separately*
**Since you will be reporting them separately, please do NOT include the program's dual professional degree/PhD students in the numbers reported for questions C16a through C17b**
[*FILL if C10c = "cannot report separately"*
**Please include the program's dual professional degree/PhD students in the numbers reported for questions C16a through C17b**
   • To preserve confidentiality, if the numbers in cells equal less than 5, the NRC will aggregate over cohorts so that the size of any reported cell is always greater than or equal to 5
   • Include doctoral students enrolled in your doctoral program, whether or not they have been admitted to candidacy

- Do not include students who only enroll with the intent of earning a master's degree and did not convert to doctoral students.
- Doctoral students who "left the program" are those who are no longer enrolled at this time.
- Doctoral students who "stopped out" (left but later enrolled again) should not be counted as students who left if they are currently enrolled or completed the doctoral degree
- Admitted to Candidacy may be defined in different ways. If your program defines and grants candidacy for a doctoral degree, please use the definition of admitted to candidacy your program uses. If it does not, please leave column 4 (Number of students admitted to doctoral candidacy) blank.
- Since you will be reporting them separately, please do NOT include the program's dual professional degree/PhD students in the numbers reported for questions C16a through C17b.

**\*C16a.          Please complete the table for the male students in your program**

|  | Number of entering doctoral students If none: enter zero | Number of students who left the program without a master's or doctoral degree | Number of students who left the program after receiving a master's degree | Number of students admitted to doctoral candidacy |
|---|---|---|---|---|
| 1996-1997 |  |  |  |  |
| 1997-1998 |  |  |  |  |
| 1998-1999 |  |  |  |  |
| 1999-2000 |  |  |  |  |
| 2000-2001 |  |  |  |  |
| 2001-2002 |  |  |  |  |
| 2002-2003 |  |  |  |  |
| 2003-2004 |  |  |  |  |
| 2004-2005 |  |  |  |  |
| 2005-2006 |  |  |  |  |

**\*C16b.  Of the male students admitted to candidacy in your program, record the number who within the various time spans listed below completed <u>doctoral</u> degrees <u>within</u> the given number of years after enrolling.**

|  | 3 years or less | 4 years | 5 years | 6 years | 7 years | 8 years | 9 years | 10 years |
|---|---|---|---|---|---|---|---|---|
| 1996-1997 |  |  |  |  |  |  |  |  |
| 1997-1998 |  |  |  |  |  |  |  |  |
| 1998-1999 |  |  |  |  |  |  |  |  |

| | | | | | | | |
|---|---|---|---|---|---|---|---|
| 1999-2000 | | | | | | | |
| 2000-2001 | | | | | | | |
| 2001-2002 | | | | | | | |
| 2002-2003 | | | | | | | |
| 2003-2004 | | | | | | | |
| 2004-2005 | | | | | | | |
| 2005-2006 | | | | | | | |

**\*C17a.      Please complete the table for the female students in your program**

| | Number of entering doctoral students If none: enter zero | Number of students who left the program without a master's or doctoral degree | Number of students who left the program after receiving a master's degree | Number of students admitted to doctoral candidacy |
|---|---|---|---|---|
| 1996-1997 | | | | |
| 1997-1998 | | | | |
| 1998-1999 | | | | |
| 1999-2000 | | | | |
| 2000-2001 | | | | |
| 2001-2002 | | | | |
| 2002-2003 | | | | |
| 2003-2004 | | | | |
| 2004-2005 | | | | |
| 2005-2006 | | | | |

**\*C17b.** **Of the female students admitted to candidacy in your program, record the number who within the various time spans listed below completed <u>doctoral</u> degrees <u>within</u> the given number of years after enrolling.**

|  | 3 years or less | 4 years | 5 years | 6 years | 7 years | 8 years | 9 years | 10 years |
|---|---|---|---|---|---|---|---|---|
| 1996-1997 | | | | | | | | |
| 1997-1998 | | | | | | | | |
| 1998-1999 | | | | | | | | |
| 1999-2000 | | | | | | | | |
| 2000-2001 | | | | | | | | |
| 2001-2002 | | | | | | | | |
| 2002-2003 | | | | | | | | |
| 2003-2004 | | | | | | | | |
| 2004-2005 | | | | | | | | |
| 2005-2006 | | | | | | | | |

*Ask C18a and C18b if C10c = can report separately*

**C18a.** **Please complete the table for the dual professional degree/PhD students in this program.**

*Dual professional degree/PhD students include students such as MD/PhD, DVM/PhD or ThD/PhD students.*

|  | Number of entering doctoral students If none: enter zero | Number of students who left the program without a master's or doctoral degree | Number of students who left the program after receiving a master's degree | Number of students admitted to doctoral candidacy |
|---|---|---|---|---|
| 1996-1997 | | | | |
| 1997-1998 | | | | |
| 1998-1999 | | | | |
| 1999-2000 | | | | |
| 2000-2001 | | | | |
| 2001-2002 | | | | |
| 2002-2003 | | | | |

| | | | | |
|---|---|---|---|---|
| 2003-2004 | | | | |
| 2004-2005 | | | | |
| 2005-2006 | | | | |

**\*C18b. Of the dual professional degree/PhD students admitted to candidacy in your program, record the number who within the various time spans listed below completed doctoral degrees within the given number of years after enrolling.**

*Dual professional degree/PhD students include students such as MD/PhD, DVM/PhD or ThD/PhD students.*

| | 3 years or less | 4 years | 5 years | 6 years | 7 years | 8 years | 9 years | 10 years | Delete col |
|---|---|---|---|---|---|---|---|---|---|
| 1996-1997 | | | | | | | | | |
| 1997-1998 | | | | | | | | | |
| 1998-1999 | | | | | | | | | |
| 1999-2000 | | | | | | | | | |
| 2000-2001 | | | | | | | | | |
| 2001-2002 | | | | | | | | | |
| 2002-2003 | | | | | | | | | |
| 2003-2004 | | | | | | | | | |
| 2004-2005 | | | | | | | | | |
| 2005-2006 | | | | | | | | | |

**C19.   In order to analyze program interdisciplinarity through a review of dissertation key words, please enter the full names of every student who was awarded a doctoral degree in this program over the past three years (2003-04 through 2005-06) and the academic year in which that degree was awarded.**

*Enter each student's name and the academic year on each line*

| **First Name** | **Middle** | **Last Name** | **Academic Year** |
|---|---|---|---|
| _____ | _____ | _____ | _____ |
| _____ | _____ | _____ | _____ |
| _____ | _____ | _____ | _____ |

[allow 300]

## Part D. Doctoral Program: Characteristics

*In this section, we ask for information about the characteristics of your doctoral program.*

**D1. Did you require GREs from all students entering this doctoral program in 2005-2006?**

    *Mark one only*

      ☐ Yes, required for all     (*skip to D4)*
      ☐ No, only required for some
      ☐ No, not required for any     (*skip to  D5)*

**D2. Which of the following criteria are used to exempt students from the GRE requirement?**

    *Mark all that apply*

      ☐ Professional experience
      ☐ Master's degree
      ☐ Undergraduate degree from same institution
      ☐ Graduate degree from same institution
      ☐ High undergraduate GPA
      ☐ Publications or research experience
      ☐ Not required for international students
      ☐ Other exam (e.g., LSAT, GMAT)   (Specify, _____ )

**D3. When applying for admission, do more than 50 percent of the entering students in your program provide GRE scores?**

    ☐ Yes
    ☐ No   *skip toD5*

**D4. Among the doctoral students enrolling for the first time in the program, please enter, for each academic year:**

1)      **The number who reported their scores**
2)      **Their median Verbal GRE**
3)      **Their median Quantitative GRE scores**

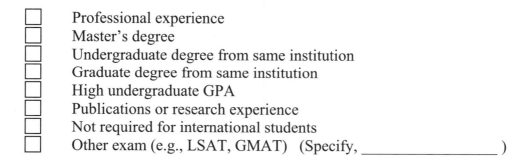

|  | **2003-04** | **2004-05** | **2005-06** |
|---|---|---|---|
| 1) Number of GRE test takers |  |  |  |
| 2) Median score, Verbal GRE |  |  |  |
| 3) Median score, Quantitative GRE |  |  |  |

*[Program will check D4(1)to make sure the numbers are less than or equal to the numbers in C3, col b]*

**D5.** **Does your program require all (or most) doctoral students to serve as teaching assistants (TAs), as part of their doctoral experience?**

☐ Yes
☐ No   skip to question D7

**D6.** **For how many terms are they required to TA?**

*If none:  enter zero*
Number of Terms Required:   ☐☐

**D7.** **Among doctoral students who teach in return for their stipend or salary...**

a. **In the fall of 2005, how many doctoral students in this program were assigned to <u>assist faculty</u> by teaching lab or recitation sections?**

*If none:  enter zero*
Number of Students: ☐☐☐

b. **On average, <u>how many course sections</u> do doctoral students who assist faculty by teaching lab or recitation sections teach in a given term?**

*If none:  enter zero*
Number of Course Sections: ☐

c. **In the fall of 2005, how many doctoral students were appointed with <u>sole responsibility</u> for instruction of one or more courses or course sections?**

*If none:  enter zero*
Number of Students
With Sole Responsibility:   ☐☐☐

d. **On average, <u>how many course sections</u> do those doctoral students with sole responsibility for instruction teach?**

*If none:  enter zero*
Number of Course Sections: ☐

e. **On average, how many students are enrolled in classes taught by doctoral students with sole responsibility for their instruction?**

*If none: enter zero*

Number of students enrolled: ☐☐☐

**D8. Please indicate whether your institution and/or your program provides the following kinds of support for doctoral students or doctoral education.**

| | Institutional Support Only | Program Support Only | Both Institutional and Program Support | Neither Institutional nor Program Support |
|---|---|---|---|---|
| Orientation for new graduate students | ☐ | ☐ | ☐ | ☐ |
| International student orientation | ☐ | ☐ | ☐ | ☐ |
| Language screening/support prior to teaching | ☐ | ☐ | ☐ | ☐ |
| Instruction in writing (outside of program requirements) | ☐ | ☐ | ☐ | ☐ |
| Instruction in statistics (outside of program requirements) | ☐ | ☐ | ☐ | ☐ |
| Prizes/awards to doctoral students for teaching and/or research | ☐ | ☐ | ☐ | ☐ |
| Assistance/training in proposal preparation | ☐ | ☐ | ☐ | ☐ |
| On-campus, graduate student research conferences | ☐ | ☐ | ☐ | ☐ |
| Formal training in academic integrity/ethics | ☐ | ☐ | ☐ | ☐ |
| Active graduate student association | ☐ | ☐ | ☐ | ☐ |
| Staff assigned to the graduate student association | ☐ | ☐ | ☐ | ☐ |
| Financial support for the graduate student association | ☐ | ☐ | ☐ | ☐ |
| Posted academic grievance procedure | ☐ | ☐ | ☐ | ☐ |
| Dispute resolution procedure | ☐ | ☐ | ☐ | ☐ |
| Regular graduate program directors/coordinators meetings | ☐ | ☐ | ☐ | ☐ |
| Annual review of all enrolled doctoral students | ☐ | ☐ | ☐ | ☐ |
| Organized training to help students improve teaching skills | ☐ | ☐ | ☐ | ☐ |
| Travel support to attend professional meetings | ☐ | ☐ | ☐ | ☐ |

**D9.  Does your program confer awards to honor faculty for mentoring or other activities that promote scholarship of doctoral students?**

 Yes
☐ No

**D10. Does your program collect data about employment outcomes for all of your doctoral graduates?**

☐ Yes
☐ No   skip to question D12

**D11. Do you provide potential applicants with this information?**

 Yes
☐ No

**D12. Approximately what percentage of the doctoral students in your program have a workspace for their <u>exclusive use</u>? (For example: a carrel in the library, a desk in an office or other place where they can keep books, papers and materials)**

*If none:  enter zero*
Percentage with exclusive work space:  ☐☐☐%

**D13. Please list the interdisciplinary centers, programs, or clinics in which the greatest number of doctoral students from your program participate (conduct research, teach, or gain clinical experience).  Please list no more then 10.**

*If none: check this box:*        ☐    *and continue*

NAMES OF INTERDISCIPLINARY CENTERS, PROGRAMS, OR CLINICS:

_____

_____

_____

_____

[allow 10]

**D14. What other programs does your program collaborate with for organized training activities (e.g. training grants, certificate programs, joint degree programs)?**

     *If none: check this box:* ☐ *and continue*

     NAMES OF OTHER PROGRAMS

_____

_____

_____

[allow 10]

**Part E. Doctoral Program: Financial Support for Full -Time Students**

*In this section, we ask for information about the financial support your program provides to its full-time doctoral students.*

**E1.** **For the 2005-2006 academic year, what did your institution charge full-time first-year doctoral students in your program for tuition, mandatory fees, and health insurance premiums?**

- *Enter dollar amounts without commas or dollar signs ($).*
- *Public Institutions: Please answer separately for in-state and out-of-state students*

| | Public Institutions | | Private Institutions |
|---|---|---|---|
| | In-state students | Out-of-state students | |
| Tuition and fees for full-time enrollment: | $_____ | $_____ | $_____ |
| Health Insurance premiums: | $_____ | $_____ | $_____ |

**E2.** **For the 2005-2006 academic year, not including summer 2006, what was the <u>modal amount of total financial support</u> your program provided to funded full-time first-year doctoral students?**

- *Financial support is funding provided by your institution or program or by an external funding agency or organization. It does not include personal, spousal, or family support, wages from work unrelated to the program, or loans*

- *Enter dollar amounts without commas or dollar signs ($).*

- *Public Institutions:  Please answer separately for in-state and out-of-state students.*

|  | **Public Institutions** | | **Private Institutions** |
|---|---|---|---|
|  | In-state students | Out-of-state students |  |
| **Modal Amount Of Total Support** | $_____ | $_____ | $_____ |

**E3.** **For the 2005-2006 academic year, not including summer 2006, what was the <u>modal amount of financial support</u> your program provided to funded full-time first-year doctoral students in these three categories?**

- *Enter dollar amounts without commas or dollar signs ($).*
- *Public Institutions:  Please answer separately for in-state and out-of-state students*

|  | **Public Institutions** | | **Private Institutions** |
|---|---|---|---|
|  | In-state students | Out-of-state students |  |
| Tuition and fees for full-time enrollment: | $_____ | $_____ | $_____ |
| Health Insurance premiums: | $_____ | $_____ | $_____ |
| Academic year support (stipend/salary) | $_____ | $_____ | $_____ |

**E4. What was the modal amount of summer 2006 support your program provided to funded full-time first-year doctoral students?**

    If none:  check this box ☐ and continue

- *Enter dollar amounts without commas or dollar signs ($).*
- *Public Institutions:  Please answer separately for in-state and out-of-state students.*

|  | **Public Institutions** | **Private Institutions** |
|---|---|---|

|  | In-state students | Out-of-state students |  |
|---|---|---|---|
| Summer support: | $_____ | $_____ | $_____ |

**E5.** **How many of the <u>full-time first-year</u> doctoral students (FFDs) who entered your program in the 2005-06 academic year had…..**

**Number of Students**
*If none: enter zero*

| | |
|---|---|
| Full financial support: | ☐☐☐ |
| Partial financial support: | ☐☐☐ |
| No financial support: | ☐☐☐ |
| **Total number of FFD doctoral students:** | ☐☐☐ |

*[Program will check that the first three numbers add to the last number]*

**E6.** **Does a majority of the full-time doctoral students in your program receive a typical pattern of financial support over their first five years?**

☐ Yes
☐ No  *skip to E8*

**E7** **Please indicate your program's typical five-year pattern of financial support by recording, for each funding mechanism listed, how many years of support a student would  typically receive during his or her first five years of enrollment.**

- *For the types of support that are not applicable, enter 0*
- *When entering a number that includes a decimal, please type in the decimal.*

**Typical Five-Year Pattern**

| | |
|---|---|
| Number of fellowship support years: | ☐.☐ |
| Number of traineeship support years: | ☐.☐ |
| Number of teaching assistantship years: | ☐.☐ |
| Number of research assistantship years: | ☐.☐ |
| Number of other assistantship years: | ☐.☐ |
| Number of years without support: | ☐.☐ |

**E8.** **Including all of the** *[program automatically enters the number from C9a (full-time)]* **Fall term 2005 <u>full-time</u> doctoral students, record the number who received the various types of support indicated below:**

- *Financial support is funding provided by your institution or program or by an external funding agency or organization. It does not include personal, spouse, or family support, wages from work unrelated to the program, or loans*

| | Fall Term 2005 Doctoral Students by Year in Program | | | | | | |
|---|---|---|---|---|---|---|---|
| | Yr 1 | Yr 2 | Yr 3 | Yr 4 | Yr 5 | Yr 6 | >6 Yr |
| Full support | | | | | | | |
|    a) Externally funded fellowships only | | | | | | | |
|    b) Externally funded traineeships only | | | | | | | |
|    c) Institutional fellowships only | | | | | | | |
|    d) Teaching assistantships only | | | | | | | |
|    e) Research assistantships only | | | | | | | |
|    f) Administration (other) assistantship only | | | | | | | |
|    g) Combination of externally funded fellowship or traineeship (a or b) with internal support (c, d, e, and/or f) | | | | | | | |
|    h) Combination of internal fellowship(s) with internal assistantships (d, e, and/or f) | | | | | | | |
|    i) Combination of internal assistantships (d, e, and/or f) | | | | | | | |
|    j) Other _____ | | | | | | | |
| Funded with less than full support | | | | | | | |
| Unfunded | | | | | | | |
| **TOTAL NUMBER OF STUDENTS** | | | | | | | |

**E9.** During the 2005-2006 academic year, did your program use externally-funded <u>training grants</u> to support doctoral students?

      ☐ Yes
      ☐ No

## Part F. Postdoctoral Scholars

*In this section, we ask for information about the postdoctoral scholars (postdocs) associated with your program*

*Please use this **definition of a postdoctoral scholar** developed by the Association of American Universities:*

- *The appointee was recently awarded a Ph.D. or equivalent doctorate (e.g., Sc.D., M.D.) in an appropriate field; and*
- *the appointment is temporary; and*
- *the appointment involves substantially full-time research or scholarship; and*
- *the appointment is viewed as preparatory for a full-time academic and/or research career; and*

- *the appointment is not part of a clinical training program; and*
- *the appointee works under the supervision of a senior scholar or a department in a university or similar research institution (e.g., national laboratory, NIH, etc.); and*
- *the appointee has the freedom, and is expected, to publish the results of his or her research or scholarship during the period of the appointment.*

(See: *http://www.aau.edu/reports/PostDocRpt.html.* Accessed 6/27/06)

**F1. During the 2005 Fall term, were any postdoctoral scholars, including those who are university employees or those on external or portable fellowships, working with core or new faculty in your program?**

☐ Yes
☐ No  *skip to exit screen*

**F2. During the 2005 Fall term, how many postdoctoral scholars, including those who are university employees or those on external or portable fellowships, were working with core or new faculty in your program?**

Number of Postdocs: ☐☐☐

**a. Of the** [program enters the number from F2] **postdoctoral scholars, how many were ...**

Male: ☐☐☐
Female: ☐☐☐

*[Should total to the number in F2]*

**b. Of the** *[program enters the number from F2]* **postdoctoral scholars, how many were ...**

If none: enter zero

U.S. Citizens: ☐☐☐
Permanent Residents: ☐☐☐
Temporary Visa Holders: ☐☐☐
Citizenship Unknown: ☐☐☐
*[Should total to the number in F2]*

**c. Of the** *[program enters the number of US citizens and permanent residents from F2b]* **postdoctoral students who were U.S. citizens or permanent residents, how many were...**

*If none: enter zero*

White, Non-Hispanic: ☐☐☐
Black, Non-Hispanic: ☐☐☐
Hispanic: ☐☐☐

Asian or Pacific Islander:            ☐☐☐
American Indian or Alaska Native:     ☐☐☐
Race/ethnicity Unknown:               ☐☐☐

*[Program will check to make sure the total of responses to this question equal the numbers entered for U.S. citizens and permanent residents in F2b]*

**F3.** Among the *[program enters the number from F2]* postdoctoral scholars associated with this program, which <u>four countries of origin</u> provide the largest percentage of postdoctoral scholars on temporary visas to the program and what percentage of all postdoctoral scholars in the program do citizens of these countries comprise?

**Country of Origin**        **Percentage of All Postdoctoral Scholars in the Program**

_____  ☐☐%
_____  ☐☐%
_____  ☐☐%
_____  ☐☐%

**F4.** Of the *[program enters the number from F2]* postdoctoral scholars associated with this program, how many had <u>portable fellowships</u> (i.e., fellowships awarded directly to postdoctoral scholars rather than through institutions and which can be used at an institution of the individual's choosing)?

*If none: enter zero*

*Please fill in number:* ☐☐☐

## Part IN: Possible Ineligible Program

**IN1.** Is this program ineligible because it:

> *Mark All That Apply*
> ☐ a. Does NOT enroll doctoral students?
> ☐ b. Does NOT have designated faculty?
> ☐ c. Has NO developed curriculum for doctoral study?
> ☐ d. Makes NO recommendations for the award of degrees?
> ☐ e. Awarded fewer than 5 Ph.D.s between 2001/2 to 2005/6?

*[If "e" is marked, go to exit screen.]*
*[If "e" is not marked and there is only one item marked in a-d, go to 2.]*

**IN2.** According to the eligibility criteria for the 2006 NRC Assessment, your program is eligible and you may continue.

*[Return to eligibility page of questionnaire.]*

**National Research Council**

**Assessment of Research Doctorate Programs**

**2006**

**Program Questionnaire for Emerging Fields**

Every ten or so years, the National Research Council conducts a study of national importance regarding the quality and characteristics of doctoral programs in the United States.  This comparative assessment is designed to assist prospective doctoral students with selecting programs that best fit their interests and to permit programs to benchmark themselves against similar programs.

The 2006 Assessment of Research Doctorate Programs collects data about the doctoral programs in over 60 areas of study in American universities.

Your institution has identified your program in:

_____(Name of program that was identified by the institution)_____

as an area of doctoral study that corresponds to the following emerging field in the NRC

taxonomy:

_____(Name of field in the NRC taxonomy)_____

**Your program was selected because it satisfies at least three of the following four criteria for a doctoral program:**

1. Enrolls doctoral students
2. Has a designated faculty
3. Develops a curriculum for doctoral study
4. Makes recommendations for the award of degrees.

In addition, the program must have awarded 5 Ph.D.s during the period 2001/2 to 2005/6.

**If more than one doctoral degree granting program in this field exists at your institution:** data and faculty lists for those programs will be provided to the NRC <u>separately</u>.

The following other program(s) at your institution will also be part of the study in the field of_(Name of field in the NRC taxonomy):

____(Name of program that was identified by the institution)_____
____(Name of program that was identified by the institution)_____etc.

**We are interested in the number of core, new, and associated faculty in your program.**

**Core Faculty** are faculty members who:

1) have served as a chair or member of a program dissertation committee in the past 5

academic years (2001-2002 through 2005-2006), OR

2) are serving as a member of the graduate admissions or curriculum committee

The faculty member must be currently (2006-2007) and formally designated as faculty in the program, and not be an outside reader who reads the dissertation but does not contribute substantially to its development. Include emeritus faculty only if the faculty member has, within the past three years, either chaired a dissertation committee or been the primary instructor for a regular Ph. D. course.

**New Faculty** are faculty members who:

1) do not meet the criteria for core faculty, but who have been hired in tenured or tenure-track positions within the past three academic years (2003-2004 through 2005-2006) AND

2)  are currently employed at your university and are expected to become involved in doctoral education in your program

**Associated Faculty** are faculty members who:

1) have chaired or served on program dissertation committees in the past five years (2001 2002 through 2005-2006), AND

2) have a current (2006-2007) faculty appointment at your institution, but who are not designated faculty in the program.

They should not be outside readers, or faculty currently employed at other universities. Include emeritus faculty only if the faculty member has, within the past three years, either chaired a dissertation committee or been the primary instructor for a regular Ph.D. course.

## A. 1. *Based on the definitions above, please provide for this program...*

The number of core faculty: ☐☐☐
The number of new faculty: ☐☐☐
The number of associated faculty: ☐☐☐

**2. How many students were enrolled in doctoral study in this program during the 2005-2006 academic year?**

Number of Students ☐☐☐

**3. How many of this program's currently enrolled doctoral students were in the candidacy stage as of the 2005-2006 academic year?**

Number of Students ☐☐☐

# The National Academies
# National Research Council
# Assessment of Research Doctorate Programs

## Survey of Program Quality

Thank you for agreeing to participate as a rater in **{taxonomy field name}** in the Survey of Program Quality, a critical component of the National Research Council's Assessment of Research Doctorate Programs.  This survey asks for your judgment—and the judgment of other faculty members like you—about the quality of a sample of doctoral programs in your field.

**How your judgments will be used.** The judgments of over 200 raters in each field will be used to calculate ratings of perceived quality for a sample of the programs, rather than all the programs in a field.  Previous research (Ostriker & Kuh, 2003[1]) has shown us how to use faculty views on the strength of different PhD programs combined with objective data concerning program characteristics to produce ratings of additional programs. These new ratings are based on objectively measured characteristics, such as publications, citations and time to degree, but imitate, to the extent achievable, the judgment criteria of the initially surveyed faculty.

**Thinking about your perception of a program's quality.**  As part of this survey, you will be asked to rate 15 programs on a scale of 1 to 6 (1=a program not sufficient for graduate education, 6=a distinguished program).  *We urge you to keep two things in mind as you decide on your ratings:*

- Prior to rating these 15 programs, you will have the opportunity to view a list of all programs in your field.  Keep this "universe" of programs in mind as you rate each of the 15 programs <u>relative to this universe</u>, not to each other.

- <u>Please reflect on what you consider important in a doctoral program</u> as you decide on your ratings.  To assist you, a link below each program's name goes to an information page that lists several program and faculty characteristics, a list of the program's faculty and a link to the program's web site as well, should you want to seek additional information before finalizing your rating.

Your efforts will improve doctoral education through benchmarking and better information about programs.  The survey is being conducted by Mathematica Policy Research (MPR), an organization experienced in the conduct of confidential surveys. Your responses will be compiled by MPR and provided to the NRC for their analyses. The National Research Council staff who analyze the data will sign non-disclosure confidentiality agreements to protect the identity of individuals participating in the survey.  The survey will be conducted using secure

---

[1] Link to citation url.

web-based survey technology and any information that could be used to identify or link responses to an individual respondent for any survey question will be maintained in storage that is secure. Your identity will be known only to the National Research Council and Mathematica Policy Research who have signed non-disclosure agreements. Only aggregate information from the survey, such as means and distributions of ratings for programs, will be included in publications from the project. If you have any questions about the study or this questionnaire, please email us at *NRC-Assessment@mathematica-mpr.com.*

I provide my informed consent to participate in this study ☐ Yes ☐ No

**Instructions**

1.  Listed below are the 15 programs in your field that you are being asked to rate. Given the range of programs within some fields, you may or may not be familiar with all of the programs you are being asked to rate. Consequently, you will be asked two questions about each program. The first asks how familiar you are with the program and the second asks you to rate its quality.

2.  Before considering programs individually, please take a moment to familiarize yourself with the larger range of programs in your field. To do so, please click on this link:

## Click here for a list of all institutions in the study with programs in this field:

☐

3.  To begin considering programs individually, click on the link provided for each institution. You will be taken to that program's information page. If it was provided to the NRC, the information pages will also list a link to that program's home page.

    **NOTE: The two rating questions for each program will appear at the bottom of that program's information page. Your rating will only be considered valid if both questions are answered.**

4.  Finally, after you have rated all 15 programs, a summary page will appear with all of your responses. Please review your responses and make any final changes at that point. Once submitted, your responses are final.

| Names of Programs to be Rated | Information Link |
|---|---|
| Cornell University | link to information page |
| Duke University | link to information page |
| **Etc.** | |
| | |
| | |
| | |
| | |
| | |

|  |  |
|---|---|

| SAVE<br>QUIT FOR NOW | SAVE—GO TO<br>SUMMARY PAGE |
|---|---|

**Institution:** {name}    **Location:** {place}
**Program:** {name}    **Program URL:** {URL}

Two types of information are presented about this program – the names of the faculty who are currently working with doctoral students, followed by a few facts about the program and its faculty.

**Faculty Names (Faculty spreadsheet)**

| Core[2] | New[3] | Associated[4] |
|---|---|---|
|  |  |  |
|  |  |  |
|  |  |  |
|  |  |  |
|  |  |  |
|  |  |  |
|  |  |  |
|  |  |  |
|  |  |  |
|  |  |  |
|  |  |  |
|  |  |  |
|  |  |  |
|  |  |  |
|  |  |  |
|  |  |  |
|  |  |  |
|  |  |  |
|  |  |  |
|  |  |  |
|  |  |  |
|  |  |  |
|  |  |  |

[2] There will be a link to explain this term.
[3] There will be a link to explain this term.
[4] There will be a link to explain this term.

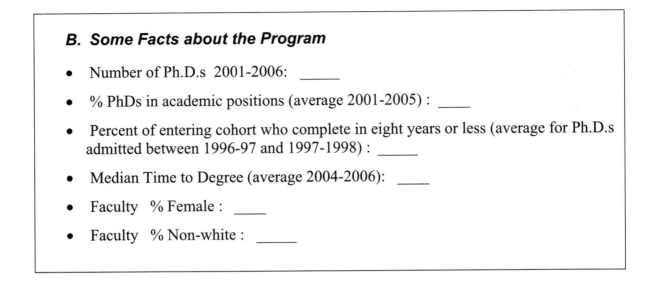

**B. Some Facts about the Program**

- Number of Ph.D.s 2001-2006: _____

- % PhDs in academic positions (average 2001-2005) : ____

- Percent of entering cohort who complete in eight years or less (average for Ph.D.s admitted between 1996-97 and 1997-1998) : _____

- Median Time to Degree (average 2004-2006): ____

- Faculty  % Female : ____

- Faculty  % Non-white : _____

## The Rating Questions

1. On a scale from 1 to 3, where 1 means you have little or no familiarity with this program and 3 means that you have considerable familiarity, how familiar are you with this program?

| Little or None | Some | Considerable |
|---|---|---|
| 1 | 2 | 3 |
| ☐ | ☐ | ☐ |

2. On a scale from 1 to 6, where 1 equals not adequate for doctoral education and 6 equals a distinguished program, how would you rate this program?

| Not Adequate for Doctoral Education | Marginal | Adequate | Good | Strong | Distinguished | Don't Know Well Enough to Evaluate |
|---|---|---|---|---|---|---|
| 1 | 2 | 3 | 4 | 5 | 6 | 9 |
| ☐ | ☐ | ☐ | ☐ | ☐ | ☐ | ☐ |
| ☐ | ☐ | ☐ | ☐ | ☐ | ☐ | ☐ |

| SAVE QUIT FOR NOW | SAVE—GO TO SUMMARY PAGE | SAVE/GO TO NEXT PROGRAM |
|---|---|---|

Listed below are your responses to the rating questions you answered. Please review them carefully.

- NOTE - If you wish to review a program's information sheet once again, click on the link under the university's name
- If you wish to change a response, you can do so by making the change on this page.
  The correct question will be updated automatically for you

| University/Program Name | Familiarity Rating | Quality Rating |
|---|---|---|
| {name-link to info page} | {inserted automatically} | {inserted automatically} |
| | | |
| | | |
| | | |
| | | |
| | | |
| | | |
| | | |
| | | |
| | | |
| | | |
| | | |
| | | |
| | | |
| | | |
| | | |
| | | |
| | | |
| | | |

**CAUTION: Please make sure you have <u>thoroughly reviewed</u> your answers.
Once you click the "submit button" your responses are final.**

SUBMIT MY FINAL
RESPONSES

**Thank you for your time!**

# Welcome to the National Research Council's

# 2006 Assessment of Research Doctorate Programs

# Faculty Questionnaire

Every 10 or so years, the National Research Council conducts a study of national importance regarding the quality and characteristics of doctoral programs in the United States. The **2006 Assessment of Research Doctorate Programs** collects data on the doctoral programs and doctoral faculty in over 60 areas of study in American universities, along with some student data. This comparative assessment, the most comprehensive to date, is designed to assist prospective doctoral students with selecting programs that best fit their interests and to permit programs to benchmark themselves against similar programs.

**Your participation is important**. By completing this questionnaire, you are providing information that will: (1) help the NRC identify the characteristics of successful graduate programs, (2) enable the NRC with collecting data on grants, citations, and publications from other sources; and (3) permit a statistical description of the faculty in the graduate program(s) or programs with which you are affiliated. For further information about the assessment, see *www7.nationalacademies.org/resdoc/index.html.* This site also has a list of Frequently Asked Questions and contains an Email link to request answers to questions you might have concerning the study or the questionnaire.

**All of the information you provide will be treated as confidential.** The survey is being conducted by Mathematica Policy Research (MPR), an organization experienced in the conduct of confidential surveys. Your responses will be compiled by MPR and provided to the NRC for their analyses. Personally identifiable information, such as past employment and ZIP Codes, will be used to obtain data on publications, grants and awards and honors from other databases. The National Research Council staff who analyze the data will sign non-disclosure confidentiality agreements to protect the identity of individuals participating in the survey. The survey will be conducted using secure web-based survey technology and any information that could be used to identify or link responses to an individual respondent for any survey question will be maintained in storage that is secure. Any data, including race/ethnicity and gender, that is not currently available to the public will only be used in an aggregated form that cannot be used to discern the identity of any survey participant in any report or presentation concerning the survey or in the public use file that will be made available to the public at the conclusion of this study. The link between your name and the data you provide in this questionnaire will only be used to obtain publications and, awards and honors data from other databases and will be removed prior to the publication of the public use file.

**Your participation is voluntary.** Completing the questionnaire averages about 14 minutes, not counting the time required to list or upload publications, which will vary from person to person. You may refuse to answer any question or discontinue participation at any point. There is no personal risk to you in responding to this questionnaire. Your identity will be known to only the National Research Council and Mathematica Policy Research. No information concerning respondents will be given to your institution. If you have any questions about the study or this questionnaire, please email us at *NRC-Assessment@mathematica-mpr.com.* Faculty must submit their competed questionnaire by February 15, 2007 if they wish to be considered as a program rater for the Rating Survey that follows this spring. Otherwise, the end date is April 1, 2007.

**Click here to indicate your informed consent to participate in this study**                          ☐

## A.    Program Identification

You have been identified by your institution as a faculty member who participates in doctoral education in one or more graduate programs that fall under one or more fields in the NRC taxonomy. The names of these programs are listed below in questions A2i and A2. However, if you are involved in a doctoral program that is <u>not</u> on this list, it is not part of this study and should not be considered when responding to this questionnaire.

**A1.    In what year did you become a faculty member at this institution?**

Year:

   **a. Do you have emeritus status?**

   ☐ Yes    *(ask A1b)*
   ☐ No   (skip to *A2*)

   **b.  During the last 3 years have you been the primary instructor for a regular PhD course?**

   ☐ Yes
   ☐ No

**A2i.  Using the drop down list of graduate programs at this institution that are eligible for this study, please select the doctoral program or programs in which you are involved.  <u>Do not include</u> programs for which you serve/ have served as an "outside reader."**

   **For each please enter the number of  doctoral dissertation committees  you have <u>chaired</u> (that is, been the principal advisor for) during your last 3 years at this institution.**

   **Do Not include committee memberships in programs that are not part of the study.**

| **Program Name**<br>(Drop down list of institution's<br>participating program) | **Number of**<br>**Committees Chaired**<br>*If none, enter zero* |
| --- | --- |
| | |

*[If A1b = yes, skip to A4]*
*[If A1b = no and A2i (Number of committees chaired) is > zero, skip to A4]*
*[If A1b = no and A2i (Number of committees chaired) is < zero, go to exit screen]*

**A2.   Using the drop down list, please select the doctoral program or programs in which you are involved.  <u>Do not include</u> programs for which you serve/ have served as an "outside reader".  For each please enter:**

   • *Column 1: The number of  doctoral dissertation committees  you have <u>chaired</u> (that is, been the principal advisor for) during your last 5 years at this institution*

- *Column 2: The total number of committees that you have <u>either served on or chaired</u> <u>during the period 2001-2006.</u> Please include committees on which you are <u>currently</u> serving or chairing*

| **Program Name** (Drop down list of institution's participating program) | Column 1 **Number of Committees Chaired** *If none, enter zero* | Column 2 **Number of Committees Served On or Chaired** *If none, enter zero* |
|---|---|---|
| _____ | _____ | _____ |

*(If A1 = 2003 or later or A2 contains a number greater than zero, skip to A4, otherwise ask A3)*

**A3.** **Are you currently serving on <u>doctoral admissions or curriculum committees</u> in one or more of the programs you indicated?   [LIST PROGRAM NAMES FROM A2]**

 Yes
☐ No

*1.(If A3 equals "Yes" go to A4, otherwise skip to the exit "thank you" screen)*

**A4.** **Please record your <u>primary</u> area of specialization.  Then, using the drop down list, please select the field that comes closest to describing or including your primary area of specialization.**

**Primary Area of Specialization:** _____

a.        (Drop down Taxonomy list – including subfields)        _____

**A5.** **Please record any additional areas of specialization you currently have.  Then, using the drop down list, please select the field that comes closest to describing or including that additional area of specialization.**

IF NONE: CHECK THIS BOX:        ☐ *(should not skip to C1 but continue to A6)*

a.    **Area of Specialization:** _____

(Drop down list of Taxonomy fields and subfields

b.    **Area of Specialization:** _____

(Drop down list of Taxonomy fields and subfields

c.    **Area of Specialization:** _____

(Drop down list of Taxonomy fields and subfields

d.    **Area of Specialization:** _____

e.    **Area of Specialization:** _____

f.    **Area of Specialization:** _____

**A6.    In your current position at this institution, on which <u>two</u> work activities listed below do you work the most hours, on average?**

|  | **Activity Worked <u>Most</u> Hours** *Mark One Only* | **Activity Worked the <u>Second Most</u> Hours** *Mark One Only* |
|---|:---:|:---:|
| Research and development | ☐ | ☐ |
| Teaching | ☐ | ☐ |
| Management or Administration | ☐ | ☐ |
| Professional services to individuals | ☐ | ☐ |
| Other – Specify activity worked <u>most</u> hours: ☐ | | ☐ |
| Other – Specify activity worked <u>second most</u> hours:_____ ☐ | | ☐ |

# B.    Prior Experience

**B1.    What was your status <u>immediately</u> prior to your employment as a faculty member at your current institution?**

*Mark One Only*

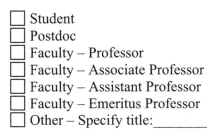

☐ Student
☐ Postdoc
☐ Faculty – Professor
☐ Faculty – Associate Professor
☐ Faculty – Assistant Professor
☐ Faculty – Emeritus Professor
☐ Other – Specify title:_____

**B2.  Please provide the name and location of your previous employer**

Previous employer: _____
City:_____
State:_____ Zip Code: _____
Country:_____

*Ask B3 if B1 = any response except student*

**B3.  Which of the following employment sectors <u>best</u> describes your last employer immediately before being hired by this institution?**

*Mark One Only*

EDUCATION
- ☐ U.S. 4-year college or university other than medical school
- ☐ U.S. medical school (including university-affiliated hospital or medical center)
- ☐ U.S. university-affiliated research institute
- ☐ U.S. community college or technical institute
- ☐ U.S. preschool, elementary, middle, secondary school or school system
- ☐ Non-U.S. educational institution

GOVERNMENT (other than education institution)
- ☐ Foreign government
- ☐ U.S. federal government
- ☐ U.S. state government
- ☐ U.S. local government

PRIVATE SECTOR (other than education institution)
- ☐ Not-for-profit institution
- ☐ U. S. based industry or business (for profit)
- ☐ Non-U. S. based industry or business (for profit)

OTHER
- ☐ Self-employed
- ☐ Other:_____

**B4.  Thinking about the job you held immediately before being hired by your current institution, on which <u>two</u> work activities listed below did you work the most hours?**

| | Activity Worked <u>Most</u> Hours | Activity Worked the <u>Second Most</u> Hours |
|---|---|---|
| | *Mark One Only* | *Mark One Only* |
| Research and development | ☐ | ☐ |
| Teaching | ☐ | ☐ |
| Management or Administration | ☐ | ☐ |
| Professional services to individuals | ☐ | ☐ |
| Other – Specify activity worked <u>most</u> hours:_____ | ☐ | ☐ |
| Other – Specify activity worked <u>second most</u> hours:_____ | ☐ | ☐ |

# C. Educational Background

**C1.** **Please indicate all degrees earned beyond your bachelor's degree**

*Mark All That Apply*

☐ Doctorate (e.g. PhD DSc EdD etc.)
☐ Other professional degree (e.g. JD LLB MD DDS DVM etc.)
☐ Master's degree (e.g. MS MA MBA MFA)
☐ Other – Specify degree:_____

**C2.** **What institution conferred your Ph.D. or equivalent degree?  If a U.S. institution, please use the dropdown list to select the school.   If a foreign institution, please enter the name and address of that institution below**

Drop down list
of U.S. Institutions

Foreign Institution (record below)

Institution Name:_____
City: _____
Country: _____

**C3.** **Using the drop down list, please pick the field that comes closest to the field of your Ph.D. or equivalent degree.**

_____[Drop down Taxonomy list—including subfields]_____

Other field – please specify:

_____

**C4.** **In what year was your Ph.D. or equivalent degree conferred?**

Year: ☐☐☐☐

**C5.** **Using the Association of American Universities (AAU) definition detailed below, have you ever held a postdoctoral position (postdoc)?**

The AAU **definition of a postdoctoral scholar** states:

- The appointee was recently awarded a Ph.D. or equivalent doctorate (e.g., Sc.D., M.D.) in an appropriate field; and
- the appointment is temporary; and
- the appointment involves substantially full-time research or scholarship; and
- the appointment is viewed as preparatory for a full-time academic and/or research career; and
- the appointment is not part of a clinical training program; and

- the appointee works under the supervision of a senior scholar or a department in a university or similar research institution (e.g., national laboratory, NIH, etc.); and
- the appointee has the freedom, and is expected, to publish the results of his or her research or scholarship during the period of the appointment.

(See: *http://www.aau.edu/reports/PostDocRpt.html.*)

☐ Yes
☐ No *skip to D1*

**C6.  How many postdoctoral appointments have you held?**

Number of Postdocs Held: ☐

**C7.  For each postdoc held, please enter the number of years that you held the postdoc and the sector in which you were working.**

- *If you have held more than 4 postdoctoral appointments, please list the four most recent*

|  | Number of Years | Sector (drop down list from B3) |
|---|---|---|
| Most Recent |  |  |
| Second Most Recent |  |  |
| Third Most Recent |  |  |
| Fourth Most Recent |  |  |

## D.    Scholarly Activity

*The questions in this section will help us match productivity data such as publications, citations, research grants and other types of scholarly productivity with the faculty who participate in the graduate program There will be two primary sources of data. The first will be the data provided by the journals monitored by the Institute for Scientific Information (ISI). The list can be found at: http://scientific.thomson.com/mjl/. The second will be your answers to the questions below. In counting publications, in most cases, the NRC will limit itself to books, monographs, and articles and reviews in refereed journals. It is especially important that you list books, monographs, and articles in edited volumes and in specialist journals not covered by ISI so that we have a full picture of your scholarly productivity. In addition, if there are other kinds of scholarly production that you feel give a complete picture of your scholarship, please list them below in D5*

**D1.**    **Under what names or variants of your name have you published books or articles in the past five years (e.g. Jane Doe, Jane H. Doe, J. H. Doe or other prior names)?**

- *If you are in the Humanities, please include the names or variants of your name under which you have published books or articles in the past 10 years (1996-2006).*

_____
_____
_____

**D2.**    **Please list the Zip Codes that appeared on your publications as a reflection of your professional location between 2001 and 2006.**

- *If you are in the Humanities, please list the zip codes that appeared on your publications in the past 10 years (1996-2006).*

            Zip Code 1 _____
            Zip Code 2 _____
            Zip Code 3 _____
            Zip Code 4 _____
            Zip Code 5 _____
            Zip Code 6 _____
            Zip Code 7 _____
            Zip Code 8 _____

**D3.**    **Please list the titles of books that you have authored, co-authored or edited from 2001 to 2006.**

- *If you are in the Humanities, please list the titles of books you have authored, co-authored or edited in the past 10 years (1996-2006).*

- *If you have an electronic version of your CV, you may want to cut and paste the requested information*

**Books Authored or Co-authored**
Book 1:_____
Book 2:_____
Book 3:_____
Book 4:_____
Book 5:_____

**Books Edited**
Book 1:_____
Book 2:_____
Book 3:_____
Book 4:_____
Book 5:_____

*[allow up to Book 30}*

**D4.   Please list any papers you authored or co-authored from 2001 to 2006.**

- *Faculty in the Arts and Humanities:* Since ISI coverage of publications in the Arts and Humanities is spotty,  it is important that these faculty provide as complete a listing as possible of papers authored or co-authored in the **past 10 years (1996-2006).** If you would    like    to    browse    the    ISI    website,    here    is    the    link: http://scientific.thomson.com/mjl/
- *Papers listed on your CV:* If you  upload your CV, there is no need to reenter papers already listed there.  You will have an opportunity to upload your CV when you reach the end of the questionnaire
- *Additional papers not included on your CV.* To include papers not on your CV, you *can* upload a list of these papers by using this link [LINK].
- *For journal articles*, please remember to add the volume number.
- *For articles in edited volumes.*  Please enter these in D5.

| Authors | Title | Journal | Year of Publication |
|---------|-------|---------|---------------------|
| _____ | _____ | _____ | ☐☐☐☐ |
| _____ | _____ | _____ | ☐☐☐☐ |
| _____ | _____ | _____ | ☐☐☐☐ |
| _____ | _____ | _____ | ☐☐☐☐ |
| _____ | _____ | _____ | ☐☐☐☐ |

*[allow up to 30 articles]*

**D5.   Please list any other scholarly product (e.g. shows curated, databases assembled, etc.) from the period 2001 to 2006 not covered above.**

- *If you are in the Humanities, please list any other scholarly product from the past 10 years (1996-2006) not covered above.*
- *For All Faculty,  If you wish to list chapters contributed to edited volumes, please list them here showing chapter title and volume title.  Alternatively, we can extract them from your CV, which you should attach.*

| Authors | Title | Year |
|---------|-------|------|
| _____ | _____ | ☐☐☐☐ |
| _____ | _____ | ☐☐☐☐ |
| _____ | _____ | ☐☐☐☐ |
| _____ | _____ | ☐☐☐☐ |
| _____ | _____ | ☐☐☐☐ |
| _____ | _____ | ☐☐☐☐ |

*[allow up to 30 products]*

**D6.**    **To what scholarly or professional societies do you belong?**

- *If you have an electronic version of your CV, you may want to cut and paste the requested information.*

_____

_____

_____

_____

_____

*[allow 8]*


# E.    Research Activity

**E1.**    **Is any of your work currently supported by an extramural grant or contract?**

☐ Yes
☐ No   *skip to E4*

*Ask E2 if E1 = yes*


**E2.**      **How many extramural grants or contracts currently fund your work?**

Number of Current Grants/Contracts:      [___]

**a. For how many of these extramural grants or contracts do you currently serve as:**

**Number of Grants/Contracts**
*If None: Enter Zero*

1. The sole principal investigator . . . . . . . . . .[   ]
2. A co-principal investigator . . . . . . . . . . . .[   ]

**E3. Currently, how many doctoral students are supported on your extramural funding (grants or contracts)?**

*If None: Enter Zero*

Number of Supported
Doctoral Students:                                   [__]__]

**E4. Since July 1, 2001, have you either: 1) submitted a disclosure to your university's licensing or tech transfer office, 2) filed for a patent or 3) were named as an inventor on a licensed patent?**

☐ Yes
☐ No   *skip to E5*

*Ask E4a if E4 = yes*

**E4a.  Since July 1, 2001 . . .**

*If none, enter zero*
**Enter Number**

1.  How many disclosures have you submitted to your university's licensing or tech transfer office?                                                                    _____
2.  How many patents applications have you filed?                                _____
3.  How many patents have been granted to you as an inventor?                     _____
4.  Of the patents that have been granted to you as an inventor since July 1, 2001 (item 3 above), how many have resulted in commercialized products or processes or have been licensed?                                                                 _____

[program will check that E4a3 > 0, if E4a3 >0 then E4a4 >0 and not less than E4a3]

**E5.     To what extent is your current research related to the field of your Ph.D. or equivalent degree?**

☐ Closely related
☐ Somewhat related
☐ Not related

*Ask E6 if C5 = yes*
E6.To what extent is your current research related to your postdoc experience immediately prior to becoming a faculty member?

☐ Closely related
☐ Somewhat related
☐ Not related

## F.  Doctoral Students

**F1.**    Please provide a list of doctoral students at your current institution for whom you served as primary dissertation adviser who have completed their studies and received their doctorate in the past five (5) years (2001-02 through 2005-06).  For each doctorate holder, please indicate the year in which the degree was awarded and current position and employer, if known.

| Name | Degree Year | Current Position | Current Employer | City | State | Country |
|------|------|------|------|------|------|------|
|  |  |  |  |  |  |  |
|  |  |  |  |  |  |  |

*[allow 40]*

## G. Program Quality

*The charge to the Committee on an Assessment of Research-Doctorate Programs includes the design and calculation of program ratings that use collected data to quantitatively estimate program quality. The committee will construct one set of ratings based on the perceptions of graduate faculty of the relative importance of program characteristics to the quality of doctoral programs. This section of the questionnaire asks you to describe the relative importance of program characteristics as determinants or indicators of program quality.*

### *Specific Characteristics:  Program Faculty Quality (Category I)*

**G1.**  In Column A, please select the characteristics in this category (up to FOUR*)* that you feel are the most important to program quality.  In Column B, if you selected more than two characteristics, please select the TWO you feel are the most important.

| CATEGORY I -- Program Faculty Quality | Column A Most Important Characteristics (*Mark Up to Four*) | Column B Two Most important Characteristics |
|------|------|------|
| a.   Number of publications (books, articles, etc.) per faculty member | ☐ | ☐ |
| b.   Number of citations per faculty member | ☐ | ☐ |
| c.   Receipt of extramural grants for research | ☐ | ☐ |
| d.   Involvement in interdisciplinary work | ☐ | ☐ |
| e.   Racial/ethnic diversity of the program faculty | ☐ | ☐ |
| f.   Gender diversity of the program faculty | ☐ | ☐ |
| g.   Reception by peers of a faculty member's work as measured by honors and awards | ☐ | ☐ |

## *Specific Characteristics:  Student Characteristics (Category II)*

**G2.  In Column A, please select the characteristics in this category (up to FOUR) that you feel are the most important to program quality.  In Column B, if you selected more than two characteristics, please select the TWO you feel are the most important.**

| CATEGORY II -- Student Characteristics | Column A Most Important Characteristics (*Mark Up to Four*) | Column B Two Most important Characteristics |
|---|---|---|
| a.  Median GRE scores of entering students | ☐ | ☐ |
| b.  Percentage of students receiving full financial support | ☐ | ☐ |
| c.  Percentage of students with portable fellowships | ☐ | ☐ |
| d.  Number of student publications and presentations | ☐ | ☐ |
| e.  Racial/ethnic diversity of the student population | ☐ | ☐ |
| f.  Gender diversity of the student population | ☐ | ☐ |
| g.  A high percentage of international students | ☐ | ☐ |

## *Specific Characteristics:  Program Characteristics (Category III)*

**G3.  In Column A, please select the characteristics in this category (up to FOUR) that you feel are the most important to program quality.  In Column B, if you selected more than two characteristics, please select the TWO you feel are the most important.**

| CATEGORY III -- Program Characteristics | Column A Most Important Characteristics (*Mark Up to Four*) | Column B Two Most important Characteristics |
|---|---|---|
| a.  Average number of Ph.D.s granted over the last five years | ☐ | ☐ |
| b.  Percentage of entering students who complete a doctoral degree | ☐ | ☐ |
| c.  Time to degree | ☐ | ☐ |
| d.  Placement of students after graduation | ☐ | ☐ |
| e.  Percentage of students with individual work space | ☐ | ☐ |
| f.  Percentage of health insurance premiums covered by the institution or program | ☐ | ☐ |
| g.  Number of student support activities provided at either the institutional or program level (This variable will be a tally of whether the following services are provided to graduate students at either the institutional or program level: orientation for new students, prizes/awards to doctoral students for teaching and/or research, formal training in academic integrity/ethics, travel funds to attend professional meetings, grievance/dispute resolution procedures, annual review of all enrolled doctoral students, training to improve teaching skills, institutionally-supported graduate student association, information about | ☐ | ☐ |

| CATEGORY III -- Program Characteristics | Column A Most Important Characteristics (*Mark Up to Four*) | Column B Two Most important Characteristics |
|---|---|---|
| employment outcomes of graduates and on-campus graduate student research conferences). | | |

## *General Characteristics*

**G4.** **Please assign a score to each category with the total adding up to 100, where 0 indicates the category has no importance to your judgment of quality and 100 indicates it is the only category that is important.**

| Category | Score |
|---|---|
| Category 1: Program Faculty Quality Characteristics | |
| Category 2: Student Characteristics | |
| Category 3: Program Characteristics | |
| **Total** | **100** |

# H.   Demographic Information

**H1.In what year were you born?**

Year of birth: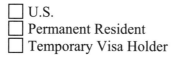

**H2.Are you:**

☐ Male
☐ Female

**H3.What is your citizenship status?**

☐ U.S.
☐ Permanent Resident
☐ Temporary Visa Holder

**H4.   Are you Hispanic (or Latino).**

☐ Yes
☐ No  *skip to H6*

**H5.   Which of the following best describes your Hispanic origin or descent?**
*Mark one only*

☐ Mexican or Chicano
☐ Puerto Rican
☐ Cuban
☐ Other Hispanic descent – specify_____

**H6.   What is your racial background**

*Mark all that apply*

☐ American Indian or Alaska Native
☐ Native Hawaiian or other Pacific Islander
☐ Asian
☐ Black or African-American
☐ White

**I1.  To help us understand the characteristics of faculty in doctoral programs without asking additional questions, and to enable us to access data from national databases (e.g., on citation counts), please attach your current C.V. when you submit this questionnaire.**

☐ C. V. attached

**J1. Would you be willing to answer an additional questionnaire that would ask you to rate the overall quality of other doctoral programs in your field?**

☐ Yes
☐ No

*Ask J2 if J1 = yes*

**J2.   Good contact information is needed for those selected.  Please fill in your preferred contact information below.**

ADDRESS: _____

_____

_____

_____

CITY: _____ STATE: _____ ZIP CODE: _____

**J3.   Please provide your preferred e-mail address where you can be reached if there are responses in your questionnaire that require clarification or if you prefer to be contacted about the program ratings by email.**

Email address: _____

**Thank you for your time.**

## Rationale for Questions on the Faculty Questionnaire

A.  **Program Identification**—The questions in this section are designed to confirm data provided by the program about faculty who participate in doctoral education in the program and to determine if the faculty member meets the criteria that they have served on doctoral committees or are recent hires. These data will also be used to apportion faculty effort, for those who are associated with more than one program.

    A1. This question will be useful in knowing that productivity information on publications, awards, and honors can be linked to the current institution.

    A2. The faculty spreadsheets/program questionnaire asked for a list of faculty members that chaired or served on a doctoral committee in a field. The intent of this question is to determine if a faculty member actually served on a committee in the past five years and to determine the number of such committees. It is important to ask for committee service, since the number of committees will determine the faculty member's effort in the programs. This can be used to proportion the productivity measures related to publications, grants and awards. All of an institution's programs that are participating in the assessment will be on a drop down list. The faculty members will use this list to identify the programs with which he or she is involved and the number of committees.

    A3. This question is asked because service of a doctoral admissions or curriculum committee is an alternate criterion for Core Program Faculty if they have no dissertation committee service in that program.

    A4. The answer to this question will permit a description of research specializations of faculty.

    A5. These questions will identify the primary or core faculty in a program and the subfields that are represented by the faculty members. It will allow individuals when using the data on programs to compare programs with like characteristics and will help prospective students match their interests to that of a program.

    A6. This information will be compared with the information in B4 to see if the work activity of the faculty member has changed from their previous institution.

B.  **Prior Experience**—This section asks for prior employment and primary and secondary employment activity in that employment. Such information is useful in describing the research-intensity of faculty and their previous research experience.

    B1.-
    B3. These questions ask for information about prior employment and will provide information about the origins of the program faculty. It will also be useful in the matching the faculty to productivity data, if they are recent hires at their current institution.

    B4. This question will provide information on whether the work activity of the faculty member has changed.

C.  **Educational Background**—This section asks about degrees, institutions, Ph.D. field as well as year Ph.D. conferred. Further, the questions ask about post doctoral appointment experience.

C1. While many of the faculty members will have the Ph.D. as their highest degree, it will be important to know if the faculty have received other degrees. These data are not available from other data sources and are especially important in describing the background of faculty in the biomedical sciences.

C2. The doctoral origins of the faculty for a program will provide data on the career paths of graduates from different institutions and provide a count of the number of foreign degree holders on faculties at U.S. doctoral institutions. It provides information about the segmentation of the academic labor market and is an indirect outcomes measure for those doctorate-awarding origins of those who are academically employed.

C3. Field of Ph.D. or equivalent will provide information on whether the faculty member has changed research fields. It may also give a measure of interdisciplinarity.

C4. Year of Ph.D. or equivalent will allow for cohort analyses and in conjunction with the next question will provide information about the postdoctoral experience.

C5.-
C7. There is very little known about the postdoctoral experience and these questions will provide information on the career paths of individuals who have held postdocs in terms of the number and duration and how that has changed over time for doctoral faculty.

D. **Scholarly Activity**—The questions in this section of the questionnaire are designed to gather information that will be helpful in matching the faculty in a program to data from national databases of publications, citations and grants.

D1. The request for the names faculty use on their publications will help in the matching process by eliminating false matches and by finding publications written before a name change, for example the name used before marriage.

D2. In addition to using author names in the matching process, the ZIP Code for the location of the author will be used, since it is the only uniquely identifiable numeric piece of information that appears on a publication. Institutional names may be available, but they vary in form and it will be difficult to identify all forms that pertain to a particular institution. Also, if a faculty member moves from one institution to another, the ZIP Code of the prior institution will help in matching the earlier publications to the faculty member.

D3. There is no good data source for matching the faculty in a program to the books they have authored. Sources, such as the Library of Congress and Books in Print, do not carry geographic information about the author and matching on name alone will provide multiple matches. The titles of the books can then be used to eliminate false matches.

D4. ISI does not cover all possible journals. In particular, its coverage of highly specialized journals in the humanities may be very limited. A listing of these publications will be useful in obtaining more complete data on faculty productivity.

D5. This question is intended to obtain a list of non-journal and non-print scholarly contributions.

D6. This information will be an indicator of professional involvement and interdisciplinary activity.

**E.**    **Research Activity**—This section asks about their current and recent research/scholarly activities.

     E1.   This question is important to the calculation of the percentage of faculty supported by outside grants.

     E2. Since grant data from the federal agencies and other organizations will not be matched to program faculty, the information from this question will assist in providing a measure of research productivity

     E3. These questions will provide added information about grant and contract support related to the support of graduate students.

     E4. Patents, disclosures, and licenses in some fields are very important measures of research productivity, and there is no good source for this information at the program level.

     E5-
     E6. This question will provide additional information on trends in research and mobility across fields over a career.

**F.**    **Doctoral Students**—Information from this question will be used to identify the career outcomes of doctoral students that completed the program. Knowing the career paths for graduates of the program is important since it helps in characterizing program goals. It will assist students who use the data from the study to select a degree program that meets their own career objectives.

**G.**    **Program Quality**—This section collects data pertinent to the design and calculation of program ratings.

     G1.-G3. These questions ask for those characteristics of doctoral programs that the faculty member considers important.

     G4. This question will provide information about characteristics that faculty think are valuable in determining program quality. The varying weights that faculty put on these items will be used to calculate weights to be applied to observed data for the explicit ratings of programs.

**H.**    **Demographic Information**—This section asks for basic demographic information about the faculty. This information is not available from any other source, except a population sample from the National Survey of Postsecondary Faculty, which is not available at the program level.

**I.**    The C.V. for the faculty is requested to verify publication and career path data.

# Welcome to the National Research Council's

# 2006 Assessment of Research Doctorate Programs

## Admitted-to-Candidacy Doctoral Student Questionnaire

This questionnaire is part of the National Research Council's **2006 Assessment of Research Doctoral Programs**. The National Research Council (NRC) is the operating arm of the National Academy of Sciences, an institution that conducts studies on issues relevant to questions of importance to educational, scientific and technological policy. Its reports are highly respected and have important impact on national and institutional policymakers.

This is the first NRC assessment of doctoral programs in over ten years. The study is an effort to gather data about doctoral programs nationwide and provide data that will be helpful to students, faculty, administrators and those who make educational policy.

For the first time, the assessment is including a survey of doctoral students. By completing this questionnaire, you provide information that will: (1) bring a student perspective to the study; (2) permit a statistical description of the advanced doctoral students in your field, and (3) help the NRC identify the multiple dimensions of successful graduate programs.

Further information about the assessment may be found at www7.nationalacademies.org/resdoc/ index.html. This site also has a list of Frequently Asked Questions and contains an Email link for submitting questions you might have about the study or the questionnaire.

**As a graduate student, this is an important opportunity for you to be heard on issues related to graduate education, both in your program and in general.** If you and your fellow students respond at a high rate, the results will provide important information about and to your program that will help facilitate change in graduate education at the program level.

Your responses to this online questionnaire will be entered directly into our database and treated as completely confidential by the NRC. Your individual answers will not be shared with faculty or administrators of your doctoral program. Any data, including race/ethnicity and gender, that is not currently available to the public will only be used in aggregated form that cannot be used to discern the identity of any survey participant in any report or presentation concerning the survey or in the public use file that will be made available to the public at the conclusion of this study. The link between your name and the data you provide will be removed prior to the publication of the public use file. In the case of questions with an open-ended response, comments will be reported only in an anonymous form that does not disclose the identity of the respondent.

**Your participation is voluntary.** You may refuse to answer any question or discontinue participation at any point. There is no personal risk to you in responding to this questionnaire since your identify will be known only to the National Research Council and Mathematica Policy Research. No information concerning respondents will be given to your institution. If you have any questions related to the study or this questionnaire, please send an email *to NRC-Assessment@mathematica-mpr.com*

**II.    Please click here to indicate your informed consent to participate in this study** ☐

222

**Part A.  Education**

The questions in this section are designed to collect information on your education and how you have been financially supported during your doctoral program.

**A1.**     **When did you <u>first enroll</u> in this doctoral program?**

Month ☐☐     Year ☐☐☐☐

**A2.**     **When were you <u>admitted to candidacy</u> for the doctorate?**

Month ☐☐     Year ☐☐☐☐

**A2a.**     **Please record your <u>primary</u> area of specialization.  Then, using the drop down list, please select the field that comes closest to describing or including your primary area of specialization.**

**Primary Area
of Specialization:** _____

(Drop down Taxonomy list – including subfields)

**A2b.**     **Please record any additional areas of specialization you currently have.  Then, using the drop down list, please select the field that comes closest to describing or including that additional area of specialization.**

*IF NONE:  MARK THIS BOX:* ☐

1.   **Area of Specialization:** _____

(Drop down list of Taxonomy fields and subfields

2.   **Area of Specialization:** _____

(Drop down list of Taxonomy fields and subfields

3.   **Area of Specialization:** _____

(Drop down list of Taxonomy fields and subfields

**A3.**     **When do you expect to be awarded your doctorate?**

Month ☐☐     Year ☐☐☐☐

**A4.** **Before entering this doctorate program, had you already completed a master's degree in:**

**Yes**

a. Your current field?................................................................... ☐

b. Another field - specify:.......................................................... ☐

_____

**A5.** **While studying for your doctorate, will you also receive any of the following as part of a joint, concurrent, or combined degree program:**

*(c) Mark Yes or No fo*

**Yes**

a. Professional doctorate (e.g., MD, DDS, OD, JD)?.............. ☐

b. Professional master's degree (e.g., MBA, MPA, MPH, PSM)?......................... ☐

c. Master's degree in your current doctoral program?...... ☐

d. Master's degree in a different field?........................ ☐

*Ask A6 if any "yes" responses to A4 or A5c or A5d*

**A6.** **Did you write a master's thesis?**

☐ Yes
☐ No

**A7.** **While studying for the doctorate, will you receive a <u>certificate</u> in another field or skill area?**

☐ Yes
☐ No

A8.     While in your program, how many <u>research presentations</u> (including poster presentations) have you made at:

**Number**
*Enter Zero if None*

    a.  Research conferences on your campus
       (including other units of a multi-
       campus system)?                                                     ☐☐

    b.  At regional, national, or international
       meetings?                                                                   ☐☐

**A9.     Have you received <u>travel funds</u> for research presentations at regional, national, or international meetings?**

      ☐ Yes
      ☐ No *(skip to A11)*

*Ask A10 if A9 = yes*

**A10.    From which of the following sources have you received travel funds for research presentations?**
                 IF NOT KNOWN:  MARK THIS BOX: ☐

*Mark up to three*

      ☐ National Fellowship
      ☐ Traineeship
      ☐ Professional Society
      ☐ Graduate program
      ☐ University or school/college
      ☐ Extramural grant
      ☐ Other – Specify source: _____

**A11.    How many research publications have you <u>authored or coauthored</u> before and during your doctoral studies (include pieces accepted for publication but not yet published)?**

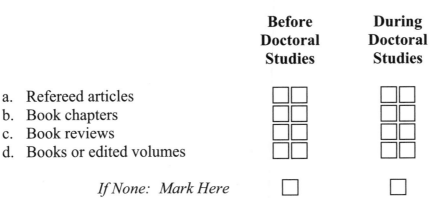

|  | Before Doctoral Studies | During Doctoral Studies |
|---|---|---|
| a.  Refereed articles | ☐☐ | ☐☐ |
| b.  Book chapters | ☐☐ | ☐☐ |
| c.  Book reviews | ☐☐ | ☐☐ |
| d.  Books or edited volumes | ☐☐ | ☐☐ |
| *If None:  Mark Here* | ☐ | ☐ |

**A12.** **Which of the following have been your <u>largest</u> sources of financial support during your doctoral program?**

Mark up to three sources

- ☐ *National Fellowship/Scholarship*
- ☐ *Institutional Fellowship/Stipend*
- ☐ *Traineeship*
- ☐ *Teaching assistantship (TA)*
- ☐ *Research assistantship (RA)*
- ☐ *Other assistantship (e.g., general assistantship)*
- ☐ *Internship, clinical residency*
- ☐ *Personal earnings during graduate school (other than sources listed above)*
- ☐ *Loans (from any source)*
- ☐ *Personal savings*
- ☐ *Spouse's, partner's, or family earnings or savings*
- ☐ *Employer's reimbursement/assistance*
- ☐ *Foreign (non-U.S.)*
- ☐ *Other – Specify source:_____*

Ask A13 if any of the first 7 categories in A12 are checked

**A13.** **If you had a fellowship, scholarship, traineeship, or assistantship, with what degree of support did it provide you?**

Mark one only
- ☐ Full
- ☐ Partial

**Part B: Postgraduation Plans**

*The questions in this section are designed to collect information on your career plans and whether and how they have changed over time.*

**B1.** **When you entered your doctoral program, what were your primary and secondary career goals?**

*Mark One in Each Column*

| | **Primary** | **Secondary** |
|---|---|---|
| a. Research and development ............................ | ☐ | ☐ |
| b. Teaching .................................................. | ☐ | ☐ |
| c. Management or administration ...................... | ☐ | ☐ |
| d. Professional services to individuals ................ | ☐ | ☐ |
| e. Other – Specify goal: ................................. | ☐ | ☐ |

*If No Secondary Career Goals:  Mark this Box*      ☐

**B2.** <u>**At this time**</u>**, what are your primary and secondary career goals?**

*Mark  One in Each Column*

| | **Primary** | **Secondary** |
|---|---|---|
| a. Research and development ................................. | ☐ | ☐ |
| b. Teaching .................................................... | ☐ | ☐ |
| c. Management or administration ............................ | ☐ | ☐ |
| d. Professional services to individuals ..................... | ☐ | ☐ |
| e. Other - specify: ......................................... | ☐ | ☐ |

*If No Secondary Career Goal:  Mark this Box*      ☐

**B3.** **Do you feel supported by your advisor in your current career goals?**

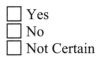

☐ Yes
☐ No
☐ Not Certain

**B4.**     **When you entered your doctoral program, for what type of employer did you believe you would work when you graduated?**

                                                 (i)      Mark one only

**III.     EDUCATION**
- [ ] U.S. 4-year college or university other than medical school
- [ ] U.S. medical school (including university-affiliated hospital or medical center)
- [ ] U.S. university-affiliated research institute
- [ ] U.S. community college or technical institute
- [ ] U.S. preschool, elementary, middle, secondary school or school system
- [ ] Non-U.S. educational institution

**IV.     GOVERNMENT (other than education institution)**
- [ ] Foreign government
- [ ] U.S. federal government
- [ ] U.S. state government
- [ ] U.S. local government

**V.     PRIVATE SECTOR (other than education institution)**
- [ ] Not-for-profit institution
- [ ] U. S. based industry or business (for profit)
- [ ] Non-U.S. based industry or business (for profit)

OTHER
- [ ] Self-employed
- [ ] Other – Specify sector: _____

 

**B5.**     <u>At this time</u>, **for what type of employer do you expect to work when you graduate?**

*Mark one only*

**VI.     EDUCATION**
- [ ] U.S. 4-year college or university other than medical school
- [ ] U.S. medical school (including university-affiliated hospital or medical center)
- [ ] U.S. university-affiliated research institute
- [ ] U.S. community college or technical institute
- [ ] U.S. preschool, elementary, middle, secondary school or school system
- [ ] Non-U.S. educational institution

**VII.     GOVERNMENT (other than education institution)**
- [ ] Foreign government
- [ ] U.S. federal government
- [ ] U.S. state government
- [ ] U.S. local government

**VIII.     PRIVATE SECTOR (other than education institution)**
- [ ] Not-for-profit institution
- [ ] Industry or business (for profit)
- [ ] Non-U.S. based industry or business (for profit)

**IX.     OTHER**
- [ ] Self-employed
- [ ] Other – Specify sector: _____

## Part C: Program Characteristics

*We are interested in the characteristics of your program and your perception of the program's quality.*

**C1.**    **Did your institution or graduate program provide you with an <u>orientation</u> when you matriculated?**

☐ Yes
☐ No

**C2.**    **When you entered your doctoral program, did the program provide you with <u>written</u> expectations (e.g., a handbook) about academic progress?**

☐ Yes
☐ No

**C3.**    **During your doctoral program, have you or will you participate in formal *(e.g., school- or program-sponsored class or seminar)* or informal *(e.g., individual conversations with mentor)* instruction, practice or professional development training in:**

*Mark one for each activity*

| | Formal Only | Informal Only | Both Formal and Informal | Neither |
|---|---|---|---|---|
| a. Oral communication and presentation skills? | ☐ | ☐ | ☐ | ☐ |
| b. Speaking to nonacademic audiences? | ☐ | ☐ | ☐ | ☐ |
| c. Writing proposals for funding? | ☐ | ☐ | ☐ | ☐ |
| d. Preparing articles for publication? | ☐ | ☐ | ☐ | ☐ |
| e. Working in collaborative groups? | ☐ | ☐ | ☐ | ☐ |
| f. Conducting independent research/scholarship? | ☐ | ☐ | ☐ | ☐ |
| g. Project management? | ☐ | ☐ | ☐ | ☐ |
| h. Research/professional ethics? | ☐ | ☐ | ☐ | ☐ |
| i. Teaching/pedagogy? | ☐ | ☐ | ☐ | ☐ |
| j. Supervision and evaluation? | ☐ | ☐ | ☐ | ☐ |
| k. Preparation for job interviews? | ☐ | ☐ | ☐ | ☐ |

*230*                                                                 *APPENDIX D*

**C4.**     **During your doctoral program have you, or do you, expect to:**

        **X.**                                                              *Mark Yes or No for*
                                                                  *each*

        **XI.**                                                          **Yes**               **No**

        **XII.**............................................................................**a.**

.......................................................................................

        **Mentor or tutor a high school student?** ........................   ☐         ☐

        b.   Mentor or tutor an undergraduate student?.................................   ☐         ☐

        c.   Mentor or tutor a graduate student?...........................................   ☐         ☐

        d.   Grade papers for undergraduate or graduate courses?..................   ☐         ☐

        e.   Lead discussion sections of undergraduate or graduate courses?..   ☐         ☐

        f.    Lead laboratory sections of undergraduate or graduate courses?..   ☐         ☐

        g.   Guest lecture in undergraduate or graduate courses?.....................   ☐         ☐

        h.   Teach a course based on a previously set curriculum? ..................   ☐         ☐

        i.    Teach a course based on a curriculum you developed?.................   ☐         ☐

**C5.**     **Other than course grades, does your program provide <u>an annual or more frequent</u> <u>assessment</u> of your academic progress? (examples: a letter from the program, a meeting with your dissertation committee)**

        ☐ Yes
        ☐ No *(skip to C7)*

*Ask C6 if C5 = Yes*

**C6.**     **Are these assessments helpful?**

        ☐ Yes
        ☐ No

**C7.**     **Have you begun your doctoral dissertation research?**

        ☐ Yes
        ☐ No *(skip to C10)*

*Ask C8 if C7 = Yes*

**C8.**     **Have you received <u>timely</u> feedback on this research?**

        ☐ Yes
        ☐ No *(skip to C10)*

*a)*

*Ask C9 if C8 = Yes*

**C9.** **Has this feedback been helpful?**

☐ Yes
☐ No

**C10.** **Are there one or more faculty members at your institution whom you consider as mentors, either in your program or external to it?**

- *A **mentor** is an individual from whom you seek advice about your education, career development or other matters of concern to you as a graduate student*

1.                                                                                          *Mark Yes or No for each*

**XIII.**

|  | **Yes** | **No** |
|---|---|---|
| a. I have a mentor in my program............................................. | ☐ | ☐ |
| b. I have a mentor external to my program............................. | ☐ | ☐ |

**C11.** **Do you have access to career advice?**

☐ Yes
☐ No *(skip to C16)*

*Ask C12 if C11 = Yes*

**C12.** **Have you taken advantage of the opportunity for career advice?**

☐ Yes
☐ No *(skip to C16)*

*Ask C13 and C14 if C12 = Yes*

**C13.** **Who has provided the advice?**

*Mark all that apply*

☐ An individual who serves as both advisor and mentor
☐ Advisor
☐ Mentor
☐ Graduate program director/coordinator
☐ Program staff
☐ University-wide career office
☐ Other – Specify who advised you:

_____

**C14.** **Does the advice cover a variety of employment sectors (e.g., employment outside of academic institutions)?**

☐ Yes
☐ No
☐ Don't Know

**C15.** **Which source of career advice did you find __most__ helpful?**

*Mark one only*

☐ An individual who serves as both advisor and mentor
☐ Advisor
☐ Mentor
☐ Graduate program director/coordinator
☐ Program staff
☐ University-wide career office
☐ Other – Specify most helpful source:

_____

**C16.** **On a scale of 1 to 5 where 1 is distant and 5 is interactive, how would you characterize your overall relationship with:**

*Mark one for each category*

| | Highly Interactive, Supportive | | Neutral | | Distant, Antagonistic or Hostile |
|---|---|---|---|---|---|
| | 5 | 4 | 3 | 2 | 1 |
| a. your faculty advisor? .................................. | ☐ | ☐ | ☐ | ☐ | ☐ |
| b. the faculty in your program?...................... | ☐ | ☐ | ☐ | ☐ | ☐ |

**C17.** **On a scale of 1 to 5, how supportive are students in your program of one another?**

*Mark one only*

☐ 5 Very supportive
☐ 4
☐ 3 Somewhat supportive
☐ 2
☐ 1 Not supportive

**C18.** **Does your program encourage students to interact with faculty outside of your program?**

☐ Yes
☐ No

**C19.** **Thinking about your doctoral program, how satisfied are you with the quality of the:**

|  | *Mark one for each category* | | |
| --- | :---: | :---: | :---: |
|  | **Very Satisfied** | **Somewhat Satisfied** | **Not Satisfied** |
| a. Teaching by the faculty?.................................... | ☐ | ☐ | ☐ |
| b. The dissertation supervision?.............................. | ☐ | ☐ | ☐ |
| c. Your research experience in the program? .......... | ☐ | ☐ | ☐ |
| d. Your program's curriculum? .............................. | ☐ | ☐ | ☐ |
| e. The <u>overall</u> quality of the program?.................... | ☐ | ☐ | ☐ |

**C20.** **How much do you feel you have benefited from the:**

|  | *Mark one for each category* | | |
| --- | :---: | :---: | :---: |
|  | **A Lot** | **Some** | **Not At All** |
| a. Intellectual environment of your program? .............. | ☐ | ☐ | ☐ |
| b. Intellectual environment of your institution?............ | ☐ | ☐ | ☐ |

**C21.** **How satisfied are you with the quality of program-sponsored activities designed to promote social interaction of students with faculty and with other students?**

☐ Very satisfied
☐ Somewhat satisfied
☐ Not satisfied

**C22.** **How much do you feel you belong to your program?**

☐ A lot
☐ Some
☐ Not at all

**C23.** **In the space below, please provide any additional comments you would like to make about your doctoral program, its characteristics or quality:**

_____

_____

_____

**Part D:  Resources**

*We are interested in your perception of the adequacy of the resources available to you for your graduate work and dissertation research.*

**D1.** **Thinking about your graduate education and dissertation research, please rate the adequacy of the support that has been available to you in each of the following areas:**

*Mark one for each category*

|  | **Excellent** | **Good** | **Fair** | **Poor** | **Not Applicable** | **Don't Know** |
|---|---|---|---|---|---|---|
| a. Computer resources? | ☐ | ☐ | ☐ | ☐ | ☐ | ☐ |
| b. Other research, laboratory, clinical or studio facilities? | ☐ | ☐ | ☐ | ☐ | ☐ | ☐ |
| c. Library resources? | ☐ | ☐ | ☐ | ☐ | ☐ | ☐ |
| d. Your on campus personal work space? | ☐ | ☐ | ☐ | ☐ | ☐ | ☐ |
| e. Space available for social interaction among students in your program (e.g., coffee nook, lunch room)? | ☐ | ☐ | ☐ | ☐ | ☐ | ☐ |
| f. University-provided housing or housing support? | ☐ | ☐ | ☐ | ☐ | ☐ | ☐ |
| g. University-provided child care facilities or child care support? | ☐ | ☐ | ☐ | ☐ | ☐ | ☐ |
| h. University recreational/athletic facilities? | ☐ | ☐ | ☐ | ☐ | ☐ | ☐ |
| i. Healthcare and/or health services provided by your program or university? | ☐ | ☐ | ☐ | ☐ | ☐ | ☐ |

**D2.** **In the space below, please provide any additional comments you would like to make about program or university resources available to you:**

_____

_____

_____

**Part E:  Background Information**

**E1.**      **Are you:**

☐ Male
☐ Female

**E2.**      **What is your marital status?**

*Mark one only*

☐ Married
☐ Living in a marriage-like relationship
☐ Widowed
☐ Divorced
☐ Separated
☐ Never married

**E3.**      **Not including yourself or your spouse/partner, how many <u>dependents</u> do you have—that is, how many others receive at least one half of their <u>financial</u> support from you?**

*If No Dependents:  Mark this box:* ☐

                                                    **Number**

a.  5 years of age or younger......... ☐☐
b.  6 to 18 years........................... ☐☐
c.  19 years or older ..................... ☐☐

**E4.**      **Including children, elderly parents or others, as appropriate, for how many people are you a primary caregiver?**

Number: ☐☐

**E5.**      **What is the highest educational attainment of your mother and father (or guardian)?**

*Mark one for each*

| | **Mother** | **Father** |
|---|---|---|
| a.  Less than high/secondary school graduation | ☐ | ☐ |
| b.  High/secondary school graduate | ☐ | ☐ |
| c.  Some college | ☐ | ☐ |
| d.  Bachelor's degree | ☐ | ☐ |
| e.  Master's degree (e.g., MA, MS, MBS, MSW, etc.) | ☐ | ☐ |
| f.  Professional degree (e.g., JD, LLB, D.Min, MD, DDS, etc.) | ☐ | ☐ |
| g.  Doctoral degree | ☐ | ☐ |
| h.  Not applicable | ☐ | ☐ |

**E6.**      **In what year were you born?**

Year of Birth: ☐☐☐☐

**E7.**      **What is your citizenship status?**

*Mark one only*

U.S. Citizen
☐ Since birth
☐ Naturalized

Non-U.S. Citizen
☐ With a Permanent U.S. Resident Visa ("Green Card")
☐ With a Temporary U.S. Visa

**E8.**      **Are you Hispanic (or Latino)?**

☐ Yes
☐ No *(skip to E10)*

**E9.**      **Which of the following best describes your Hispanic origin or descent?**

*Mark one only*

☐ Mexican or Chicano
☐ Puerto Rican
☐ Cuban
☐ Other Hispanic – Specify Hispanic descent:

_____

**E10.**     **What is your racial background?**

(i)      Mark all that apply

☐ American Indian or Alaska Native
☐ Native Hawaiian or other Pacific Islander
☐ Asian
☐ Black or African-American
☐ White

**Thank you for your time!**

# Admitted to Candidacy Student Questionnaire

# Question Rationale

## General Rationale for Questionnaire

The data collected from the student questionnaire will provide important information for prospective students seeking to compare programs within a field; academic administrators seeking to examine program quality within a field, within an institution, or across institutions; and education policy researchers seeking to explore changes or potential changes in doctoral education and their implications.

Since this is the first time a student questionnaire has been administered as part of the Assessment of Doctoral Programs, its administration will be limited to five fields: English, economics, chemical engineering, physics, and neuroscience/neurobiology.

## Part A. Education

The questions in this section are designed to collect information on your area of research, your educational progress and financial support.

**Time to Degree:** Questions 1-3 obtain data on when you enrolled, what your research specialty is, when you were admitted to candidacy and when you expect to complete. In combination with completion data provided by programs, these data will provide a picture of how students progress through their programs.

**Post-Baccalaureate Credentials:** Questions 4-8 obtain data on the master's and other degrees and certificates you may have obtained before or en route to the doctorate. This information provides a fuller picture of the post-baccalaureate credentials that students in a given program obtain in order to matriculate into a program or to prepare themselves for their career.

**Research Opportunity:** Questions 9-10 obtain data on the number of research publications you may have written and presentations given. These data provide an indication of the research experiences that students obtain in a program and offer an indicator of the extent to which students are encouraged to develop their own research interests and skills

**Financial Support:** Questions 11-13 obtain information on the level and type of financial support that students in a program have. This information, in combination with other data on the program and institutional questionnaires, will provide valuable information on financial support.

**Part B: Postgraduation Plans**

The questions in this section are designed to collect information on the career plans and goals of doctoral students and whether and how they have changed over time.

**Career Goals:** Questions 1-2 obtain data on career goals both when the respondents entered the program and now. Similarly, questions 4-5 obtain data on the type of employer the respondents expected to work for when they entered their program and now. These questions will provide a picture of the kinds of career goals students in different programs have and how they change over time.

**Faculty Support for Career Goals:** Question 3 is designed to obtain information on how supportive faculty are of students who seek a variety of career aspirations, particularly those outside of academia.

**Part C: Program Characteristics**

This section obtains data on program characteristics and the respondent's perception of program quality.

**Career Skills:** Numerous reports, beginning with the COSEPUP's *Reshaping the Graduate Education of Scientists and Engineers* (1995), have advocated that graduate students learn a variety of career skills in addition to the substance of their discipline. Question 1 will collect data on the opportunity to acquire written and oral communication skills, proposal writing, teamwork, independent research, project management, ethics, pedagogy, and others. Question 2 focuses more specifically on opportunities to acquire teaching skills and experience.

**Academic Progress:** Questions 3-8 and 14 collect data on how students acquire information about the expectations of their program for academic progress and the kinds and quality of feedback on their progress that they receive.

**Mentoring and Career Counseling**: The availability of a mentor has been identified as an important key to success in graduate education. Question 9 asks whether respondents have a faculty member they consider a mentor. The availability of career advice—particularly advice that covers the range of potential employment sectors is important potentially for both student retention and career preparation. Questions 10-13 obtain data on the availability and source of career advice for doctoral students. Question 15 also asks respondents about the quality of the relationships they have with their advisors.

**Social Integration:** Barbara Lovitts' book, *Leaving the Ivy Hall*, identified the degree to which a student feels part of a department as a critical factor in determining whether a student completes a doctoral program. Questions C15, C16, C17, C18, C20, C21, and D1 collect data on the degree to which students feel supported by faculty and peers, have opportunities to interact with faculty and students, and the quality of the interaction.

**Program Quality:** Questions 19-24 provide respondents with an opportunity to provide their perceptions of program quality (curriculum, research experience, faculty teaching ability, dissertation supervision, and intellectual environment).

**Part D: Resources**

This section collects data on respondent perceptions of the adequacy of the resources and benefits available for doctoral students.

**Education and Research Resources:** The availability of adequate resources is important to both the speed and quality of a student's academic progress. Questions 1-4 collect data on respondents' perceptions of the resources available (from the institution or program) to support their education and research. They ask for perceptions of the adequacy of computer resources, research, laboratory, or studio facilities, library resources, and on-campus work-space.

**Social Integration:** As noted above, the degree to which a student feels part of a department as a critical factor in determining whether a student completes a doctoral program. Question D5, along with other questions, collects data on opportunities for social interaction.

**Quality of Life:** In addition to financial support and health care benefits, support for doctoral students may also include provision of housing or housing assistance, provision of child care or financial support for child care, and recreational facilities. These pieces of the support package a doctoral student can expect—particularly students with children—may affect the ability of students to matriculate, complete in a timely manner, or complete at all. Questions 6-8 collect data on respondent perceptions of these benefits.

**Part E: Background Information**

The information collected in this section of the questionnaire will allow analysts to examine the comparative demographics of programs, and also examine how the answers to questions in Parts A-D of the questionnaire may vary across such dimensions as age, gender, race/ethnicity, citizenship status, family background, marital status, and responsibility for dependents. The participation in doctoral education of students from a variety of backgrounds is important to the academic enterprise, the conduct of research, and society in general, so understanding how doctoral education works for students across groups will provide the opportunity to evaluate success to date and areas where further progress is necessary.

# APPENDIX E
## List of Variables

**VARIABLES USED IN THE RATINGS CALCULATION**

**Publications per Allocated Faculty,** [*] **2001-2006 (Non-Humanities):** Data from the Thomson Reuters (formerly Institute for Scientific Information) were used to construct this variable. It is the average over the seven years, 2000-2006, of the number of articles for each allocated faculty member divided by the total number of faculty allocated to the program. Data were obtained by matching faculty lists supplied by the programs to the Thomson-Reuters list of publications and cover publications extending back to 1981. For multi-authored articles, a publication is awarded for each author on the paper who is also on a faculty list. For computer science, refereed papers from conferences were used as well as articles.[1] The list of journals included in the ISI database can be found here: http://science.thomsonreuters.com/mjl/. To find the precise journal coverage for the 2005-2006 period, contact Thomson Reuters. Books were not counted for the non-humanities.

**Number of Published Books and Articles per Allocated Faculty (Humanities):** Data from résumés submitted by the humanities faculty were used to construct this variable. It is made up of two measures; the number of published books and the number of articles published during the period 1986 to 2006 that were listed on the résumé. The calculated measure was the sum of five times the number of books plus the number articles for each allocated faculty member divided by the faculty allocated to the program. In computing the allocated faculty to the program, only the allocations of the faculty who submitted résumés were added to get the allocation. Book reviews were counted as articles.

**Average Citations per Publication (Non-Humanities):** Data from Thomson Reuters were used to construct this variable. It is the per-year average of the number of allocated citations in the years 2000-2006 to papers published during the period 1981-2006 by program faculty divided by the allocated publications that could contribute to the citations. For example, the number of allocated citations for a faculty member in 2003 is found by taking the 2003 citations to that faculty member's publications between 1981 and 2003. These counts are summed over the entire faculty in the program and divided by the sum of the allocated publications to the program in 2003.

---

[*] Because many faculty members supervise dissertations in more than one program, faculty members were allocated across the programs that they were associated with so that the total, taken across all programs, equaled one.

[1] These papers were compiled from the résumés of individual faculty members.

**Percent of Faculty with Grants:** Data from the faculty questionnaire were used to construct this variable. The faculty questionnaire asks whether a faculty member's work is currently supported by an extramural grant or contract (E1). The total of faculty who answered this question in the affirmative was divided by the total respondents in the program and the percentage was then calculated.

**Percent Interdisciplinary:** Data from the program questionnaire were used for this variable. Faculty were identified as either core, new, or associated. Percent interdisciplinary is the ratio of associated to the sum of core, new, and associated faculty. Allocations were not used in the construction of this variable.

**Percent Non-Asian Minority Faculty of Core and New Faculty, 2006[**]:** Data from the program questionnaire were used for this variable. For each program the data reported for question B7, the race/ethnicity of core and new faculty in the program, was used to compute the ratio of non-Hispanic Blacks, Hispanic, and American Indians or Alaska Natives to that of non-Hispanic Whites, non-Hispanic Blacks, Hispanic, Asian or Pacific Islanders, and American Indians or Alaska Natives. Faculty with Race/Ethnicity Unknown were excluded from the ratio, as were faculty who were neither American citizens not permanent residents. Allocations were not used in the construction of this variable.

**Percent Female Faculty of Core and New Faculty, 2006:** Data from the program questionnaire were used for this variable. For each program the data reported for question B5, the gender of core and new faculty in the program, was used to compute the ratio of core or new female faculty to the total of core and new faculty as described above. Allocations were not used in the construction of this variable.

**Awards per Allocated Faculty:** Data from a review of 1,393 awards and honors from various scholarly organizations were used for this variable. The awards were identified by the committee as "Highly Prestigious" or "Prestigious" with the former given a weight of 5. The award recipients were matched to the faculty in all programs, and the total awards for a faculty member in a program was the sum of the weighted awards times the faculty member's allocation in that program. These awards were added across the faculty in a program and divided by the total allocation of the faculty to the program. Even though the awards spreadsheet provided on the website is separated by field, award recipients were matched to faculty members in all programs by broad field. Therefore, just because an award was omitted from a field on the online spreadsheet, this does not mean that faculty did not get credit for awards outside their field.

**Average GRE, 2004-2006 (Verbal Measure for the Humanities, Quantitative Measure for All Other Fields):** Data from the program questionnaire were used for this variable. For each program, question D4 reported the average GRE verbal and

---

[**] "Core" faculty are those whose primary appointment is in the doctoral program. "New" faculty are those with tenure track appointments who were appointed in 2003-2006.

quantitative scores for the 2003-2004, 2004-2005, and 2005-2006 academic years and the number of individuals who reported their scores. A weighted average was used to compute the average GRE, which was calculated by multiplying the number of individuals reporting scores by the reported average GRE score for each year, adding these three quantities and dividing by the sum of the individuals reporting scores.

**Percent Students Receiving Full Support in the First Year (Fall 2005):** Data from the program questionnaire were used for this variable. For each program question E5 reported the type of support that full-time graduate students received during the fall term each year of enrollment. For this variable the data for the first year were added for all types of support and divided by the total number of students.

**Percent First-Year Students with External Funding, 2005:** Data from the program questionnaire were used for this variable. For each program question E8 reported the type of support full-time graduate students received during fall term each year of enrollment. For this variable the data for the first year were added for support by externally funded fellowships and combinations of external fellowships and other internal support and then divided by the total number of first year students.

**Percent First-Year Students with Institutional Fellowships Alone, Fall 2005:** Data from the program questionnaire were used for this variable. For each program question E8 reported the type of support full-time graduate students received during fall term each year of enrollment. This variable is defined as the data for first-year students who were supported by institutional fellowships alone divided by the total number of first year students.

**Percent First-Year Students with Combination of Fellowships and Traineeships, Fall 2005:** Data from the program questionnaire were used for this variable. For each program question E8 reported the type of support full-time graduate students received during fall term each year of enrollment. This variable is defined as the data for first year students who were supported by a combination of fellowships and traineeships divided by the total number of first-year students.

**Percent First-Year Students with Both Internal Fellowships and Internal Assistantships, Fall 2005:** Data from the program questionnaire were used for this variable. For each program question E8 reported the type of support full-time graduate students received during fall term each year of enrollment. This variable is defined as the data for first-year students who were supported by both internal fellowships and internal assistantships divided by the total number of first year students.

**Percent First-Year Students with Multiple Internal Assistantships, Fall 2005:** Data from the program questionnaire were used for this variable. For each program question E8 reported the type of support full-time graduate students received during fall term each year of enrollment. This variable is defined as the data for first year students who were supported by multiple internal assistantships divided by the total number of first-year students.

**Percent Non-Asian Minority Students, 2005:** Data from the program questionnaire were used for this variable. Question C9c reported the race/ethnicity of doctoral students in the program. This was used to compute the ratio of non-Hispanic Blacks, Hispanics, and American Indians or Alaska Natives to that of non-Hispanic Whites, non-Hispanic Blacks, Hispanics, Asian or Pacific Islanders, and American Indians or Alaska Natives. Respondents with Race/Ethnicity Unknown where excluded from the ratio as were international students.

**Percent Female Students, 2005:** Data from the program questionnaire were used for this variable. Question C9 reported the gender of doctoral students in the program. This was used to compute the percentage by taking the number of female graduate students divided by the total number of doctoral students.

**Percent International Students, 2006:** Data from the program questionnaire were used for this variable. Question C9b reported the citizenship of graduate students in the program. These data were used to compute the percentage of international graduate students by taking the number with temporary visas and dividing it by the number of doctoral students with known citizenship status.

**Average Annual Ph.D.'s Graduated 2002-2006:** Data from the program questionnaire were used for this variable. Question C1 reported the number of doctoral degrees awarded each academic year from 2001-2002 to 2005-2006. The average of these numbers was used for this variable. If no data were provided for a particular year, the average was taken over the years for which there were data.

**Average Completion Percentage (8-Year Completion Percentage for Humanities Fields, 6 Years for Other Fields):** Data from the program questionnaire were used for this variable. Questions C16 and C17 reported for males and females separately the number of graduate students who entered in different cohorts from 1996-1997 to 2005-2006 and the number in each cohort who completed in 3 years or less, in their 4th, 5th, 6th, 7th, 8th, 9th years, and in 10 or more years. To compute the completion rate, the number of doctoral students for a given entering cohort who completed their doctorate in 3 years or less and in their 4th, 5th, 6th years were totaled and the total was divided by the entering students in that cohort. This computation was made for each cohort that entered from 1996-1997 to 1998-1999 for the humanities and 1996-1997 to 2000-2001 for the other fields. Cohorts beyond these years were not considered, since the students could complete in a year that was after the final year 2005-2006 for which data were collected. To compute the average completion rate, an average was taken over 3 cohorts for the humanities and over 5 cohorts for other fields.

**Time to Degree (for Full- and Part-Time Graduates):** Data from the program questionnaire were used for this variable. Question C2 reported the median time to degree for full-time and part-time students averaged over the years 2004-2006. That reported number was used for this variable.

**Percent Ph.D.'s with Definite Plans for an Academic Position, 2001-2005**: Data from the National Science Foundation 2005 Doctorate Records File (DRF) were used for this variable. A crosswalk was generated between the DRF Specialty Fields of Study and the fields in the study taxonomy. Data from the DRF for 5 years (2001-2005) were matched by field and institution to the programs in the research-doctorate study. The percentage was computed by taking the number of individuals who have a signed contract or are negotiating a contract for a position at an educational institution and dividing by the number of doctorates in those years. Positions included employment and postdoctoral fellowships. In the final version, this definition has changed. The denominator is now the number of survey respondents instead of the number of doctorates in those years.

**Student Work Space:** Data from the program questionnaire were used for this variable. Question D12 reported the percentage of graduate students who have work space for their exclusive use. If reported percentage was 100 percent, then a value of 1 was given to this variable. Otherwise the value was -1.

**Health Insurance:** Data from the institutional questionnaire were used for this variable. Question A1 reported whether or not the institution provided health care insurance for its graduate students. If the response to this question was yes, then a value of 1 was given to this variable. If it was no, then the value was -1.

**Student Activities:** Data from the program questionnaire were used for this variable. Question D8 listed 18 different kinds of support for doctoral students or doctoral education. This variable is a count of the number of support mechanisms proved by the program or the institution.

Data Not Used in Ranking Calculations but Presented in the On-line Tables

**Total Faculty:** Sum of core, new, and associated faculty 2006 (Question B1 through B3 on the program questionnaire)

**Number of Allocated Faculty:** Number of allocated faculty in 2006 (described in footnote on p. 46)

**Assistant Professors (%):** Number of assistant professors as a percent of core and new faculty 2006 (Question B1 and B2 on the program questionnaire)

**Tenured Faculty (% of Core and new Faculty):** Number of faculty with tenure as a percent of core and new faculty 2006 (Questions B1 and B2)
**Number of Core and New Faculty:** Sum of core (B1) and new faculty (B2)

**Total Students Enrolled:** Number of Students Enrolled Fall 2005 (C8)

**Average 1st Yr Enrollment:** Average annual first year enrollment, 2002-2006 (C3)

**Research Assistants (%):** Percent of students with research assistantships fall 2005   as a percent of enrollment. (E8)

**Teaching Assistants (%) (Percent of enrollment):** Number of students with teaching assistantships, fall 2005 as a percent of enrollment (E8)

**Regional Code**: 1=North East (Maine, New Hampshire, Vermont, Massachusetts, Rhode Island, Connecticut, New York, Pennsylvania, New Jersey) 2=Mid-West (Wisconsin, Michigan, Illinois, Indiana, Ohio, Missouri, North Dakota, South Dakota, Nebraska, Kansas, Minnesota, Iowa)  3=South Atlantic (Delaware, Maryland, District of Columbia, Virginia, West Virginia, North Carolina, South Carolina, Georgia, Florida) 4=South Central (Kentucky, Tennessee, Mississippi, Alabama, Oklahoma, Texas, Arkansas, Louisiana) 5=West (Idaho, Montana, Wyoming, Nevada, Utah, Colorado, Arizona, New Mexico, Alaska, Washington, Oregon, California, Hawaii)

# APPENDIX F

# R AND S COEFFICIENTS BY FIELDS

| Aerospace Engineering | R-Based .05 | R-Based .95 | R-Based Stdev | S-Based .05 | S-Based .95 | S-Based Stdev |
|---|---|---|---|---|---|---|
| Publications per Allocated Faculty | 0.077 | 0.112 | 0.012 | 0.077 | 0.112 | 0.012 |
| Cites Per Publication | -0.065 | 0.023 | 0.025 | -0.065 | 0.023 | 0.025 |
| Grants per Allocated Faculty | -0.005 | 0.035 | 0.013 | -0.005 | 0.035 | 0.013 |
| Percent Faculty Interdisciplinary | -0.042 | 0.014 | 0.018 | -0.042 | 0.014 | 0.018 |
| percent Non-Asian Minority Faculty | -0.080 | 0.019 | 0.029 | -0.080 | 0.019 | 0.029 |
| Percent Female Faculty | 0.052 | 0.079 | 0.009 | 0.052 | 0.079 | 0.009 |
| Awards per Allocated Faculty | 0.087 | 0.123 | 0.011 | 0.087 | 0.123 | 0.011 |
| Average GRE-Q | -0.002 | 0.063 | 0.020 | -0.002 | 0.063 | 0.020 |
| Percent First-Year Students with Full Support | -0.053 | -0.006 | 0.014 | -0.053 | -0.006 | 0.014 |
| Percent First-Year Students with Portable Fellowships | -0.071 | -0.009 | 0.021 | -0.071 | -0.009 | 0.021 |
| Percent Non-Asian Minority Students | -0.083 | 0.004 | 0.028 | -0.083 | 0.004 | 0.028 |
| Percent Female Students | -0.020 | 0.012 | 0.013 | -0.020 | 0.012 | 0.013 |
| Percent International Students | -0.116 | -0.082 | 0.012 | -0.116 | -0.082 | 0.012 |
| Average PhDs 2002 to 2006 | 0.163 | 0.214 | 0.015 | 0.163 | 0.214 | 0.015 |
| Percent Completing within 6 Years | -0.007 | 0.067 | 0.019 | -0.007 | 0.067 | 0.019 |
| Time to Degree Full and Part Time | -0.045 | 0.009 | 0.017 | -0.045 | 0.009 | 0.017 |
| Percent Students in Academic Positions | 0.011 | 0.082 | 0.021 | 0.011 | 0.082 | 0.021 |
| Student Workspace | -0.005 | 0.048 | 0.017 | -0.005 | 0.048 | 0.017 |
| Health Insurance | 0.011 | 0.056 | 0.014 | 0.011 | 0.056 | 0.014 |
| Number of Student Activities | 0.006 | 0.065 | 0.020 | 0.006 | 0.065 | 0.020 |

| Agricultural. And Resource Economics | R-Based .05 | R-Based .95 | R-Based Stdev | S-Based .05 | S-Based .95 | S-Based Stdev |
|---|---|---|---|---|---|---|
| Publications per Allocated Faculty | -0.032 | 0.068 | 0.038 | 0.170 | 0.184 | 0.004 |
| Cites Per Publication | 0.114 | 0.249 | 0.046 | 0.130 | 0.145 | 0.004 |
| Grants per Allocated Faculty | 0.024 | 0.100 | 0.027 | 0.105 | 0.118 | 0.004 |
| Percent Faculty Interdisciplinary | -0.037 | -0.019 | 0.006 | 0.037 | 0.048 | 0.003 |
| percent Non-Asian Minority Faculty | -0.004 | 0.071 | 0.022 | 0.006 | 0.011 | 0.001 |
| Percent Female Faculty | -0.096 | -0.011 | 0.031 | 0.006 | 0.010 | 0.001 |
| Awards per Allocated Faculty | -0.005 | 0.116 | 0.035 | 0.076 | 0.088 | 0.004 |
| Average GRE-Q | 0.082 | 0.124 | 0.013 | 0.078 | 0.088 | 0.003 |
| Percent First-Year Students with Full Support | -0.036 | 0.052 | 0.028 | 0.047 | 0.055 | 0.003 |
| Percent First-Year Students with Portable Fellowships | -0.017 | 0.043 | 0.018 | 0.025 | 0.031 | 0.002 |
| Percent Non-Asian Minority Students | -0.022 | 0.048 | 0.018 | 0.012 | 0.016 | 0.002 |
| Percent Female Students | -0.112 | -0.049 | 0.023 | 0.008 | 0.012 | 0.001 |
| Percent International Students | -0.005 | 0.031 | 0.012 | 0.009 | 0.013 | 0.001 |
| Average PhDs 2002 to 2006 | 0.116 | 0.219 | 0.039 | 0.033 | 0.040 | 0.002 |
| Percent Completing within 6 Years | -0.025 | 0.042 | 0.023 | 0.040 | 0.048 | 0.003 |
| Time to Degree Full and Part Time | -0.025 | 0.048 | 0.024 | -0.027 | -0.021 | 0.002 |
| Percent Students in Academic Positions | -0.032 | 0.022 | 0.016 | 0.089 | 0.098 | 0.003 |
| Student Workspace | -0.023 | 0.023 | 0.014 | 0.004 | 0.006 | 0.001 |
| Health Insurance | -0.056 | 0.016 | 0.021 | 0.001 | 0.003 | 0.001 |
| Number of Student Activities | -0.007 | 0.048 | 0.017 | 0.027 | 0.034 | 0.002 |

| American Studies | R-Based .05 | R-Based .95 | R-Based Stdev | S-Based .05 | S-Based .95 | S-Based Stdev |
|---|---|---|---|---|---|---|
| Publications per Allocated Faculty | -0.018 | 0.052 | 0.022 | 0.128 | 0.151 | 0.007 |
| Cites Per Publication | None | None | None | None | None | None |
| Grants per Allocated Faculty | -0.050 | -0.016 | 0.011 | 0.019 | 0.034 | 0.004 |
| Percent Faculty Interdisciplinary | -0.060 | -0.001 | 0.015 | 0.086 | 0.106 | 0.006 |
| percent Non-Asian Minority Faculty | 0.032 | 0.097 | 0.022 | 0.080 | 0.097 | 0.005 |
| Percent Female Faculty | -0.053 | 0.004 | 0.017 | 0.042 | 0.055 | 0.004 |
| Awards per Allocated Faculty | 0.083 | 0.131 | 0.015 | 0.070 | 0.093 | 0.007 |
| Average GRE-Q | 0.131 | 0.172 | 0.012 | 0.024 | 0.035 | 0.004 |
| Percent First-Year Students with Full Support | 0.012 | 0.049 | 0.010 | 0.074 | 0.087 | 0.004 |
| Percent First-Year Students with Portable Fellowships | -0.007 | 0.026 | 0.011 | 0.015 | 0.024 | 0.003 |
| Percent Non-Asian Minority Students | 0.018 | 0.075 | 0.015 | 0.071 | 0.082 | 0.004 |
| Percent Female Students | -0.020 | 0.034 | 0.016 | 0.036 | 0.045 | 0.003 |
| Percent International Students | -0.068 | 0.012 | 0.023 | 0.006 | 0.012 | 0.002 |
| Average PhDs 2002 to 2006 | 0.104 | 0.145 | 0.014 | 0.018 | 0.027 | 0.003 |
| Percent Completing within 6 Years | -0.031 | 0.024 | 0.017 | 0.059 | 0.071 | 0.004 |
| Time to Degree Full and Part Time | -0.079 | -0.025 | 0.015 | -0.030 | -0.021 | 0.003 |
| Percent Students in Academic Positions | 0.043 | 0.096 | 0.017 | 0.078 | 0.091 | 0.004 |
| Student Workspace | -0.045 | 0.003 | 0.014 | 0.001 | 0.004 | 0.001 |
| Health Insurance | -0.016 | 0.044 | 0.019 | 0.011 | 0.019 | 0.003 |
| Number of Student Activities | 0.096 | 0.138 | 0.012 | 0.044 | 0.057 | 0.004 |
| **Animal Science** | **R-Based .05** | **R-Based .95** | **R-Based Stdev** | **S-Based .05** | **S-Based .95** | **S-Based Stdev** |
| Publications per Allocated Faculty | 0.026 | 0.105 | 0.026 | 0.150 | 0.159 | 0.003 |
| Cites Per Publication | -0.090 | 0.034 | 0.041 | 0.081 | 0.091 | 0.003 |
| Grants per Allocated Faculty | -0.040 | 0.019 | 0.018 | 0.143 | 0.153 | 0.003 |
| Percent Faculty Interdisciplinary | -0.028 | 0.034 | 0.022 | 0.066 | 0.075 | 0.003 |
| percent Non-Asian Minority Faculty | -0.085 | -0.014 | 0.023 | 0.007 | 0.011 | 0.001 |
| Percent Female Faculty | -0.013 | 0.050 | 0.017 | 0.009 | 0.013 | 0.001 |
| Awards per Allocated Faculty | 0.028 | 0.085 | 0.017 | 0.058 | 0.068 | 0.003 |
| Average GRE-Q | 0.051 | 0.126 | 0.028 | 0.059 | 0.067 | 0.002 |
| Percent First-Year Students with Full Support | -0.043 | 0.020 | 0.021 | 0.067 | 0.075 | 0.002 |
| Percent First-Year Students with Portable Fellowships | -0.047 | 0.050 | 0.029 | 0.022 | 0.027 | 0.002 |
| Percent Non-Asian Minority Students | -0.077 | 0.031 | 0.029 | 0.014 | 0.017 | 0.001 |
| Percent Female Students | -0.014 | 0.074 | 0.030 | 0.014 | 0.018 | 0.001 |
| Percent International Students | 0.000 | 0.118 | 0.038 | 0.007 | 0.011 | 0.001 |
| Average PhDs 2002 to 2006 | 0.102 | 0.170 | 0.026 | 0.036 | 0.042 | 0.002 |
| Percent Completing within 6 Years | -0.034 | 0.055 | 0.021 | 0.055 | 0.062 | 0.002 |
| Time to Degree Full and Part Time | -0.083 | -0.004 | 0.025 | -0.029 | -0.024 | 0.001 |
| Percent Students in Academic Positions | -0.027 | 0.056 | 0.030 | 0.086 | 0.094 | 0.002 |
| Student Workspace | -0.080 | -0.016 | 0.021 | 0.003 | 0.005 | 0.001 |
| Health Insurance | -0.020 | 0.061 | 0.027 | 0.005 | 0.007 | 0.001 |
| Number of Student Activities | 0.066 | 0.120 | 0.020 | 0.031 | 0.036 | 0.002 |

| Anthropology | R-Based .05 | R-Based .95 | R-Based Stdev | S-Based .05 | S-Based .95 | S-Based Stdev |
|---|---|---|---|---|---|---|
| Publications per Allocated Faculty | 0.025 | 0.055 | 0.012 | 0.149 | 0.157 | 0.002 |
| Cites Per Publication | 0.025 | 0.062 | 0.016 | 0.076 | 0.084 | 0.002 |
| Grants per Allocated Faculty | -0.022 | 0.012 | 0.010 | 0.104 | 0.113 | 0.003 |
| Percent Faculty Interdisciplinary | 0.006 | 0.056 | 0.015 | 0.053 | 0.059 | 0.002 |
| percent Non-Asian Minority Faculty | -0.048 | 0.033 | 0.026 | 0.030 | 0.035 | 0.002 |
| Percent Female Faculty | -0.028 | 0.010 | 0.011 | 0.026 | 0.031 | 0.001 |
| Awards per Allocated Faculty | 0.108 | 0.143 | 0.017 | 0.059 | 0.066 | 0.002 |
| Average GRE-Q | 0.035 | 0.091 | 0.019 | 0.043 | 0.048 | 0.001 |
| Percent First-Year Students with Full Support | 0.003 | 0.040 | 0.012 | 0.063 | 0.069 | 0.002 |
| Percent First-Year Students with Portable Fellowships | 0.037 | 0.123 | 0.028 | 0.035 | 0.039 | 0.001 |
| Percent Non-Asian Minority Students | -0.008 | 0.078 | 0.023 | 0.032 | 0.036 | 0.001 |
| Percent Female Students | -0.031 | 0.044 | 0.023 | 0.018 | 0.022 | 0.001 |
| Percent International Students | 0.036 | 0.064 | 0.009 | 0.017 | 0.021 | 0.001 |
| Average PhDs 2002 to 2006 | 0.107 | 0.153 | 0.012 | 0.021 | 0.024 | 0.001 |
| Percent Completing within 6 Years | -0.037 | 0.076 | 0.034 | 0.060 | 0.065 | 0.001 |
| Time to Degree Full and Part Time | -0.018 | 0.039 | 0.016 | -0.028 | -0.025 | 0.001 |
| Percent Students in Academic Positions | 0.057 | 0.083 | 0.010 | 0.082 | 0.087 | 0.002 |
| Student Workspace | -0.025 | 0.024 | 0.014 | 0.005 | 0.007 | 0.001 |
| Health Insurance | 0.043 | 0.111 | 0.019 | 0.008 | 0.010 | 0.001 |
| Number of Student Activities | 0.047 | 0.090 | 0.016 | 0.043 | 0.048 | 0.001 |

| Applied Mathematics | R-Based .05 | R-Based .95 | R-Based Stdev | S-Based .05 | S-Based .95 | S-Based Stdev |
|---|---|---|---|---|---|---|
| Publications per Allocated Faculty | 0.040 | 0.069 | 0.010 | 0.131 | 0.143 | 0.004 |
| Cites Per Publication | 0.069 | 0.093 | 0.010 | 0.120 | 0.134 | 0.004 |
| Grants per Allocated Faculty | 0.061 | 0.131 | 0.020 | 0.126 | 0.139 | 0.004 |
| Percent Faculty Interdisciplinary | 0.031 | 0.083 | 0.014 | 0.055 | 0.066 | 0.003 |
| percent Non-Asian Minority Faculty | -0.025 | 0.019 | 0.014 | 0.004 | 0.008 | 0.001 |
| Percent Female Faculty | -0.036 | -0.005 | 0.009 | 0.006 | 0.010 | 0.001 |
| Awards per Allocated Faculty | 0.041 | 0.084 | 0.012 | 0.086 | 0.099 | 0.004 |
| Average GRE-Q | 0.061 | 0.093 | 0.013 | 0.062 | 0.071 | 0.003 |
| Percent First-Year Students with Full Support | -0.037 | 0.036 | 0.019 | 0.059 | 0.068 | 0.003 |
| Percent First-Year Students with Portable Fellowships | 0.004 | 0.041 | 0.011 | 0.042 | 0.050 | 0.003 |
| Percent Non-Asian Minority Students | -0.025 | 0.037 | 0.017 | 0.010 | 0.014 | 0.001 |
| Percent Female Students | -0.045 | -0.030 | 0.006 | 0.013 | 0.018 | 0.001 |
| Percent International Students | -0.085 | -0.009 | 0.026 | 0.015 | 0.022 | 0.002 |
| Average PhDs 2002 to 2006 | 0.058 | 0.113 | 0.019 | 0.037 | 0.044 | 0.002 |
| Percent Completing within 6 Years | 0.021 | 0.044 | 0.007 | 0.044 | 0.051 | 0.002 |
| Time to Degree Full and Part Time | 0.011 | 0.073 | 0.017 | -0.027 | -0.022 | 0.002 |
| Percent Students in Academic Positions | -0.031 | 0.057 | 0.023 | 0.069 | 0.076 | 0.002 |
| Student Workspace | 0.074 | 0.117 | 0.015 | 0.005 | 0.008 | 0.001 |
| Health Insurance | -0.034 | 0.052 | 0.036 | 0.003 | 0.005 | 0.001 |
| Number of Student Activities | -0.065 | 0.019 | 0.034 | 0.018 | 0.024 | 0.002 |

| Art History | R-Based .05 | R-Based .95 | R-Based Stdev | S-Based .05 | S-Based .95 | S-Based Stdev |
|---|---|---|---|---|---|---|
| Publications per Allocated Faculty | 0.022 | 0.124 | 0.035 | 0.171 | 0.184 | 0.004 |
| Cites Per Publication | None | None | None | None | None | None |
| Grants per Allocated Faculty | 0.001 | 0.077 | 0.028 | 0.073 | 0.085 | 0.004 |
| Percent Faculty Interdisciplinary | 0.032 | 0.083 | 0.015 | 0.070 | 0.083 | 0.004 |
| percent Non-Asian Minority Faculty | -0.037 | 0.033 | 0.024 | 0.025 | 0.032 | 0.002 |
| Percent Female Faculty | -0.010 | 0.064 | 0.025 | 0.034 | 0.042 | 0.003 |
| Awards per Allocated Faculty | 0.016 | 0.072 | 0.017 | 0.095 | 0.109 | 0.004 |
| Average GRE-Q | 0.100 | 0.148 | 0.015 | 0.053 | 0.061 | 0.003 |
| Percent First-Year Students with Full Support | 0.080 | 0.124 | 0.014 | 0.071 | 0.079 | 0.002 |
| Percent First-Year Students with Portable Fellowships | 0.028 | 0.066 | 0.012 | 0.022 | 0.028 | 0.002 |
| Percent Non-Asian Minority Students | 0.022 | 0.069 | 0.015 | 0.025 | 0.031 | 0.002 |
| Percent Female Students | -0.025 | 0.091 | 0.040 | 0.016 | 0.021 | 0.001 |
| Percent International Students | -0.062 | -0.003 | 0.017 | 0.021 | 0.028 | 0.002 |
| Average PhDs 2002 to 2006 | 0.138 | 0.223 | 0.033 | 0.026 | 0.033 | 0.002 |
| Percent Completing within 6 Years | -0.002 | 0.039 | 0.015 | 0.064 | 0.072 | 0.002 |
| Time to Degree Full and Part Time | -0.031 | 0.015 | 0.016 | -0.029 | -0.023 | 0.002 |
| Percent Students in Academic Positions | 0.022 | 0.081 | 0.019 | 0.085 | 0.093 | 0.002 |
| Student Workspace | -0.051 | 0.031 | 0.029 | 0.003 | 0.005 | 0.001 |
| Health Insurance | 0.027 | 0.078 | 0.017 | 0.006 | 0.010 | 0.001 |
| Number of Student Activities | -0.018 | 0.028 | 0.015 | 0.042 | 0.050 | 0.002 |
| **Astrophysics and Astronomy** | **R-Based .05** | **R-Based .95** | **R-Based Stdev** | **S-Based .05** | **S-Based .95** | **S-Based Stdev** |
| Publications per Allocated Faculty | 0.058 | 0.102 | 0.012 | 0.126 | 0.139 | 0.004 |
| Cites Per Publication | 0.012 | 0.042 | 0.010 | 0.146 | 0.159 | 0.004 |
| Grants per Allocated Faculty | 0.035 | 0.074 | 0.013 | 0.144 | 0.155 | 0.004 |
| Percent Faculty Interdisciplinary | 0.002 | 0.054 | 0.017 | 0.016 | 0.023 | 0.002 |
| percent Non-Asian Minority Faculty | 0.006 | 0.037 | 0.010 | 0.003 | 0.006 | 0.001 |
| Percent Female Faculty | -0.007 | 0.028 | 0.012 | 0.018 | 0.023 | 0.002 |
| Awards per Allocated Faculty | 0.104 | 0.149 | 0.016 | 0.080 | 0.092 | 0.003 |
| Average GRE-Q | 0.099 | 0.117 | 0.006 | 0.059 | 0.066 | 0.002 |
| Percent First-Year Students with Full Support | -0.016 | 0.056 | 0.025 | 0.050 | 0.058 | 0.002 |
| Percent First-Year Students with Portable Fellowships | 0.026 | 0.048 | 0.008 | 0.038 | 0.046 | 0.002 |
| Percent Non-Asian Minority Students | -0.036 | -0.007 | 0.009 | 0.007 | 0.010 | 0.001 |
| Percent Female Students | -0.050 | -0.017 | 0.011 | 0.024 | 0.030 | 0.002 |
| Percent International Students | -0.004 | 0.030 | 0.010 | 0.007 | 0.010 | 0.001 |
| Average PhDs 2002 to 2006 | 0.152 | 0.176 | 0.011 | 0.022 | 0.027 | 0.002 |
| Percent Completing within 6 Years | -0.054 | -0.005 | 0.016 | 0.052 | 0.059 | 0.002 |
| Time to Degree Full and Part Time | 0.051 | 0.091 | 0.013 | -0.032 | -0.027 | 0.002 |
| Percent Students in Academic Positions | 0.021 | 0.097 | 0.025 | 0.078 | 0.085 | 0.002 |
| Student Workspace | -0.025 | 0.017 | 0.012 | 0.006 | 0.009 | 0.001 |
| Health Insurance | -0.062 | -0.008 | 0.020 | 0.004 | 0.007 | 0.001 |
| Number of Student Activities | 0.019 | 0.058 | 0.011 | 0.025 | 0.031 | 0.002 |

| Biochemistry, Biophysics, and Structural Biology | R-Based .05 | R-Based .95 | R-Based Stdev | S-Based .05 | S-Based .95 | S-Based Stdev |
|---|---|---|---|---|---|---|
| Publications per Allocated Faculty | 0.071 | 0.116 | 0.013 | 0.138 | 0.144 | 0.002 |
| Cites Per Publication | 0.108 | 0.123 | 0.008 | 0.098 | 0.104 | 0.002 |
| Grants per Allocated Faculty | 0.011 | 0.056 | 0.015 | 0.167 | 0.172 | 0.002 |
| Percent Faculty Interdisciplinary | -0.035 | 0.057 | 0.032 | 0.041 | 0.046 | 0.002 |
| percent Non-Asian Minority Faculty | -0.034 | 0.007 | 0.015 | 0.008 | 0.010 | 0.001 |
| Percent Female Faculty | -0.044 | 0.036 | 0.025 | 0.014 | 0.016 | 0.001 |
| Awards per Allocated Faculty | 0.109 | 0.149 | 0.012 | 0.058 | 0.063 | 0.002 |
| Average GRE-Q | 0.054 | 0.102 | 0.017 | 0.077 | 0.082 | 0.002 |
| Percent First-Year Students with Full Support | -0.017 | 0.051 | 0.022 | 0.054 | 0.059 | 0.001 |
| Percent First-Year Students with Portable Fellowships | 0.029 | 0.087 | 0.019 | 0.043 | 0.047 | 0.001 |
| Percent Non-Asian Minority Students | -0.021 | 0.011 | 0.011 | 0.019 | 0.022 | 0.001 |
| Percent Female Students | -0.071 | -0.039 | 0.011 | 0.016 | 0.019 | 0.001 |
| Percent International Students | -0.052 | -0.012 | 0.014 | 0.008 | 0.010 | 0.001 |
| Average PhDs 2002 to 2006 | 0.077 | 0.120 | 0.013 | 0.025 | 0.028 | 0.001 |
| Percent Completing within 6 Years | -0.046 | 0.029 | 0.025 | 0.053 | 0.057 | 0.001 |
| Time to Degree Full and Part Time | -0.006 | 0.052 | 0.018 | -0.033 | -0.030 | 0.001 |
| Percent Students in Academic Positions | -0.053 | 0.029 | 0.025 | 0.075 | 0.079 | 0.001 |
| Student Workspace | -0.068 | 0.005 | 0.021 | 0.004 | 0.005 | 0.000 |
| Health Insurance | -0.014 | 0.029 | 0.014 | 0.004 | 0.006 | 0.000 |
| Number of Student Activities | 0.035 | 0.076 | 0.014 | 0.032 | 0.035 | 0.001 |
| **Biomedical Engineering and Bioengineering** | R-Based .05 | R-Based .95 | R-Based Stdev | S-Based .05 | S-Based .95 | S-Based Stdev |
| Publications per Allocated Faculty | 0.096 | 0.141 | 0.011 | 0.123 | 0.132 | 0.003 |
| Cites Per Publication | 0.012 | 0.053 | 0.016 | 0.099 | 0.109 | 0.003 |
| Grants per Allocated Faculty | 0.032 | 0.063 | 0.012 | 0.153 | 0.161 | 0.002 |
| Percent Faculty Interdisciplinary | -0.021 | 0.023 | 0.012 | 0.058 | 0.065 | 0.002 |
| percent Non-Asian Minority Faculty | -0.021 | -0.006 | 0.005 | 0.009 | 0.013 | 0.001 |
| Percent Female Faculty | -0.040 | -0.018 | 0.006 | 0.010 | 0.014 | 0.001 |
| Awards per Allocated Faculty | 0.040 | 0.071 | 0.009 | 0.056 | 0.063 | 0.002 |
| Average GRE-Q | 0.069 | 0.101 | 0.009 | 0.065 | 0.071 | 0.002 |
| Percent First-Year Students with Full Support | 0.069 | 0.097 | 0.008 | 0.060 | 0.066 | 0.002 |
| Percent First-Year Students with Portable Fellowships | -0.006 | 0.030 | 0.009 | 0.053 | 0.059 | 0.002 |
| Percent Non-Asian Minority Students | -0.035 | 0.017 | 0.015 | 0.019 | 0.023 | 0.001 |
| Percent Female Students | 0.032 | 0.068 | 0.014 | 0.016 | 0.019 | 0.001 |
| Percent International Students | -0.052 | -0.028 | 0.012 | 0.006 | 0.009 | 0.001 |
| Average PhDs 2002 to 2006 | 0.141 | 0.177 | 0.011 | 0.038 | 0.043 | 0.002 |
| Percent Completing within 6 Years | -0.002 | 0.056 | 0.014 | 0.047 | 0.052 | 0.002 |
| Time to Degree Full and Part Time | 0.058 | 0.092 | 0.009 | -0.026 | -0.022 | 0.001 |
| Percent Students in Academic Positions | 0.022 | 0.086 | 0.014 | 0.074 | 0.080 | 0.002 |
| Student Workspace | -0.038 | -0.014 | 0.006 | 0.006 | 0.008 | 0.001 |
| Health Insurance | -0.005 | 0.035 | 0.012 | 0.004 | 0.006 | 0.001 |
| Number of Student Activities | 0.024 | 0.059 | 0.014 | 0.029 | 0.033 | 0.001 |

| Cell and Developmental Biology | R-Based .05 | R-Based .95 | R-Based Stdev | S-Based .05 | S-Based .95 | S-Based Stdev |
|---|---|---|---|---|---|---|
| Publications per Allocated Faculty | -0.027 | 0.101 | 0.051 | 0.127 | 0.133 | 0.002 |
| Cites Per Publication | 0.039 | 0.111 | 0.026 | 0.097 | 0.104 | 0.002 |
| Grants per Allocated Faculty | -0.034 | 0.091 | 0.044 | 0.165 | 0.170 | 0.002 |
| Percent Faculty Interdisciplinary | 0.017 | 0.093 | 0.024 | 0.039 | 0.044 | 0.002 |
| percent Non-Asian Minority Faculty | -0.056 | 0.000 | 0.017 | 0.010 | 0.012 | 0.001 |
| Percent Female Faculty | -0.059 | 0.037 | 0.027 | 0.017 | 0.020 | 0.001 |
| Awards per Allocated Faculty | 0.068 | 0.153 | 0.026 | 0.056 | 0.061 | 0.002 |
| Average GRE-Q | 0.040 | 0.085 | 0.016 | 0.077 | 0.082 | 0.002 |
| Percent First-Year Students with Full Support | -0.006 | 0.064 | 0.022 | 0.056 | 0.061 | 0.001 |
| Percent First-Year Students with Portable Fellowships | -0.027 | 0.061 | 0.028 | 0.040 | 0.044 | 0.001 |
| Percent Non-Asian Minority Students | -0.042 | 0.016 | 0.022 | 0.023 | 0.026 | 0.001 |
| Percent Female Students | -0.005 | 0.069 | 0.021 | 0.018 | 0.022 | 0.001 |
| Percent International Students | -0.025 | 0.015 | 0.013 | 0.007 | 0.009 | 0.001 |
| Average PhDs 2002 to 2006 | 0.094 | 0.161 | 0.024 | 0.021 | 0.024 | 0.001 |
| Percent Completing within 6 Years | 0.022 | 0.140 | 0.043 | 0.058 | 0.062 | 0.001 |
| Time to Degree Full and Part Time | 0.002 | 0.117 | 0.041 | -0.034 | -0.031 | 0.001 |
| Percent Students in Academic Positions | -0.044 | 0.010 | 0.017 | 0.077 | 0.081 | 0.001 |
| Student Workspace | -0.094 | 0.041 | 0.041 | 0.004 | 0.005 | 0.000 |
| Health Insurance | -0.039 | 0.035 | 0.025 | 0.004 | 0.005 | 0.000 |
| Number of Student Activities | -0.004 | 0.060 | 0.018 | 0.035 | 0.039 | 0.001 |

| Chemical Engineering | R-Based .05 | R-Based .95 | R-Based Stdev | S-Based .05 | S-Based .95 | S-Based Stdev |
|---|---|---|---|---|---|---|
| Publications per Allocated Faculty | 0.049 | 0.129 | 0.029 | 0.146 | 0.154 | 0.002 |
| Cites Per Publication | 0.055 | 0.091 | 0.011 | 0.133 | 0.141 | 0.003 |
| Grants per Allocated Faculty | 0.029 | 0.054 | 0.007 | 0.136 | 0.143 | 0.002 |
| Percent Faculty Interdisciplinary | 0.017 | 0.066 | 0.015 | 0.037 | 0.044 | 0.002 |
| percent Non-Asian Minority Faculty | 0.002 | 0.048 | 0.015 | 0.005 | 0.008 | 0.001 |
| Percent Female Faculty | -0.057 | 0.000 | 0.017 | 0.007 | 0.010 | 0.001 |
| Awards per Allocated Faculty | 0.074 | 0.113 | 0.011 | 0.086 | 0.095 | 0.003 |
| Average GRE-Q | 0.028 | 0.088 | 0.021 | 0.062 | 0.068 | 0.002 |
| Percent First-Year Students with Full Support | 0.029 | 0.059 | 0.009 | 0.061 | 0.067 | 0.002 |
| Percent First-Year Students with Portable Fellowships | -0.118 | -0.011 | 0.036 | 0.049 | 0.055 | 0.002 |
| Percent Non-Asian Minority Students | -0.063 | -0.019 | 0.014 | 0.012 | 0.015 | 0.001 |
| Percent Female Students | -0.011 | 0.077 | 0.032 | 0.013 | 0.016 | 0.001 |
| Percent International Students | -0.070 | 0.022 | 0.032 | 0.006 | 0.008 | 0.001 |
| Average PhDs 2002 to 2006 | 0.115 | 0.242 | 0.046 | 0.053 | 0.057 | 0.001 |
| Percent Completing within 6 Years | -0.009 | 0.068 | 0.027 | 0.035 | 0.039 | 0.001 |
| Time to Degree Full and Part Time | -0.026 | 0.028 | 0.017 | -0.023 | -0.020 | 0.001 |
| Percent Students in Academic Positions | -0.019 | 0.046 | 0.023 | 0.065 | 0.071 | 0.002 |
| Student Workspace | 0.017 | 0.036 | 0.006 | 0.003 | 0.005 | 0.000 |
| Health Insurance | -0.004 | 0.044 | 0.016 | 0.002 | 0.003 | 0.000 |
| Number of Student Activities | -0.012 | 0.076 | 0.029 | 0.021 | 0.025 | 0.001 |

| Chemistry | R-Based .05 | R-Based .95 | R-Based Stdev | S-Based .05 | S-Based .95 | S-Based Stdev |
|---|---|---|---|---|---|---|
| Publications per Allocated Faculty | -0.022 | 0.156 | 0.070 | 0.146 | 0.151 | 0.002 |
| Cites Per Publication | 0.018 | 0.076 | 0.017 | 0.125 | 0.130 | 0.002 |
| Grants per Allocated Faculty | 0.053 | 0.110 | 0.017 | 0.163 | 0.167 | 0.001 |
| Percent Faculty Interdisciplinary | -0.022 | 0.059 | 0.031 | 0.033 | 0.036 | 0.001 |
| percent Non-Asian Minority Faculty | -0.007 | 0.043 | 0.014 | 0.007 | 0.009 | 0.000 |
| Percent Female Faculty | -0.049 | 0.001 | 0.014 | 0.011 | 0.013 | 0.001 |
| Awards per Allocated Faculty | 0.074 | 0.142 | 0.021 | 0.081 | 0.086 | 0.001 |
| Average GRE-Q | -0.017 | 0.054 | 0.022 | 0.066 | 0.070 | 0.001 |
| Percent First-Year Students with Full Support | 0.041 | 0.080 | 0.013 | 0.053 | 0.057 | 0.001 |
| Percent First-Year Students with Portable Fellowships | -0.049 | -0.007 | 0.014 | 0.043 | 0.047 | 0.001 |
| Percent Non-Asian Minority Students | -0.051 | 0.045 | 0.024 | 0.015 | 0.017 | 0.001 |
| Percent Female Students | -0.044 | 0.019 | 0.019 | 0.016 | 0.018 | 0.001 |
| Percent International Students | -0.074 | -0.030 | 0.013 | 0.007 | 0.009 | 0.001 |
| Average PhDs 2002 to 2006 | 0.096 | 0.222 | 0.039 | 0.038 | 0.041 | 0.001 |
| Percent Completing within 6 Years | -0.056 | -0.002 | 0.018 | 0.045 | 0.048 | 0.001 |
| Time to Degree Full and Part Time | -0.021 | 0.038 | 0.021 | -0.025 | -0.023 | 0.001 |
| Percent Students in Academic Positions | 0.005 | 0.085 | 0.026 | 0.067 | 0.069 | 0.001 |
| Student Workspace | 0.022 | 0.076 | 0.019 | 0.005 | 0.006 | 0.000 |
| Health Insurance | 0.011 | 0.078 | 0.020 | 0.003 | 0.004 | 0.000 |
| Number of Student Activities | 0.031 | 0.096 | 0.020 | 0.022 | 0.024 | 0.001 |
| **Civil and Environmental Engineering** | **R-Based .05** | **R-Based .95** | **R-Based Stdev** | **S-Based .05** | **S-Based .95** | **S-Based Stdev** |
| Publications per Allocated Faculty | 0.059 | 0.125 | 0.021 | 0.148 | 0.155 | 0.002 |
| Cites Per Publication | -0.047 | 0.033 | 0.029 | 0.096 | 0.102 | 0.002 |
| Grants per Allocated Faculty | 0.011 | 0.060 | 0.015 | 0.140 | 0.146 | 0.002 |
| Percent Faculty Interdisciplinary | 0.010 | 0.097 | 0.029 | 0.047 | 0.052 | 0.002 |
| percent Non-Asian Minority Faculty | -0.031 | 0.029 | 0.019 | 0.008 | 0.011 | 0.001 |
| Percent Female Faculty | -0.044 | 0.008 | 0.016 | 0.010 | 0.013 | 0.001 |
| Awards per Allocated Faculty | -0.022 | 0.056 | 0.029 | 0.077 | 0.083 | 0.002 |
| Average GRE-Q | 0.020 | 0.082 | 0.023 | 0.065 | 0.071 | 0.002 |
| Percent First-Year Students with Full Support | -0.026 | 0.024 | 0.016 | 0.068 | 0.072 | 0.002 |
| Percent First-Year Students with Portable Fellowships | -0.043 | 0.000 | 0.014 | 0.047 | 0.052 | 0.002 |
| Percent Non-Asian Minority Students | -0.052 | 0.000 | 0.016 | 0.015 | 0.018 | 0.001 |
| Percent Female Students | -0.007 | 0.063 | 0.022 | 0.015 | 0.018 | 0.001 |
| Percent International Students | -0.024 | 0.040 | 0.021 | 0.009 | 0.012 | 0.001 |
| Average PhDs 2002 to 2006 | 0.267 | 0.334 | 0.025 | 0.055 | 0.059 | 0.001 |
| Percent Completing within 6 Years | -0.070 | 0.007 | 0.024 | 0.034 | 0.038 | 0.001 |
| Time to Degree Full and Part Time | 0.043 | 0.104 | 0.019 | -0.021 | -0.018 | 0.001 |
| Percent Students in Academic Positions | -0.013 | 0.078 | 0.029 | 0.072 | 0.076 | 0.001 |
| Student Workspace | -0.012 | 0.057 | 0.022 | 0.007 | 0.009 | 0.001 |
| Health Insurance | -0.092 | -0.051 | 0.015 | 0.003 | 0.004 | 0.000 |
| Number of Student Activities | 0.029 | 0.070 | 0.014 | 0.026 | 0.030 | 0.001 |

| Classics | R-Based .05 | R-Based .95 | R-Based Stdev | S-Based .05 | S-Based .95 | S-Based Stdev |
|---|---|---|---|---|---|---|
| Publications per Allocated Faculty | 0.103 | 0.168 | 0.021 | 0.172 | 0.189 | 0.005 |
| Cites Per Publication | None | None | None | None | None | None |
| Grants per Allocated Faculty | -0.038 | 0.022 | 0.020 | 0.047 | 0.062 | 0.004 |
| Percent Faculty Interdisciplinary | -0.037 | 0.084 | 0.036 | 0.066 | 0.082 | 0.005 |
| percent Non-Asian Minority Faculty | -0.045 | 0.019 | 0.021 | 0.004 | 0.007 | 0.001 |
| Percent Female Faculty | 0.024 | 0.106 | 0.025 | 0.026 | 0.037 | 0.003 |
| Awards per Allocated Faculty | 0.006 | 0.069 | 0.020 | 0.100 | 0.117 | 0.005 |
| Average GRE-Q | 0.109 | 0.160 | 0.021 | 0.066 | 0.079 | 0.004 |
| Percent First-Year Students with Full Support | 0.079 | 0.157 | 0.024 | 0.084 | 0.096 | 0.004 |
| Percent First-Year Students with Portable Fellowships | -0.031 | 0.068 | 0.030 | 0.019 | 0.026 | 0.002 |
| Percent Non-Asian Minority Students | -0.028 | 0.015 | 0.017 | 0.010 | 0.015 | 0.002 |
| Percent Female Students | -0.024 | 0.020 | 0.018 | 0.020 | 0.026 | 0.002 |
| Percent International Students | -0.027 | 0.037 | 0.019 | 0.019 | 0.028 | 0.003 |
| Average PhDs 2002 to 2006 | 0.129 | 0.181 | 0.016 | 0.030 | 0.040 | 0.003 |
| Percent Completing within 6 Years | -0.008 | 0.050 | 0.019 | 0.067 | 0.080 | 0.004 |
| Time to Degree Full and Part Time | -0.061 | 0.010 | 0.020 | -0.041 | -0.032 | 0.003 |
| Percent Students in Academic Positions | 0.009 | 0.101 | 0.028 | 0.093 | 0.106 | 0.004 |
| Student Workspace | -0.033 | 0.043 | 0.028 | 0.003 | 0.006 | 0.001 |
| Health Insurance | 0.032 | 0.092 | 0.020 | 0.006 | 0.011 | 0.002 |
| Number of Student Activities | -0.036 | 0.024 | 0.018 | 0.039 | 0.049 | 0.003 |
| **Communication** | R-Based .05 | R-Based .95 | R-Based Stdev | S-Based .05 | S-Based .95 | S-Based Stdev |
| Publications per Allocated Faculty | -0.064 | 0.096 | 0.048 | 0.164 | 0.172 | 0.002 |
| Cites Per Publication | -0.114 | 0.129 | 0.078 | 0.091 | 0.099 | 0.003 |
| Grants per Allocated Faculty | -0.035 | 0.122 | 0.053 | 0.065 | 0.072 | 0.002 |
| Percent Faculty Interdisciplinary | 0.000 | 0.123 | 0.042 | 0.058 | 0.065 | 0.002 |
| percent Non-Asian Minority Faculty | -0.038 | 0.091 | 0.040 | 0.030 | 0.035 | 0.002 |
| Percent Female Faculty | -0.081 | 0.100 | 0.055 | 0.024 | 0.028 | 0.001 |
| Awards per Allocated Faculty | -0.049 | 0.093 | 0.041 | 0.081 | 0.089 | 0.002 |
| Average GRE-Q | -0.066 | 0.114 | 0.057 | 0.062 | 0.067 | 0.002 |
| Percent First-Year Students with Full Support | -0.056 | 0.152 | 0.067 | 0.053 | 0.057 | 0.001 |
| Percent First-Year Students with Portable Fellowships | -0.067 | 0.049 | 0.033 | 0.011 | 0.014 | 0.001 |
| Percent Non-Asian Minority Students | -0.090 | 0.031 | 0.037 | 0.035 | 0.039 | 0.001 |
| Percent Female Students | -0.053 | 0.130 | 0.060 | 0.018 | 0.021 | 0.001 |
| Percent International Students | -0.074 | 0.085 | 0.049 | 0.012 | 0.014 | 0.001 |
| Average PhDs 2002 to 2006 | -0.112 | 0.082 | 0.055 | 0.026 | 0.029 | 0.001 |
| Percent Completing within 6 Years | -0.082 | 0.091 | 0.047 | 0.063 | 0.068 | 0.001 |
| Time to Degree Full and Part Time | -0.088 | 0.052 | 0.044 | -0.027 | -0.023 | 0.001 |
| Percent Students in Academic Positions | -0.041 | 0.097 | 0.042 | 0.083 | 0.088 | 0.002 |
| Student Workspace | -0.066 | 0.110 | 0.060 | 0.003 | 0.005 | 0.000 |
| Health Insurance | -0.081 | 0.102 | 0.057 | 0.008 | 0.010 | 0.001 |
| Number of Student Activities | -0.076 | 0.107 | 0.056 | 0.043 | 0.048 | 0.002 |

| **Comparative Literature.** | **R-Based .05** | **R-Based .95** | **R-Based Stdev** | **S-Based .05** | **S-Based .95** | **S-Based Stdev** |
|---|---|---|---|---|---|---|
| Publications per Allocated Faculty | 0.033 | 0.108 | 0.027 | 0.150 | 0.166 | 0.005 |
| Cites Per Publication | None | None | None | None | None | None |
| Grants per Allocated Faculty | -0.048 | 0.000 | 0.017 | 0.030 | 0.041 | 0.003 |
| Percent Faculty Interdisciplinary | 0.001 | 0.060 | 0.022 | 0.097 | 0.112 | 0.005 |
| percent Non-Asian Minority Faculty | 0.061 | 0.103 | 0.017 | 0.038 | 0.048 | 0.003 |
| Percent Female Faculty | -0.056 | 0.059 | 0.043 | 0.033 | 0.043 | 0.003 |
| Awards per Allocated Faculty | 0.064 | 0.314 | 0.097 | 0.079 | 0.095 | 0.005 |
| Average GRE-Q | -0.060 | 0.020 | 0.028 | 0.038 | 0.049 | 0.003 |
| Percent First-Year Students with Full Support | -0.006 | 0.077 | 0.028 | 0.073 | 0.083 | 0.003 |
| Percent First-Year Students with Portable Fellowships | 0.030 | 0.075 | 0.018 | 0.022 | 0.030 | 0.002 |
| Percent Non-Asian Minority Students | 0.048 | 0.123 | 0.028 | 0.036 | 0.044 | 0.002 |
| Percent Female Students | 0.034 | 0.110 | 0.026 | 0.026 | 0.033 | 0.002 |
| Percent International Students | -0.075 | -0.038 | 0.014 | 0.036 | 0.046 | 0.003 |
| Average PhDs 2002 to 2006 | -0.024 | 0.003 | 0.009 | 0.023 | 0.029 | 0.002 |
| Percent Completing within 6 Years | -0.079 | -0.031 | 0.015 | 0.064 | 0.073 | 0.003 |
| Time to Degree Full and Part Time | -0.063 | -0.015 | 0.017 | -0.030 | -0.023 | 0.002 |
| Percent Students in Academic Positions | 0.021 | 0.066 | 0.017 | 0.085 | 0.095 | 0.003 |
| Student Workspace | -0.034 | 0.054 | 0.035 | 0.002 | 0.004 | 0.001 |
| Health Insurance | 0.004 | 0.038 | 0.011 | 0.010 | 0.016 | 0.002 |
| Number of Student Activities | -0.013 | 0.023 | 0.011 | 0.045 | 0.054 | 0.003 |

| **Computer Science** | **R-Based .05** | **R-Based .95** | **R-Based Stdev** | **S-Based .05** | **S-Based .95** | **S-Based Stdev** |
|---|---|---|---|---|---|---|
| Publications per Allocated Faculty | 0.096 | 0.193 | 0.023 | 0.157 | 0.166 | 0.002 |
| Cites Per Publication | None | None | None | None | None | None |
| Grants per Allocated Faculty | 0.005 | 0.089 | 0.023 | 0.153 | 0.160 | 0.002 |
| Percent Faculty Interdisciplinary | 0.017 | 0.063 | 0.014 | 0.051 | 0.056 | 0.002 |
| percent Non-Asian Minority Faculty | 0.024 | 0.074 | 0.015 | 0.006 | 0.008 | 0.001 |
| Percent Female Faculty | 0.029 | 0.073 | 0.014 | 0.009 | 0.012 | 0.001 |
| Awards per Allocated Faculty | 0.084 | 0.130 | 0.014 | 0.122 | 0.130 | 0.003 |
| Average GRE-Q | 0.052 | 0.135 | 0.025 | 0.069 | 0.074 | 0.002 |
| Percent First-Year Students with Full Support | -0.011 | 0.015 | 0.007 | 0.078 | 0.082 | 0.001 |
| Percent First-Year Students with Portable Fellowships | -0.058 | -0.025 | 0.010 | 0.050 | 0.055 | 0.001 |
| Percent Non-Asian Minority Students | -0.061 | 0.005 | 0.020 | 0.013 | 0.015 | 0.001 |
| Percent Female Students | -0.065 | 0.007 | 0.027 | 0.017 | 0.020 | 0.001 |
| Percent International Students | -0.031 | 0.006 | 0.012 | 0.011 | 0.014 | 0.001 |
| Average PhDs 2002 to 2006 | 0.065 | 0.155 | 0.029 | 0.044 | 0.048 | 0.001 |
| Percent Completing within 6 Years | 0.019 | 0.050 | 0.009 | 0.043 | 0.047 | 0.001 |
| Time to Degree Full and Part Time | -0.001 | 0.059 | 0.017 | -0.021 | -0.019 | 0.001 |
| Percent Students in Academic Positions | 0.054 | 0.092 | 0.012 | 0.082 | 0.086 | 0.001 |
| Student Workspace | -0.009 | 0.026 | 0.011 | 0.009 | 0.011 | 0.000 |
| Health Insurance | -0.027 | 0.040 | 0.019 | 0.003 | 0.004 | 0.000 |
| Number of Student Activities | 0.033 | 0.088 | 0.020 | 0.027 | 0.030 | 0.001 |

| Earth Sciences | R-Based .05 | R-Based .95 | R-Based Stdev | S-Based .05 | S-Based .95 | S-Based Stdev |
|---|---|---|---|---|---|---|
| Publications per Allocated Faculty | -0.018 | 0.057 | 0.023 | 0.138 | 0.144 | 0.002 |
| Cites Per Publication | 0.101 | 0.160 | 0.017 | 0.118 | 0.126 | 0.002 |
| Grants per Allocated Faculty | -0.053 | 0.007 | 0.020 | 0.138 | 0.144 | 0.002 |
| Percent Faculty Interdisciplinary | 0.015 | 0.077 | 0.019 | 0.053 | 0.059 | 0.002 |
| percent Non-Asian Minority Faculty | -0.043 | 0.037 | 0.026 | 0.006 | 0.008 | 0.001 |
| Percent Female Faculty | -0.057 | 0.012 | 0.021 | 0.014 | 0.017 | 0.001 |
| Awards per Allocated Faculty | 0.053 | 0.102 | 0.015 | 0.066 | 0.072 | 0.002 |
| Average GRE-Q | 0.089 | 0.180 | 0.026 | 0.063 | 0.068 | 0.002 |
| Percent First-Year Students with Full Support | -0.016 | 0.044 | 0.020 | 0.067 | 0.072 | 0.001 |
| Percent First-Year Students with Portable Fellowships | -0.075 | 0.020 | 0.028 | 0.038 | 0.042 | 0.001 |
| Percent Non-Asian Minority Students | 0.011 | 0.063 | 0.016 | 0.011 | 0.014 | 0.001 |
| Percent Female Students | -0.033 | 0.028 | 0.019 | 0.018 | 0.021 | 0.001 |
| Percent International Students | -0.100 | -0.054 | 0.014 | 0.007 | 0.010 | 0.001 |
| Average PhDs 2002 to 2006 | 0.051 | 0.101 | 0.015 | 0.037 | 0.040 | 0.001 |
| Percent Completing within 6 Years | -0.007 | 0.068 | 0.022 | 0.048 | 0.052 | 0.001 |
| Time to Degree Full and Part Time | 0.002 | 0.059 | 0.018 | -0.028 | -0.025 | 0.001 |
| Percent Students in Academic Positions | 0.047 | 0.121 | 0.021 | 0.076 | 0.081 | 0.001 |
| Student Workspace | 0.010 | 0.065 | 0.017 | 0.005 | 0.006 | 0.000 |
| Health Insurance | -0.044 | 0.040 | 0.025 | 0.004 | 0.005 | 0.000 |
| Number of Student Activities | 0.035 | 0.072 | 0.011 | 0.028 | 0.032 | 0.001 |
| **Ecology and Evolutionary Biology.** | R-Based .05 | R-Based .95 | R-Based Stdev | S-Based .05 | S-Based .95 | S-Based Stdev |
| Publications per Allocated Faculty | 0.034 | 0.072 | 0.015 | 0.139 | 0.146 | 0.002 |
| Cites Per Publication | 0.044 | 0.062 | 0.007 | 0.102 | 0.110 | 0.002 |
| Grants per Allocated Faculty | -0.026 | 0.023 | 0.021 | 0.129 | 0.136 | 0.002 |
| Percent Faculty Interdisciplinary | -0.061 | -0.041 | 0.008 | 0.054 | 0.061 | 0.002 |
| percent Non-Asian Minority Faculty | -0.061 | -0.031 | 0.013 | 0.010 | 0.013 | 0.001 |
| Percent Female Faculty | 0.055 | 0.075 | 0.008 | 0.022 | 0.025 | 0.001 |
| Awards per Allocated Faculty | 0.067 | 0.087 | 0.007 | 0.054 | 0.061 | 0.002 |
| Average GRE-Q | 0.086 | 0.108 | 0.014 | 0.056 | 0.061 | 0.002 |
| Percent First-Year Students with Full Support | -0.016 | 0.044 | 0.024 | 0.067 | 0.073 | 0.002 |
| Percent First-Year Students with Portable Fellowships | -0.052 | -0.023 | 0.010 | 0.047 | 0.052 | 0.001 |
| Percent Non-Asian Minority Students | -0.012 | 0.024 | 0.017 | 0.020 | 0.023 | 0.001 |
| Percent Female Students | 0.040 | 0.052 | 0.005 | 0.020 | 0.023 | 0.001 |
| Percent International Students | -0.029 | 0.005 | 0.013 | 0.008 | 0.011 | 0.001 |
| Average PhDs 2002 to 2006 | 0.098 | 0.155 | 0.024 | 0.026 | 0.029 | 0.001 |
| Percent Completing within 6 Years | -0.018 | -0.002 | 0.007 | 0.050 | 0.054 | 0.001 |
| Time to Degree Full and Part Time | -0.026 | -0.019 | 0.009 | -0.026 | -0.022 | 0.001 |
| Percent Students in Academic Positions | 0.080 | 0.105 | 0.011 | 0.078 | 0.082 | 0.001 |
| Student Workspace | -0.072 | -0.044 | 0.010 | 0.007 | 0.009 | 0.001 |
| Health Insurance | -0.027 | 0.032 | 0.024 | 0.005 | 0.007 | 0.001 |
| Number of Student Activities | 0.055 | 0.078 | 0.009 | 0.038 | 0.043 | 0.001 |

| **Economics** | **R-Based .05** | **R-Based .95** | **R-Based Stdev** | **S-Based .05** | **S-Based .95** | **S-Based Stdev** |
|---|---|---|---|---|---|---|
| Publications per Allocated Faculty | -0.032 | 0.068 | 0.038 | 0.200 | 0.207 | 0.002 |
| Cites Per Publication | 0.114 | 0.249 | 0.046 | 0.198 | 0.205 | 0.002 |
| Grants per Allocated Faculty | 0.024 | 0.100 | 0.027 | 0.075 | 0.081 | 0.002 |
| Percent Faculty Interdisciplinary | -0.037 | -0.019 | 0.006 | 0.016 | 0.020 | 0.001 |
| percent Non-Asian Minority Faculty | -0.004 | 0.071 | 0.022 | 0.005 | 0.006 | 0.001 |
| Percent Female Faculty | -0.096 | -0.011 | 0.031 | 0.006 | 0.008 | 0.001 |
| Awards per Allocated Faculty | -0.005 | 0.116 | 0.035 | 0.089 | 0.096 | 0.002 |
| Average GRE-Q | 0.082 | 0.124 | 0.013 | 0.080 | 0.084 | 0.001 |
| Percent First-Year Students with Full Support | -0.036 | 0.052 | 0.028 | 0.055 | 0.059 | 0.001 |
| Percent First-Year Students with Portable Fellowships | -0.017 | 0.043 | 0.018 | 0.028 | 0.032 | 0.001 |
| Percent Non-Asian Minority Students | -0.022 | 0.048 | 0.018 | 0.007 | 0.009 | 0.001 |
| Percent Female Students | -0.112 | -0.049 | 0.023 | 0.006 | 0.007 | 0.000 |
| Percent International Students | -0.005 | 0.031 | 0.012 | 0.015 | 0.018 | 0.001 |
| Average PhDs 2002 to 2006 | 0.116 | 0.219 | 0.039 | 0.021 | 0.023 | 0.001 |
| Percent Completing within 6 Years | -0.025 | 0.042 | 0.023 | 0.036 | 0.039 | 0.001 |
| Time to Degree Full and Part Time | -0.025 | 0.048 | 0.024 | -0.032 | -0.029 | 0.001 |
| Percent Students in Academic Positions | -0.032 | 0.022 | 0.016 | 0.075 | 0.079 | 0.001 |
| Student Workspace | -0.023 | 0.023 | 0.014 | 0.005 | 0.006 | 0.000 |
| Health Insurance | -0.056 | 0.016 | 0.021 | 0.001 | 0.002 | 0.000 |
| Number of Student Activities | -0.007 | 0.048 | 0.017 | 0.017 | 0.019 | 0.001 |
| **Electrical and Computer Engineering** | **R-Based .05** | **R-Based .95** | **R-Based Stdev** | **S-Based .05** | **S-Based .95** | **S-Based Stdev** |
| Publications per Allocated Faculty | 0.098 | 0.140 | 0.017 | 0.138 | 0.144 | 0.002 |
| Cites Per Publication | 0.032 | 0.063 | 0.010 | 0.125 | 0.131 | 0.002 |
| Grants per Allocated Faculty | 0.009 | 0.064 | 0.021 | 0.135 | 0.141 | 0.002 |
| Percent Faculty Interdisciplinary | 0.039 | 0.075 | 0.013 | 0.041 | 0.045 | 0.001 |
| percent Non-Asian Minority Faculty | -0.041 | 0.002 | 0.014 | 0.006 | 0.008 | 0.001 |
| Percent Female Faculty | -0.040 | -0.019 | 0.007 | 0.006 | 0.008 | 0.000 |
| Awards per Allocated Faculty | 0.024 | 0.122 | 0.033 | 0.088 | 0.094 | 0.002 |
| Average GRE-Q | 0.037 | 0.096 | 0.022 | 0.065 | 0.069 | 0.001 |
| Percent First-Year Students with Full Support | -0.019 | 0.053 | 0.028 | 0.071 | 0.075 | 0.001 |
| Percent First-Year Students with Portable Fellowships | 0.015 | 0.054 | 0.015 | 0.045 | 0.049 | 0.001 |
| Percent Non-Asian Minority Students | -0.025 | 0.005 | 0.011 | 0.012 | 0.014 | 0.001 |
| Percent Female Students | -0.058 | -0.018 | 0.012 | 0.011 | 0.013 | 0.001 |
| Percent International Students | -0.037 | 0.005 | 0.015 | 0.011 | 0.014 | 0.001 |
| Average PhDs 2002 to 2006 | 0.137 | 0.182 | 0.019 | 0.055 | 0.058 | 0.001 |
| Percent Completing within 6 Years | 0.028 | 0.097 | 0.026 | 0.038 | 0.041 | 0.001 |
| Time to Degree Full and Part Time | 0.014 | 0.074 | 0.021 | -0.020 | -0.018 | 0.001 |
| Percent Students in Academic Positions | -0.071 | -0.019 | 0.016 | 0.071 | 0.075 | 0.001 |
| Student Workspace | -0.043 | 0.008 | 0.017 | 0.006 | 0.008 | 0.000 |
| Health Insurance | 0.001 | 0.032 | 0.009 | 0.002 | 0.003 | 0.000 |
| Number of Student Activities | 0.051 | 0.095 | 0.016 | 0.022 | 0.024 | 0.001 |

| **English Language and Literature** | R-Based .05 | R-Based .95 | R-Based Stdev | S-Based .05 | S-Based .95 | S-Based Stdev |
|---|---|---|---|---|---|---|
| Publications per Allocated Faculty | -0.018 | 0.052 | 0.022 | 0.168 | 0.174 | 0.002 |
| Cites Per Publication | None | None | None | None | None | None |
| Grants per Allocated Faculty | -0.050 | -0.016 | 0.011 | 0.036 | 0.040 | 0.001 |
| Percent Faculty Interdisciplinary | -0.060 | -0.001 | 0.015 | 0.057 | 0.061 | 0.001 |
| percent Non-Asian Minority Faculty | 0.032 | 0.097 | 0.022 | 0.051 | 0.055 | 0.001 |
| Percent Female Faculty | -0.053 | 0.004 | 0.017 | 0.042 | 0.046 | 0.001 |
| Awards per Allocated Faculty | 0.083 | 0.131 | 0.015 | 0.100 | 0.106 | 0.002 |
| Average GRE-Q | 0.131 | 0.172 | 0.012 | 0.057 | 0.061 | 0.001 |
| Percent First-Year Students with Full Support | 0.012 | 0.049 | 0.010 | 0.080 | 0.084 | 0.001 |
| Percent First-Year Students with Portable Fellowships | -0.007 | 0.026 | 0.011 | 0.022 | 0.024 | 0.001 |
| Percent Non-Asian Minority Students | 0.018 | 0.075 | 0.015 | 0.046 | 0.049 | 0.001 |
| Percent Female Students | -0.020 | 0.034 | 0.016 | 0.030 | 0.032 | 0.001 |
| Percent International Students | -0.068 | 0.012 | 0.023 | 0.008 | 0.010 | 0.001 |
| Average PhDs 2002 to 2006 | 0.104 | 0.145 | 0.014 | 0.017 | 0.020 | 0.001 |
| Percent Completing within 6 Years | -0.031 | 0.024 | 0.017 | 0.062 | 0.066 | 0.001 |
| Time to Degree Full and Part Time | -0.079 | -0.025 | 0.015 | -0.032 | -0.029 | 0.001 |
| Percent Students in Academic Positions | 0.043 | 0.096 | 0.017 | 0.093 | 0.096 | 0.001 |
| Student Workspace | -0.045 | 0.003 | 0.014 | 0.003 | 0.004 | 0.000 |
| Health Insurance | -0.016 | 0.044 | 0.019 | 0.016 | 0.018 | 0.001 |
| Number of Student Activities | 0.096 | 0.138 | 0.012 | 0.051 | 0.054 | 0.001 |
| **Entomology** | R-Based .05 | R-Based .95 | R-Based Stdev | S-Based .05 | S-Based .95 | S-Based Stdev |
| Publications per Allocated Faculty | 0.057 | 0.157 | 0.028 | 0.159 | 0.173 | 0.004 |
| Cites Per Publication | 0.007 | 0.063 | 0.032 | 0.072 | 0.086 | 0.004 |
| Grants per Allocated Faculty | 0.016 | 0.073 | 0.019 | 0.150 | 0.165 | 0.004 |
| Percent Faculty Interdisciplinary | -0.038 | 0.050 | 0.027 | 0.061 | 0.073 | 0.004 |
| percent Non-Asian Minority Faculty | -0.025 | 0.052 | 0.023 | 0.007 | 0.012 | 0.002 |
| Percent Female Faculty | -0.064 | -0.003 | 0.029 | 0.009 | 0.014 | 0.002 |
| Awards per Allocated Faculty | -0.008 | 0.079 | 0.031 | 0.052 | 0.063 | 0.003 |
| Average GRE-Q | 0.025 | 0.082 | 0.018 | 0.061 | 0.072 | 0.004 |
| Percent First-Year Students with Full Support | 0.015 | 0.098 | 0.027 | 0.056 | 0.065 | 0.003 |
| Percent First-Year Students with Portable Fellowships | -0.064 | 0.023 | 0.028 | 0.028 | 0.036 | 0.003 |
| Percent Non-Asian Minority Students | -0.020 | 0.027 | 0.015 | 0.015 | 0.021 | 0.002 |
| Percent Female Students | -0.002 | 0.055 | 0.015 | 0.013 | 0.019 | 0.002 |
| Percent International Students | -0.023 | 0.045 | 0.023 | 0.007 | 0.011 | 0.001 |
| Average PhDs 2002 to 2006 | 0.123 | 0.226 | 0.035 | 0.036 | 0.044 | 0.003 |
| Percent Completing within 6 Years | 0.008 | 0.052 | 0.014 | 0.049 | 0.057 | 0.003 |
| Time to Degree Full and Part Time | 0.005 | 0.111 | 0.028 | -0.029 | -0.022 | 0.002 |
| Percent Students in Academic Positions | 0.008 | 0.058 | 0.015 | 0.082 | 0.091 | 0.003 |
| Student Workspace | -0.073 | 0.029 | 0.031 | 0.003 | 0.006 | 0.001 |
| Health Insurance | 0.025 | 0.104 | 0.024 | 0.004 | 0.007 | 0.001 |
| Number of Student Activities | 0.016 | 0.114 | 0.031 | 0.031 | 0.039 | 0.002 |

| **Food Science** | R-Based .05 | R-Based .95 | R-Based Stdev | S-Based .05 | S-Based .95 | S-Based Stdev |
|---|---|---|---|---|---|---|
| Publications per Allocated Faculty | 0.057 | 0.157 | 0.028 | 0.152 | 0.167 | 0.005 |
| Cites Per Publication | 0.007 | 0.063 | 0.032 | 0.068 | 0.083 | 0.004 |
| Grants per Allocated Faculty | 0.016 | 0.073 | 0.019 | 0.150 | 0.165 | 0.005 |
| Percent Faculty Interdisciplinary | -0.038 | 0.050 | 0.027 | 0.063 | 0.077 | 0.004 |
| percent Non-Asian Minority Faculty | -0.025 | 0.052 | 0.023 | 0.005 | 0.011 | 0.002 |
| Percent Female Faculty | -0.064 | -0.003 | 0.029 | 0.005 | 0.009 | 0.001 |
| Awards per Allocated Faculty | -0.008 | 0.079 | 0.031 | 0.055 | 0.069 | 0.004 |
| Average GRE-Q | 0.025 | 0.082 | 0.018 | 0.055 | 0.066 | 0.003 |
| Percent First-Year Students with Full Support | 0.015 | 0.098 | 0.027 | 0.061 | 0.072 | 0.003 |
| Percent First-Year Students with Portable Fellowships | -0.064 | 0.023 | 0.028 | 0.024 | 0.032 | 0.002 |
| Percent Non-Asian Minority Students | -0.020 | 0.027 | 0.015 | 0.017 | 0.024 | 0.002 |
| Percent Female Students | -0.002 | 0.055 | 0.015 | 0.008 | 0.012 | 0.001 |
| Percent International Students | -0.023 | 0.045 | 0.023 | 0.007 | 0.013 | 0.002 |
| Average PhDs 2002 to 2006 | 0.123 | 0.226 | 0.035 | 0.043 | 0.052 | 0.003 |
| Percent Completing within 6 Years | 0.008 | 0.052 | 0.014 | 0.046 | 0.057 | 0.003 |
| Time to Degree Full and Part Time | 0.005 | 0.111 | 0.028 | -0.037 | -0.028 | 0.003 |
| Percent Students in Academic Positions | 0.008 | 0.058 | 0.015 | 0.081 | 0.091 | 0.003 |
| Student Workspace | -0.073 | 0.029 | 0.031 | 0.004 | 0.008 | 0.001 |
| Health Insurance | 0.025 | 0.104 | 0.024 | 0.003 | 0.007 | 0.001 |
| Number of Student Activities | 0.016 | 0.114 | 0.031 | 0.031 | 0.040 | 0.003 |
| **Forestry and Forest Sciences** | R-Based .05 | R-Based .95 | R-Based Stdev | S-Based .05 | S-Based .95 | S-Based Stdev |
| Publications per Allocated Faculty | 0.057 | 0.157 | 0.028 | 0.139 | 0.152 | 0.004 |
| Cites Per Publication | 0.007 | 0.063 | 0.032 | 0.083 | 0.096 | 0.004 |
| Grants per Allocated Faculty | 0.016 | 0.073 | 0.019 | 0.137 | 0.149 | 0.004 |
| Percent Faculty Interdisciplinary | -0.038 | 0.050 | 0.027 | 0.071 | 0.084 | 0.004 |
| percent Non-Asian Minority Faculty | -0.025 | 0.052 | 0.023 | 0.007 | 0.012 | 0.001 |
| Percent Female Faculty | -0.064 | -0.003 | 0.029 | 0.011 | 0.016 | 0.002 |
| Awards per Allocated Faculty | -0.008 | 0.079 | 0.031 | 0.047 | 0.059 | 0.004 |
| Average GRE-Q | 0.025 | 0.082 | 0.018 | 0.059 | 0.070 | 0.003 |
| Percent First-Year Students with Full Support | 0.015 | 0.098 | 0.027 | 0.070 | 0.079 | 0.003 |
| Percent First-Year Students with Portable Fellowships | -0.064 | 0.023 | 0.028 | 0.024 | 0.032 | 0.003 |
| Percent Non-Asian Minority Students | -0.020 | 0.027 | 0.015 | 0.015 | 0.021 | 0.002 |
| Percent Female Students | -0.002 | 0.055 | 0.015 | 0.015 | 0.020 | 0.002 |
| Percent International Students | -0.023 | 0.045 | 0.023 | 0.012 | 0.018 | 0.002 |
| Average PhDs 2002 to 2006 | 0.123 | 0.226 | 0.035 | 0.038 | 0.045 | 0.002 |
| Percent Completing within 6 Years | 0.008 | 0.052 | 0.014 | 0.048 | 0.057 | 0.003 |
| Time to Degree Full and Part Time | 0.005 | 0.111 | 0.028 | -0.027 | -0.020 | 0.002 |
| Percent Students in Academic Positions | 0.008 | 0.058 | 0.015 | 0.080 | 0.093 | 0.004 |
| Student Workspace | -0.073 | 0.029 | 0.031 | 0.006 | 0.011 | 0.001 |
| Health Insurance | 0.025 | 0.104 | 0.024 | 0.004 | 0.008 | 0.001 |
| Number of Student Activities | 0.016 | 0.114 | 0.031 | 0.028 | 0.036 | 0.002 |

| French and Francophone Language and Literature | R-Based .05 | R-Based .95 | R-Based Stdev | S-Based .05 | S-Based .95 | S-Based Stdev |
|---|---|---|---|---|---|---|
| Publications per Allocated Faculty | -0.032 | 0.026 | 0.017 | 0.165 | 0.180 | 0.005 |
| Cites Per Publication | None | None | None | None | None | None |
| Grants per Allocated Faculty | -0.017 | 0.046 | 0.020 | 0.037 | 0.049 | 0.004 |
| Percent Faculty Interdisciplinary | -0.080 | 0.027 | 0.041 | 0.088 | 0.103 | 0.005 |
| percent Non-Asian Minority Faculty | 0.088 | 0.170 | 0.022 | 0.020 | 0.028 | 0.003 |
| Percent Female Faculty | 0.020 | 0.130 | 0.032 | 0.031 | 0.041 | 0.003 |
| Awards per Allocated Faculty | -0.027 | 0.024 | 0.016 | 0.080 | 0.098 | 0.005 |
| Average GRE-Q | 0.046 | 0.099 | 0.019 | 0.053 | 0.065 | 0.004 |
| Percent First-Year Students with Full Support | -0.094 | 0.006 | 0.037 | 0.075 | 0.087 | 0.004 |
| Percent First-Year Students with Portable Fellowships | -0.080 | -0.022 | 0.021 | 0.018 | 0.026 | 0.002 |
| Percent Non-Asian Minority Students | -0.088 | -0.007 | 0.022 | 0.023 | 0.030 | 0.002 |
| Percent Female Students | 0.006 | 0.120 | 0.038 | 0.018 | 0.025 | 0.002 |
| Percent International Students | -0.001 | 0.073 | 0.024 | 0.030 | 0.039 | 0.003 |
| Average PhDs 2002 to 2006 | -0.030 | 0.047 | 0.026 | 0.028 | 0.038 | 0.003 |
| Percent Completing within 6 Years | 0.107 | 0.181 | 0.024 | 0.066 | 0.077 | 0.004 |
| Time to Degree Full and Part Time | -0.072 | -0.010 | 0.018 | -0.036 | -0.028 | 0.002 |
| Percent Students in Academic Positions | -0.069 | -0.034 | 0.010 | 0.088 | 0.100 | 0.004 |
| Student Workspace | 0.015 | 0.058 | 0.014 | 0.001 | 0.003 | 0.001 |
| Health Insurance | -0.069 | -0.034 | 0.010 | 0.008 | 0.014 | 0.002 |
| Number of Student Activities | 0.015 | 0.058 | 0.014 | 0.046 | 0.056 | 0.003 |

| Genetics and Genomics | R-Based .05 | R-Based .95 | R-Based Stdev | S-Based .05 | S-Based .95 | S-Based Stdev |
|---|---|---|---|---|---|---|
| Publications per Allocated Faculty | 0.017 | 0.068 | 0.014 | 0.127 | 0.138 | 0.003 |
| Cites Per Publication | 0.087 | 0.113 | 0.009 | 0.099 | 0.109 | 0.003 |
| Grants per Allocated Faculty | 0.022 | 0.093 | 0.026 | 0.162 | 0.171 | 0.003 |
| Percent Faculty Interdisciplinary | -0.050 | 0.001 | 0.017 | 0.043 | 0.051 | 0.002 |
| percent Non-Asian Minority Faculty | -0.001 | 0.051 | 0.017 | 0.008 | 0.012 | 0.001 |
| Percent Female Faculty | -0.038 | -0.003 | 0.011 | 0.017 | 0.023 | 0.002 |
| Awards per Allocated Faculty | 0.088 | 0.108 | 0.007 | 0.051 | 0.060 | 0.003 |
| Average GRE-Q | 0.057 | 0.089 | 0.011 | 0.073 | 0.081 | 0.003 |
| Percent First-Year Students with Full Support | -0.043 | -0.007 | 0.012 | 0.057 | 0.064 | 0.002 |
| Percent First-Year Students with Portable Fellowships | 0.057 | 0.092 | 0.014 | 0.039 | 0.046 | 0.002 |
| Percent Non-Asian Minority Students | 0.020 | 0.055 | 0.012 | 0.020 | 0.025 | 0.002 |
| Percent Female Students | 0.016 | 0.058 | 0.014 | 0.018 | 0.022 | 0.001 |
| Percent International Students | -0.055 | -0.015 | 0.013 | 0.006 | 0.009 | 0.001 |
| Average PhDs 2002 to 2006 | 0.069 | 0.139 | 0.022 | 0.020 | 0.025 | 0.001 |
| Percent Completing within 6 Years | -0.030 | 0.026 | 0.017 | 0.058 | 0.064 | 0.002 |
| Time to Degree Full and Part Time | -0.006 | 0.041 | 0.014 | -0.033 | -0.028 | 0.001 |
| Percent Students in Academic Positions | 0.035 | 0.067 | 0.015 | 0.076 | 0.082 | 0.002 |
| Student Workspace | -0.004 | 0.057 | 0.017 | 0.003 | 0.005 | 0.001 |
| Health Insurance | -0.004 | 0.032 | 0.013 | 0.005 | 0.007 | 0.001 |
| Number of Student Activities | 0.084 | 0.107 | 0.010 | 0.029 | 0.034 | 0.002 |

| **Geography** | **R-Based .05** | **R-Based .95** | **R-Based Stdev** | **S-Based .05** | **S-Based .95** | **S-Based Stdev** |
|---|---|---|---|---|---|---|
| Publications per Allocated Faculty | -0.005 | 0.060 | 0.024 | 0.157 | 0.168 | 0.003 |
| Cites Per Publication | -0.028 | 0.072 | 0.033 | 0.103 | 0.114 | 0.004 |
| Grants per Allocated Faculty | -0.051 | 0.031 | 0.024 | 0.115 | 0.126 | 0.003 |
| Percent Faculty Interdisciplinary | -0.009 | 0.034 | 0.015 | 0.052 | 0.061 | 0.003 |
| percent Non-Asian Minority Faculty | -0.074 | -0.021 | 0.017 | 0.016 | 0.022 | 0.002 |
| Percent Female Faculty | 0.016 | 0.070 | 0.023 | 0.020 | 0.027 | 0.002 |
| Awards per Allocated Faculty | 0.116 | 0.158 | 0.014 | 0.063 | 0.074 | 0.003 |
| Average GRE-Q | 0.043 | 0.105 | 0.020 | 0.053 | 0.060 | 0.002 |
| Percent First-Year Students with Full Support | 0.010 | 0.073 | 0.023 | 0.054 | 0.061 | 0.002 |
| Percent First-Year Students with Portable Fellowships | 0.006 | 0.117 | 0.032 | 0.027 | 0.033 | 0.002 |
| Percent Non-Asian Minority Students | -0.057 | 0.004 | 0.021 | 0.021 | 0.026 | 0.001 |
| Percent Female Students | 0.016 | 0.080 | 0.018 | 0.021 | 0.026 | 0.002 |
| Percent International Students | -0.038 | 0.032 | 0.024 | 0.013 | 0.018 | 0.001 |
| Average PhDs 2002 to 2006 | 0.082 | 0.156 | 0.029 | 0.034 | 0.040 | 0.002 |
| Percent Completing within 6 Years | -0.054 | -0.012 | 0.015 | 0.049 | 0.055 | 0.002 |
| Time to Degree Full and Part Time | -0.009 | 0.049 | 0.023 | -0.026 | -0.021 | 0.001 |
| Percent Students in Academic Positions | 0.011 | 0.088 | 0.024 | 0.072 | 0.079 | 0.002 |
| Student Workspace | 0.029 | 0.081 | 0.018 | 0.005 | 0.007 | 0.001 |
| Health Insurance | -0.022 | 0.104 | 0.037 | 0.004 | 0.006 | 0.001 |
| Number of Student Activities | -0.019 | 0.128 | 0.061 | 0.033 | 0.039 | 0.002 |
| **German Language and Literature** | **R-Based .05** | **R-Based .95** | **R-Based Stdev** | **S-Based .05** | **S-Based .95** | **S-Based Stdev** |
| Publications per Allocated Faculty | -0.015 | 0.051 | 0.031 | 0.167 | 0.193 | 0.008 |
| Cites Per Publication | None | None | None | None | None | None |
| Grants per Allocated Faculty | -0.055 | -0.011 | 0.014 | 0.039 | 0.056 | 0.005 |
| Percent Faculty Interdisciplinary | -0.082 | -0.025 | 0.020 | 0.091 | 0.110 | 0.006 |
| percent Non-Asian Minority Faculty | -0.104 | -0.043 | 0.026 | 0.011 | 0.021 | 0.003 |
| Percent Female Faculty | -0.039 | 0.002 | 0.016 | 0.032 | 0.045 | 0.004 |
| Awards per Allocated Faculty | 0.049 | 0.071 | 0.019 | 0.079 | 0.097 | 0.006 |
| Average GRE-Q | 0.028 | 0.063 | 0.013 | 0.055 | 0.070 | 0.004 |
| Percent First-Year Students with Full Support | -0.029 | 0.032 | 0.023 | 0.065 | 0.078 | 0.004 |
| Percent First-Year Students with Portable Fellowships | -0.023 | 0.015 | 0.023 | 0.019 | 0.035 | 0.005 |
| Percent Non-Asian Minority Students | -0.049 | -0.009 | 0.025 | 0.014 | 0.023 | 0.003 |
| Percent Female Students | -0.075 | -0.021 | 0.019 | 0.023 | 0.032 | 0.003 |
| Percent International Students | -0.106 | 0.001 | 0.028 | 0.020 | 0.029 | 0.003 |
| Average PhDs 2002 to 2006 | 0.070 | 0.107 | 0.016 | 0.025 | 0.035 | 0.003 |
| Percent Completing within 6 Years | 0.081 | 0.130 | 0.019 | 0.062 | 0.074 | 0.004 |
| Time to Degree Full and Part Time | 0.060 | 0.101 | 0.016 | -0.036 | -0.026 | 0.003 |
| Percent Students in Academic Positions | 0.043 | 0.066 | 0.014 | 0.092 | 0.109 | 0.005 |
| Student Workspace | -0.030 | 0.033 | 0.021 | 0.003 | 0.007 | 0.001 |
| Health Insurance | 0.055 | 0.075 | 0.009 | 0.006 | 0.012 | 0.002 |
| Number of Student Activities | -0.026 | 0.013 | 0.017 | 0.048 | 0.061 | 0.004 |

| History | R-Based .05 | R-Based .95 | R-Based Stdev | S-Based .05 | S-Based .95 | S-Based Stdev |
|---|---|---|---|---|---|---|
| Publications per Allocated Faculty | 0.002 | 0.035 | 0.015 | 0.174 | 0.181 | 0.002 |
| Cites Per Publication | None | None | None | None | None | None |
| Grants per Allocated Faculty | -0.012 | 0.030 | 0.015 | 0.065 | 0.070 | 0.002 |
| Percent Faculty Interdisciplinary | -0.023 | 0.028 | 0.015 | 0.042 | 0.046 | 0.001 |
| percent Non-Asian Minority Faculty | 0.010 | 0.063 | 0.018 | 0.038 | 0.042 | 0.001 |
| Percent Female Faculty | -0.025 | -0.003 | 0.008 | 0.037 | 0.040 | 0.001 |
| Awards per Allocated Faculty | 0.137 | 0.167 | 0.010 | 0.120 | 0.126 | 0.002 |
| Average GRE-Q | 0.107 | 0.167 | 0.018 | 0.060 | 0.065 | 0.001 |
| Percent First-Year Students with Full Support | 0.034 | 0.063 | 0.010 | 0.081 | 0.085 | 0.001 |
| Percent First-Year Students with Portable Fellowships | -0.002 | 0.023 | 0.009 | 0.026 | 0.029 | 0.001 |
| Percent Non-Asian Minority Students | 0.055 | 0.078 | 0.008 | 0.034 | 0.037 | 0.001 |
| Percent Female Students | 0.007 | 0.025 | 0.006 | 0.027 | 0.030 | 0.001 |
| Percent International Students | 0.056 | 0.086 | 0.010 | 0.015 | 0.018 | 0.001 |
| Average PhDs 2002 to 2006 | 0.128 | 0.156 | 0.010 | 0.022 | 0.025 | 0.001 |
| Percent Completing within 6 Years | -0.081 | -0.014 | 0.022 | 0.060 | 0.064 | 0.001 |
| Time to Degree Full and Part Time | -0.037 | 0.011 | 0.017 | -0.029 | -0.026 | 0.001 |
| Percent Students in Academic Positions | 0.024 | 0.112 | 0.025 | 0.084 | 0.088 | 0.001 |
| Student Workspace | 0.021 | 0.060 | 0.012 | 0.002 | 0.003 | 0.000 |
| Health Insurance | 0.024 | 0.082 | 0.016 | 0.009 | 0.011 | 0.001 |
| Number of Student Activities | -0.009 | 0.037 | 0.017 | 0.042 | 0.046 | 0.001 |

| Immunology and infectious Disease | R-Based .05 | R-Based .95 | R-Based Stdev | S-Based .05 | S-Based .95 | S-Based Stdev |
|---|---|---|---|---|---|---|
| Publications per Allocated Faculty | 0.039 | 0.108 | 0.025 | 0.131 | 0.139 | 0.003 |
| Cites Per Publication | 0.085 | 0.133 | 0.018 | 0.085 | 0.094 | 0.003 |
| Grants per Allocated Faculty | 0.063 | 0.132 | 0.021 | 0.165 | 0.172 | 0.002 |
| Percent Faculty Interdisciplinary | -0.006 | 0.058 | 0.020 | 0.046 | 0.053 | 0.002 |
| percent Non-Asian Minority Faculty | -0.047 | 0.024 | 0.020 | 0.013 | 0.016 | 0.001 |
| Percent Female Faculty | -0.034 | 0.042 | 0.023 | 0.016 | 0.020 | 0.001 |
| Awards per Allocated Faculty | 0.019 | 0.079 | 0.019 | 0.048 | 0.055 | 0.002 |
| Average GRE-Q | -0.002 | 0.048 | 0.017 | 0.074 | 0.081 | 0.002 |
| Percent First-Year Students with Full Support | -0.011 | 0.047 | 0.018 | 0.052 | 0.058 | 0.002 |
| Percent First-Year Students with Portable Fellowships | 0.012 | 0.064 | 0.016 | 0.034 | 0.039 | 0.002 |
| Percent Non-Asian Minority Students | -0.021 | 0.042 | 0.019 | 0.026 | 0.030 | 0.001 |
| Percent Female Students | -0.021 | 0.063 | 0.026 | 0.019 | 0.022 | 0.001 |
| Percent International Students | -0.158 | -0.085 | 0.023 | 0.005 | 0.007 | 0.001 |
| Average PhDs 2002 to 2006 | 0.065 | 0.138 | 0.022 | 0.025 | 0.029 | 0.001 |
| Percent Completing within 6 Years | 0.005 | 0.066 | 0.017 | 0.062 | 0.067 | 0.002 |
| Time to Degree Full and Part Time | 0.008 | 0.075 | 0.021 | -0.036 | -0.031 | 0.001 |
| Percent Students in Academic Positions | 0.000 | 0.071 | 0.023 | 0.079 | 0.084 | 0.002 |
| Student Workspace | -0.079 | -0.011 | 0.021 | 0.003 | 0.004 | 0.000 |
| Health Insurance | 0.018 | 0.103 | 0.026 | 0.003 | 0.005 | 0.001 |
| Number of Student Activities | -0.040 | 0.039 | 0.023 | 0.033 | 0.038 | 0.001 |

| Integrated Biology/Integrated Biomedical Sciences | R-Based .05 | R-Based .95 | R-Based Stdev | S-Based .05 | S-Based .95 | S-Based Stdev |
|---|---|---|---|---|---|---|
| Publications per Allocated Faculty | 0.087 | 0.133 | 0.014 | 0.138 | 0.144 | 0.002 |
| Cites Per Publication | 0.046 | 0.077 | 0.010 | 0.094 | 0.100 | 0.002 |
| Grants per Allocated Faculty | 0.074 | 0.104 | 0.009 | 0.160 | 0.165 | 0.002 |
| Percent Faculty Interdisciplinary | -0.018 | 0.046 | 0.022 | 0.042 | 0.046 | 0.001 |
| percent Non-Asian Minority Faculty | -0.022 | 0.048 | 0.023 | 0.010 | 0.012 | 0.001 |
| Percent Female Faculty | -0.041 | -0.001 | 0.013 | 0.018 | 0.020 | 0.001 |
| Awards per Allocated Faculty | 0.051 | 0.120 | 0.018 | 0.059 | 0.064 | 0.001 |
| Average GRE-Q | 0.090 | 0.130 | 0.012 | 0.073 | 0.077 | 0.001 |
| Percent First-Year Students with Full Support | -0.001 | 0.059 | 0.018 | 0.056 | 0.060 | 0.001 |
| Percent First-Year Students with Portable Fellowships | -0.014 | 0.052 | 0.021 | 0.041 | 0.045 | 0.001 |
| Percent Non-Asian Minority Students | -0.023 | 0.033 | 0.017 | 0.020 | 0.023 | 0.001 |
| Percent Female Students | -0.043 | -0.002 | 0.013 | 0.016 | 0.019 | 0.001 |
| Percent International Students | -0.057 | 0.001 | 0.020 | 0.007 | 0.008 | 0.001 |
| Average PhDs 2002 to 2006 | 0.098 | 0.146 | 0.018 | 0.026 | 0.028 | 0.001 |
| Percent Completing within 6 Years | -0.017 | 0.017 | 0.012 | 0.058 | 0.061 | 0.001 |
| Time to Degree Full and Part Time | -0.008 | 0.049 | 0.019 | -0.033 | -0.030 | 0.001 |
| Percent Students in Academic Positions | 0.011 | 0.070 | 0.020 | 0.077 | 0.080 | 0.001 |
| Student Workspace | -0.020 | 0.065 | 0.023 | 0.004 | 0.005 | 0.000 |
| Health Insurance | 0.044 | 0.110 | 0.024 | 0.005 | 0.007 | 0.000 |
| Number of Student Activities | 0.016 | 0.069 | 0.017 | 0.033 | 0.036 | 0.001 |

| Kinesiology | R-Based .05 | R-Based .95 | R-Based Stdev | S-Based .05 | S-Based .95 | S-Based Stdev |
|---|---|---|---|---|---|---|
| Publications per Allocated Faculty | 0.023 | 0.143 | 0.041 | 0.167 | 0.180 | 0.004 |
| Cites Per Publication | 0.064 | 0.086 | 0.010 | 0.083 | 0.097 | 0.004 |
| Grants per Allocated Faculty | -0.022 | 0.108 | 0.044 | 0.153 | 0.167 | 0.004 |
| Percent Faculty Interdisciplinary | 0.035 | 0.088 | 0.014 | 0.053 | 0.066 | 0.004 |
| percent Non-Asian Minority Faculty | -0.103 | 0.010 | 0.033 | 0.009 | 0.014 | 0.002 |
| Percent Female Faculty | -0.059 | 0.028 | 0.025 | 0.010 | 0.015 | 0.002 |
| Awards per Allocated Faculty | -0.034 | 0.054 | 0.029 | 0.047 | 0.058 | 0.003 |
| Average GRE-Q | 0.060 | 0.153 | 0.031 | 0.060 | 0.069 | 0.003 |
| Percent First-Year Students with Full Support | -0.039 | 0.041 | 0.025 | 0.062 | 0.071 | 0.003 |
| Percent First-Year Students with Portable Fellowships | -0.066 | 0.067 | 0.047 | 0.015 | 0.021 | 0.002 |
| Percent Non-Asian Minority Students | -0.118 | -0.031 | 0.027 | 0.016 | 0.021 | 0.002 |
| Percent Female Students | -0.082 | 0.019 | 0.032 | 0.012 | 0.018 | 0.002 |
| Percent International Students | 0.005 | 0.087 | 0.025 | 0.001 | 0.004 | 0.001 |
| Average PhDs 2002 to 2006 | -0.058 | 0.098 | 0.050 | 0.026 | 0.034 | 0.002 |
| Percent Completing within 6 Years | -0.071 | 0.030 | 0.034 | 0.053 | 0.062 | 0.002 |
| Time to Degree Full and Part Time | -0.063 | 0.012 | 0.029 | -0.031 | -0.024 | 0.002 |
| Percent Students in Academic Positions | -0.029 | 0.046 | 0.024 | 0.084 | 0.092 | 0.002 |
| Student Workspace | 0.049 | 0.120 | 0.024 | 0.004 | 0.007 | 0.001 |
| Health Insurance | -0.004 | 0.092 | 0.030 | 0.004 | 0.007 | 0.001 |
| Number of Student Activities | 0.005 | 0.033 | 0.011 | 0.038 | 0.046 | 0.002 |

| Linguistics | R-Based .05 | R-Based .95 | R-Based Stdev | S-Based .05 | S-Based .95 | S-Based Stdev |
|---|---|---|---|---|---|---|
| Publications per Allocated Faculty | -0.027 | 0.079 | 0.037 | 0.149 | 0.162 | 0.004 |
| Cites Per Publication | 0.043 | 0.116 | 0.030 | 0.117 | 0.130 | 0.004 |
| Grants per Allocated Faculty | 0.024 | 0.082 | 0.020 | 0.094 | 0.105 | 0.003 |
| Percent Faculty Interdisciplinary | -0.051 | 0.019 | 0.029 | 0.061 | 0.074 | 0.004 |
| percent Non-Asian Minority Faculty | -0.031 | 0.001 | 0.011 | 0.009 | 0.014 | 0.001 |
| Percent Female Faculty | -0.067 | -0.002 | 0.022 | 0.011 | 0.016 | 0.002 |
| Awards per Allocated Faculty | 0.077 | 0.132 | 0.016 | 0.053 | 0.063 | 0.003 |
| Average GRE-Q | 0.056 | 0.104 | 0.018 | 0.047 | 0.054 | 0.002 |
| Percent First-Year Students with Full Support | -0.007 | 0.039 | 0.022 | 0.079 | 0.088 | 0.003 |
| Percent First-Year Students with Portable Fellowships | -0.048 | 0.015 | 0.030 | 0.030 | 0.037 | 0.002 |
| Percent Non-Asian Minority Students | -0.015 | 0.085 | 0.035 | 0.014 | 0.019 | 0.002 |
| Percent Female Students | -0.068 | -0.044 | 0.014 | 0.008 | 0.012 | 0.001 |
| Percent International Students | -0.052 | 0.050 | 0.038 | 0.018 | 0.024 | 0.002 |
| Average PhDs 2002 to 2006 | 0.004 | 0.072 | 0.029 | 0.021 | 0.026 | 0.002 |
| Percent Completing within 6 Years | -0.090 | -0.069 | 0.010 | 0.052 | 0.058 | 0.002 |
| Time to Degree Full and Part Time | 0.050 | 0.084 | 0.020 | -0.034 | -0.028 | 0.002 |
| Percent Students in Academic Positions | -0.045 | 0.017 | 0.023 | 0.081 | 0.088 | 0.002 |
| Student Workspace | 0.003 | 0.124 | 0.053 | 0.009 | 0.013 | 0.001 |
| Health Insurance | 0.031 | 0.098 | 0.023 | 0.004 | 0.006 | 0.001 |
| Number of Student Activities | 0.001 | 0.070 | 0.026 | 0.041 | 0.048 | 0.002 |
| **Materials Science and Engineering** | **R-Based .05** | **R-Based .95** | **R-Based Stdev** | **S-Based .05** | **S-Based .95** | **S-Based Stdev** |
| Publications per Allocated Faculty | 0.116 | 0.149 | 0.009 | 0.125 | 0.134 | 0.003 |
| Cites Per Publication | 0.017 | 0.060 | 0.014 | 0.121 | 0.130 | 0.003 |
| Grants per Allocated Faculty | -0.001 | 0.041 | 0.017 | 0.131 | 0.140 | 0.003 |
| Percent Faculty Interdisciplinary | -0.026 | 0.036 | 0.025 | 0.043 | 0.051 | 0.002 |
| percent Non-Asian Minority Faculty | -0.054 | -0.033 | 0.008 | 0.006 | 0.010 | 0.001 |
| Percent Female Faculty | 0.016 | 0.037 | 0.006 | 0.009 | 0.013 | 0.001 |
| Awards per Allocated Faculty | 0.059 | 0.072 | 0.004 | 0.080 | 0.089 | 0.003 |
| Average GRE-Q | 0.073 | 0.088 | 0.009 | 0.068 | 0.074 | 0.002 |
| Percent First-Year Students with Full Support | 0.027 | 0.056 | 0.011 | 0.059 | 0.065 | 0.002 |
| Percent First-Year Students with Portable Fellowships | -0.045 | -0.024 | 0.008 | 0.050 | 0.057 | 0.002 |
| Percent Non-Asian Minority Students | -0.067 | -0.030 | 0.013 | 0.013 | 0.017 | 0.001 |
| Percent Female Students | -0.001 | 0.036 | 0.013 | 0.018 | 0.022 | 0.001 |
| Percent International Students | -0.047 | -0.023 | 0.007 | 0.008 | 0.012 | 0.001 |
| Average PhDs 2002 to 2006 | 0.134 | 0.156 | 0.007 | 0.052 | 0.058 | 0.002 |
| Percent Completing within 6 Years | 0.018 | 0.042 | 0.011 | 0.042 | 0.048 | 0.002 |
| Time to Degree Full and Part Time | 0.023 | 0.053 | 0.015 | -0.027 | -0.022 | 0.001 |
| Percent Students in Academic Positions | -0.028 | -0.012 | 0.008 | 0.067 | 0.073 | 0.002 |
| Student Workspace | 0.065 | 0.089 | 0.008 | 0.004 | 0.007 | 0.001 |
| Health Insurance | 0.025 | 0.035 | 0.004 | 0.002 | 0.003 | 0.000 |
| Number of Student Activities | 0.024 | 0.059 | 0.013 | 0.022 | 0.026 | 0.001 |

| **Mathematics** | **R-Based .05** | **R-Based .95** | **R-Based Stdev** | **S-Based .05** | **S-Based .95** | **S-Based Stdev** |
|---|---|---|---|---|---|---|
| Publications per Allocated Faculty | 0.075 | 0.091 | 0.006 | 0.144 | 0.149 | 0.002 |
| Cites Per Publication | 0.044 | 0.096 | 0.023 | 0.119 | 0.125 | 0.002 |
| Grants per Allocated Faculty | 0.090 | 0.103 | 0.008 | 0.138 | 0.144 | 0.002 |
| Percent Faculty Interdisciplinary | 0.044 | 0.050 | 0.004 | 0.031 | 0.035 | 0.001 |
| percent Non-Asian Minority Faculty | -0.024 | 0.007 | 0.013 | 0.005 | 0.006 | 0.000 |
| Percent Female Faculty | -0.010 | 0.020 | 0.011 | 0.008 | 0.010 | 0.001 |
| Awards per Allocated Faculty | 0.088 | 0.116 | 0.013 | 0.106 | 0.112 | 0.002 |
| Average GRE-Q | 0.034 | 0.070 | 0.016 | 0.061 | 0.065 | 0.001 |
| Percent First-Year Students with Full Support | -0.033 | -0.007 | 0.009 | 0.056 | 0.060 | 0.001 |
| Percent First-Year Students with Portable Fellowships | -0.022 | 0.010 | 0.011 | 0.039 | 0.042 | 0.001 |
| Percent Non-Asian Minority Students | -0.026 | -0.002 | 0.011 | 0.008 | 0.009 | 0.000 |
| Percent Female Students | -0.031 | -0.004 | 0.011 | 0.012 | 0.014 | 0.001 |
| Percent International Students | 0.007 | 0.051 | 0.020 | 0.022 | 0.025 | 0.001 |
| Average PhDs 2002 to 2006 | 0.113 | 0.163 | 0.022 | 0.038 | 0.040 | 0.001 |
| Percent Completing within 6 Years | 0.056 | 0.087 | 0.012 | 0.051 | 0.055 | 0.001 |
| Time to Degree Full and Part Time | 0.037 | 0.052 | 0.006 | -0.028 | -0.026 | 0.001 |
| Percent Students in Academic Positions | 0.001 | 0.029 | 0.013 | 0.075 | 0.078 | 0.001 |
| Student Workspace | 0.036 | 0.062 | 0.011 | 0.004 | 0.006 | 0.000 |
| Health Insurance | 0.007 | 0.037 | 0.013 | 0.003 | 0.004 | 0.000 |
| Number of Student Activities | 0.075 | 0.104 | 0.012 | 0.021 | 0.024 | 0.001 |

| **Mechanical Engineering** | **R-Based .05** | **R-Based .95** | **R-Based Stdev** | **S-Based .05** | **S-Based .95** | **S-Based Stdev** |
|---|---|---|---|---|---|---|
| Publications per Allocated Faculty | 0.077 | 0.112 | 0.012 | 0.143 | 0.149 | 0.002 |
| Cites Per Publication | -0.065 | 0.023 | 0.025 | 0.118 | 0.124 | 0.002 |
| Grants per Allocated Faculty | -0.005 | 0.035 | 0.013 | 0.138 | 0.144 | 0.002 |
| Percent Faculty Interdisciplinary | -0.042 | 0.014 | 0.018 | 0.044 | 0.049 | 0.001 |
| percent Non-Asian Minority Faculty | -0.080 | 0.019 | 0.029 | 0.006 | 0.008 | 0.001 |
| Percent Female Faculty | 0.052 | 0.079 | 0.009 | 0.006 | 0.009 | 0.001 |
| Awards per Allocated Faculty | 0.087 | 0.123 | 0.011 | 0.077 | 0.083 | 0.002 |
| Average GRE-Q | -0.002 | 0.063 | 0.020 | 0.067 | 0.072 | 0.001 |
| Percent First-Year Students with Full Support | -0.053 | -0.006 | 0.014 | 0.070 | 0.075 | 0.001 |
| Percent First-Year Students with Portable Fellowships | -0.071 | -0.009 | 0.021 | 0.052 | 0.057 | 0.001 |
| Percent Non-Asian Minority Students | -0.083 | 0.004 | 0.028 | 0.013 | 0.015 | 0.001 |
| Percent Female Students | -0.020 | 0.012 | 0.013 | 0.013 | 0.015 | 0.001 |
| Percent International Students | -0.116 | -0.082 | 0.012 | 0.009 | 0.012 | 0.001 |
| Average PhDs 2002 to 2006 | 0.163 | 0.214 | 0.015 | 0.053 | 0.057 | 0.001 |
| Percent Completing within 6 Years | -0.007 | 0.067 | 0.019 | 0.035 | 0.039 | 0.001 |
| Time to Degree Full and Part Time | -0.045 | 0.009 | 0.017 | -0.020 | -0.018 | 0.001 |
| Percent Students in Academic Positions | 0.011 | 0.082 | 0.021 | 0.069 | 0.073 | 0.001 |
| Student Workspace | -0.005 | 0.048 | 0.017 | 0.005 | 0.007 | 0.000 |
| Health Insurance | 0.011 | 0.056 | 0.014 | 0.002 | 0.003 | 0.000 |
| Number of Student Activities | 0.006 | 0.065 | 0.020 | 0.024 | 0.027 | 0.001 |

| Microbiology | R-Based .05 | R-Based .95 | R-Based Stdev | S-Based .05 | S-Based .95 | S-Based Stdev |
|---|---|---|---|---|---|---|
| Publications per Allocated Faculty | -0.006 | 0.050 | 0.019 | 0.142 | 0.151 | 0.003 |
| Cites Per Publication | 0.031 | 0.211 | 0.045 | 0.085 | 0.096 | 0.003 |
| Grants per Allocated Faculty | 0.026 | 0.080 | 0.016 | 0.167 | 0.176 | 0.003 |
| Percent Faculty Interdisciplinary | -0.059 | -0.021 | 0.012 | 0.037 | 0.044 | 0.002 |
| percent Non-Asian Minority Faculty | 0.000 | 0.054 | 0.017 | 0.009 | 0.012 | 0.001 |
| Percent Female Faculty | -0.077 | 0.006 | 0.027 | 0.017 | 0.022 | 0.001 |
| Awards per Allocated Faculty | 0.137 | 0.194 | 0.019 | 0.058 | 0.066 | 0.002 |
| Average GRE-Q | 0.007 | 0.079 | 0.022 | 0.074 | 0.082 | 0.002 |
| Percent First-Year Students with Full Support | -0.003 | 0.061 | 0.020 | 0.050 | 0.057 | 0.002 |
| Percent First-Year Students with Portable Fellowships | -0.020 | 0.011 | 0.010 | 0.034 | 0.040 | 0.002 |
| Percent Non-Asian Minority Students | -0.052 | 0.010 | 0.018 | 0.023 | 0.028 | 0.002 |
| Percent Female Students | -0.047 | 0.008 | 0.017 | 0.017 | 0.021 | 0.001 |
| Percent International Students | -0.073 | -0.029 | 0.014 | 0.004 | 0.006 | 0.001 |
| Average PhDs 2002 to 2006 | 0.096 | 0.149 | 0.016 | 0.023 | 0.028 | 0.001 |
| Percent Completing within 6 Years | 0.011 | 0.076 | 0.022 | 0.055 | 0.060 | 0.002 |
| Time to Degree Full and Part Time | 0.012 | 0.075 | 0.019 | -0.032 | -0.027 | 0.001 |
| Percent Students in Academic Positions | -0.006 | 0.067 | 0.022 | 0.077 | 0.084 | 0.002 |
| Student Workspace | -0.029 | 0.025 | 0.019 | 0.005 | 0.007 | 0.001 |
| Health Insurance | 0.025 | 0.067 | 0.013 | 0.005 | 0.007 | 0.001 |
| Number of Student Activities | 0.019 | 0.055 | 0.011 | 0.032 | 0.038 | 0.002 |

| Music (Except Performance) | R-Based .05 | R-Based .95 | R-Based Stdev | S-Based .05 | S-Based .95 | S-Based Stdev |
|---|---|---|---|---|---|---|
| Publications per Allocated Faculty | 0.052 | 0.109 | 0.021 | 0.162 | 0.176 | 0.004 |
| Cites Per Publication | None | None | None | None | None | None |
| Grants per Allocated Faculty | -0.073 | 0.057 | 0.043 | 0.036 | 0.046 | 0.003 |
| Percent Faculty Interdisciplinary | -0.012 | 0.081 | 0.026 | 0.060 | 0.072 | 0.003 |
| percent Non-Asian Minority Faculty | 0.002 | 0.094 | 0.025 | 0.026 | 0.032 | 0.002 |
| Percent Female Faculty | 0.045 | 0.107 | 0.018 | 0.031 | 0.039 | 0.003 |
| Awards per Allocated Faculty | 0.107 | 0.183 | 0.023 | 0.114 | 0.127 | 0.004 |
| Average GRE-Q | 0.080 | 0.144 | 0.022 | 0.048 | 0.057 | 0.003 |
| Percent First-Year Students with Full Support | -0.036 | 0.063 | 0.029 | 0.080 | 0.091 | 0.004 |
| Percent First-Year Students with Portable Fellowships | -0.054 | 0.045 | 0.027 | 0.013 | 0.019 | 0.002 |
| Percent Non-Asian Minority Students | -0.009 | 0.088 | 0.030 | 0.029 | 0.035 | 0.002 |
| Percent Female Students | -0.052 | 0.017 | 0.028 | 0.028 | 0.035 | 0.002 |
| Percent International Students | -0.033 | 0.056 | 0.027 | 0.018 | 0.024 | 0.002 |
| Average PhDs 2002 to 2006 | -0.019 | 0.102 | 0.034 | 0.025 | 0.031 | 0.002 |
| Percent Completing within 6 Years | 0.010 | 0.085 | 0.028 | 0.070 | 0.080 | 0.003 |
| Time to Degree Full and Part Time | 0.003 | 0.056 | 0.016 | -0.029 | -0.023 | 0.002 |
| Percent Students in Academic Positions | 0.017 | 0.092 | 0.024 | 0.101 | 0.111 | 0.003 |
| Student Workspace | -0.046 | 0.082 | 0.037 | 0.003 | 0.006 | 0.001 |
| Health Insurance | 0.029 | 0.097 | 0.021 | 0.007 | 0.011 | 0.001 |
| Number of Student Activities | -0.026 | 0.077 | 0.033 | 0.050 | 0.058 | 0.002 |

| Neuroscience and Neurobiology | R-Based .05 | R-Based .95 | R-Based Stdev | S-Based .05 | S-Based .95 | S-Based Stdev |
|---|---|---|---|---|---|---|
| Publications per Allocated Faculty | -0.073 | 0.087 | 0.059 | 0.117 | 0.124 | 0.002 |
| Cites Per Publication | 0.066 | 0.124 | 0.020 | 0.103 | 0.110 | 0.002 |
| Grants per Allocated Faculty | 0.042 | 0.105 | 0.018 | 0.163 | 0.170 | 0.002 |
| Percent Faculty Interdisciplinary | 0.001 | 0.052 | 0.018 | 0.048 | 0.054 | 0.002 |
| percent Non-Asian Minority Faculty | 0.030 | 0.089 | 0.019 | 0.008 | 0.010 | 0.001 |
| Percent Female Faculty | -0.048 | 0.010 | 0.020 | 0.016 | 0.020 | 0.001 |
| Awards per Allocated Faculty | 0.059 | 0.134 | 0.024 | 0.058 | 0.064 | 0.002 |
| Average GRE-Q | 0.051 | 0.123 | 0.023 | 0.074 | 0.079 | 0.002 |
| Percent First-Year Students with Full Support | -0.026 | 0.023 | 0.015 | 0.055 | 0.060 | 0.002 |
| Percent First-Year Students with Portable Fellowships | 0.031 | 0.098 | 0.022 | 0.039 | 0.044 | 0.002 |
| Percent Non-Asian Minority Students | 0.000 | 0.045 | 0.014 | 0.020 | 0.023 | 0.001 |
| Percent Female Students | -0.037 | 0.027 | 0.020 | 0.020 | 0.023 | 0.001 |
| Percent International Students | -0.130 | -0.058 | 0.019 | 0.006 | 0.009 | 0.001 |
| Average PhDs 2002 to 2006 | 0.076 | 0.154 | 0.030 | 0.021 | 0.024 | 0.001 |
| Percent Completing within 6 Years | -0.024 | 0.034 | 0.021 | 0.060 | 0.064 | 0.001 |
| Time to Degree Full and Part Time | 0.010 | 0.078 | 0.020 | -0.033 | -0.029 | 0.001 |
| Percent Students in Academic Positions | -0.064 | 0.010 | 0.025 | 0.080 | 0.085 | 0.001 |
| Student Workspace | -0.027 | 0.042 | 0.020 | 0.004 | 0.006 | 0.000 |
| Health Insurance | -0.007 | 0.058 | 0.023 | 0.004 | 0.005 | 0.000 |
| Number of Student Activities | -0.017 | 0.029 | 0.016 | 0.032 | 0.036 | 0.001 |

| Nursing | R-Based .05 | R-Based .95 | R-Based Stdev | S-Based .05 | S-Based .95 | S-Based Stdev |
|---|---|---|---|---|---|---|
| Publications per Allocated Faculty | 0.068 | 0.109 | 0.014 | 0.134 | 0.142 | 0.002 |
| Cites Per Publication | -0.016 | 0.043 | 0.020 | 0.041 | 0.047 | 0.002 |
| Grants per Allocated Faculty | 0.115 | 0.205 | 0.029 | 0.153 | 0.160 | 0.002 |
| Percent Faculty Interdisciplinary | 0.013 | 0.024 | 0.003 | 0.081 | 0.089 | 0.002 |
| percent Non-Asian Minority Faculty | -0.030 | -0.002 | 0.008 | 0.032 | 0.037 | 0.002 |
| Percent Female Faculty | -0.029 | -0.009 | 0.004 | 0.005 | 0.008 | 0.001 |
| Awards per Allocated Faculty | 0.005 | 0.085 | 0.022 | 0.041 | 0.048 | 0.002 |
| Average GRE-Q | -0.029 | 0.076 | 0.035 | 0.059 | 0.064 | 0.002 |
| Percent First-Year Students with Full Support | -0.003 | 0.069 | 0.019 | 0.042 | 0.047 | 0.002 |
| Percent First-Year Students with Portable Fellowships | -0.025 | 0.136 | 0.031 | 0.023 | 0.027 | 0.001 |
| Percent Non-Asian Minority Students | -0.029 | 0.018 | 0.017 | 0.050 | 0.054 | 0.001 |
| Percent Female Students | -0.079 | 0.010 | 0.025 | 0.011 | 0.014 | 0.001 |
| Percent International Students | 0.084 | 0.216 | 0.036 | 0.005 | 0.008 | 0.001 |
| Average PhDs 2002 to 2006 | -0.015 | 0.124 | 0.034 | 0.032 | 0.037 | 0.002 |
| Percent Completing within 6 Years | -0.048 | 0.029 | 0.020 | 0.083 | 0.088 | 0.002 |
| Time to Degree Full and Part Time | -0.023 | 0.007 | 0.007 | -0.047 | -0.042 | 0.002 |
| Percent Students in Academic Positions | -0.066 | 0.042 | 0.040 | 0.062 | 0.068 | 0.002 |
| Student Workspace | 0.010 | 0.023 | 0.004 | 0.003 | 0.005 | 0.001 |
| Health Insurance | 0.033 | 0.060 | 0.006 | 0.002 | 0.004 | 0.001 |
| Number of Student Activities | -0.026 | 0.082 | 0.035 | 0.049 | 0.055 | 0.002 |

| Nutrition | R-Based .05 | R-Based .95 | R-Based Stdev | S-Based .05 | S-Based .95 | S-Based Stdev |
|---|---|---|---|---|---|---|
| Publications per Allocated Faculty | -0.008 | 0.115 | 0.049 | 0.132 | 0.144 | 0.004 |
| Cites Per Publication | -0.023 | 0.083 | 0.034 | 0.063 | 0.075 | 0.003 |
| Grants per Allocated Faculty | -0.027 | 0.029 | 0.018 | 0.148 | 0.159 | 0.003 |
| Percent Faculty Interdisciplinary | 0.001 | 0.060 | 0.020 | 0.059 | 0.070 | 0.003 |
| percent Non-Asian Minority Faculty | -0.069 | -0.006 | 0.021 | 0.012 | 0.018 | 0.002 |
| Percent Female Faculty | -0.014 | 0.080 | 0.026 | 0.008 | 0.013 | 0.002 |
| Awards per Allocated Faculty | 0.040 | 0.081 | 0.015 | 0.057 | 0.067 | 0.003 |
| Average GRE-Q | 0.026 | 0.095 | 0.023 | 0.073 | 0.081 | 0.003 |
| Percent First-Year Students with Full Support | 0.019 | 0.129 | 0.043 | 0.063 | 0.072 | 0.003 |
| Percent First-Year Students with Portable Fellowships | -0.057 | 0.112 | 0.068 | 0.022 | 0.029 | 0.002 |
| Percent Non-Asian Minority Students | -0.114 | -0.018 | 0.025 | 0.024 | 0.030 | 0.002 |
| Percent Female Students | -0.066 | -0.018 | 0.017 | 0.010 | 0.014 | 0.001 |
| Percent International Students | -0.101 | -0.034 | 0.022 | 0.005 | 0.009 | 0.001 |
| Average PhDs 2002 to 2006 | 0.111 | 0.193 | 0.026 | 0.035 | 0.042 | 0.002 |
| Percent Completing within 6 Years | 0.032 | 0.074 | 0.012 | 0.061 | 0.069 | 0.002 |
| Time to Degree Full and Part Time | -0.020 | 0.042 | 0.022 | -0.033 | -0.027 | 0.002 |
| Percent Students in Academic Positions | -0.039 | 0.024 | 0.021 | 0.082 | 0.090 | 0.003 |
| Student Workspace | -0.015 | 0.008 | 0.009 | 0.004 | 0.008 | 0.001 |
| Health Insurance | 0.013 | 0.055 | 0.014 | 0.003 | 0.005 | 0.001 |
| Number of Student Activities | -0.066 | 0.003 | 0.023 | 0.037 | 0.046 | 0.003 |

| Oceanography, Atmospheric Sciences and Meteorology | R-Based .05 | R-Based .95 | R-Based Stdev | S-Based .05 | S-Based .95 | S-Based Stdev |
|---|---|---|---|---|---|---|
| Publications per Allocated Faculty | -0.007 | 0.070 | 0.025 | 0.128 | 0.137 | 0.003 |
| Cites Per Publication | 0.038 | 0.132 | 0.030 | 0.110 | 0.119 | 0.003 |
| Grants per Allocated Faculty | -0.033 | 0.009 | 0.014 | 0.144 | 0.152 | 0.003 |
| Percent Faculty Interdisciplinary | 0.002 | 0.089 | 0.028 | 0.049 | 0.056 | 0.002 |
| percent Non-Asian Minority Faculty | -0.013 | 0.062 | 0.030 | 0.006 | 0.008 | 0.001 |
| Percent Female Faculty | -0.022 | 0.049 | 0.018 | 0.014 | 0.018 | 0.001 |
| Awards per Allocated Faculty | 0.047 | 0.088 | 0.014 | 0.066 | 0.074 | 0.002 |
| Average GRE-Q | 0.031 | 0.041 | 0.006 | 0.068 | 0.075 | 0.002 |
| Percent First-Year Students with Full Support | 0.000 | 0.097 | 0.030 | 0.065 | 0.071 | 0.002 |
| Percent First-Year Students with Portable Fellowships | -0.021 | 0.103 | 0.036 | 0.036 | 0.041 | 0.002 |
| Percent Non-Asian Minority Students | -0.031 | 0.080 | 0.038 | 0.014 | 0.017 | 0.001 |
| Percent Female Students | 0.004 | 0.088 | 0.033 | 0.019 | 0.023 | 0.001 |
| Percent International Students | -0.057 | 0.051 | 0.036 | 0.006 | 0.009 | 0.001 |
| Average PhDs 2002 to 2006 | 0.081 | 0.231 | 0.046 | 0.032 | 0.037 | 0.001 |
| Percent Completing within 6 Years | -0.011 | 0.076 | 0.026 | 0.047 | 0.052 | 0.001 |
| Time to Degree Full and Part Time | -0.076 | 0.007 | 0.025 | -0.034 | -0.030 | 0.001 |
| Percent Students in Academic Positions | 0.060 | 0.133 | 0.026 | 0.077 | 0.083 | 0.002 |
| Student Workspace | -0.038 | 0.069 | 0.034 | 0.004 | 0.006 | 0.001 |
| Health Insurance | 0.007 | 0.067 | 0.022 | 0.003 | 0.005 | 0.001 |
| Number of Student Activities | -0.017 | 0.075 | 0.034 | 0.030 | 0.035 | 0.001 |

| Operations Research, Systems Engineering and Industrial Engineering | R-Based .05 | R-Based .95 | R-Based Stdev | S-Based .05 | S-Based .95 | S-Based Stdev |
|---|---|---|---|---|---|---|
| Publications per Allocated Faculty | -0.038 | 0.081 | 0.041 | 0.147 | 0.158 | 0.003 |
| Cites Per Publication | 0.068 | 0.152 | 0.025 | 0.112 | 0.123 | 0.004 |
| Grants per Allocated Faculty | 0.000 | 0.097 | 0.031 | 0.129 | 0.139 | 0.003 |
| Percent Faculty Interdisciplinary | -0.060 | 0.034 | 0.029 | 0.047 | 0.055 | 0.002 |
| percent Non-Asian Minority Faculty | -0.067 | -0.014 | 0.016 | 0.005 | 0.008 | 0.001 |
| Percent Female Faculty | -0.062 | 0.006 | 0.022 | 0.005 | 0.009 | 0.001 |
| Awards per Allocated Faculty | 0.096 | 0.178 | 0.027 | 0.088 | 0.098 | 0.003 |
| Average GRE-Q | 0.072 | 0.097 | 0.008 | 0.073 | 0.080 | 0.002 |
| Percent First-Year Students with Full Support | -0.022 | 0.059 | 0.024 | 0.059 | 0.066 | 0.002 |
| Percent First-Year Students with Portable Fellowships | -0.051 | 0.033 | 0.024 | 0.034 | 0.040 | 0.002 |
| Percent Non-Asian Minority Students | -0.028 | 0.043 | 0.022 | 0.012 | 0.016 | 0.001 |
| Percent Female Students | -0.037 | 0.032 | 0.019 | 0.011 | 0.014 | 0.001 |
| Percent International Students | -0.055 | 0.019 | 0.022 | 0.008 | 0.012 | 0.001 |
| Average PhDs 2002 to 2006 | 0.125 | 0.194 | 0.022 | 0.046 | 0.052 | 0.002 |
| Percent Completing within 6 Years | -0.048 | 0.044 | 0.026 | 0.039 | 0.045 | 0.002 |
| Time to Degree Full and Part Time | -0.015 | 0.062 | 0.025 | -0.023 | -0.019 | 0.001 |
| Percent Students in Academic Positions | -0.057 | 0.018 | 0.022 | 0.075 | 0.083 | 0.002 |
| Student Workspace | -0.056 | 0.052 | 0.031 | 0.005 | 0.007 | 0.001 |
| Health Insurance | -0.034 | 0.093 | 0.036 | 0.002 | 0.003 | 0.000 |
| Number of Student Activities | 0.040 | 0.110 | 0.020 | 0.024 | 0.029 | 0.001 |
| **Pharmacology, Toxicology and Environmental Health** | R-Based .05 | R-Based .95 | R-Based Stdev | S-Based .05 | S-Based .95 | S-Based Stdev |
| Publications per Allocated Faculty | 0.000 | 0.056 | 0.016 | 0.137 | 0.145 | 0.002 |
| Cites Per Publication | 0.074 | 0.116 | 0.013 | 0.087 | 0.095 | 0.002 |
| Grants per Allocated Faculty | -0.045 | 0.033 | 0.022 | 0.166 | 0.173 | 0.002 |
| Percent Faculty Interdisciplinary | -0.062 | -0.031 | 0.010 | 0.048 | 0.055 | 0.002 |
| percent Non-Asian Minority Faculty | -0.054 | -0.011 | 0.012 | 0.007 | 0.010 | 0.001 |
| Percent Female Faculty | -0.019 | 0.033 | 0.016 | 0.011 | 0.014 | 0.001 |
| Awards per Allocated Faculty | 0.043 | 0.101 | 0.018 | 0.055 | 0.061 | 0.002 |
| Average GRE-Q | -0.067 | 0.019 | 0.025 | 0.073 | 0.080 | 0.002 |
| Percent First-Year Students with Full Support | -0.014 | 0.033 | 0.014 | 0.056 | 0.062 | 0.002 |
| Percent First-Year Students with Portable Fellowships | -0.011 | 0.023 | 0.009 | 0.037 | 0.042 | 0.002 |
| Percent Non-Asian Minority Students | 0.019 | 0.045 | 0.008 | 0.019 | 0.023 | 0.001 |
| Percent Female Students | 0.025 | 0.054 | 0.009 | 0.014 | 0.017 | 0.001 |
| Percent International Students | -0.109 | -0.023 | 0.025 | 0.004 | 0.006 | 0.001 |
| Average PhDs 2002 to 2006 | 0.141 | 0.200 | 0.018 | 0.030 | 0.034 | 0.001 |
| Percent Completing within 6 Years | 0.073 | 0.103 | 0.010 | 0.059 | 0.065 | 0.002 |
| Time to Degree Full and Part Time | 0.047 | 0.080 | 0.010 | -0.038 | -0.033 | 0.001 |
| Percent Students in Academic Positions | 0.049 | 0.083 | 0.012 | 0.078 | 0.083 | 0.001 |
| Student Workspace | -0.057 | 0.029 | 0.025 | 0.004 | 0.006 | 0.000 |
| Health Insurance | -0.023 | 0.017 | 0.012 | 0.003 | 0.005 | 0.000 |
| Number of Student Activities | 0.048 | 0.076 | 0.009 | 0.030 | 0.034 | 0.001 |

| Philosophy | R-Based .05 | R-Based .95 | R-Based Stdev | S-Based .05 | S-Based .95 | S-Based Stdev |
|---|---|---|---|---|---|---|
| Publications per Allocated Faculty | -0.049 | -0.024 | 0.008 | 0.195 | 0.208 | 0.004 |
| Cites Per Publication | None | None | None | None | None | None |
| Grants per Allocated Faculty | -0.003 | 0.026 | 0.008 | 0.038 | 0.045 | 0.002 |
| Percent Faculty Interdisciplinary | -0.055 | -0.019 | 0.012 | 0.037 | 0.044 | 0.002 |
| percent Non-Asian Minority Faculty | -0.051 | -0.020 | 0.009 | 0.014 | 0.018 | 0.001 |
| Percent Female Faculty | -0.058 | -0.041 | 0.006 | 0.027 | 0.033 | 0.002 |
| Awards per Allocated Faculty | 0.135 | 0.163 | 0.008 | 0.133 | 0.145 | 0.004 |
| Average GRE-Q | 0.090 | 0.111 | 0.006 | 0.079 | 0.086 | 0.002 |
| Percent First-Year Students with Full Support | 0.021 | 0.058 | 0.010 | 0.087 | 0.094 | 0.002 |
| Percent First-Year Students with Portable Fellowships | -0.085 | -0.036 | 0.014 | 0.021 | 0.025 | 0.001 |
| Percent Non-Asian Minority Students | -0.031 | 0.008 | 0.014 | 0.015 | 0.019 | 0.001 |
| Percent Female Students | 0.024 | 0.056 | 0.011 | 0.026 | 0.030 | 0.001 |
| Percent International Students | 0.047 | 0.068 | 0.006 | 0.010 | 0.014 | 0.001 |
| Average PhDs 2002 to 2006 | 0.047 | 0.084 | 0.011 | 0.020 | 0.024 | 0.001 |
| Percent Completing within 6 Years | -0.041 | -0.005 | 0.011 | 0.060 | 0.066 | 0.002 |
| Time to Degree Full and Part Time | 0.003 | 0.046 | 0.014 | -0.035 | -0.030 | 0.001 |
| Percent Students in Academic Positions | 0.138 | 0.170 | 0.010 | 0.103 | 0.112 | 0.003 |
| Student Workspace | 0.035 | 0.062 | 0.008 | 0.005 | 0.008 | 0.001 |
| Health Insurance | 0.008 | 0.019 | 0.005 | 0.009 | 0.011 | 0.001 |
| Number of Student Activities | 0.018 | 0.049 | 0.010 | 0.035 | 0.040 | 0.002 |
| **Physics** | **R-Based .05** | **R-Based .95** | **R-Based Stdev** | **S-Based .05** | **S-Based .95** | **S-Based Stdev** |
| Publications per Allocated Faculty | 0.058 | 0.102 | 0.012 | 0.126 | 0.130 | 0.001 |
| Cites Per Publication | 0.012 | 0.042 | 0.010 | 0.146 | 0.151 | 0.002 |
| Grants per Allocated Faculty | 0.035 | 0.074 | 0.013 | 0.150 | 0.154 | 0.001 |
| Percent Faculty Interdisciplinary | 0.002 | 0.054 | 0.017 | 0.022 | 0.025 | 0.001 |
| percent Non-Asian Minority Faculty | 0.006 | 0.037 | 0.010 | 0.005 | 0.006 | 0.000 |
| Percent Female Faculty | -0.007 | 0.028 | 0.012 | 0.010 | 0.012 | 0.001 |
| Awards per Allocated Faculty | 0.104 | 0.149 | 0.016 | 0.094 | 0.099 | 0.001 |
| Average GRE-Q | 0.099 | 0.117 | 0.006 | 0.072 | 0.076 | 0.001 |
| Percent First-Year Students with Full Support | -0.016 | 0.056 | 0.025 | 0.056 | 0.059 | 0.001 |
| Percent First-Year Students with Portable Fellowships | 0.026 | 0.048 | 0.008 | 0.040 | 0.043 | 0.001 |
| Percent Non-Asian Minority Students | -0.036 | -0.007 | 0.009 | 0.009 | 0.011 | 0.000 |
| Percent Female Students | -0.050 | -0.017 | 0.011 | 0.016 | 0.018 | 0.001 |
| Percent International Students | -0.004 | 0.030 | 0.010 | 0.012 | 0.014 | 0.001 |
| Average PhDs 2002 to 2006 | 0.152 | 0.176 | 0.011 | 0.035 | 0.038 | 0.001 |
| Percent Completing within 6 Years | -0.054 | -0.005 | 0.016 | 0.049 | 0.052 | 0.001 |
| Time to Degree Full and Part Time | 0.051 | 0.091 | 0.013 | -0.029 | -0.026 | 0.001 |
| Percent Students in Academic Positions | 0.021 | 0.097 | 0.025 | 0.074 | 0.077 | 0.001 |
| Student Workspace | -0.025 | 0.017 | 0.012 | 0.004 | 0.005 | 0.000 |
| Health Insurance | -0.062 | -0.008 | 0.020 | 0.003 | 0.004 | 0.000 |
| Number of Student Activities | 0.019 | 0.058 | 0.011 | 0.021 | 0.023 | 0.001 |

| Physiology | R-Based .05 | R-Based .95 | R-Based Stdev | S-Based .05 | S-Based .95 | S-Based Stdev |
|---|---|---|---|---|---|---|
| Publications per Allocated Faculty | 0.022 | 0.164 | 0.045 | 0.132 | 0.142 | 0.003 |
| Cites Per Publication | 0.013 | 0.098 | 0.026 | 0.085 | 0.096 | 0.003 |
| Grants per Allocated Faculty | -0.015 | 0.126 | 0.046 | 0.165 | 0.174 | 0.003 |
| Percent Faculty Interdisciplinary | -0.004 | 0.046 | 0.013 | 0.047 | 0.055 | 0.002 |
| percent Non-Asian Minority Faculty | -0.096 | 0.122 | 0.057 | 0.007 | 0.011 | 0.001 |
| Percent Female Faculty | -0.038 | 0.061 | 0.030 | 0.010 | 0.014 | 0.001 |
| Awards per Allocated Faculty | -0.042 | 0.106 | 0.042 | 0.059 | 0.068 | 0.003 |
| Average GRE-Q | 0.047 | 0.201 | 0.043 | 0.078 | 0.086 | 0.002 |
| Percent First-Year Students with Full Support | -0.002 | 0.096 | 0.032 | 0.054 | 0.061 | 0.002 |
| Percent First-Year Students with Portable Fellowships | -0.025 | 0.082 | 0.034 | 0.036 | 0.042 | 0.002 |
| Percent Non-Asian Minority Students | -0.082 | -0.004 | 0.024 | 0.020 | 0.025 | 0.001 |
| Percent Female Students | -0.042 | 0.069 | 0.033 | 0.014 | 0.019 | 0.001 |
| Percent International Students | -0.107 | 0.016 | 0.035 | 0.004 | 0.007 | 0.001 |
| Average PhDs 2002 to 2006 | -0.001 | 0.146 | 0.041 | 0.026 | 0.031 | 0.002 |
| Percent Completing within 6 Years | -0.037 | 0.081 | 0.036 | 0.056 | 0.063 | 0.002 |
| Time to Degree Full and Part Time | -0.003 | 0.088 | 0.027 | -0.037 | -0.031 | 0.002 |
| Percent Students in Academic Positions | -0.047 | 0.059 | 0.033 | 0.079 | 0.085 | 0.002 |
| Student Workspace | -0.029 | 0.051 | 0.027 | 0.003 | 0.005 | 0.001 |
| Health Insurance | 0.001 | 0.110 | 0.032 | 0.003 | 0.005 | 0.001 |
| Number of Student Activities | 0.032 | 0.091 | 0.018 | 0.030 | 0.035 | 0.002 |

| Plant Sciences | R-Based .05 | R-Based .95 | R-Based Stdev | S-Based .05 | S-Based .95 | S-Based Stdev |
|---|---|---|---|---|---|---|
| Publications per Allocated Faculty | 0.057 | 0.157 | 0.028 | 0.152 | 0.159 | 0.002 |
| Cites Per Publication | 0.007 | 0.063 | 0.032 | 0.080 | 0.088 | 0.002 |
| Grants per Allocated Faculty | 0.016 | 0.073 | 0.019 | 0.145 | 0.153 | 0.002 |
| Percent Faculty Interdisciplinary | -0.038 | 0.050 | 0.027 | 0.066 | 0.073 | 0.002 |
| percent Non-Asian Minority Faculty | -0.025 | 0.052 | 0.023 | 0.008 | 0.011 | 0.001 |
| Percent Female Faculty | -0.064 | -0.003 | 0.029 | 0.012 | 0.015 | 0.001 |
| Awards per Allocated Faculty | -0.008 | 0.079 | 0.031 | 0.054 | 0.060 | 0.002 |
| Average GRE-Q | 0.025 | 0.082 | 0.018 | 0.060 | 0.065 | 0.002 |
| Percent First-Year Students with Full Support | 0.015 | 0.098 | 0.027 | 0.062 | 0.068 | 0.002 |
| Percent First-Year Students with Portable Fellowships | -0.064 | 0.023 | 0.028 | 0.031 | 0.035 | 0.001 |
| Percent Non-Asian Minority Students | -0.020 | 0.027 | 0.015 | 0.017 | 0.020 | 0.001 |
| Percent Female Students | -0.002 | 0.055 | 0.015 | 0.015 | 0.017 | 0.001 |
| Percent International Students | -0.023 | 0.045 | 0.023 | 0.006 | 0.009 | 0.001 |
| Average PhDs 2002 to 2006 | 0.123 | 0.226 | 0.035 | 0.038 | 0.042 | 0.001 |
| Percent Completing within 6 Years | 0.008 | 0.052 | 0.014 | 0.052 | 0.057 | 0.001 |
| Time to Degree Full and Part Time | 0.005 | 0.111 | 0.028 | -0.030 | -0.026 | 0.001 |
| Percent Students in Academic Positions | 0.008 | 0.058 | 0.015 | 0.085 | 0.090 | 0.002 |
| Student Workspace | -0.073 | 0.029 | 0.031 | 0.006 | 0.008 | 0.001 |
| Health Insurance | 0.025 | 0.104 | 0.024 | 0.005 | 0.007 | 0.001 |
| Number of Student Activities | 0.016 | 0.114 | 0.031 | 0.034 | 0.038 | 0.001 |

| Political Science | R-Based .05 | R-Based .95 | R-Based Stdev | S-Based .05 | S-Based .95 | S-Based Stdev |
|---|---|---|---|---|---|---|
| Publications per Allocated Faculty | 0.043 | 0.064 | 0.007 | 0.178 | 0.185 | 0.002 |
| Cites Per Publication | 0.057 | 0.081 | 0.008 | 0.141 | 0.149 | 0.002 |
| Grants per Allocated Faculty | 0.009 | 0.040 | 0.010 | 0.075 | 0.082 | 0.002 |
| Percent Faculty Interdisciplinary | 0.005 | 0.034 | 0.010 | 0.032 | 0.037 | 0.001 |
| percent Non-Asian Minority Faculty | -0.012 | 0.006 | 0.006 | 0.021 | 0.025 | 0.001 |
| Percent Female Faculty | -0.016 | 0.005 | 0.007 | 0.019 | 0.022 | 0.001 |
| Awards per Allocated Faculty | 0.096 | 0.114 | 0.007 | 0.096 | 0.102 | 0.002 |
| Average GRE-Q | 0.144 | 0.169 | 0.006 | 0.069 | 0.074 | 0.002 |
| Percent First-Year Students with Full Support | -0.061 | -0.041 | 0.008 | 0.061 | 0.065 | 0.001 |
| Percent First-Year Students with Portable Fellowships | 0.005 | 0.034 | 0.008 | 0.021 | 0.025 | 0.001 |
| Percent Non-Asian Minority Students | -0.039 | -0.017 | 0.007 | 0.020 | 0.022 | 0.001 |
| Percent Female Students | 0.035 | 0.050 | 0.005 | 0.014 | 0.016 | 0.001 |
| Percent International Students | -0.019 | -0.006 | 0.004 | 0.011 | 0.013 | 0.001 |
| Average PhDs 2002 to 2006 | 0.152 | 0.166 | 0.004 | 0.021 | 0.024 | 0.001 |
| Percent Completing within 6 Years | -0.084 | -0.054 | 0.010 | 0.045 | 0.049 | 0.001 |
| Time to Degree Full and Part Time | -0.062 | -0.035 | 0.012 | -0.025 | -0.022 | 0.001 |
| Percent Students in Academic Positions | 0.009 | 0.021 | 0.004 | 0.074 | 0.079 | 0.001 |
| Student Workspace | 0.002 | 0.047 | 0.012 | 0.004 | 0.006 | 0.000 |
| Health Insurance | 0.012 | 0.030 | 0.005 | 0.005 | 0.006 | 0.000 |
| Number of Student Activities | 0.051 | 0.075 | 0.008 | 0.030 | 0.033 | 0.001 |
| **Psychology** | **R-Based .05** | **R-Based .95** | **R-Based Stdev** | **S-Based .05** | **S-Based .95** | **S-Based Stdev** |
| Publications per Allocated Faculty | 0.056 | 0.156 | 0.029 | 0.153 | 0.158 | 0.001 |
| Cites Per Publication | 0.053 | 0.136 | 0.026 | 0.121 | 0.126 | 0.002 |
| Grants per Allocated Faculty | 0.094 | 0.151 | 0.020 | 0.137 | 0.142 | 0.001 |
| Percent Faculty Interdisciplinary | -0.022 | 0.068 | 0.028 | 0.036 | 0.039 | 0.001 |
| percent Non-Asian Minority Faculty | -0.027 | 0.059 | 0.030 | 0.021 | 0.023 | 0.001 |
| Percent Female Faculty | -0.032 | 0.051 | 0.028 | 0.016 | 0.018 | 0.001 |
| Awards per Allocated Faculty | 0.052 | 0.109 | 0.015 | 0.062 | 0.066 | 0.001 |
| Average GRE-Q | 0.016 | 0.095 | 0.025 | 0.069 | 0.073 | 0.001 |
| Percent First-Year Students with Full Support | -0.065 | 0.039 | 0.036 | 0.062 | 0.065 | 0.001 |
| Percent First-Year Students with Portable Fellowships | -0.050 | 0.021 | 0.019 | 0.025 | 0.027 | 0.001 |
| Percent Non-Asian Minority Students | -0.051 | 0.014 | 0.023 | 0.028 | 0.030 | 0.001 |
| Percent Female Students | -0.004 | 0.057 | 0.018 | 0.012 | 0.014 | 0.000 |
| Percent International Students | -0.017 | 0.036 | 0.018 | 0.003 | 0.003 | 0.000 |
| Average PhDs 2002 to 2006 | 0.060 | 0.135 | 0.024 | 0.022 | 0.023 | 0.001 |
| Percent Completing within 6 Years | 0.015 | 0.053 | 0.015 | 0.056 | 0.059 | 0.001 |
| Time to Degree Full and Part Time | -0.051 | 0.029 | 0.026 | -0.028 | -0.026 | 0.001 |
| Percent Students in Academic Positions | 0.032 | 0.093 | 0.018 | 0.079 | 0.081 | 0.001 |
| Student Workspace | -0.014 | 0.100 | 0.043 | 0.006 | 0.007 | 0.000 |
| Health Insurance | -0.039 | 0.039 | 0.026 | 0.005 | 0.006 | 0.000 |
| Number of Student Activities | -0.012 | 0.080 | 0.031 | 0.036 | 0.039 | 0.001 |

| Public Affairs, Public Policy and Public Administration | R-Based .05 | R-Based .95 | R-Based Stdev | S-Based .05 | S-Based .95 | S-Based Stdev |
|---|---|---|---|---|---|---|
| Publications per Allocated Faculty | -0.065 | -0.044 | 0.007 | 0.164 | 0.175 | 0.004 |
| Cites Per Publication | -0.068 | -0.053 | 0.006 | 0.109 | 0.123 | 0.004 |
| Grants per Allocated Faculty | 0.042 | 0.060 | 0.006 | 0.093 | 0.103 | 0.003 |
| Percent Faculty Interdisciplinary | -0.072 | -0.034 | 0.012 | 0.047 | 0.058 | 0.003 |
| percent Non-Asian Minority Faculty | -0.091 | -0.065 | 0.009 | 0.020 | 0.025 | 0.002 |
| Percent Female Faculty | -0.029 | -0.004 | 0.009 | 0.014 | 0.020 | 0.002 |
| Awards per Allocated Faculty | 0.127 | 0.148 | 0.006 | 0.068 | 0.080 | 0.003 |
| Average GRE-Q | 0.047 | 0.061 | 0.005 | 0.072 | 0.081 | 0.003 |
| Percent First-Year Students with Full Support | -0.003 | 0.014 | 0.006 | 0.053 | 0.060 | 0.002 |
| Percent First-Year Students with Portable Fellowships | -0.074 | -0.057 | 0.006 | 0.019 | 0.024 | 0.002 |
| Percent Non-Asian Minority Students | -0.048 | -0.031 | 0.005 | 0.028 | 0.033 | 0.002 |
| Percent Female Students | 0.043 | 0.051 | 0.004 | 0.015 | 0.019 | 0.001 |
| Percent International Students | 0.061 | 0.073 | 0.005 | 0.007 | 0.010 | 0.001 |
| Average PhDs 2002 to 2006 | 0.037 | 0.068 | 0.010 | 0.024 | 0.031 | 0.002 |
| Percent Completing within 6 Years | -0.023 | -0.007 | 0.005 | 0.054 | 0.060 | 0.002 |
| Time to Degree Full and Part Time | 0.023 | 0.040 | 0.006 | -0.026 | -0.021 | 0.001 |
| Percent Students in Academic Positions | 0.016 | 0.032 | 0.005 | 0.078 | 0.088 | 0.003 |
| Student Workspace | 0.107 | 0.126 | 0.007 | 0.005 | 0.007 | 0.001 |
| Health Insurance | -0.031 | -0.009 | 0.008 | 0.002 | 0.004 | 0.001 |
| Number of Student Activities | -0.027 | 0.009 | 0.011 | 0.036 | 0.042 | 0.002 |
| **Public Health** | **R-Based .05** | **R-Based .95** | **R-Based Stdev** | **S-Based .05** | **S-Based .95** | **S-Based Stdev** |
| Publications per Allocated Faculty | 0.105 | 0.151 | 0.014 | 0.131 | 0.139 | 0.002 |
| Cites Per Publication | 0.029 | 0.087 | 0.018 | 0.071 | 0.079 | 0.002 |
| Grants per Allocated Faculty | -0.024 | 0.035 | 0.019 | 0.142 | 0.149 | 0.002 |
| Percent Faculty Interdisciplinary | 0.024 | 0.107 | 0.024 | 0.069 | 0.075 | 0.002 |
| percent Non-Asian Minority Faculty | -0.016 | 0.068 | 0.024 | 0.021 | 0.024 | 0.001 |
| Percent Female Faculty | -0.100 | -0.035 | 0.021 | 0.016 | 0.019 | 0.001 |
| Awards per Allocated Faculty | -0.069 | 0.034 | 0.027 | 0.044 | 0.050 | 0.002 |
| Average GRE-Q | 0.054 | 0.143 | 0.025 | 0.071 | 0.076 | 0.002 |
| Percent First-Year Students with Full Support | -0.019 | 0.038 | 0.017 | 0.058 | 0.063 | 0.002 |
| Percent First-Year Students with Portable Fellowships | -0.055 | 0.030 | 0.024 | 0.021 | 0.025 | 0.001 |
| Percent Non-Asian Minority Students | -0.013 | 0.054 | 0.021 | 0.035 | 0.039 | 0.001 |
| Percent Female Students | 0.047 | 0.102 | 0.018 | 0.016 | 0.019 | 0.001 |
| Percent International Students | -0.077 | 0.044 | 0.033 | 0.009 | 0.012 | 0.001 |
| Average PhDs 2002 to 2006 | 0.003 | 0.085 | 0.026 | 0.028 | 0.032 | 0.001 |
| Percent Completing within 6 Years | 0.025 | 0.094 | 0.022 | 0.064 | 0.069 | 0.001 |
| Time to Degree Full and Part Time | -0.039 | 0.044 | 0.024 | -0.035 | -0.031 | 0.001 |
| Percent Students in Academic Positions | -0.036 | 0.019 | 0.019 | 0.082 | 0.087 | 0.001 |
| Student Workspace | -0.051 | -0.001 | 0.015 | 0.006 | 0.008 | 0.001 |
| Health Insurance | 0.024 | 0.077 | 0.016 | 0.004 | 0.005 | 0.001 |
| Number of Student Activities | 0.026 | 0.067 | 0.011 | 0.037 | 0.041 | 0.001 |

| Religion | R-Based .05 | R-Based .95 | R-Based Stdev | S-Based .05 | S-Based .95 | S-Based Stdev |
|---|---|---|---|---|---|---|
| Publications per Allocated Faculty | -0.026 | 0.056 | 0.027 | 0.168 | 0.179 | 0.004 |
| Cites Per Publication | None | None | None | None | None | None |
| Grants per Allocated Faculty | -0.013 | 0.052 | 0.023 | 0.036 | 0.046 | 0.003 |
| Percent Faculty Interdisciplinary | -0.090 | -0.014 | 0.025 | 0.061 | 0.072 | 0.003 |
| percent Non-Asian Minority Faculty | -0.048 | 0.040 | 0.029 | 0.043 | 0.051 | 0.003 |
| Percent Female Faculty | -0.021 | 0.033 | 0.014 | 0.039 | 0.047 | 0.002 |
| Awards per Allocated Faculty | 0.013 | 0.059 | 0.017 | 0.091 | 0.103 | 0.004 |
| Average GRE-Q | -0.007 | 0.079 | 0.026 | 0.077 | 0.086 | 0.003 |
| Percent First-Year Students with Full Support | 0.045 | 0.098 | 0.019 | 0.073 | 0.081 | 0.002 |
| Percent First-Year Students with Portable Fellowships | 0.005 | 0.066 | 0.020 | 0.011 | 0.016 | 0.001 |
| Percent Non-Asian Minority Students | -0.049 | 0.011 | 0.020 | 0.036 | 0.042 | 0.002 |
| Percent Female Students | -0.076 | 0.032 | 0.036 | 0.033 | 0.039 | 0.002 |
| Percent International Students | -0.087 | -0.041 | 0.017 | 0.013 | 0.017 | 0.001 |
| Average PhDs 2002 to 2006 | 0.118 | 0.273 | 0.057 | 0.026 | 0.032 | 0.002 |
| Percent Completing within 6 Years | -0.024 | 0.028 | 0.018 | 0.070 | 0.077 | 0.002 |
| Time to Degree Full and Part Time | -0.034 | 0.039 | 0.021 | -0.032 | -0.026 | 0.002 |
| Percent Students in Academic Positions | 0.064 | 0.165 | 0.027 | 0.085 | 0.093 | 0.002 |
| Student Workspace | -0.007 | 0.070 | 0.025 | 0.002 | 0.003 | 0.000 |
| Health Insurance | 0.056 | 0.146 | 0.030 | 0.006 | 0.009 | 0.001 |
| Number of Student Activities | 0.008 | 0.074 | 0.020 | 0.035 | 0.042 | 0.002 |

| Sociology | R-Based .05 | R-Based .95 | R-Based Stdev | S-Based .05 | S-Based .95 | S-Based Stdev |
|---|---|---|---|---|---|---|
| Publications per Allocated Faculty | -0.014 | 0.081 | 0.032 | 0.161 | 0.168 | 0.002 |
| Cites Per Publication | 0.040 | 0.108 | 0.022 | 0.107 | 0.114 | 0.002 |
| Grants per Allocated Faculty | -0.069 | -0.008 | 0.020 | 0.100 | 0.107 | 0.002 |
| Percent Faculty Interdisciplinary | -0.089 | 0.024 | 0.036 | 0.034 | 0.039 | 0.002 |
| percent Non-Asian Minority Faculty | -0.016 | 0.059 | 0.023 | 0.036 | 0.040 | 0.001 |
| Percent Female Faculty | -0.021 | 0.014 | 0.010 | 0.027 | 0.031 | 0.001 |
| Awards per Allocated Faculty | 0.056 | 0.124 | 0.025 | 0.081 | 0.089 | 0.002 |
| Average GRE-Q | 0.069 | 0.114 | 0.013 | 0.052 | 0.057 | 0.001 |
| Percent First-Year Students with Full Support | 0.021 | 0.079 | 0.019 | 0.054 | 0.058 | 0.001 |
| Percent First-Year Students with Portable Fellowships | 0.044 | 0.098 | 0.017 | 0.021 | 0.024 | 0.001 |
| Percent Non-Asian Minority Students | -0.034 | 0.018 | 0.015 | 0.032 | 0.035 | 0.001 |
| Percent Female Students | 0.002 | 0.065 | 0.016 | 0.018 | 0.020 | 0.001 |
| Percent International Students | -0.053 | 0.058 | 0.028 | 0.010 | 0.012 | 0.001 |
| Average PhDs 2002 to 2006 | 0.060 | 0.101 | 0.012 | 0.022 | 0.025 | 0.001 |
| Percent Completing within 6 Years | -0.088 | -0.053 | 0.011 | 0.053 | 0.057 | 0.001 |
| Time to Degree Full and Part Time | 0.024 | 0.086 | 0.022 | -0.025 | -0.022 | 0.001 |
| Percent Students in Academic Positions | -0.014 | 0.051 | 0.018 | 0.077 | 0.081 | 0.001 |
| Student Workspace | -0.010 | 0.064 | 0.022 | 0.005 | 0.007 | 0.000 |
| Health Insurance | 0.025 | 0.100 | 0.027 | 0.006 | 0.008 | 0.000 |
| Number of Student Activities | 0.005 | 0.111 | 0.031 | 0.039 | 0.042 | 0.001 |

| Spanish Language and Literature | R-Based .05 | R-Based .95 | R-Based Stdev | S-Based .05 | S-Based .95 | S-Based Stdev |
|---|---|---|---|---|---|---|
| Publications per Allocated Faculty | 0.072 | 0.122 | 0.016 | 0.171 | 0.182 | 0.003 |
| Cites Per Publication | None | None | None | None | None | None |
| Grants per Allocated Faculty | -0.044 | -0.010 | 0.010 | 0.048 | 0.058 | 0.003 |
| Percent Faculty Interdisciplinary | -0.074 | -0.029 | 0.015 | 0.073 | 0.083 | 0.003 |
| percent Non-Asian Minority Faculty | 0.008 | 0.066 | 0.021 | 0.035 | 0.043 | 0.002 |
| Percent Female Faculty | -0.012 | 0.041 | 0.016 | 0.028 | 0.035 | 0.002 |
| Awards per Allocated Faculty | 0.061 | 0.113 | 0.016 | 0.072 | 0.085 | 0.004 |
| Average GRE-Q | 0.061 | 0.164 | 0.036 | 0.040 | 0.047 | 0.002 |
| Percent First-Year Students with Full Support | 0.016 | 0.051 | 0.011 | 0.072 | 0.080 | 0.002 |
| Percent First-Year Students with Portable Fellowships | -0.055 | 0.043 | 0.038 | 0.017 | 0.022 | 0.002 |
| Percent Non-Asian Minority Students | -0.077 | -0.052 | 0.008 | 0.032 | 0.037 | 0.002 |
| Percent Female Students | -0.062 | 0.018 | 0.024 | 0.019 | 0.024 | 0.001 |
| Percent International Students | -0.014 | 0.080 | 0.030 | 0.043 | 0.049 | 0.002 |
| Average PhDs 2002 to 2006 | 0.099 | 0.147 | 0.015 | 0.039 | 0.046 | 0.002 |
| Percent Completing within 6 Years | -0.057 | -0.003 | 0.016 | 0.062 | 0.069 | 0.002 |
| Time to Degree Full and Part Time | 0.004 | 0.092 | 0.031 | -0.036 | -0.030 | 0.002 |
| Percent Students in Academic Positions | 0.040 | 0.085 | 0.014 | 0.091 | 0.098 | 0.002 |
| Student Workspace | -0.029 | 0.008 | 0.011 | 0.002 | 0.004 | 0.001 |
| Health Insurance | 0.001 | 0.085 | 0.026 | 0.010 | 0.014 | 0.001 |
| Number of Student Activities | 0.035 | 0.070 | 0.012 | 0.048 | 0.056 | 0.002 |
| **Statistics** | **R-Based .05** | **R-Based .95** | **R-Based Stdev** | **S-Based .05** | **S-Based .95** | **S-Based Stdev** |
| Publications per Allocated Faculty | 0.007 | 0.058 | 0.014 | 0.147 | 0.158 | 0.004 |
| Cites Per Publication | 0.094 | 0.129 | 0.012 | 0.114 | 0.126 | 0.004 |
| Grants per Allocated Faculty | 0.031 | 0.074 | 0.013 | 0.124 | 0.135 | 0.003 |
| Percent Faculty Interdisciplinary | 0.007 | 0.040 | 0.011 | 0.076 | 0.086 | 0.003 |
| percent Non-Asian Minority Faculty | 0.015 | 0.073 | 0.018 | 0.005 | 0.008 | 0.001 |
| Percent Female Faculty | -0.049 | -0.012 | 0.012 | 0.008 | 0.012 | 0.001 |
| Awards per Allocated Faculty | 0.012 | 0.054 | 0.011 | 0.079 | 0.091 | 0.004 |
| Average GRE-Q | -0.028 | 0.013 | 0.012 | 0.059 | 0.066 | 0.002 |
| Percent First-Year Students with Full Support | -0.048 | 0.005 | 0.017 | 0.052 | 0.058 | 0.002 |
| Percent First-Year Students with Portable Fellowships | -0.069 | -0.032 | 0.010 | 0.021 | 0.026 | 0.001 |
| Percent Non-Asian Minority Students | -0.022 | 0.033 | 0.018 | 0.013 | 0.017 | 0.001 |
| Percent Female Students | -0.129 | -0.089 | 0.013 | 0.013 | 0.017 | 0.001 |
| Percent International Students | -0.007 | 0.052 | 0.015 | 0.014 | 0.019 | 0.001 |
| Average PhDs 2002 to 2006 | 0.120 | 0.154 | 0.012 | 0.037 | 0.043 | 0.002 |
| Percent Completing within 6 Years | -0.079 | -0.054 | 0.008 | 0.043 | 0.048 | 0.002 |
| Time to Degree Full and Part Time | -0.048 | 0.002 | 0.016 | -0.026 | -0.021 | 0.002 |
| Percent Students in Academic Positions | 0.057 | 0.079 | 0.008 | 0.077 | 0.086 | 0.003 |
| Student Workspace | 0.058 | 0.100 | 0.011 | 0.006 | 0.009 | 0.001 |
| Health Insurance | 0.006 | 0.046 | 0.013 | 0.002 | 0.004 | 0.001 |
| Number of Student Activities | -0.041 | 0.014 | 0.015 | 0.024 | 0.029 | 0.001 |

| Theater and Performance Studies | R-Based .05 | R-Based .95 | R-Based Stdev | S-Based .05 | S-Based .95 | S-Based Stdev |
|---|---|---|---|---|---|---|
| Publications per Allocated Faculty | -0.018 | 0.052 | 0.022 | 0.145 | 0.166 | 0.006 |
| Cites Per Publication | None | None | None | None | None | None |
| Grants per Allocated Faculty | -0.050 | -0.016 | 0.011 | 0.025 | 0.037 | 0.004 |
| Percent Faculty Interdisciplinary | -0.060 | -0.001 | 0.015 | 0.078 | 0.095 | 0.005 |
| percent Non-Asian Minority Faculty | 0.032 | 0.097 | 0.022 | 0.048 | 0.062 | 0.004 |
| Percent Female Faculty | -0.053 | 0.004 | 0.017 | 0.041 | 0.055 | 0.004 |
| Awards per Allocated Faculty | 0.083 | 0.131 | 0.015 | 0.076 | 0.096 | 0.006 |
| Average GRE-Q | 0.131 | 0.172 | 0.012 | 0.037 | 0.049 | 0.004 |
| Percent First-Year Students with Full Support | 0.012 | 0.049 | 0.010 | 0.065 | 0.081 | 0.005 |
| Percent First-Year Students with Portable Fellowships | -0.007 | 0.026 | 0.011 | 0.009 | 0.017 | 0.002 |
| Percent Non-Asian Minority Students | 0.018 | 0.075 | 0.015 | 0.046 | 0.057 | 0.003 |
| Percent Female Students | -0.020 | 0.034 | 0.016 | 0.034 | 0.045 | 0.003 |
| Percent International Students | -0.068 | 0.012 | 0.023 | 0.015 | 0.024 | 0.003 |
| Average PhDs 2002 to 2006 | 0.104 | 0.145 | 0.014 | 0.019 | 0.027 | 0.003 |
| Percent Completing within 6 Years | -0.031 | 0.024 | 0.017 | 0.065 | 0.079 | 0.004 |
| Time to Degree Full and Part Time | -0.079 | -0.025 | 0.015 | -0.035 | -0.023 | 0.004 |
| Percent Students in Academic Positions | 0.043 | 0.096 | 0.017 | 0.094 | 0.107 | 0.004 |
| Student Workspace | -0.045 | 0.003 | 0.014 | 0.001 | 0.004 | 0.001 |
| Health Insurance | -0.016 | 0.044 | 0.019 | 0.009 | 0.016 | 0.002 |
| Number of Student Activities | 0.096 | 0.138 | 0.012 | 0.053 | 0.065 | 0.004 |

# Appendix G
## Correlation of the Median R and S Rankings by Broad Field

| Fields by Broad Field | Correlation of median R and S-ranking |
|---|---|
| Agricultural Sciences | |
| Animal Sciences | 0.548 |
| Entomology | 0.818 |
| Food Science | 0.801 |
| Forestry and Forest Sciences | 0.750 |
| Nutrition | 0.792 |
| Plant Sciences | 0.853 |
| Biological and Health Sciences | |
| Biochemistry, Biophysics, and Structural Biology | 0.886 |
| Cell and Developmental Biology | 0.857 |
| Ecology and Evolutionary Biology | 0.786 |
| Genetics and Genomics | 0.846 |
| Immunology and Infectious Disease | 0.795 |
| Biology/Integrated Biology/Integrated Biomedical Sciences | 0.904 |
| Kinesiology | 0.811 |
| Microbiology | 0.841 |
| Neuroscience and Neurobiology | 0.836 |
| Nursing | 0.891 |
| Pharmacology, Toxicology and Environmental Health | 0.644 |
| Physiology | 0.866 |
| Public Health | 0.853 |
| Engineering | |
| Aerospace Engineering | 0.833 |
| Biomedical Engineering and Bioengineering | 0.891 |
| Chemical Engineering | 0.875 |
| Civil and Environmental Engineering | 0.677 |
| Electrical and Computer Engineering | 0.842 |
| Materials Science and Engineering | 0.779 |
| Mechanical Engineering | 0.748 |
| Operations Research, Systems Engineering and Industrial Engineering | 0.858 |
| Humanities | |
| American Studies | 0.844 |
| History of Art, Architecture and Archaeology | 0.842 |
| Classics | 0.879 |
| Comparative Literature | 0.659 |
| English Language and Literature | 0.780 |
| French and Francophone Language and Literature | 0.543 |
| German Language and Literature | 0.314 |
| History | 0.828 |
| Music (except performance) | 0.835 |
| Philosophy | 0.733 |
| Religion | 0.731 |

| Spanish and Portuguese Language and Literature | 0.542 |
| Theatre and Performance Studies | 0.757 |

| Fields by Broad Field | Correlation of median R and S-ranking |
|---|---|
| Physical Sciences | |
| Applied Mathematics | 0.853 |
| Astrophysics and Astronomy | 0.774 |
| Chemistry | 0.863 |
| Computer Sciences | 0.889 |
| Earth Sciences | 0.877 |
| Mathematics | 0.935 |
| Oceanography, Atmospheric Sciences and Meteorology | 0.863 |
| Physics | 0.842 |
| Statistics and Probability | 0.765 |
| Social and Behavioral Sciences | |
| Agricultural and Resource Economics | 0.764 |
| Anthropology | 0.771 |
| Communication | 0.789 |
| Economics | 0.844 |
| Geography | 0.713 |
| Linguistics | 0.579 |
| Political Science | 0.819 |
| Psychology | 0.958 |
| Public Affairs, Public Policy and Public Administration | 0.783 |
| Sociology | 0.570 |

# Appendix H
## Detail for the Rating Study

| Field | No. of Programs in Sample | No. of Raters in Sample | Average Count of Raters per Program | Max Number of Ratings for a Program in the Field | Min Number of Ratings for a Program in the Field |
|---|---|---|---|---|---|
| Animal Sciences | 36 | 135 | 40.4 | 54 | 21 |
| Anthropology | 50 | 163 | 43.3 | 51 | 33 |
| Applied Mathematics | 26 | 110 | 48.1 | 65 | 35 |
| Biochemistry, Biophysics, and Structural Biology | 49 | 143 | 40.3 | 45 | 30 |
| Biology/Integrated Biology/Integrated Biomedical Sciences | 50 | 172 | 37.4 | 48 | 27 |
| Biomedical Engineering and Bioengineering | 50 | 162 | 41.9 | 55 | 29 |
| Cell and Developmental Biology | 50 | 170 | 40.0 | 56 | 21 |
| Chemical Engineering | 50 | 160 | 47.2 | 54 | 23 |
| Chemistry | 50 | 173 | 44.0 | 58 | 37 |
| Civil and Environmental Engineering | 50 | 162 | 43.4 | 53 | 32 |
| Classics | 18 | 73 | 41.7 | 47 | 36 |
| Communication | 49 | 169 | 50.0 | 57 | 28 |
| Comparative Literature | 29 | 91 | 39.1 | 54 | 31 |
| Computer Sciences | 49 | 186 | 50.1 | 61 | 41 |
| Earth Sciences | 50 | 197 | 48.5 | 64 | 26 |
| Ecology and Evolutionary Biology | 49 | 158 | 40.3 | 53 | 26 |
| Economics | 49 | 166 | 44.6 | 52 | 34 |
| Electrical and Computer Engineering | 50 | 261 | 68.9 | 82 | 52 |
| English Language and Literature | 50 | 172 | 45.6 | 63 | 30 |
| French and Francophone Language and Literature | 30 | 91 | 42.3 | 51 | 36 |
| Genetics and Genomics | 40 | 116 | 36.5 | 51 | 28 |
| Geography | 40 | 136 | 47.1 | 56 | 35 |
| German Language and Literature | 23 | 91 | 49.9 | 56 | 45 |
| History | 49 | 159 | 41.8 | 57 | 31 |
| History of Art, Architecture, and Archeology | 39 | 121 | 40.4 | 48 | 16 |
| Immunology and Infectious Disease | 50 | 176 | 38.3 | 56 | 26 |
| Kinesiology | 30 | 83 | 36.2 | 44 | 29 |
| Linguistics | 30 | 108 | 48.4 | 58 | 22 |
| Materials Science and Engineering | 49 | 171 | 45.6 | 56 | 27 |
| Mathematics | 48 | 181 | 48.4 | 56 | 39 |
| Mechanical Engineering | 48 | 265 | 70.5 | 85 | 53 |
| Microbiology | 48 | 141 | 35.5 | 43 | 26 |
| Music (Except Performance) | 43 | 137 | 40.9 | 52 | 24 |
| Neuroscience and Neurobiology | 50 | 160 | 41.9 | 51 | 32 |
| Nursing | 28 | 101 | 44.1 | 54 | 32 |
| Nutrition | 29 | 119 | 47.6 | 61 | 38 |
| Oceanography, Atmospheric Sciences and Meteorology | 30 | 141 | 49.5 | 72 | 28 |
| Operations Research, Systems Engineering and Industrial Engineering | 48 | 146 | 38.0 | 52 | 28 |
| Pharmacology, Toxicology and Environmental Health | 50 | 195 | 46.7 | 60 | 36 |

| Field | No. of Programs in Sample | No. of Raters in Sample | Average Count of Raters per Program | Max Number of Ratings for a Program in the Field | Min Number of Ratings for a Program in the Field |
|---|---|---|---|---|---|
| Philosophy | 50 | 171 | 46.7 | 57 | 34 |
| Physics | 50 | 177 | 43.7 | 58 | 23 |
| Physiology | 46 | 140 | 35.6 | 48 | 27 |
| Plant Sciences | 43 | 153 | 39.3 | 54 | 25 |
| Political Science | 50 | 154 | 40.9 | 48 | 29 |
| Psychology | 50 | 231 | 50.9 | 69 | 28 |
| Public Affairs, Public Policy and Public Administration | 35 | 119 | 38.3 | 51 | 29 |
| Public Health | 32 | 157 | 49.0 | 73 | 27 |
| Religion | 30 | 95 | 40.1 | 54 | 28 |
| Sociology | 51 | 214 | 43.0 | 53 | 27 |
| Spanish and Portuguese Language and Literature | 49 | 161 | 44.0 | 54 | 36 |
| Statistics and Probability | 48 | 163 | 47.2 | 60 | 38 |

# APPENDIX I

## COUNT OF RANKED AND UNRANKED PROGRAMS BY FIELD

| Broad Field | Field | Total Ranked | Total Unranked |
|---|---|---|---|
| **Agricultural Sciences** | Animal Sciences | 60 | 1 |
| | Entomology | 28 | 0 |
| | Food Science | 31 | 0 |
| | Forestry and Forest Sciences | 33 | 1 |
| | Nutrition | 44 | 1 |
| | Plant Sciences | 116 | 2 |
| **Agricultural Sciences Total** | | 312 | 5 |
| **Biological and Health Sciences** | Biochemistry, Biophysics, and Structural Biology | 157 | 1 |
| | Biology/Integrated Biology/Integrated Biomedical Sciences (Note: Use this field only if the degree field is not specialized.) | 121 | 0 |
| | Cell and Developmental Biology | 122 | 0 |
| | Ecology and Evolutionary Biology | 94 | 0 |
| | Genetics and Genomics | 65 | 1 |
| | Immunology and Infectious Disease | 78 | 0 |
| | Kinesiology | 41 | 0 |
| | Microbiology | 74 | 0 |
| | Neuroscience and Neurobiology | 94 | 0 |
| | Nursing | 52 | 3 |
| | Pharmacology, Toxicology and Environmental Health | 116 | 2 |
| | Physiology | 63 | 0 |
| | Public Health | 91 | 1 |
| **Biological and Health Sciences Total** | | 1168 | 8 |
| **Engineering** | Aerospace Engineering | 31 | 0 |
| | Biomedical Engineering and Bioengineering | 74 | 0 |
| | Chemical Engineering | 106 | 0 |
| | Civil and Environmental Engineering | 130 | 1 |
| | Computer Engineering | 0 | 20 |
| | Electrical and Computer Engineering | 136 | 0 |
| | Engineering Science and Materials (not elsewhere classified) | 0 | 14 |
| | Materials Science and Engineering | 83 | 1 |
| | Mechanical Engineering | 127 | 1 |
| | Operations Research, Systems Engineering and Industrial Engineering | 72 | 2 |
| **Engineering Total** | | 759 | 39 |
| | | | |
| | | | |

| Broad Field | Field | Total Ranked | Total Unrankedl |
|---|---|---|---|
| **Humanities** | American Studies | 22 | 1 |
| | Classics | 31 | 3 |
| | Comparative Literature | 46 | 0 |
| | English Language and Literature | 119 | 0 |
| | French and Francophone Language and Literature | 43 | 0 |
| | German Language and Literature | 29 | 2 |
| | History | 137 | 1 |
| | History of Art, Architecture and Archaeology | 58 | 0 |
| | Languages, Societies and Cultures | 0 | 94 |
| | Music (except performance) | 62 | 1 |
| | Philosophy | 90 | 0 |
| | Religion | 40 | 0 |
| | Spanish and Portuguese Language and Literature | 60 | 0 |
| | Theatre and Performance Studies | 27 | 0 |
| **Humanities Total** | | 764 | 102 |
| **Physical and Mathematical Sciences** | Applied Mathematics | 33 | 1 |
| | Astrophysics and Astronomy | 33 | 0 |
| | Chemistry | 178 | 2 |
| | Computer Sciences | 127 | 1 |
| | Earth Sciences | 141 | 1 |
| | Mathematics | 127 | 0 |
| | Oceanography, Atmospheric Sciences and Meteorology | 50 | 0 |
| | Physics | 161 | 1 |
| | Statistics and Probability | 61 | 0 |
| **Physical and Mathematical Sciences Total** | | 911 | 6 |
| **Social and Behavioral Sciences** | Agricultural and Resource Economics | 28 | 0 |
| | Anthropology | 82 | 0 |
| | Communication | 83 | 0 |
| | Economics | 117 | 1 |
| | Geography | 49 | 0 |
| | Linguistics | 52 | 1 |
| | Political Science | 105 | 1 |
| | Psychology | 236 | 1 |
| | Public Affairs, Public Policy and Public Administration | 54 | 0 |
| | Sociology | 118 | 2 |
| **Social and Behavioral Sciences Total** | | 924 | 0 |
| **Grand Total** | | 4838 | 166 |

# APPENDIX J

# A Technical Discussion of the Process of Rating and Ranking Programs in a Field

This appendix explains in detail how the various parts of the rating and ranking process for graduate programs fit together and how the process is carried out. Figure J-1 provides a graphical overview of the entire process and forms the basis for this appendix. The appendix addresses each of the boxes in Figure J-1 separately, starting at the top and generally working downward and to the right. The topics in this appendix include:

- a summary of the sources of data used in the rating and ranking process,
- the survey (S)-based weights, the regression (R)-based weights, and the details of the calculations of the endpoints of the 90 percent ranges
- the simulation of the uncertainty in the weights by random-halves sampling,
- the simulation of the uncertainty in the values of the program variables,
- the combination of the simulated weights for the significant program variables with the simulated standardized values of the program variables to obtain simulated rankings, and
- the resulting 90 percent ranges of rankings that are the primary rating and ranking quantities that we report.
- a description of an alternative ranking methodology that combines measures of interest to the user.

285

# THE METHOD FOR CALCULATING THE R AND S RANKINGS

**Figure J-1** A graphical summary of the NRC's approach to
rating and thereby ranking graduate programs.

### The three sets of data: X, P, and R.

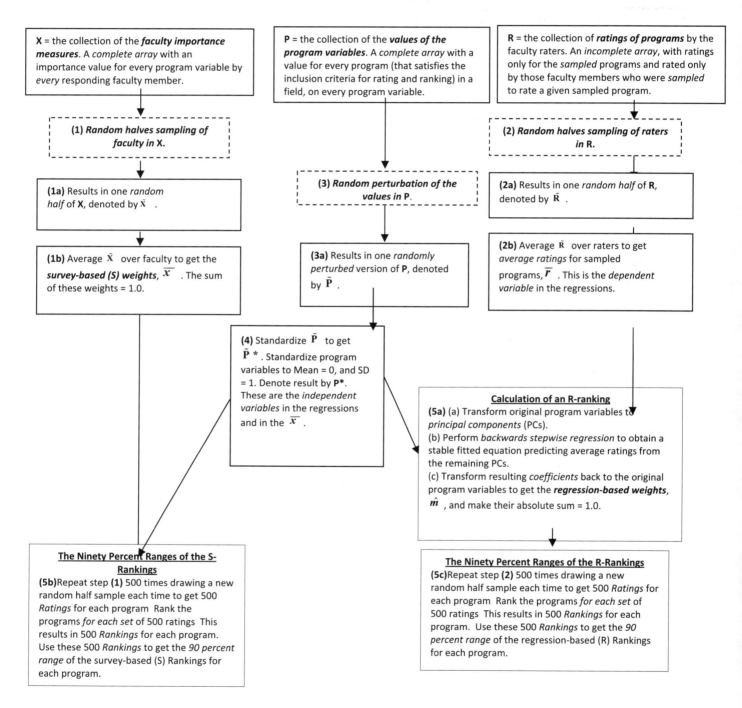

X = the collection of the **faculty importance measures**. A *complete array* with an importance value for every program variable by *every* responding faculty member.

P = the collection of the **values of the program variables**. A *complete array* with a value for every program (that satisfies the inclusion criteria for rating and ranking) in a field, on every program variable.

R = the collection of **ratings of programs** by the faculty raters. An *incomplete array*, with ratings only for the *sampled* programs and rated only by those faculty members who were *sampled* to rate a given sampled program.

**(1)** *Random halves sampling of faculty in X.*

**(2)** *Random halves sampling of raters in R.*

**(3)** *Random perturbation of the values in P.*

**(1a)** Results in one *random half* of **X**, denoted by $\tilde{X}$ .

**(2a)** Results in one *random half* of **R**, denoted by $\tilde{R}$ .

**(1b)** Average $\tilde{X}$ over faculty to get the **survey-based (S) weights**, $\overline{x}$ . The sum of these weights = 1.0.

**(3a)** Results in one *randomly perturbed* version of **P**, denoted by $\tilde{P}$ .

**(2b)** Average $\tilde{R}$ over raters to get *average ratings* for sampled programs, $\overline{r}$ . This is the *dependent variable* in the regressions.

**(4)** Standardize $\tilde{P}$ to get $\tilde{P}*$ . Standardize program variables to Mean = 0, and SD = 1. Denote result by **P\***. These are the *independent variables* in the regressions and in the $\overline{x}$ .

**Calculation of an R-ranking**
**(5a)** (a) Transform original program variables to *principal components* (PCs).
(b) Perform *backwards stepwise regression* to obtain a stable fitted equation predicting average ratings from the remaining PCs.
(c) Transform resulting *coefficients* back to the original program variables to get the **regression-based weights**, $\hat{m}$ , and make their absolute sum = 1.0.

**The Ninety Percent Ranges of the S-Rankings**
**(5b)** Repeat step **(1)** 500 times drawing a new random half sample each time to get 500 *Ratings* for each program Rank the programs *for each set* of 500 ratings This results in 500 *Rankings* for each program. Use these 500 *Rankings* to get the *90 percent range* of the survey-based (S) Rankings for each program.

**The Ninety Percent Ranges of the R-Rankings**
**(5c)** Repeat step **(2)** 500 times drawing a new random half sample each time to get 500 *Ratings* for each program Rank the programs *for each set* of 500 ratings This results in 500 *Rankings* for each program. Use these 500 *Rankings* to get the *90 percent range* of the regression-based (R) Rankings for each program.

## The Three Data Sets

The empirical basis of the NRC ratings and rankings are the three data sets indicated in the three unlabeled boxes at the top of Figure J-1. The first, denoted by **X**, is the collection of faculty *importance measures* that were derived from data that were collected in the faculty questionnaire. The data in **X** are used to derive the *direct or survey-based (S) weights* discussed more extensively below. The second data set, denoted by **P**, is the collection of the values of the 20 *program variables* that were collected from various sources for each program. The data in **P** are used in the final ratings and rankings of the programs and are discussed in greater detail below. The third, denoted by **R**, is the collection of *ratings of programs by faculty raters*. These ratings were made separately from the faculty questionnaire and involved only a sample of programs from each field and only a sample of faculty raters from that field. This sample of faculty ratings plays a crucial role in the derivation of the *regression-based weights*, discussed more extensively below.

## Box (1b): The Direct Weights From the Faculty Questionnaire[1]

Let us turn first to the *survey (S) or direct weights* in box (1b) in Figure J-1, leaving boxes (1) and (1a) to the later discussion of how the uncertainty in these data was simulated.

The faculty questionnaire asks each graduate-program faculty respondent to indicate how important each of 21 characteristics is to the quality of a program in his or her field of study.[2] This information is then used to derive the *survey (S) or direct weights* for each surveyed faculty member, as described below.

The original 21 program characteristics listed on the faculty questionnaire are shown in Table J-1, and they were divided into three categories—faculty, student, and program characteristics. Of the original 21, there are 20 for which adequate data were deemed to be available to use in the rating process, and these 20 data values for each program became the 20 *program variables* used in this study to which we repeatedly refer.

Faculty respondents were first asked to indicate up to four characteristics in each category that they thought were "most important" to program quality. Each characteristic that was listed received an initial score of 1 for that faculty respondent. These preferences were then narrowed by asking the faculty members to further identify a maximum of *two* characteristics in each category that they thought were the most important. Each of these selected characteristics received an additional point, resulting in a score of 2. Given this approach, at most, 12 of the program characteristics can have a non-zero value for any given faculty member; and of these 12, 6, at most, will have a score of 2, and the rest will have a score of 1. At least 8 program characteristics will have a score of 0 for each faculty respondent, more than 8 would be zero if the respondent selected less than 4 as the "important" or 2 as the "most important" characteristics. A final question asked faculty respondents to indicate the *relative importance* of each of the three categories by assigning them values that summed to 100 over the three

---

[1] The importance of program attributes to program quality is surveyed in Section G of the faculty questionnaire.
[2] The number of student publications and presentations was not used because consistent data on it were unavailable. The direct or survey-based and regression-based weights were calculated without it.

categories.[3] For each faculty respondent, his or her *importance measure* for each program characteristic was calculated as the product of the score that it received times the relative importance value assigned to its category. Finally, the 20 importance measures for each faculty respondent were transformed by dividing each one by the sum of his or her importance measures across the 20 program variables.

---

**Faculty characteristics**

    i.   Number of publications per faculty member

    ii.   Number of citations per publication (for non-humanities fields)

    iii.   Percent of faculty holding grants

    iv. Involvement in interdisciplinary work

    v. Racial/ethnic diversity of program faculty

    vi. Gender diversity of program faculty

    vii. Reception by peers of a faculty member's work as measured by honors and awards

**Student characteristics**

    i. Median GRE scores of entering students

    ii. Percentage of students receiving full financial support

    iii.   Percentage of students with external funding

    iv.   Number of student publications and presentations (not used)

    v. Racial/ethnic diversity of the student population

    vi. Gender diversity of the student population

    vii. A high percentage of international students

**Program characteristics**

    i. Average number of Ph.D.'s granted in last five years

    ii. Percentage of entering students who complete a doctoral degree in a given time (6 years for non-humanities, 8 years for humanities).

    iii. Time to degree

    iv. Placement of students after graduation (percent in either positions or postdoctoral fellowships in academia)

    v. Percentage of students with individual work space

    vi. Percentage of health insurance premiums covered by institution or program

---

[3] The faculty task can be thought of as asking faculty how many percentage points should be assigned to each category. The sum of the percentage point weights adds up to 100.

We will use the following notation consistently: $i$ for a *faculty respondent*, $j$ for a *program* in a field, and $k$ for one of the 20 *program variables*. Thus, $x_{ik}$ denotes the measure of importance placed on program variable $k$ by faculty respondent $i$. The values, $x_{ik}$, are non-negative and, over $k$, sum to 1.0 for each faculty respondent $i$. The *importance measure vector* for faculty respondent $i$ is the collection of these 20 values,

$$x_i = (x_{i1}, x_{i2}, \ldots, x_{i20}). \qquad (1)$$

The entries in these $x$-vectors are non-negative and sum to 1.00. Denote the vector of *average importance weights*, averaged across the entire set of faculty respondents in a field, by

$$\overline{x} = (\overline{x}_1, \overline{x}_2, \ldots, \overline{x}_{20}). \qquad (2)$$

The mean value, $\overline{x}_k$, is the average weight of the importance given to the $k^{\text{th}}$ program variable by all the surveyed faculty respondents in the field. The averages, $\{\overline{x}_k\}$, are the *direct or survey-based weights* of the faculty respondents because they directly give the average relative importance of each program variable, as indicated by the faculty questionnaire responses in the field of study. Thus, the final 20 importance measures of the program characteristics for each faculty respondent are non-negative and sum to 1.0.

### Boxes (2b), (4): The Regression-Based Weights

We next consider the processes in boxes (2b) and (4) in Figure J-1 that lead to the *regression-based weights*. Again, we leave boxes (2) and (2a) to our later discussion of how we simulated the uncertainty in these data.

The regression-based weights represent our attempt to ascertain how much weight is implicitly given to each program variable by faculty members when they rate programs by using their own *perceived* quality of the programs they are rating. We used linear regression to predict average faculty ratings from the 20 program variables and interpreted the resulting regression coefficients as indicating the *implicit importance* of each program variable for faculty ratings. This is different from the survey or direct weights that were just described. We have broken down the process of obtaining the regression-based weights into the three parts indicated by boxes (2b) and (4) which we now discuss in turn.

### Box (2b): The average ratings for the sampled programs

The ratings data in R of Figure J-1 are the ratings given by the sampled faculty members to the sample of programs that they were requested to rate. A randomly selected faculty member, $i$, rates a randomly selected program, $j$, on a scale of 1 to 6 in terms of his or her *perception* of its quality. Denote this rating by $r_{ij}$. The matrix sampling plan used was designed so that a sample of up to 50 of the programs in a field was rated by a sample of the graduate faculty members in that same field. Each rater rated about 15 programs, and none rated his or her own program. On average, each rated program was rated by about 44 faculty raters. The rater sample was stratified to ensure proportionality by geographic region, program size (measured by number of faculty), and academic rank. The program sample was stratified to ensure proportionality by geographic region and program size.

R is the array of all the values of $r_{ij}$. Note that R is an *incomplete array* because many faculty members who responded to the questionnaire did *not* rate programs and many programs in a field were *not* rated, except for the small fields. Box (2b) indicates that we compute the average of these ratings for program $j$, and denote this average rating by $\bar{r}_j$. Because each program's average rating is determined by a different random sample of graduate faculty raters, it is highly unlikely that any two programs will be evaluated by exactly the same set of raters. Denote the *vector* of the average ratings for the sampled programs in a field by $\bar{r}$.

The values of the average ratings in $\bar{r}$ are the *dependent variable* in the regression analyses used to form the regression-based weights.

*Box (4): The program variables and standardizing*

Denote the value of program variable $k$ for program $j$ by $p_{jk}$, and define the vector of all program variables for program $j$ by

$$\boldsymbol{p}_j = (p_{j1}, p_{j2}, \ldots, p_{j20}), \tag{3}$$

and the array with rows given by $\boldsymbol{p}_j$ by P. A cursory examination of the program characteristics listed in Table A-1 shows that they are on *different scales*. For example, the number of publications per faculty member (numbers in the fives and tens), the median GRE scores of entering students (numbers in the hundreds), and the percentage of entering students who complete a doctoral degree in 10 years or less (fractions) are reported in values that are of very different *orders of magnitude*. If these values are left as they are, the size of any regression coefficient based on them will be influenced by *both* the importance of that program variable for predicting the average ratings (which is what we are interested in), as well as the scale of that variable (which is arbitrary and does not interest us). The program variables with *large values*, such as the median GRE scores, will have very small coefficients to reflect the change in scale in going from GRE scores (in the hundreds) to ratings (in the 1 to 6 range). Conversely, program variables with *small values*, such as proportions, will have larger regression coefficients to reflect the change in scale in going from numbers less than 1 to ratings (in the 1 to 6 range).

To avoid the ambiguity between the influence of the scale and the real predictive importance of a variable, we needed to modify the values of the different program variables so they have *similar scales*. This would ensure that program variables with the same influence on the prediction of faculty ratings would have similar regression-coefficient values. Our solution is the very common one of *standardizing* the $p_{jk}$-values by subtracting their mean across the programs in a field and dividing by the corresponding standard deviation. This will result in program variables that have the same mean (0.0) and standard deviation (1.0) across the programs in the field. In this way, no program variable will have substantially larger or smaller values than any other program variable across the programs in a field. For the regressions of box (4), the standardization was done only over the programs that were sampled for rating.

We denote the values of the standardized program variables with an asterisk ($p_{jk}*$ and **P***). Two program variables (Student Work Space and Health Insurance) were coded as 1 (present) or -1 (absent). We felt that there was no need for additional standardization of these two program variables and they were not standardized to have mean 0 and variance 1.

The standardized program variables for the sampled and rated programs served as the *predictor or independent variables* in the regressions that lead to the regression-based weights.

### *Box (5a): The regressions and the regression-based weights*

The statistical problem addressed in box (4) is to use $\bar{r}$ and $\mathbf{P}^*$ as the *dependent* and *independent* variables, respectively, in a linear regression, to obtain the vector of regression-based weights, $\hat{m}$, using least squares. It should be noted that only the data in $\mathbf{P}^*$ for the *sampled* programs are used. The data for the non-sampled programs in $\mathbf{P}^*$ are not used in this step of the process.

Two immediate problems arise. These are: (1) the number of observations (i.e., the number of sampled programs in a field) is 50 or less, while the number of independent variables (i.e., the program variables in $\mathbf{P}^*$) is 20, and (2) a number of the program variables are correlated with each other across the programs in a field. This is less than an ideal situation for obtaining *stable* regression coefficients. There are too few observations to hope for stable estimates of the coefficients for 20 variables. The fact that these variables are also correlated does not help matters either. If we had ignored these two problems, least-squares regression methods would have tended to assign coefficients rather arbitrarily to one particular variable or to other variables that are correlated with it, and how this worked out would depend on which programs were included in the sample of rated programs. The resulting unstable regression coefficients would have been unusable for our purposes.

For example, as expected, when we fit a linear model that included all 20 of the program variables, we found that for a number of the variables, the coefficients and their signs did not make intuitive sense. However, we found, as expected, that they made more sense when we used various step-wise selection methods for reducing the number of variables used as predictors. With only 50 cases, we had to expect that we could not use all 20 variables in the prediction equations without adjustments.

After examining a variety of approaches, we settled on using a backwards, step-wise selection method applied to the 20 *principal component* (PC) variables formed from the 20 program variables (rather than using the original 20 program variables). The regression coefficients obtained for the remaining PC variables were then transformed back to scale of the original 20 program variables, with the result that all 20 program variables now had non-zero coefficients, but these coefficients were subject to several linear constraints implied by the deleted PC variables.

The principal component variables are linear combinations of the original 20 program variables that have two properties: (1) they are uncorrelated in the sample, and (2) they can give exactly the same predictions as do the original variables—that is, every prediction equation that is possible with the original variables is also possible to form using the PC variables, using different regression coefficients. The PC variables are usually ordered by their variances from largest to smallest, but this plays no role here. There are as many PC variables as there are original variables—in our case, 20.

If we denote the array of original 20 standardized variables for the sample of rated programs as $\mathbf{P}^*$, then the corresponding array of the 20 PC variables, $\mathbf{C}$, is given by the matrix multiplication, $\mathbf{C} = \mathbf{P}^*\mathbf{V}$, where $\mathbf{V}$ is the 20 by 20 orthogonal matrix specified by, among other things, the *singular value decomposition* of $\mathbf{P}^*$. After the regression coefficients are estimated using the PC variables, we get back to the coefficients for the original standardized variables in **P\*** by transforming the vector of regression coefficients by the transformation, **V**.

  Our step-wise use of the PC variables proceeded as follows. We begin with a least-squares prediction equation, predicting $\bar{r}$ from **C**, that includes all of the PC variables. Then a series of analyses is performed, with one PC variable at a time being left out of the prediction equation; the PC variable that has the least impact on the fit of the predicted ratings (as measured by its t-statistic) is removed. This process is repeated, removing one PC variable each time, until the remaining PC variables each add statistically significant improvements to the fit of the predictions of the ratings (at the 0.05 level). The result is a set of regression coefficients, the *PC coefficients*, $\hat{\gamma}$.which predict the sample of program ratings from a subset of the PC variables, i.e.,

$$\hat{\bar{r}} = \mathbf{C}\,\tilde{\hat{\gamma}} \tag{4}$$

  In Equation 5, the caret denotes estimation. Moreover, for the PC variables that have been eliminated during the backwards selection process, the corresponding PC-coefficients, $\hat{\gamma}_k$, are zero. These zeros mean that we are setting the *coefficients* of certain *linear combinations of the original variables* to zero rather than setting the coefficients for some of the original program variables to zero. This was regarded as a virtue, because we did not *necessarily* eliminate any of the original program variables from the prediction equation used to find the regression-based weights. By proceeding this way, we are not forced to give a zero weight to one of two collinear variables in the step-wise procedure. Instead, both collinear variables will typically load onto the same principal components and get some weight when the matrix **V** is applied to the PC coefficients to obtain the coefficients for the original program variables, i.e.,

$$\hat{m} = \mathbf{V}\,\hat{\gamma}. \tag{5}$$

In the same way, the matrix of estimated variances and covariances of $\hat{\gamma}$, obtained from the least-squares output, may be transformed to the corresponding matrix for $\hat{m}$.[4]

  The regression coefficient for the $k^{\text{th}}$ program variable, denoted by $\hat{m}$, is the *regression-based weight* for program characteristic $k$ as a predictor of the average ratings of the programs by the faculty raters, and $\hat{m} = (\hat{m}_1, \hat{m}_2, ..., \hat{m}_{20})$.

  The predicted perceived quality rating for a sampled program can be expected to *differ* somewhat from the actual average rating for that program. For example, for the two fields studied in *Assessing Research Doctorate Programs: A Methodology Study*, the root-mean-square deviation between the predictions and the average ratings was 0.42 on a 1-to-6 rating scale for both mathematics and English. In addition, the (adjusted) $R^2$ of the regressions of average ratings on measured program characteristics was 0.82 for mathematics and 0.80 for English. These values indicate that the predictions account for about 80 percent of the variability in average

---

[4] If the weights from the R and S measures were to be combined, the variances from this matrix would be used later [in box (6) of the computation of combined weights] in the computation of the "optimal fraction" for combining the survey-based and regression-based weights.

ratings. We regarded this as satisfactory levels of agreement between predicted and actual to use these methods in this study.

These results show that the *predicted* perceived quality ratings agree fairly well with the *actual* ratings. However, these results do not indicate how well a prediction equation that was based on a *sample of programs* will reproduce the predictions of the equation for the *whole population of programs* in a field. The data for mathematics, reported in *Assessing Research Doctorate Programs: A Methodology Study*, indicate that using 49 programs did a reasonably good job of reproducing the predictions based on the whole field of 147 mathematics programs.[5] Thus, we decided that in developing the regression-based ratings, we would use a sample of 50 programs from a field if it had more than 50 programs and use almost all of the programs in fields with 50 or fewer programs. When there were fewer than 30 programs in a field, it was combined with a larger discipline with similar direct weights for the purposes of estimating the regression-based weights.[6] In two cases, computer engineering and engineering science and materials, there were fewer than 25 programs, and these fields were not ranked, although data are reported for all 20 characteristics.[7]

There is one final alteration in the values of $\hat{m}$ that needs to be mentioned. The survey-based or direct weights, $\{\bar{x}_k\}$, have absolute values that sum to 1.0. This is not necessarily true of the regression coefficients, $\{\hat{m}_k\}$. The scale of $m_k$ depends on both the scale of $p_{jk}$ and the scale of the average ratings, $\{\bar{r}_j\}$. We decided, because initially our intent was to *combine* these two sources of the importance of the various program variables, that they needed to be on similar scales. We decided to force them *both* to sum to 1.0 in absolute value[8]. This allows the direct and regression-based weights to have negative values where they arise, typically in the regression-based weights, without requiring anything complicated to deal with this. Using the sum of absolute values allows the sign of the regression-based weights to be determined by the data rather than by an a priori hypothesis. Thus, we divided each regression coefficient, $\hat{m}_k$, by the sum of the absolute values of all the regression coefficients. In this way, both the direct and

---

[5] See Appendix G of *Assessing Research Doctorate Programs: A Methodology Study*, National Research Council (2003)

[6] The fields for which this was done were:

| Small Field | Surrogate Field |
|---|---|
| Aerospace engineering | Mechanical engineering |
| Agricultural economics | Economics |
| American studies | English literature |
| Astrophysics and astronomy | Physics |
| Entomology | Plant science |
| Forestry | Plant science |
| Food science | Plant science |
| Theatre and performance | English literature |

[7] Ranges of rankings are not provided for three fields that were in the original taxonomy: 1)Languages, Societies, and Cultures, for which the sub-fields were too diverse to it as a coherent field; and 2)Engineering Science and Materials and 3) Computer Engineering, which fell below the minimum of 25 programs to permit the calculation of rankings for a field. The committee had not anticipated this when it developed the taxonomy, or the fields would not have been included as a separate field.

[8] We use the absolute value here because, for time to degree, a higher value should receive a negative weight. Note that normalization has no effect on relative rankings, since it is simply a linear transformation.

regression-based weights are fractional values, mostly positive but some negative, whose absolute sums equal 1.0[9].

## Boxes (1), (1a), (2) and (2a): Simulating the Uncertainty in the Direct and Regression-Based Weights

The survey-based (S) or direct weight vector, $\bar{x}$, is subject to uncertainty; that is, a different set of respondent faculty would have led to different values in $\bar{x}$. Disagreement among the graduate faculty on the relative importance of the 20 program variables is the source of the uncertainty of the direct or survey-based weights. The average ratings of the sampled faculty in $\bar{r}$ are also subject to uncertainty; a different sample of raters or programs would have produced different values in $\bar{r}$. One way to reflect this uncertainty is to use the sampling distributions of $\bar{x}$ and $\bar{r}$. There are various ways that these sampling distributions may be realized. We chose an empirical approach that made no assumptions about the shapes of the various distributions involved, but this allowed us to use computer-intensive methods to let the sampling variability of both $\bar{x}$ and $\bar{r}$ influence the final ratings and rankings. We examined two empirical approaches, Efron's *bootstrap* and a *random-halves* (RH) procedure suggested by the committee chairman. We found that both gave very similar final results in terms of the final ranges of rankings and ratings. The bootstrap requires taking a sample of $N$ with replacement from the relevant empirical distribution. The RH procedure requires taking a sample of $N/2$ without replacement from the same empirical distribution. We chose to use the RH procedure because it cut the sampling computations in half, is fairly easy to explain, and as far as we could tell, gave essentially the same results as the bootstrap for ranking and rating.

### Boxes (1) and (2): The random halves procedure

The RH procedure for both $\bar{x}$ and $\bar{r}$ are nearly the same, and with the same justifications. **X** is a complete array whose rows denote the $N$ faculty respondents, while **R** is an incomplete array whose rows denote the $n$ sampled faculty raters for a field. In the case of **X**, the RH procedure requires a random sample of size $N/2$ of the *faculty respondents*. In the case of **R**, the RH procedure requires a random sample of size $n/2$ of the *faculty raters*. Repeated draws from these random half samples are then used to simulate the uncertainty in $\bar{x}$ and $\bar{r}$, respectively.

Alert readers may worry that these half samples will exhibit *too much* variability in the resulting averages; after all, a half sample has only half the number of cases as a full sample— and the bootstrap always takes a full sample of $N$ or $n$. The explanation of why a half sample without replacement has essentially the same variability as a full sample with replacement is most easily seen by considering the variance of the mean of a sample without replacement from a finite population. It is well known from sampling theory that the variance of the mean from a sample of size $N/2$, from a population of size $N$ is, essentially,

---

[9] The estimated standard deviations of the $\{\hat{m}_k\}$, obtained in standard ways from the regression output, were also divided by this sum to make them the correct size for use in the process of combining the direct and regression-based weights, discussed below.

$$\text{Var}(\bar{x}_k) = \frac{\sigma^2_{x_k}}{\left(\dfrac{N}{2}\right)}(1 - \frac{N}{2}/N) = \frac{\sigma^2_{x_k}}{N}. \tag{6}$$

That is, because of the "finite sampling correction," the variance from a random half sample without replacement is exactly the same as the variance of a random sample of twice the size with replacement (there is a small "$N$ versus $N-1$" effect that Formula 11 ignores). This is why the bootstrap and the RH methods give such similar results in our application to the uncertainty of the direct weights. There are other reasons to expect the RH method to produce a useful simulation of the uncertainty of averages.[10]

The same reasoning applies to the RH sampling of the faculty raters in **R** to simulate the uncertainty in the average ratings, $\bar{r}$, used to obtain the regression-based weights. The procedure was to sample a random half of all raters for programs in a field and compute the average rating for each program from that half sample.

The regression-based weights are subject to uncertainty from *two* sources. The first is the uncertainty arising from sampling the faculty raters and, as indicated above, the RH sampling directly addresses this source. The second is from using average ratings from a sample of programs rather than all the programs to develop the regression equation from which the regression-based weights are derived. In the discussion of box (4), above, we gave our reasoning for believing the sample of 50 programs is adequate, and how we pool the data from other related fields when the number of programs in a field is smaller than 50. In addition, while the use of ratings for a sample of programs has the practical value of reducing the workload of the faculty raters, our *implicit* use of the predicted average ratings, $\{M_j\}$, from Equation 5 above, rather than actual average ratings, $\{\bar{r}_j\}$, also reduces some of the uncertainty due to the sampling of the programs to be rated. For these two reasons, we believe that this second source of uncertainty is not as important as that simulated by the RH procedure for the uncertainty in the average ratings, and consequently, for the regression-based weights, $\hat{m}$.

We always drew the RH samples 500 times, and those for $\bar{x}$ were statistically independent of those for $\bar{r}$. This gives us 500 replications of the direct or survey-based weights and 500 replications of the regression-based weights.

### Boxes (3) and (3a): Incorporating Uncertainty into the Program Variables

In addition to the uncertainty in the survey-based (direct) and regression-based weights discussed above, there is also some uncertainty in the values of the program variables themselves. Some of the 20 program variables used to calculate the ratings also vary or have an error associated with their values due to year-to-year fluctuations. Data for five of the variables (publications per faculty, citations per publications, GRE scores, Ph.D. completion, and number of Ph.D.'s) were collected over time, and averages over a number of years were used as the values of these program variables. If a different time period had been used, the values would have been

---

[10] The random-halves procedure has a place in the statistical literature, but with other names. It is an example of the "deleted-d" jackknife as described in Efron and Tibshirani, (1993) *An Introduction to the Bootstrap.* New York: Chapman and Hall. p. 149, with d = n/2. It is described by Kirk Wolter in a private communication as an example of the "balanced repeated replication" or "balanced half samples," and described in Wolter, K. M. (2007) *Introduction to Variance Estimation.*, 2nd ed. New York: Springer-Verlag.

different. To express this type of uncertainty, a *relative error factor, $e_{jk}$,* was associated with each program variable value, $p_{jk}$. The relative error factor was calculated by dividing the standard deviation over the series by the square root of the number of observations in the series, and then dividing that number by the value of the variable $p_{kj}$. For example, the publications per faculty variable is the average number of allocated publications per allocated faculty over 7 years, and a standard error value was calculated for this variable as $SD/\sqrt{7}$. This standard error was then divided by the value of the publications per faculty variable to get the relative error factor for this program variable.

For the other 15 program variables that are used in the ratings, no data on variability were directly obtained during the study, and we assigned a relative error of 0, 0.1 or 0.2 to these variables. The relative error for the variables Student Workspace and Health Insurance were given an error of 0, because they were thought to have little or no temporal fluctuation over the interval considered; and for Percent of Faculty Holding Grants, the error assigned was 0.2, because an examination of data from the *National Science Foundation Survey of Research Expenditure* indicated this to be an appropriate estimate. The remaining 12 program variables were assigned a relative error of 0.1. Each program had its own relative error factor for each program variable, $e_{jk}$.

Just as we had simulated values from the sampling distributions of $\bar{x}$ and $\bar{r}$ via RH sampling, we also wanted to reflect the uncertainty in the values of the program variables themselves rather than using the fixed values, $\{p_{kj}\}$, in computing program ratings. We did this in the following way. The value, $p_{kj}$, was *perturbed* by drawing randomly from the Gaussian distribution, $N(p_{kj}, (e_k p_{kj})^2)$. This distribution has a mean equal to the variable value $p_{kj}$ and a standard deviation equal to the relative error, $e_k$, times the variable value, $p_{kj}$. Thus, the entire array **P** is randomly perturbed to a new array, $\tilde{\mathbf{P}}$. This perturbing process is repeated 500 times, and each one is standardized to have mean 0.0 and standard deviation 1.0 for each of the 20 program variables to produce 500 standardized arrays, $\tilde{\mathbf{P}}*$.

## Boxes (5b) and (5c): The Ninety Percent Ranges of the S and R Rankings

In box (5b) we have already calculated 500 replications of the survey-based weights and in box (5c) we have done the same for the Regression-based weights for the given field [from box (2b)] and from 500 replications of the steps in boxes 5b and 5c we have 500 replications of the standardized perturbed version of **P** that contains the program variable data for all of the programs to be rated in the field.

For either measure, denote the $k^{th}$ replication of $R_j$ by $R_j^{(k)}$. To obtain the $k^{th}$ replication of the *rankings* of the programs, sort the values of $R_j^{(k)}$ over $j$ from high to low and assign the rank of 1 to the program with the highest rating in this set. In case of tied ratings, we use the standard procedure in which the ranks are averaged for the tied cases, and the common rank given to the tied programs is the average of the ranks that would have been given to the tied set of programs. For each of the replications of the ratings, there is a corresponding replication of the rankings of the programs, resulting in 500 replications of the ranking of each program.

Instead of reporting a single ranking of the programs in a field, we report the ninety percent range of the rankings for each program. This is an interval starting with the rank that was at the 5th percentile in the distribution of the 500 replications of the ranks for the given program, and ending at the 95th percentile of this distribution. The interpretation of the ninety percent range is that it is *range that covers the middle ninety percent of the rankings* and reflects the uncertainty in the survey-based (direct) and regression-based weights and in the program data values five percent of a program's rankings in our process are less than this interval and five percent are higher. The interval itself represents what we would expect the typical rankings for that program to be, given the uncertainty in the process and the ratings of the other programs in the field.[11] These ninety percent ranges are reported for the R and S measures, as well as for the three dimensional measures.

## AN ALTERNATIVE APPROACH TO CONSTRUCTING RANKINGS: COMBINING THE R AND S MEASURES

The prepublication version of the revised Methodology Guide appeared in July 2009 and explained the methodology developed by the committee at that time, that is, one that combined the R-based and S-based measures in a way that will be described below. In July 2009, the committee had estimated ranges of rankings for only a handful of fields and assumed that this method of estimation would be generally satisfactory. In theory it is, but when applied to data for additional fields it became clear that there were some fields for which the range of program rankings based on the S-measure differed considerably from that based on the R-measure. Further, the committee came to view any set of ranges of rankings that it might develop as

---

[11]In an earlier draft of this guide, we chose an inter-quartile range, but this choice, rather than some other range (eliminating the top and bottom quintile, for example) is arbitrary. The current approach uses broader ranges which result in greater overlap of ranges, but has the advantage of covering most of the rankings a program might achieve. The point of introducing uncertainty in our calculations is that we do not know the "true" ranking of a program. The purpose of presenting a ninety percent range is to provide a range in which a program's ranking is likely to fall.

illustrative, that is, any range of rankings depended critically on the characteristics chosen and the weights applied to those characteristics. The R- and S- based ranges of rankings were two examples of data-based ranking schemes, but there are others. In fact, the dimensional measures described in the body of this Guide, are an example[12]. The technical description of further steps that the committee carried out to obtain ranges of rankings using the combined measures are described in this section—beginning with an alternative conceptual diagram.

---

[12] In most cases, it would not make sense to combine the dimensional measures because they yield differing results for most programs.

# Figure J-2  A graphical summary of the alternative method.

## The three sets of data: X, P, and R.

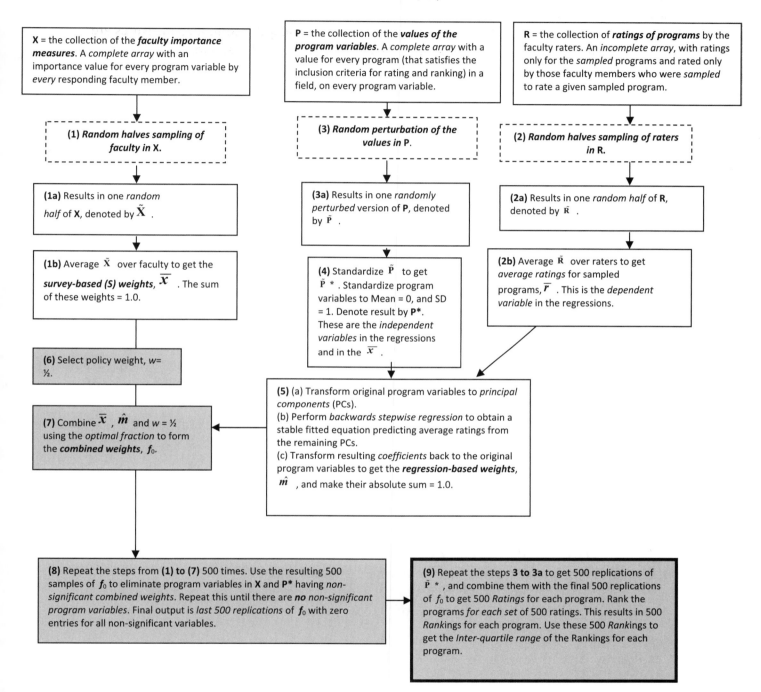

**X** = the collection of the *faculty importance measures*. A *complete array* with an importance value for every program variable by *every* responding faculty member.

**P** = the collection of the *values of the program variables*. A *complete array* with a value for every program (that satisfies the inclusion criteria for rating and ranking) in a field, on every program variable.

**R** = the collection of *ratings of programs* by the faculty raters. An *incomplete array*, with ratings only for the *sampled* programs and rated only by those faculty members who were *sampled* to rate a given sampled program.

**(1)** *Random halves sampling of faculty in* X.

**(3)** *Random perturbation of the values in* P.

**(2)** *Random halves sampling of raters in* R.

**(1a)** Results in one *random half* of **X**, denoted by $\tilde{X}$ .

**(3a)** Results in one *randomly perturbed* version of **P**, denoted by $\tilde{P}$ .

**(2a)** Results in one *random half* of **R**, denoted by $\tilde{R}$ .

**(1b)** Average $\tilde{X}$ over faculty to get the *survey-based (S) weights*, $\overline{x}$ . The sum of these weights = 1.0.

**(4)** Standardize $\tilde{P}$ to get $\tilde{P}$ * . Standardize program variables to Mean = 0, and SD = 1. Denote result by **P***. These are the *independent variables* in the regressions and in the $\overline{x}$ .

**(2b)** Average $\tilde{R}$ over raters to get *average ratings* for sampled programs, $\overline{r}$ . This is the *dependent variable* in the regressions.

**(6)** Select policy weight, *w* = ½.

**(5)** (a) Transform original program variables to *principal components* (PCs).
(b) Perform *backwards stepwise regression* to obtain a stable fitted equation predicting average ratings from the remaining PCs.
(c) Transform resulting *coefficients* back to the original program variables to get the *regression-based weights*, $\hat{m}$ , and make their absolute sum = 1.0.

**(7)** Combine $\overline{x}$ , $\hat{m}$ and *w* = ½ using the *optimal fraction* to form the **combined weights**, $f_0$.

**(8)** Repeat the steps from **(1)** to **(7)** 500 times. Use the resulting 500 samples of $f_0$ to eliminate program variables in **X** and **P*** having *non-significant combined weights*. Repeat this until there are *no non-significant program variables*. Final output is *last 500 replications* of $f_0$ with zero entries for all non-significant variables.

**(9)** Repeat the steps **3 to 3a** to get 500 replications of $\tilde{P}$ *, and combine them with the final 500 replications of $f_0$ to get 500 *Ratings* for each program. Rank the programs *for each set* of 500 ratings. This results in 500 *Rankings* for each program. Use these 500 *Rankings* to get the *Inter-quartile range* of the Rankings for each program.

*Note: Shaded boxes indicate steps used in an alternative technique and are omitted from the technique used to generate the current rankings*

## Boxes (6) and (7): The Combined Weights

To motivate our method of combining of the direct and regression-based weights, we start by describing the direct and regression-based *ratings*. Remembering that the standardized values of the program variables for program $j$ are denoted by $p_{jk}*$, the *direct rating* for program $j$, using the average direct weight vector, $\bar{x}$, is $X_j$, is given by

$$X_j = \sum_{k=1}^{20} \bar{x}_k p_{jk} *. \tag{7}$$

The *regression-based rating* for program $j$, using the regression-based weight vector, $\hat{m}$, is $M_j$, is given by

$$M_j = \sum_{k=1}^{20} \hat{m}_k p_{jk} *. \tag{8}$$

Note that the regression-based rating is a linear transformation of the predicted ratings used to obtain the regression-based weights, because the constant term of the regression is deleted, and the weights have been scaled by a common value so that their absolute sum is 1.0. The procedure for computing regression-based ratings can be used for any program, sampled or not, in the given field. Simply use $M_j$ *as* defined in Equation 7 above, where $\{p_{jk}*\}$ comes from the data for program $j$ and the $\{\ddot{m}_k\}$ are the regression-based weights based on the sample of programs and raters.[13]

We combined the direct ratings with the regression-based ratings as follows. Let $w$ denote a *policy weight* and form the following *combination* of the direct and regression-based ratings:

$$R_j = wM_j + (1 - w)X_j. \tag{9}$$

The *policy weight*, $w$, is chosen in box (5) of Figure J-1, and is the amount the regression-based ratings are allowed to influence the combined rating, $R_j$. When $w = 0$, the regression-based rating has *no* influence on the $R_j$. When $w = 1$, the $R_j$s are *totally* based upon the regression-based ratings. Any *compromise value* of $w$ is somewhere between 0 and 1.

We did not actually form both the direct and regression-based ratings in our work. Instead, we exploited the simple linear form of these given by:

$$R_j = w \sum_{k=1}^{20} \hat{m}_k p_{jk} * + (1 - w) \sum_{k=1}^{20} \bar{x}_k p_{jk} * = \sum_{k=1}^{20} \bar{f}_k p_{jk} * \tag{10}$$

where the combined weight, $\bar{f}_k$, is given by

---

[13] We have throughout estimated linear regressions. Is this assumption justified? We can only say that, empirically, we tried alternative specifications that included quadratic terms for the most important variables (publications and citations) and did not find an improved fit.

$$\overline{f}_k = w\,\hat{m}_k + (1-w)\,\overline{x}_k. \tag{11}$$

The representation of the combined rating given in Equations 9 and 10 is a linear combination of the program variables that uses the *combined weights*, $\{\overline{f}_k\}$ defined in Equation 10. The combined weight $\overline{f}_k$ is applied to the $k^{\text{th}}$ standardized program characteristic, $p_{jk}{*}$ for each $k$, and then all 20 of these weighted values are summed to obtain the final combined rating for program $j$.

However, because both $\hat{m}_k$ and $\overline{x}_k$ are subject to uncertainty, we made one additional adjustment to Equation 10 that is described below, following the discussion of how we simulated the uncertainty in both the direct weights and in the average ratings used to form the regression-based weights.

*Box (7): Using the optimal fraction to combine the direct and regression-based weights.*

In deriving the ranges of ratings that reflect the uncertainty in $\hat{m}_k$ and $\overline{x}_k$, simulated values, $m_k$, and $x_k$, are drawn from the sampling distributions of $\hat{m}_k$, and $\overline{x}_k$, respectively, using independent RH samples from the appropriate parts of $\mathbf{R}$ and $\mathbf{X}$. These two simulated values are to be combined to form a simulated value, $f_k$, for $\overline{f}_k$ in Equation 11. However, the simple weighted average in Equation 11 only reflects the effect of the policy weighting, $w$, and ignores the fact that both $m_k$, and $x_k$ are independent random draws from distributions, rather than fixed values. We want to combine $m_k$, and $x_k$ in such a way as to bring the simulated value, $f_k$, as close as possible to $\overline{f}_k$ on average, and in a way that will also reflect the policy weight, $w$, appropriately. This section outlines our approach to choosing the *optimal fraction* to apply to $m_k$ to achieve this. The optimal fraction is the amount of weight applied to $m_k$ that minimizes the mean-square error of $f_k$, treating $\overline{f}_k$ as a target parameter to be estimated.

First, consider a general weighting, $f_k(u)$, that uses a fraction, $u$. This weighting has the form

$$f_k(u) = u m_k + (1-u) x_k. \tag{12}$$

By construction of the RH procedure, the mean of the distribution of $m_k$ is $\hat{m}_k$ (the regression coefficients that are obtained when the data from all $n$ faculty raters are used). Similarly, the mean of the distribution of $x_k$ is $\overline{x}_k$, the mean importance value that is obtained when the data from all $N$ faculty respondents are averaged. We may regard $f_k(u)$ as an estimator of $\phi_k$, given by

$$\phi_k = w\,\hat{m}_k + (1-w)\,\overline{x}_k. \tag{13}$$

The problem then is to find the value of $u$ that will minimize the mean-square error (MSE) of $f_k(u)$ given by

$$\text{MSE}(u) = \text{E}(f_k(u) - \phi_k)^2, \tag{14}$$

where, in Equation 14, the notation, $E(f_k(u) - \phi_k)^2$ denotes the *expectation* or *average* taken over the independent RH distributions of $\hat{m}_k$ and $\bar{x}_k$. The MSE is a measure of the combined uncertainty in $f_k(u)$.

The MSE in (14) can be written as

$$
\begin{aligned}
\text{MSE}(u) &= E(um_k + (1-u)x_k - w\hat{m}_k - (1-w)\bar{x}_k)^2 \\
&= E(u(m_k - \hat{m}_k) + (1-u)(x_k - \bar{x}_k) + (u-w)\hat{m}_k + (w-u)\bar{x}_k)^2 \\
&= E(u(m_k - \hat{m}_k) + (1-u)(x_k - \bar{x}_k) + (u-w)(\hat{m}_k - \bar{x}_k))^2.
\end{aligned}
\tag{15}
$$

The point of re-expressing Equation 14 as Equation 15 is that now when the squaring is carried out, all of the terms except the squared ones have zero expected values and can be ignored. If we denote the variance of the sampling distribution of $\hat{m}_k$ by $\sigma^2(\hat{m}_k)$ and the variance of $\bar{x}_k$ by $\sigma^2(\bar{x}_k)$, then Equation 15 becomes

$$
\text{MSE}(u) = u^2\sigma^2(\hat{m}_k) + (1-u)^2\sigma^2(\bar{x}_k) + (u-w)^2(\hat{m}_k - \bar{x}_k)^2.
\tag{16}
$$

It is now a straightforward task to differentiate Equation 16 in $u$, set the result to zero, and solve for the optimal $u$-value, $u_{0k}$, which we call the *optimal fraction*. This calculation results in

$$
u_{0k} = \frac{\sigma^2(\bar{x}_k) + w(\hat{m}_k - \bar{x}_k)^2}{\sigma^2(\bar{x}_k) + \sigma^2(\hat{m}_k) + (\hat{m}_k - \bar{x}_k)^2}.
\tag{17}
$$

The optimal fraction in Equation 12 has some useful and intuitive properties. It takes on the value $w$ when there is no uncertainty about the direct and regression-based weights. Moreover, $w$ has no influence on the optimal fraction when $\hat{m}_k$ and $\bar{x}_k$ are equal. In that case, the direct weights and regression-based weights on the $k^{th}$ program characteristic are the same, and the optimal fraction combines the two simulated values in a way that is inversely proportional to their variances, so that the value with less variation gets more weight. Note also, that the value in Equation 12 is the same for all of the RH simulated values of $m_k$ and $x_k$.

The two variances in Equation 12, $\sigma^2(\bar{x}_k)$ and $\sigma^2(\hat{m}_k)$, may be found in standard ways. The value of $\sigma^2(\bar{x}_k)$ is given by

$$
\sigma^2(\bar{x}_k) = \sigma^2(x_k)/N_F,
\tag{18}
$$

where $N_F$ denotes the number of faculty in the field who supply direct weight data, and $\sigma^2(x_k)$ denotes the variance of the individual direct weights given to the $k^{th}$ program variable by these faculty respondents. The value of $\sigma^2(\hat{m}_k)$ is obtained from the regression output that produces $\hat{m}_k$ when the data from all faculty raters in a field are used. Its square root, $\sigma(\hat{m}_k)$ is the standard error of the regression coefficient, $\hat{m}_k$. Finally, because we rescaled the $\hat{m}_k$ so that their absolute sum was 1.0, the same divisor must be applied to $\sigma(\hat{m}_k)$ to put it on the corresponding scale.

If we now replace the $u$ in Equation 17 with $u_{0k}$ given in Equation 17, we then obtain the combined weight that optimally combines the two simulated values of the weights, $m_k$, and $x_k$, into the combined rating, given by

$$R_{0j} = \sum_{k=1}^{20} f_{0k} p^*_{kj} \tag{19}$$

where

$$f_{0k} = u_{0k} m_k + (1 - u_{0k}) x_k, \tag{20}$$

and $u_{0k}$ is given by Equation 17. The vector of optimally combined weights is denoted by $f_0$[14].

The values of $R_{0j}$ from Equations 19 and 20 are used as the 500 simulated values of the combined ratings for the purposes of determining the ranking interval ranges for each program that is discussed below.

In performing the RH sampling to mimic the uncertainty in the direct and regression-based weights, it should be emphasized that the random half samples from $X$ and $R$ were statistically independent. This is our justification for assuming that the random draws, $m_k$, and $x_k$, are statistically independent in the calculation of the optimal fraction, $u_{0k}$.[15]

As a final point, we did realize that the approach to calculating the optimal fraction described above did not take into account any correlation between the direct and regression-based weights for *different* program variables. We did examine a method that did, but it simply produced a matrix version of Equation 12 that reduced to the procedure we used when the program variables were uncorrelated, but was otherwise difficult to implement with the resources available to us.

## Box 8: Eliminating Non-Significant Program Variables

After we have obtained the 500 simulated values of the combined weights by applying Equations 17 and 20 to the 500 simulated values for the direct and regression-based weights, we were in a position to examine the distributions of these 500 values of the combined weights for each program variable. The distributions of the combined weights for some of the program variables did not contain zero and were not even near zero. However, other program variables had combined weight distributions that did contain zero. If zero is inside the middle 95 percent of this distribution, we declare the combined weight for that program variable to be *non-significant* for the rating and ranking process (in analogy with the usual way that distributions of parameters are tested for statistical significance). If the combined weight for a program variable is not significantly different from zero, the variable for that coefficient is dropped from further computations. This elimination of program variables required us to recalculate everything above box (8) in Figure J-2. The eliminated program variables are ignored in calculating the direct and regression-based weights for the other variables. New RH samples are drawn, the direct weights are retransformed so that the absolute sum of the remaining direct weights was 1.0, the regressions are re-run using the reduced set of program variables as predictors, and new optimal

---

[15] The fact that the raters for each field were a subset of those who answered the faculty questionnaire may confuse some into thinking that our independence assumption may not be justified. This is an unfortunate misunderstanding of the simulation of uncertainty in the rating and ranking process. It is the statistical independence of the two RH sampling processes that matters, nothing else.

fractions are computed to combine the direct and regression-based weights. Finally, the 500 simulated combined coefficients are again tested for statistical significance from zero. This process is repeated until a final set of combined weights, each of which is significantly different from zero, is obtained. Only after this testing and retesting process is performed are the final sets of 500 combined coefficients ready for use in the computation of the intervals of rankings that are discussed in box (5) of Figure J-1. The values for the combined weights that correspond to the eliminated variables are set to 0.0 in each of the final 500 simulated values of $f_0$. These 500 vectors of combined weights are used in the production of the ratings that are used to produce the final intervals of rankings for each program, as discussed later.

Empirically, the examination of three fields suggests that this process has two useful effects. First, the middle of the inter-quartile ranges of rankings of programs is changed very little, so that the ranges before eliminating nonsignificant program variables and those after this elimination are centered in nearly the same places[16]. Second, the widths of these inter-quartile ranges are slightly reduced or are unchanged. These are the effects that we would expect from eliminating variables that are having only a noisy effect on the ranking and rating process, and for this reason, we have continued to include box (8) in our rating and ranking process. Nonetheless, the inter-quartile intervals do shift more markedly than the medians, when estimated coefficients are set to zero—largely for those departments near the middle of the rankings. This is because quartile estimates are more variable than median estimates. There are even rare instances in which the intervals calculated both ways do not overlap.

From this point on, the calculation of the ranges of rankings is carried out as described in the section about the R-and S- ranges of rankings.

---

[16] Examination of the effect of this procedure gave correlations between the median rankings with and without the elimination of nonsignificant variables of .99.